If

BRIDELESS IN WEMBLEY

Brideless in Wembley

SANJAY SURI

PENGUIN
VIKING

VIKING
Published by the Penguin Group
Penguin Books India Pvt. Ltd, 11 Community Centre, Panchsheel Park, New Delhi 110017, India
Penguin Group (USA) Inc., 375 Hudson Street, New York, NY 10014, USA
Penguin Group (Canada), 90 Eglinton Avenue East, Suite 700, Toronto, Ontario, M4P 2Y3, Canada (a division of Pearson Penguin Canada Inc.)
Penguin Books Ltd, 80 Strand, London WC2R 0RL, England
Penguin Ireland, 25 St Stephen's Green, Dublin 2, Ireland (a division of Penguin Books Ltd)
Penguin Group (Australia), 250 Camberwell Road, Camberwell, Victoria 3124, Australia (a division of Pearson Australia Group Pty Ltd)
Penguin Group (NZ), cnr Airborne and Rosedale Roads, Albany, Auckland 1310, New Zealand (a division of Pearson New Zealand Ltd)
Penguin Group (South Africa) (Pty) Ltd, 24 Sturdee Avenue, Rosebank, Johannesburg 2196, South Africa

Penguin Books Ltd, Registered Offices: 80 Strand, London WC2R 0RL, England

First published by Penguin Books India 2006
Copyright © Sanjay Suri 2006

All rights reserved
10 9 8 7 6 5 4 3 2 1

Lines on pp 42 and 43 quoted from the poem 'Goblin Market' by Christina Rossetti, first published 1862; p 65 from *An Introduction to Swaminarayan Hinduism* by Raymond Brady Williams, Cambridge University Press, 2001; pp 68–69 from *Female Infanticide and Social Structure: A Socio-historical Study in Western and Northern India* by L.S. Vishwanath, Hindustan Publishing Corporation, 2000. Kailash Puri's letters in the section 'Aunt and Agony' printed by permission of Kailash Puri, *Des Pardes* and *Punjab Times*.

ISBN 13: 9780670058778
ISBN 10: 0670 058777

Typeset in Sabon by InoSoft Systems, Noida
Printed at Sanat Printers

Contents

Introduction

A long introduction is usually pre-chapter suicide, but before I hand this introduction over to the great Gurdev Singh Manku, a quick word or two about what this book is not. It does not offer dining-table wisdom of the 'caught-between-two-worlds' variety, enough to get anyone to abandon a more than averagely decent dinner. Nor is it a history book; I do not have a first chapter called 'Early Arrivals' followed by another called 'Settling In'.

The way Indians were being Indian, someone had to take notes, and do no more, really. So this is a book of stories. Stories born from hanging around people living their idea of 'Indian' in all sorts of ways. My principal skill in putting these stories together has been a lack of imagination; I could never have thought up the people in them.

But over to Mankuji, the Sikh poet with a dyed beard and a challenging glint in the eye I met at the Redbridge Indian Social Klub. My friend Bhandari sahib, retired from a long career in Ford where he rose to a managerial position, had invited me to a meeting of the Klub in Redbridge, east of east London.

'Why do you spell club with a "k"?' I asked him.

'Because when you spell with a "k", we can shorten the name to "RISK". We are elderly people in this Klub, you know, and they are always at risk.'

If Wodehouse could make the disgruntled 'gruntled', and in Bollywood a night can be a 'nite', Bhandari too can make a club a 'Klub'.

Bhandari sahib, who chaired the meeting in his usual black blazer and red tie that announced his managerial past, quickly invited Mankuji to address about fifty of us, mostly RISK members. Mankuji took the mike, and began to read from a piece of paper:

Ik duniya nai vasavaange
Mitran de samne baith ke,
Te ik gal sabh nu samjhavange,
Yaro Punjab nu London nai ban-ana,
Asi London nu Punjab banavange.

We will create a brave new world
We will sit with our friends
And make one thing loud and clear
Friends, Punjab will never be London,
We will make London a Punjab.

The poem went down well, the applause was undiluted by politeness. The Urdu 'wah-wah' translated as Punjabi 'vaa, ji vaa' filled the room. Everyone wanted more, and Manku was ready.

Goreya maein nai jaana
Chhad ke tera desh,
Goreya maein nai jaana
Chhad ke tera desh.

Listen to me, white guys,
I won't leave your country now
Listen to me, white guys,
I won't leave your country now.

Veleyan nu ethay roti mildi,
Dil vich fikr nai koi,
Khao piyo mauj udao,
Is da jikr nai koi.
Rajai le lao,
Sarana le lao,
Ya pher le lao khes,
Goreya main nai jana
Chhad ke tera desh ...

The jobless have plenty to eat
And little to worry about.
Eat, drink and be merry,
Nobody cares what you do.
Awake carefree, go to sleep
Just rest easy, as you like.
Listen to me, white guys,
I won't leave your country now ...

Rang roop da vehm nai koi,
Paaven hove kaala.
Ethay jamna, ethay marna,
Jeeja hove ya sala.
Bai final gal tenu samjhavan,
Toon chal ja pardes goreya,
Main nai jana chhad ke tera desh ...

Nobody cares about your colour,
Whatever it may be.
We will live here, we will die here,
Brother, or brother-in-law
Let me say this once finally,
You can leave and go abroad
White guys, but listen to me,
I'll never leave your country now.

What Manku's poems didn't say is that the country back there doesn't leave you either. But that's between the characters and these stories, and anyone who cares to read them.

A warm 'Thank You' to everyone who let me into their stories. I stepped into this world through working with Gopal Raju and Veena Merchant at *India Abroad*, and with Tarun Basu for the *Indo-Asian News Service*. This collection began with my confession, later, in *Outlook*, about my inability to find myself a wife. That was published only because Vinod Mehta has a declared policy of occasionally indulging 'controlled eccentricity' in print. Krishan Chopra at Penguin India risked my proposal to assemble some such stories into a book, which took shape in the end under the watchful eyes of Poulomi Chatterjee. Through working with the Inter Press Service, I've stepped away from Indian lives, but it's reassuring to keep dipping into that dear old mess through *Outlook* and more recently the local *South Asia World* television channel. It's the world to which I belong; one lifetime is too little to become a cultural 'other' in. Who wants to, anyway.

Leicester

BESTARD

'Nod twice when you see Silva.' Dhanjibhai Atwal spoke the words like he'd never forget them. They'd been his passport to Britain. In 1956 he might still have made it to Britain without that booklet with his photograph on it, but not without nodding to Silva.

Dhanjibhai put on his glasses as he spoke, like he was looking at the past through them, not at me. Dhanjibhai, I'd been told by a friend, was Leicester's memory, though Leicester was beginning to forget that. Few people ever dropped in to ask him where he came from, or indeed where Leicester had come from—Indian Leicester, that is. I had dropped in to see him after one of those 100-mile drives up Britain's Asian corridor, the M1 motorway on a map, the one that takes you up past Watford, Luton, Northampton, Bedford and what not.

No place is Indian like Leicester is, not even Wembley where I started from. As a Wembley man, I lived in an area of India just half an hour's drive from London, unlike my friends from India who'd have to take a nine-hour flight, but I still always looked for excuses to take the M1 to Leicester. Maybe it's because so much of Leicester is Indian; it's the first big town in the West where whites are steadily declining into minority status. Partly because more Indians and other non-whites are coming in, growing and multiplying quite busily and partly because, seeing them, white people are leaving. Or maybe it was just the feel of Indian life here; so many know one another and live around themselves, and I too was searching for at least partial immersion into a community that would shelter me occasionally from the anonymity of living in a big city. Or, who knows, I'd probably just become one of those chronic ghetto Indians that my more evolved friends kept such carefully globalized distance from. But Leicester has always called, and I go as much as I can.

At last, this time, I would be seeing Dhanjibhai. In Leicester, with the M1 behind me, I turned off the Ring Road, since Leicester is town enough to have one, into Belgrave Road, the heart of Indian Leicester that so many tens of thousands live around. Over and down the Belgrave flyover and I was on Belgrave Road proper, the bit where you smell the bhajias on those infrequent days when English weather is decent enough to let you lower your car window. The drive down that flyover always felt like a touchdown into India. Straight past the sari stores and jewellery shops, and yes, the veggie eats since this is Gujarati land, I continued into Melton Road, and looped right into Doncaster Road where Dhanjibhai lived.

Doncaster Road is an English-looking street in the usual way. The long row of houses was joined under tiled roofs that appeared to continue all the way. Invisible walls separated the little drawing rooms underneath. The one Dhanjibhai invited me into was an almost straight repeat of most Gujarati drawing rooms in the Belgrave area of Leicester. It was small—about ten feet by eight—with a sofa in the bay window and the mandatory dusty paper flowers arranged on the sill. Ganesh, done in golden clay with a sandalwood garland around him, oversaw goings-on alongside family pictures. All families are different, but for some reason their pictures all look the same, especially when you place them at about that height on the wall.

A few frames had closed in around a younger Dhanjibhai posing with various other Atwals. Dhanjibhai as he now was, still looked young for an eighty-something as he sat me down on the sofa across from him. His smallish frame and squarish head would always give him that boyish look. Past a certain stage what counts is only the 'pass-for' age. Dhanjibhai's pass-for age could be fifty-eight, particularly in those moments of relived happiness when smiles creased his face but somehow erased the years.

It was with a smile that he began to tell me of his flight from Bombay to London.

'Do you know, I used to be a Gandhi satyagrahi, but I was also a real Bombay-ka-khiladi. I paid 2800 rupees for my ticket to London. That was in 1956, the days of the Suez crisis. The ticket was for 1300 rupees but, you know, with agent and all it came to 2800. That is what agents charged those days. Of course, now they take lakhs and lakhs. Then you could still go to England easily compared to now. It was a free country. But the British government had written that too many illiterate people are coming there and they cannot find work, and so they should be stopped.

'We were a group of four. We had bought our tickets, you know, in the black market. We met at Santa Cruz airport to take a BOAC flight via Karachi, Cairo and Frankfurt to Heathrow. My ticket was for Nairobi. The agent had told us he would take care of it and someone in Karachi would change the ticket to one for London.

'But when we landed at Karachi, we got into trouble. The customs people took our passports and kept our bags on one side. They opened my bags, they were looking for addresses in England.

' "You are going to England! We will throw you behind the bars!" an officer shouted at us. I argued with him. He cannot arrest us, I told him. We are just in transit for Nairobi.

'Then one old man came out of an office. He looked at me and began to walk slowly to one side. I ran after him and shouted "Salaam waleikhum". He seemed like Khuda ka banda to me, I told him that. I said to him, we are in trouble, we want help. I told him what happened. He said to me I cannot help you, you will have to go to jail. But then he looked around and said, there is a chance. He said, talk to a customs man called Silva. He said, nod twice when you see Silva.

'I saw Silva. I nodded to him twice, many times. Silva did not see me nodding, I think. He asked me, who are you? Again I nodded twice. He got very angry. I said to him, "I am from Bombay, don't you remember me? Why didn't you come to receive me?" I am a Bombay-ka-khiladi, so that is what I said. Silva didn't seem to like it. He threw me out of the queue, and he said to me, go and stand to one side.

'I waited all day. Then at six in the evening, after the duty changed, Silva came to me. He told me I can get my passport and ticket to London. He said that, and then he just waited. I said, I want the passport and ticket first. He said I would have to go to a hotel and take the flight next morning. The other three fellows and I were taken to a hotel. There the old man came to see us—you know, that Khuda ka banda. I knew then that Khuda is not juda from us. I fell at the old man's feet, I literally begged him to help us. He said, don't worry, reach the airport at five in the morning. I gave him ten pounds, and he said, no, that is too much. I told him it is for his grandchildren, I told him I love his grandchildren. He was very happy.

'The next day we went to the airport and we found Silva waiting for us. I took him to one side and offered him a pack of cigarettes. Have a smoke, I said. He opened the packet. Inside I had put one five-pound note and one ten-pound note. He was very happy. He took me to a counter and gave me my passport and the ticket. The ticket was not for Nairobi, the ticket was for London.

'We arrived at Heathrow via Cairo and Frankfurt. There the police officer told us to stand to one side. He said he will arrest us because we have come here to settle. Then he called one army officer who had served in India. The officer came and abused us in Hindi. He called me "kutta ka bachha". Then he said so many things like "kala" and "sala". I told him to calm down. You stayed in our country for 250 years, I said, we did not abuse you. I said we were all going to Nairobi, we have just come to see London for one week. He did not know I am a Bombay-ka-khiladi.

'Then one senior officer came. I told him I am a cloth trader and my companions are also here on business. We will see the place, see if we can do business and then go away in one week. I was wearing a Gandhi cap, and he was very impressed. Then one lady came. They talked and after some time they let us go. My friend Kunwarjibhai was waiting for us outside. He had come from Wednesbury to take us to his house. We went to Victoria Station to take a train to Wednesbury. And do you know something? I have never seen Victoria Station again.'

Some time after moving to Leicester the satyagrahi must have taken over from the khiladi. It started, Dhanjibhai said, after he heard the story of Jenabhai. 'I remember that day,' he said, and again he seemed to look a long way back through his glasses, this time to the story he'd heard. 'There was heavy snow—foot and a half. Nobody was outside, nobody. That was the day on which Jenabhai appeared. When I heard what he had gone through, I knew I now I have to do something.'

Jenabhai too had arrived at Heathrow on a BOAC flight. His ticket had been arranged by an agent in Bombay who had made sure Jenabhai was not carrying any evidence on him—not even an address in Britain—that could raise an immigration officer's suspicion that he had come to settle there. He was told the only word he should speak was 'Leicester'.

'Jenabhai told us a stewardess took him to the BOAC counter at Heathrow. Then BOAC staff called a taxi to take him to St Pancras Station in London. He had some pounds and shillings with him. The driver took Jenabhai to the ticketmaster at St Pancras and asked him to put Jenabhai on a train to Leicester. The ticketmaster found a passenger who would help Jenabhai get off at Leicester. At the London Road Station in Leicester the man put him in the hands of the stationmaster, who called a taxi to take him to Stafford Road, you know, very near this house. And they were all English people, all English strangers who were helping Jenabhai.

'But after Jenabhai got to Stafford Road he did not know what to do. He had never seen snow, he had never felt so cold. After some time one white woman came. Jenabhai ran out of the telephone booth, shouting "I Indian, I Indian". The woman was frightened by this black man in the snow. She ran away, and she was screaming. She went to a laundry on Stafford Road where an Indian, Hirabhai, worked. So Hirabhai came to the telephone booth and found Jenabhai. And you know what he did? He slapped Jenabhai. Then Jenabhai had to explain he was not attacking the woman. So Hirabhai took him to 63 Loughborough Road, where a lot of Indians lived. There Jenabhai met Jeevanbhai, who was from the same village in Gujarat. They gave him hot food, and brandy and a bed in a room with fireplace.

'But, you see, the question was this: How many Jenabhais are there? And what are we going to do about them? There are Jenabhais coming in every day. We decided to do something that very week. We went to the stationmaster in Leicester and gave him 63 Loughborough Road as an address for all lost Indians. Then we took a train to St Pancras and left the same address with the stationmaster's office there. Then we went to Heathrow airport to give the address as a sort of help centre for any Indian who needs it. Many people came to us after that.'

To an Indian arriving in England without an address, the usually recommended way, just Leicester became an address. Then destination, and then home.

Britain wasn't easy destination for an Indian, not even in the pre-visa mid-fifties. Dhanjibhai Atwal had managed to get to Heathrow and, past it, to Leicester. Jenabhai had followed and then more Jenabhais. But you couldn't just get to Britain and be. The 'what next' question wasn't easy, and it rose early.

'The British people, they used to think we are a bunch of dark coolies from the Raj days,' Atwal said. 'They used to think we are mad, we have no brains, we cannot do proper work.' They were only given work that the British were too spoilt to touch, and it was as coolies that many of the first arrivals worked, Dhanjibhai with them. Like other early Indians at 63 Loughborough Road, he negotiated long years searching for better work and found mostly abuse. Until rescue came in the shape of the engineering company J.W. Bastard & Co. That unfortunately named company proved more than fortunate for Indians. It would make workers out of coolies.

'You must know how we managed to get a foothold in this city,' Dhanjibhai said. 'Otherwise all this history will die with me.' His wife had brought us some tea in the meanwhile, which had rapidly settled to room temperature. 'They do not understand,' he said, pointing towards Belgrave Road and Melton Road. 'All this could not have happened if we had not tried so hard then.' And it could not have happened without that Englishman Alberts, Dhanjibhai said, or without that man Dhanjibhai remembers only as 'Punjabi Bhai'.

Dhanjibhai and his friends had been working as coolies in a timber yard in Leicester, like all the other Indians they knew, until they ran into Alberts.

'He was the manager of the spinning mill on Frog Island. He gave work to one Punjabi bhai. He was the only Indian we knew who had a proper job, he was not a coolie. So we spoke to Punjabi bhai, we asked him to help some of us. So he spoke to Alberts, and Alberts agreed to take two more Indians. He decided he would train them for three months in the mill. You know what we did? We sent two of our men who had already worked in mills in Navasari. The men picked up in two days what they would have learnt in three months' training. Punjabi bhai could not believe it. Alberts could not believe it.

'At the end of the second day the two men told the rest that Alberts had in their presence said things like "very nice" and "very fine". Alberts asked for more Indians to come and work at the mill, so more of our men joined. I also joined. We all taught each other. We used to work on two, even four machines at a time. We would work at night, go on working. We stayed away from the unions. These British, they work with their mouths, we worked with our hands.'

It worked. Sixty more Indians joined within months, Dhanjibhai said. The factory began to work three shifts, its balance sheets began to balance a little at first and then to unbalance happily. British workers used to complain about working conditions, the Indians were ready to work no matter what the conditions.

'You know, that year when Christmas came, we arranged to have a party. We called Alberts and his wife as guests, we booked a nice place in Granby Hotel. We decided to present his wife with a gold necklace. We contributed one pound each, some even gave two. Myself, I gave two. When Alberts and his family arrived, we gave them a VIP reception. We gave his wife a gold necklace and we gave his daughter roses. Alberts put the necklace around his wife's neck. Then he gave a speech. He said thank you to us. Then he said something we were not expecting. He said that in the New Year he would take 200 more workers. He said we could do in one week what a British worker does in one month. He said, the

British had ruled India but they did not tell us about your great culture, what you are, and what you can achieve. He said, your work is like magic, I did not know you are all so intelligent. He said the production has doubled, he said the spinning mill had come out of its losses.'

'We were so grateful,' Dhanjibhai said. 'So we said this company is not Bastard. It is Bestard.'

The story spread. 'There was an annual meeting of managers from all factories of the region. We know that Alberts made a speech there praising us Indian workers sky-high. After that everything changed. One time we used to be turned away from factory gates, they used to call us mad people. Now they started inviting us in, they would say, come in, we'll sort you out. Then Alberts called a meeting of Indian workers in the canteen of J.W. Bastard. He told us we need workers in the north, in Lancashire and Yorkshire. He told me he will get our people work, but he said we must not let him down. We said, we will never let you down. So groups of our workers began to go north, fifteen people, twenty people at a time.

'People wrote to their families that there is work, come. So people came in one flight after another, and there were no complaints. Why would there be complaints? In the factory that Alberts had, our people would work, you know, eighteen hours at a time even. They would never ask for more. But Alberts would give us two pints of beer free as bonus at the end of the day. I used to talk to Alberts all the time. I took in many, many people. And to our people I said, work hard and help others from your own country. People from mills background came and they succeeded. I used to try and help people so they could work twenty-six weeks in one place. After that they could register on the Labour Exchange and work anywhere.'

Dhanjibhai became supervisor. He did okay working for himself and for the British firm, but he began to work more and more also for the planeloads of Indians flying in. He was worker, fixer and leader. 'I know how to do things for others because I was a satyagrahi with Gandhiji. But I know how to do things for myself because I am also a Bombay-ka-khiladi.'

SHIRES SHARE

Leicester lost a little England and gained a little America with the opening of The Shires. Another step in the serial surrender to jeans, burgers and shopping malls that is now getting so complete you don't notice any more. From a producing city, Leicester was turning into a consuming city. The town had stopped manufacturing but it could still buy, and switch to this new way of moving goods around.

Why just Leicester, Britain was turning from a selling to a buying country, and in this new world the mall becomes the official city magnet to draw in people and their money. And because a covered American mall is also a smart place, Leicester could begin to feel good about itself again. Feeling good and moving goods are not always separate things—so America was teaching the world, and now it was Leicester's turn.

The Shires is not quite as big as the typical American mall—what is?—but it's American to detail. The sky offered a bright blue view this Saturday through the glass roof, and showed off faces below in diffused natural light. The mall, in the lately discovered American advantage, kept those faces warm. The English high street is a cold place from where you dip in and out of variously heated stores. American cover made shopping snug and sensible; it brought the street indoors. The mall was to the high street like burger to sandwich; the Americans had simply heated it into a global business.

But as I descended down the 'scenic lift' from the roof-level parking into the arcade below, The Shires seemed in some ways to have out-Americaned the Americans. Not in the design; it had the usual square kiosks selling Madison coffee and sunglasses alternating with benches down the central arcade with shops on the sides, and an entrance or two into one of those huge chain stores that always surprise you with that unexpected space within the mall. The difference lay in what retailers like to call 'footfall'. It's hard to see such crowds in an American mall, maybe they just have too much space around, maybe even too many malls. Here, every minute you stood still in the arcade, you would be in someone's way.

All of Leicester comes to The Shires at some time. 'All of Leicester' means a varied lot; Leicester is advertised now as the city of diversity, and this morning The Shires had drawn all of its diversity to feed into that busy footfall. Strolling down the arcade I found myself making way for white people, black people, Chinese-looking people, Asians of the subcontinental sort, or simply Asians, as most Brits still like to say. Everyone was here under that same glass roof, a perfect camera picture of multicultural multitudes. It looked like a model of the way the world could be.

I parked myself on a bench across from J.D. Sports. I planned to be there five hours, until 5 p.m., doing what I dared to call to myself a rough quantitative survey, since I wouldn't have to face a methodology lecturer afterwards. I wanted to see how many had come with their ethnic own, and how many with others. I would write down the number of people in each group, and who they ethnically were. I would of course never know just how many from which group had wandered in relative to their numbers in the city. I was not pretending that an accurate cross-section of Leicester had set out to parade itself before the perfect researcher. I was only looking out for the ethnic company of those that did.

The first minute was promising. I counted seventy-two persons passing between me and J.D. Sports in that one minute. In the next there were sixty-three. Other sample minutes stood mostly between these numbers. If sixty-five was an average, I would look at 3900 people in an hour, and close to 20,000 over five hours. No doubt many people would walk by more than once, no doubt later in the afternoon the footfall could lessen, and absolutely no doubt at all that my concentration would fail now and then. But my absent-mindedness would be random too, and these factors were not likely to affect the sampling. Blacks and Indians were not more likely to walk in together at 4 p.m. than at two.

Of course, my measure of multiculturalism, or the lack of it, was purely pigmental or other visibly ethnic appearances like the 'Chinese' look. Awkward thoughts, these, and ugly word, 'pigment'. But the debate over multiculturalism rests on them, just as its failure arises from them. Pigment makes peoples out of people.

Multiculturalism would succeed the day people came together as people, and not just to share space as peoples. But a sharing of space rather than togetherness was all I was seeing from my bench minute after eye-opening minute. The Shires brought people together, and still kept them apart. Almost every group was single-ethnic coded. Group after group from different cultures appeared, but almost never different cultures within a group. Everything appeared normal, and nothing seemed right, at least not as they said it was in multicultural Leicester.

A white girl in a kilt came to sit on the backrest my side, boots on bench. She was calling out to her friends, all white, on the first floor walkway in English I struggled to follow. Three Asian girls passed by between me and J.D., then another three; there's something about girls going shopping in threes. I reminded myself that I was there to note just the colour coding of passing groups.

But why should it be remarkable that the white girl who would not use a bench as a bench be talking only to white girls? Or that the threes were all-Asian threes? That's the way it is; it just happens not to be the way the slogans go. If this was multicultural Leicester, then these ought not to be the only groups, the only conversations. And yet, through that afternoon, this was the only kind of togetherness I overwhelmingly saw.

Over five hours I scanned perhaps 12,000 to 15,000 people. Through this I counted only forty-four people in twelve mixed groups. A black guy with a white girl here, an Indian youngster with some Chinese-looking friends there, only a rare few sharing more than the roof. Most mixed groups were clearly university students, and I was beginning to feel gloomy enough to ask how long this would last past university days. Everyone else came and went with their ethnic own. If this observation was valid, we were talking zero point zero zero something by way of multicultural Leicester, which would of course make it not multicultural at all.

With so little to note by way of cross-cultural togetherness, I found myself making nonsense observations instead. White people, I found, walked a good deal faster than Asians. When they walked at the same speed, white people took longer steps. White people mostly looked ahead and moved forward efficiently, like they were going somewhere; Asians looked sideways a good deal more and walked too with a more sideward sway. Asians walked like they thought they were in a smart place, white people walked like they were in just some place. Asians walked like they would like to be looked at, the whites looked like they didn't care.

Among Asians, no one looked around more than single males; they were there for the shoppers, not the shopping. Indians had an eye for one another, the whites seemed more self-contained. White or non-white, there seemed a higher number of single gender groups, particularly female; girls obviously liked going shopping with girls. Girls in groups usually carried shopping bags; in male groups very few seemed to carry any, as though bags would lessen their dash. Whites touched one another only when they were a couple; Asians touched one another a lot more outside couple links, but almost never as a couple. Many Asian girls linked arms, I saw no white girls who did. Those who came alone were mostly white.

A lot more Indians had teenaged children with them. Many of the Muslim women came with small children. 'I told you so,' I'd have heard a Shiv Sainik on my bench say, had he been there. Asian parents kept a close eye on children; white parents let the kids keep an eye on them. Between me and J.D. Sports that afternoon, all sorts of commonplace patterns that had congealed into clichés appeared and went their way.

It was commonplace that people stick to their own, you see that every day, everywhere. What struck me this Saturday afternoon was the near completeness of the separation. People, as representative of peoples walked by each other a lot, but found no meeting ground. 'Multicultural Leicester' had declared itself different. Leicester was not really a multicultural city, only a city of adjacent cultures.

My final observation that afternoon as I got up to leave at 5 p.m. was that no wooden bench is meant to be sat upon that long.

Across the flyover that leads on from The Shires to Belgrave Road, Leicester wasn't pretending to be multicultural. This was India, and all of it Indian.

Belgrave Road is where Leicester's famous Diwali celebrations take place. It's brightly lit that evening, and closed to traffic because it has to make room for anything from 30,000 to 50,000 people. I was among them the last two Diwalis. Indians came as usual from many other places in the Midlands, and even beyond. Both times, the near complete absence of white people stood out almost as much as the size of the crowds. Whatever happened to British curiosity? They love to go out and see the world, but they don't much like it when the world moves down into the next street.

'You see, it's like you're in an aeroplane and now you're landing in India,' my friend Raksha was explaining to her little daughter one day as she drove us over Belgrave flyover in the Suzuki four-wheel drive. Children learn early about that difference in worlds from one side of the flyover to the other. Behind us was the city centre and The Shires. Down the flyover, we landed in Gujarat.

The shop signs said so, the ones in English included. Friendly Fashions—plain English words, but put them together and they can only add up to an Indian company. And who else but a store called Laheka will offer 'exclusive designer outfits for ladies'?

Friends Tandoori and a couple of other restaurants must be the only Indian places that draw some white people to the area. Nothing but a curry would bring white people here, and nothing will keep them here once they're done with it. Buses carry white people through Belgrave Road, but they never get off. Leicester will begin to get multicultural the day they begin to.

Belgrave flyover is no hyphen between white Leicester and Indian Leicester; it's a dividing line. Leicester is perhaps not a city even of adjacent cultures, it's only variously monocultural.

GIVE ME GHETTO

I wasn't expecting to step on to a metal sheet when Mrs Barot opened the door. She saw my surprise over this metal doormat.

'It's these boys,' she said. 'They had been throwing fire inside and they used to put shit through the letter box. So I put this iron sheet and I sealed the letter box.' The way she told me, she'd obviously been saying it to visitors before; matter-of-fact, like it was just sensible to let shit land on a tin sheet, not on a welcoming rug.

My friend Sheetal Singh Gill and I had dropped in at the Barots' house in Northfields in Leicester. Northfields is just about a mile or so out from the Indian heart of Leicester around Belgrave Road and Melton Road, but it is a long mile. It's mostly white working class, which is fine, but the Barots had begun to feel stranded in hostile land here. Gill had lately been very concerned about them. Gill, ex-Hoshiarpur and also ex-Indian Workers Association, that early migrant group, drove a taxi for a living but his heart was in the job of getting concerned. He had been trying to help the Barots for a while, without much success.

A few steps into the house, our feet now on carpet, we sat down to wait for her husband Kanubhai Barot. He came downstairs on a banister lift. Somehow, his wife said, he had been unwell one way or another ever since they moved into this house.

Mr Barot seemed to be in his late sixties, and Gill had told me he was now retired from very active years in the Indian community in Leicester. Since he came to Leicester in 1978, he had been joint secretary at the Shree Sanatan Mandir and then general secretary of the Gujarat Hindu Association that holds together many Gujarati organizations around Leicester. He spent years there making things happen right through the annually packed Hindu calendar. He edited two Gujarati magazines—*Amay Gujarati* and *Sanatan Sandesh*—and was vice-chairman of the Belgrave Neighbourhood Centre, the busiest Gujarati meeting place in Belgrave. Until very recently he taught Hindustani vocal music at Belgrave Road.

Kanubhai looked stronger than he must have been; tall and almost tough. His wife set a straight chair for him in the middle of the room. He lowered himself slowly on to it, looking at the window. The white blinds were letting in some insufficient winter sunshine, but Mr Barot had no eyes for sunshine, he was looking by anxious reflex to see if there was someone there. The window looked out on a world of trouble.

Mrs Barot sat at the table behind, cleaning moong dal for

dinner, 'mug' as Gujaratis call it, as in English mug. An Indian home can't get any more Indian than this—a husband retired from singing Hindustani vocal and organizing community events, at home with his wife preparing dal. But outside was an England that wouldn't let them be.

'Look, they shoot at my windows with air guns,' Mr Barot said. 'Take a closer look at the windows.' I saw little pockmarks covered with adhesive plaster, evidence of several attacks.

'Come let me show you the side,' Mrs Barot said. She opened the door to a little storeroom under the stairs. A window here had more bits of plaster with cracks spreading out around them. To the Barots every window was a weak spot; to those shooting at them, every one an opportunity.

'You are not thinking of changing the glasses?' Gill asked.

'I can't go on replacing windows, how many windows can I replace?' Mrs Barot said. 'On each window I will have to spend twenty or twenty-five pounds. How many times will I replace? They will break more. How long can this go on? If they smash the whole thing, I'll have to change it. But this hole with the air gun, chalta hai. If I start replacing the windows, they will make it a point to shoot at them again.' Replacing a glass pane wouldn't just be expensive, it would be provocative. The Barots couldn't win, and they weren't trying.

'But haven't you reported this to the police?' I asked Mr Barot back in their sitting room. An obviously naïve question.

'We have, so many times. But they say they can't do anything.'

'How long has this been going on?'

'For so many years. Every week there is something.'

'You said something every *week*?'

'Every week once or twice something or the other happens here. We are fed up, god, we are really fed up. What shall we do? We bought this house, spent so much money on it. It will be such a loss, but I think I will have to leave. Everybody who comes here, goes.'

As we'd driven up to the Barots', we'd seen signs of a fire in the shop next door that served also as post office. As was usual, the owners lived above the shop. I asked if that fire too was the racists' doing.

'Of course. I heard the alarm go off in their house,' Mr Barot said. 'They were away, they had told us to keep an eye. I rushed to the phone to call the police but my line was dead. They had cut the main line. Nobody in any house around us could use the telephone. They broke into the shop, they looted it. Next morning I found a video belonging to the shopkeeper in my garden. When our telephone was connected again, I phoned the police. I told them there's a brand new video lying in my garden and it's about to rain. They said, go and give it in at the post office.'

'You mean the police knew this was the video stolen from the post office?'

'Yes, they knew. The police had come by at about two in the night, they knew what had happened.'

'You mean there was a burglary, the stolen video was left in your garden, and the police asked you to return it to the shop?'

'Yes, they just said go and give it to the post office, or tell them to come and pick it up. We told the shop owners. They came and picked it up. What shall I say? So many of these things happen here all the time. You see, if we complain to the police, it comes into the newspaper. When they come to know we have complained, the next day we will be finished. They will destroy us, they will break our home into pieces, they will burn our home.'

'Has this sort of thing happened?'

'This is what happened at the post office right next to us. They burnt the house at night.'

'Had the owners complained to the local paper?'

'Yes, the earlier tenants had complained and it was written about in the local newspaper. They were abused endlessly and driven out. You should never let anybody know that you have a problem.'

The attack seemed to have been part punishment. The Punjabi family who had taken the post office and shop had decided to confront the children who would keep vandalizing it. Mr Barot knew better.

The Punjabi couple was younger, and angrier, and that was their fault, Mrs Barot said. 'When the kids came and sat on the wall and shouted at her, she said don't make noise here. A white person will not take that kind of talk from us, will they? She kept scolding them, so they would do it more and more. They used to write dirty things on their door, like black bastard, Paki bastard. She used to clean the wall. Then they would come and write more. One lady told her, don't react, they will do more. But she kept stopping them, and it became worse and worse. So the couple got fed up and left.'

The racists then went for the Barots. Someone needed revenge for what their Indian neighbours had dared to do, Mrs Barot said. She was downstairs watching TV that day, when she heard the door rattle. 'I thought my son is here. He has a key so I ignored the noise. I heard someone trying to open the door again and again. Then I went to look. I saw a hand coming in through the letter box and there was a fire in the hand. I shouted, Who is it? Who is it? What do you want? They ran away. Afterwards a man and a woman came from the police. I told them what had happened. They said they will take a round in the evening, but we should be careful. That was all.'

There is only one family the Barots say they can turn to—their white next door neighbours. 'He said that if we are attacked and the phone goes dead, we can bang loudly on the wall. They are very nice. We take chicken-vicken to their place sometimes.' The couple was kind, but they were elderly and struggling with their own lives. The Barots could turn to bang on their wall if the phone went dead, but the couple could do nothing to stop the Barots getting attacked. Still, while those they dreaded were white, this white couple was their only hope in trouble, even if they had very little to do with them most of the time.

'Now you know why so many people are moving out of here,' Gill said. 'Why our people like to live with our people.' He had been telling me for a while that Leicester is not that comfortably Indian in these parts.

Gill lived in another part of Northfields, down a street many Indians had moved into. From a white point of view, it was an Asian mini ghetto; for Gill and his neighbours, a little street fortress where their families were relatively safe.

Many spot that safety too late. 'People come from London, from Manchester, they see that this area is very quiet, very nice, the prices are good, so they buy,' Gill said. 'Then they realize where they have come. And then it's hard to leave. They have invested money, and they cannot find a buyer because nobody is willing to pay anything close to what they paid.'

The Barots wanted to move, but property agents knew why. 'They have brought the price of this house so low that it is becoming difficult to move,' Barot said. And he had other problems. 'Now that I am disabled, I can't get a mortgage. Where will I find another house to live in? I get so angry with all this. I say the government should give us a licence for a machine gun. I tell you, I will shoot these people.'

'Children' seemed the most terror-laden word the Barots knew. 'It's the children we fear the most,' Mr Barot said. 'You know, they are children, but they have the dirtiest abuses. What are their parents doing? These people just leave their children to themselves. They don't care what they do, whether they study or not, that they are harming others or even themselves. They just leave them. The elderly people here, they are all right. We just want the local council to do one thing. Make this an estate for the elderly. We will be all right. It's the only solution. Just take these children away from here.'

'How old are the children?'

'They are all just ten to fifteen years old.'

'Do you report them to the police?'

'I cannot say which child did this. But we have told them that it's the children who do it.'

'So what do they say?'

'They say they cannot do anything. Under the law they cannot take action against a child.'

'So that means the children can legally do all this to you?'

'Yes, that is what they say. We just want them to take the children away from here.'

It was not a suggestion Mr Barot has pursued seriously. If white British children were to leave an estate in England because an Indian had objected to them, the *Sun* would find a headline the government wouldn't want to read. The Barots had done all they could to fortify the house. Now they just waited, for that weekly assault, for time to pass, for just something to change somehow.

A lid screwed on to the letterbox would now keep out a white hand with fire and the envelopes packed with shit. But there were some defences the Barots had abandoned. They'd stopped trying to hold up the fence. Again and again the fence at the back of the little house had been torn down. White gangs would walk into the little lawn, bang on the door at the back near the kitchen. They shouted abuse in the day and at night, at home, outside. The insurance did not cover fencing because they said it's not considered a part of the house. Also, the Barots could not protect their car. A week before I met the Barots, a window of their car was smashed, the stereo taken away.

White people's cars also got broken into in the neighbourhood, but too many things happened at the Barots' house that don't to white persons. 'They abuse us when we step out. We don't use the front street any more. We take a short cut from the back to try and avoid them. It's not safe to even drive along this road. They hate us. They are jealous. They say we have a house, a car with a radio and stereo. Sometimes they don't have money in their pocket for a meal. They don't like it, they hate us for it, they want to destroy it for us.'

Mr Barot knew hundreds of people in Leicester, but none who could help. Some members of the Gujarat Hindu Association where Mr Barot had worked for years were on the police board in Leicester. 'They have been saying that the police should send people in plain clothes to keep an eye on the situation. But nothing is happening.' The leader was now a fugitive. The man of music now dreamt of a machine gun. 'The community supports people,' he said, shaking his head, 'but they don't get into these problems. If somebody is harassing me here, what can they do? Nobody gets involved in problems with the police or the white people.'

'Would you be happier in Belgrave?'

'Oh yes, if they try that in Belgrave, our people will get together and beat them up. But out here in the middle of all of them we can do nothing.'

'Is this why so many Indians stay together?'

'Yes, this is why you have the ghetto system, why everyone stays together, so that if anybody attacks us, we can get together and do something. Here there's one of our homes alone on one street, someone alone in another corner. What can we do? We can do nothing. Unless we sell this property and go away, or give it to somebody for free and go away.'

'So are you planning to sell and move?'

'We would lose our life's savings. If we had a house in Belgrave, we could sell it easily and at a good price. I think I will call an estate agent, try to exchange this for something else somewhere.'

From this house, Belgrave looked like home.

KASHMIR CAB

When Ajit Doval was made director of the Intelligence Bureau, he probably didn't list the meeting on Kashmir in Leicester that evening among his credentials. But in the shadowy style of intelligence men, he must have done his bit to make it happen.

It was always an idea waiting to happen; diplomacy from within. While India talks to Britain, Indians in Britain would talk to people in Britain, create a British Indian movement to counter the very active Pakistanis. The Pakistanis had been doing it for years. Calling meetings, meeting MPs, writing to them, lecturing at universities, lecturing in mosques, demonstrating outside India House, outside 10 Downing Street, raising Kashmir in council meetings, sourcing funds for Pakistani centres, promoting this, pushing that.

Indians had spent too long doing very little of the kind. It was time to move them, and who could start this better than local elected Indians. BJP leaders would come with their Kashmir speeches and go, but political movements are nothing if not local. There were after all more than a hundred Indian councillors elected to local government all over Britain. They'd been invited to receptions and lunches at India House. This was payback time, time for an Indian meeting on Kashmir.

The principal mover and shaker was Parmi Bhai, now walking into the hall at the Abbey Primary School by Belgrave Road. I was the first to arrive at the hall, the caretaker had cheerfully let me in: 'Come in, mate, they should be along.' Parmi Bhai walked in soon after, with that look of a man who's called the meeting, you can tell them apart at every meeting.

I'd known Parmi Bhai for years off and on. His parents had named him Paramjit Singh Bahia, but everyone knew him as Parmi Bhai. He'd been elected earlier to the city council in Southampton on a Labour ticket. He spoke often of troubled relations with the party, which considered him some local loose cannon. Only because, he said, he was a 'committed sort of chap'.

Parmi Bhai was a taxi driver, and he'd given up business for the day to drive four hours from Southampton in his red Citroën taxi for the meeting. Outside of his taxi, he was very much a politician. He was in his fifties, and balding between silver-grey hair around his ears. You might almost think he was white unless he stood next to a white man. For the meeting, he wore a dark blue suit over an immaculate white shirt with spotted red tie. An important-looking briefcase in his hand completed the picture of a man who has things to do. He looked the professor–politician.

Paul Sood, then contesting to be a Labour councillor walked in soon after. Sood, a greying Jalandhari lad, had helped Parmi Bhai organize the meeting, with of course some silent support from Doval. Abbey Primary School was in Sood's ward, his home ground for his political future. Sood joined Parmi in that host look. We all waited, and then two more turned up, Ajit Doval and Saleem Gillings, the Jamaican chairman of the National Association of Race Equality Councils.

'He's here as observer,' Parmi Bhai told me. 'Important chap. My buddy.'

But no one else appeared, and it was past time for the meeting. Sood figured the reason. Clocks had been put forward an hour to move to summer time (in that odd Western tradition, since the sun does not consult Greenwich before it rises). 'Our people, you know, they must have forgotten,' Sood said to us. 'They'll all be here an hour late.' He looked a bit agitated, fearful that his guests may not be so forgetful after all. He and Parmi had prepared their speeches; the audience was missing, but for me.

Parmi Bhai and Doval exchanged looks, and Doval tactfully took Gillings out for coffee to give the rest time to turn up.

Parmi had been waiting for the moment when Gillings would pass hearing distance. 'Where's everybody, bhenchod?' he said to Sood.

'I don't know, I told everyone,' Sood said. He'd sent letters or faxes to 130 Indian councillors, he said, then he had phoned them. Almost all had promised they would come. The front rows had been reserved for the councillors. They were vacant, and there was nobody at the back who could be moved up.

We heard some steps, and Sood smiled. 'See, they're coming.' A man with a Hindu tilak sitting large on his forehead walked in. Chandubhai Bhatt from the Hindu Council of Leicester.

'Where's everybody?' he asked.

'There's a little confusion about the time change,' Sood said.

'You mean everybody has forgotten?' Chandubhai looked at his watch brushing against rolls of rudraksh. He was not convinced, and his forehead creased up around his tilak. We were all beginning to sound a little loud in the empty hall, and Sood was losing faith that British Summer Time would save the meeting.

'Maybe it's because it is Mother's Day,' Sood ventured. No one said anything, and Sood looked like he wished he hadn't opened his mouth.

Some whispering between Sood and Parmi led to hurried telephoning, that produced another two men who arrived with their wives and children. They sat for a bit, then wandered in and out, waiting for something to happen. Sood was looking out of the window, and seeing only failure. Two young girls turned in from the road towards the hall.

'See, they're coming,' he said.

'Why you are counting the same people again and again?' Parmi barked.

He was blaming Sood, but Sood would not be blamed. 'What is happening here today in Leicester has been happening for 1300 years in India,' he said, speech-like. 'What is wrong with us, do we have blood in our veins or water?'

'Too much water my friend,' Chandubhai said. He'd seen it all before. 'If they were doing a meeting on Kashmir they would have collected thousand people in half an hour.' They. The Pakistanis, of course.

'It's these Gujaratis,' Sood said. 'They can go on getting pushed and they'll do nothing. That's why they got thrown out of East Africa.'

Vasant Kalyani, photographer for the *Leicester Mercury* walked in. Sood and Parmi were trying not to look at his camera, but Kalyani was sympathetic. 'Badokidogo, we used to say in Tanzania.' What will be will be.

Sood produced a small rescue act. Sheetal Singh Gill, that saviour to many, walked in. He mattered, as president then of the Indian Workers Association in Leicester, a leftist outfit that was strong in the fifties and sixties. Now he headed the local taxi union, of mostly Indian and Pakistani taxi drivers. The Kashmir agitation had brought him here just before a cab drivers meeting he had called later in the evening. The taxi drivers had a fight on their hands. They'd been driving their cheap Japanese cars happily enough, but now the council wanted them to buy the FX4s, familiar as the London cab. Those cabs cost £24,000 each, twice the price of a new Japanese car. Taxi drivers usually bought used Japanese cars for a few thousand, and the new requirement meant that taxi drivers were in for it. Gill was leading the agitation against the London cab being forced upon the streets of Leicester.

'Do something,' Sood said to him after explaining the emptiness of the hall. He didn't say it with hands folded, but there's a way of saying such things without using your hands. Gill left, and returned fifteen minutes later with about twenty taxi drivers. Some numbers at last, but I saw the problem immediately as they walked in, and so of course would Sood and Parmi; a good number of the taxi drivers were clearly Pakistanis. We now had an Indian meeting on Kashmir where about half the audience was Pakistani. Gill had meant well, but this was always going to be a danger if an Indian meeting on Kashmir had to borrow bodies from a meeting of Leicester taxi drivers.

'Let's get it done now,' Doval said to Parmi. This was not going to be among his successes and he wanted it to end quickly.

If a meeting meant someone speaking and someone listening, we had a meeting now. Sood stepped on to the stage with Gillings sitting on one side, Parmi on the other. I waited to hear what they would say on Kashmir before this unexpectedly mixed audience.

Sood was the chair; and left the speech to Parmi, who walked up to the mike and launched into it straightaway after a quick welcome. 'Where is human rights when they harass us at Heathrow? And they got audacity to tell us about problems affecting us? They lecture on Kashmir. What right they have to talk without full facts?' He had mentioned Kashmir, but said nothing about it. I admired him for speaking as though there were more of us.

Parmi took the mike in a settled kind of way. 'It is mothering Sunday, we have adopted some of their customs here,' he said, hoping this would explain the missing Indians and their absence of interest in Kashmir. 'This is Mother's Day but nobody thinks of Motherland Day.' He paused as speakers do before thunderous applause, which we'd have had if we weren't so short of hands.

'Comrades, you know what is first thing I do when I get up in the morning?' Parmi paused again, and it was good more people weren't around for embarrassing guesswork. 'I get up and go to bathroom.' What next?

'There is mirror there, big mirror. I look my face into it. Then I ask that mirror: WHO AM I? Mirror tells me, Parmi, you are black and don't you ever forget it. After that I have coffee and I know I am Indian. And I know I'm not going to apologize for it.'

Parmi was not going to apologize for the small numbers either. 'Mahabharat was won by five Pandavas. Guru Gobind Singh created an army out of five. Christ also had only twelve–thirteen. We can start from small number but if we have faith we will succeed, opposition *will* fail.'

Parmi was getting into the mood and no one seemed to notice that he'd forgotten all about Kashmir. 'The biggest problem is racism. Even prime minister admits it.' We were still waiting for Kashmir, but Parmi continued. 'You know what we are all farting for?' I knew Parmi, and so I knew he meant 'fighting', these things happen when you part-import an accent. And there weren't that many others who'd get him wrong. 'I will always be farting for the have-nots. When they needed soldiers we became soldiers, when they needed workers we became workers, when they needed services we became doctors and nurses. When economy was collapsing, we had the tricks. British leaders go to lay wreath on the samadhi of Gandhi, but they never talk about virginity tests here. Remember, Chair, how we ran that campaign?' Chair, recently the bhenchod, nodded the way leaders do when momentous matters are on their mind.

But now the taxi gang was getting up to leave. They had made a meeting of this, and it was time for their own. 'Wish you luck with the taxi meeting anyway,' Parmi said. He had to let the remaining six or seven of us know that this was not a walkout.

Now Parmi turned to Kashmir. The real speech could begin only after the audience was gone. He raised a sheet of paper and waved it around. It was a statement by Labour MP Clare Short. She had always been critical of India over Kashmir, and she'd just returned from Pakistan with more to say that was less than kind about the Indian government. 'It is downright wicked fiction by a woman in a dream world who only looks what she wants to see.' He paused, then said, 'Clare is not fair.' He waited, aware that he'd again said something that demanded applause pause. 'If she is not living in fool's paradise where the hell she is living? I have paper here that says 7817 people have died in Kashmir from terrorism. That's hell of lot of people, Clare. What if so many had died in London and Birmingham and Guildford? But they don't mention about it, that's what makes me sick. And they are pouring fuels on burning fires.'

In the audience the two women who had come in with their men had stopped nudging one another and whispering, they were actually listening. They had been patient. A couple of men had been loyal to the cause, the women had been loyal to their men. But Parmi's speech continued mostly to the walls of an empty school. 'When cold wind starts blowing in subcontinent, Indians and Pakistanis here start sneezing, I tell you. But we are all victims of racism. Clare should start farting about that, I tell you.' This was now becoming a communication between Parmi and the mike. Finally he stopped. We vacated the vacant hall.

'It was a bad show, how did you manage it?' Parmi asked Sood, down where the audience should have been.

'You see, I did not publicize this meeting openly.'

'Why not?'

'If it had been on the local radio there would have been Khalistanis, there would have been everyone.' The invited did not come, some who might have come were not invited. This became a secret public meeting.

TURBAN AND TROUBLE

It would have been another of those gray and dull mornings in England without the pink and peacock blue salwar kameezes on the pavement across the gurdwara on East Park Lane in Leicester. Or the yellow so prominent among the turbans this Sunday morning, the yellow of protest, or at least the colour to make a point in. It was right to pick a turban in that yellow, because the turban was what the meeting at the gurdwara this morning was about.

Somewhere in boring Brussels a bunch of Eurocrats had made the wearing of helmets compulsory in factories and other locations considered high-risk. To a Sikh that order came as an overhanging threat that a helmet must replace the turban at these locations, and this is what the Sikhs were gathering to talk about.

The ruling from Brussels set off a first dispute between Surinder Singh Dhanjol and the steel factory where he worked in Wolverhampton. He had refused to replace his turban with a 'hard hat' in the factory area. So he was confined to the boiler plant and then offered small administrative jobs that he declined. Finally, he was sacked. He appealed to an industrial tribunal in Birmingham and lost. That led to this meeting. Because it was not about Dhanjol any more, it was about Sikh honour and rights.

I ran into Dhanjol in the gurdwara basement where a quick exhibition on the Sikh struggle had been set up. It showcased mostly paintings of Sikh strength and sacrifices in the face of Mughal oppression and Operation Blue Star, and the usual pictures of Bhindranwale carrying a Sten gun. At any other place Dhanjol would be the eternal uncle, but here he was the uncle who had dared. Dhanjol was being led through the exhibition by a big man with aggressive looks, an assertively tied turban and words to match. 'If our struggles and sacrifices end, Sikhi has no meaning,' he was saying to Dhanjol, just ahead of me.

Dhanjol, the now unemployed hero, had been talking the language of sacrifice. 'I can give up my life but not my turban,' he had said on BBC Television. He now belonged to the subject of the exhibition he was walking through, comfortable amid the paintings of blood and torture.

After a short walkabout through the basement, I followed Dhanjol and his fiery companion to the gurdwara hall upstairs. The large hall was filled with people, and that unique gurdwara fragrance. Dhanjol joined the group at the front end of the hall, facing the sangat. He'd lost a job but found leadership.

The fiery man, Santokh Singh as he was introduced, began the meeting. 'They want us to take off our turbans and wear iron caps. Raise your voice against iron caps.' He spoke in Punjabi, at a pitch just right for anger. Voices went up after he spoke, saying nothing much. Santokh Singh now got louder by the sentence. 'They are testing us, they have attacked some of us already. If we don't take up the challenge, we'll all be under attack tomorrow.' Santokh Singh was loud but brief.

Lt. Gen. G.S. Clair was introduced to address the packed hall. He had retired from the Indian Army in 1987, we were all told. We all heard that unmentioned year in that statement—1984. The general had been a serving officer in the Indian army in 1984, and had not resigned despite Operation Blue Star. Everyone let that pass. As a Sikh general he had the roab due to a general; as a man he had that upright military manner you don't challenge.

'Ours has been a very honourable association with the British Empire for centuries,' the general said. 'There was an understanding we had with the British government after they took over from the East India Company.' After the uprising of 1857, that is, when several Sikh forces backed the British to set up crown rule over India. 'We were valued for our valour, our bravery. It was a very honourable profession. And then how many of us gave our lives during the two world wars to keep the Union Jack flying.'

For the general, as for many soldiers in Sikh families, that history tied in with family history. 'My father was in Third Skinner Horse in the cavalry. He served in France till he retired in 1942. My two brothers fought in the Burma War. I lost a close relative in Burma who was reported missing. I have a lot of associations with the British Empire.'

The general now turned to the point that Brussels had missed, that now the British were missing. 'When I was in the cavalry, we were never told to wear helmets. Bullets and shells were flying then—we would have needed something thicker than those plastic helmets they now want us to wear. Then we wore what the gurus gave us, we are proud of that. We have sacrificed our elders to uphold the empire through the ages, the British must now recognize our right to wear our turbans.'

It was only a small return the Sikhs were seeking for the forgotten debt. But there were no returns to be claimed for dated valour, and lives lost. It was okay for a Sikh to expose his head to bullets when it was in the cause of the empire. The Sikhs then were good for the rulers, and so the rulers were good to them. Now Sikhs have only a few votes, but they were going to make them count.

Britain has all sorts of doubts about the EU, but it was not about to sacrifice the EU for summoned memories of Sikh heroes who had fought to keep Britain intact through the world wars. There's a Remembrance Day, but it is not spent remembering Sikh soldiers. Or thinking that they might in those days have been better off in helmets. A fair bit of history hangs on that question of helmets and turbans that Brussels had never begun to suspect.

The angry speeches were routine, but everyone was waiting for Kashmir Singh, the one known for knowing everything about the turban in Britain, the intellect of the Sikh voice.

'In 1968 Sikh drivers and conductors struck in Wolverhampton because they were ordered to wear caps instead of turbans,' the suave and suited Kashmir Singh said, on a considerably lower pitch than the one Santokh Singh had produced. 'They won.' Driver Tarsem Singh Sandhu had been sacked then because the rules permitted only clean-shaven staff. Another driver, Sohan Singh Jolly, had threatened to burn himself if rules weren't changed. A supporting protest rally was held in Delhi. The Indian government stepped in to plead with the British government. Under all this weight, the managers at Wolverhampton bus depot gave in.

More turban trouble lay ahead, Kashmir Singh narrated. In

1972, Sikhs were told they couldn't ride motorcycles wearing turbans instead of helmets. 'This was ordered by the Conservative government,' Kashmir Singh told us. 'The government changed, but the Labour government didn't listen to us. Then we promised to support Margaret Thatcher and she promised to support us. Finally they changed the law in 1976 and we were allowed to ride motorcycles wearing turbans.' That you never see a Sikh riding a motorcycle is another matter. It was a battle won.

The campaign continued; it had to. A new struggle began in 1984, quite a year for Sikh struggles. A new law made helmets compulsory at construction sites. 'For five years after that we were writing to the government, we wrote two or three thousand letters. We had hundreds of meetings. We were supported by the Khalistan Council, the International Sikh Youth Federation, Akhand Kirtani Jatha, Akali Dal, Ramgarhia Board, gurdwaras, Walsall College students, Wolverhampton School students, Cambridge University students and so many others.'

And, again, the Sikhs won. They were granted exemption from helmets on construction sites under the Employment Act of 1989.

This now was the new round. If a battle on motorcycle helmets could be fought and won a little unnecessarily, Kashmir Singh offered a string of reasons for the need to win this one. Not all the bureaucrats in Brussels and London could have thought up what he did.

He presented several scenarios: A Sikh policeman is not required to wear a helmet. But what if he is chasing a thief who runs into a factory? The policeman cannot go in. If he does, he will break the law himself, and the thief will run away. A Sikh lawyer cannot represent Dhanjol. The lawyer might want to see the factory in Wolverhampton himself. If a Sikh judge like Mota Singh has to investigate what happened in the factory, he cannot. And what of a Sikh on a jury? What if the jury had to visit an accident site in a building? The Sikh on the jury would have to be replaced.

With each scenario the problem looked bigger and bigger. A Sikh architect could design a factory and watch it come up, because under British law he could enter a construction site. Once it was built he could not enter it under European law, because in its completion it had progressed from construction site to factory.

A computer engineer could set up hardware in a power station when it was being constructed. Once it was safely built, he could not enter. If he installed the hardware in time, he could not inspect the software later. A Sikh railway worker could not legally shunt a wagon any more. A Sikh householder could cut the branches of trees in his garden, but not if he was employed to do so.

A Sikh doctor could not treat anyone on a construction site accident. A Sikh ambulance driver could not drive to a dangerous area. Sikh teachers may sometimes have to show children a factory. They could not go; neither could Sikh children in class. How would Sikh businessmen win construction contracts if they could not visit what they had built? Kashmir Singh's final scenario: if right here in this gurdwara they had to paint the walls higher than six-and-a-half feet, the law said they could not do it wearing turbans.

He concluded with the argument that if this was all for the health and safety of Sikhs, they still did not need to replace turbans with helmets either for health or for safety.

Again, he had masses of data handy. Smoking 200 cigarettes a day means a one in 200 risk of death. Natural causes above age 40 bring a one in 500 chance of death, flu one in 4000, road accidents one in 5000, accidents at home one in 10,000, accidents at work one in 20,000, natural background radiation one in 40,000, radiation exposure one in 80,000, head injuries in construction work one in 500,000, head injuries in construction work to British Sikhs one in 50 million, and in non-construction areas where the new European law applies, far less than that. So what was the fuss about?

And what if that less than one in 50 million chance were to come to pass? Kashmir Singh had worked that out too.

The Health and Safety Executive in Sheffield had put the turban to a safety test, he said. For impacts to the front of the head the turban gave 141.7 per cent better protection than a helmet. For impacts to the back it gave 95.1 per cent protection, to the side 77.1 per cent, and on top 31 per cent.

And that 31 per cent figure would have been better if the kanga had been incorporated into the joorha, Kashmir Singh said. The kanga was explained to some local white leaders in the gurdwara hall as the 'wooden comb at the base of the knot of hair'. And the figure of 31 per cent would have been better if a padka had been included in the test. So the hair tied up into the joorha and strengthened with a kanga, and a padka worn within the turban would have fortified the turban that much more. And, he said, the turban tested in Sheffield should have been six to eight metres in length, not 4.5 metres. Besides, the length of the hair makes a difference. All this would have raised that 31 per cent figure quite a bit.

The turban would in fact do better than a helmet, Kashmir Singh argued. The constructional shape of the turban provided better vision. It was also higher than the head, so that the top of the turban would come into contact with structures before the head. And the turban, Kashmir Singh said, was never removed to scratch the head, as a helmet might be.

He signed off citing British authorities on the greater safety of the turban. Lt. Gen. Sir Reginald Savory, KGT, CB, DSO, MC, had written to a science officer to say he had known Sikhs pick bullets out of their turbans during and after battle, and that in fact the turban absorbed the shock of a bullet possibly rather better than a tin helmet. Col. H.A.Hughes, DSO, MBE, DL, JP, said of his regiment in the North-West Frontier Province that consisted entirely of Sikhs that he had no more head wounds here than in any other battalion wearing steel helmets.

Through the meeting, my view on the turban was changed for ever. It seemed a pity such detail should ever be necessary to defend something as sanctified as a turban. The emblem of Sikh pride had had to be offered up for cold dissection, because what do people in Brussels know? If only Kashmir Singh had never been put in a position where he had to make such a defence.

*

Who could deny the legitimacy of the campaign for the turban in that Leicester gurdwara? But it didn't feel like it was just a Sikh campaign, it had a Khalistani feel about it. Maybe it was Kashmir Singh's matter-of-fact reference to Khalistan groups among others. Or the pictures of Bhindranwale downstairs, or the ominous looking chaps at the back of the platform from the International Sikh Youth Federation.

The hidden Khalistani push came to the surface at another meeting, later, at the Guru Nanak Sikh Gurdwara in Wolverhampton, a little further west from Leicester in the Midlands. The meeting was called principally by a new group, the Sikh Secretariat. The brains behind it, again, Kashmir Singh, I was told by friends before I headed out to Wolverhampton.

The Khalistan stalls set up outside the gurdwara in Wolverhampton announced what to expect at the meeting. I can't remember another market where so many stalls all sold the same things—Bhindranwale videos, tapes, posters and books. They had taken up quite a few spaces in the gurdwara car park.

It was a bright Sunday morning, just right for stalls of a happier kind. The gurdwara was just across from a church, but the traffic down the road consisted mostly of Sikh-bearing cars headed for the gurdwara. This kind of thing had ceased to surprise anyone long back. The Wolverhampton sun had very much more of Bhindranwale's face to shine on than good Christians going to church.

Bhindranwale's face meant something to me. I had spent years reporting for the *Indian Express* on terrorist violence in Punjab and Delhi. I'd reported from Amritsar and around Punjab during Operation Blue Star. And I had managed to beat curfew and the June heat to get to Bhindranwale's village in Rode the day it was announced he had been killed.

It was a tense day; an army helicopter circled above, and a group of about 200 or so Sikhs had gathered at Bhindranwale's house. My friend Kanwar Sandhu from the *Express* had also made it to Bhindranwale's village. We'd been welcomed warmly, given a hot meal and invited to rest; that particular tradition of Punjab had been kept up for a perfect stranger, and in Bhindranwale's house, on that of all days. I felt a good deal less welcome at the gurdwara this Sunday morning in the West Midlands in England than in Rode village in Faridkot that day.

Among the few outsiders at this Khalistan mela were two white English girls in the foyer, heads covered with scarves, in blue T-shirts that said HALIFAX CAR INSURANCE. Car insurance was on offer to all within a shaheedi picture gallery of martyrs and brutal Indian police. The girls were handing out cards with smiling faces on them, pictures of happiness as known only to those who would have Halifax to call if their car were to run into another.

The girls must have been sent to take on the 'Asian' gathering here—Britain had managed to make Bhindranwale too 'an Asian'. The poor smiling girls were not going to get far; the Sikhs coming in might have one view of Bhindranwale or another, but car insurance was not going to be what they'd take away from here.

That there were two views on Bhindranwale was becoming obvious. Many Sikhs were coming in for the regular Sunday morning sangat, and then leaving. Someone on the mike was seeing this and not liking it. 'People have given the last eighteen, twenty years of their life for this, and you find it difficult to give ten minutes,' came an admonition over some hidden speaker. And this from those who should be showing the Sikhs of Punjab what true Sikhism is. 'There is no true Sikhism in Punjab. We should send them models from here. Let them follow our youngsters from here.'

I stepped into the gurdwara office to look for Kashmir Singh, but found only two quiet and unhappy looking men. 'This is the gurdwara office,' one said. 'We don't know anything. We have nothing to do with what they are saying.' 'Ask someone in a yellow turban, don't ask us,' said the other.

Donations were being announced between speeches. I heard all sorts of figures, £25, £11, Coventry £4000, Southampton £2000, Singh family £300, the Wolverhampton gurdwara £2500. If all this was true, it was adding up nicely.

The voice over the mike was now becoming a bit hoarse, but that helped turn it into a low-key roar that sounded earnest and heartfelt. 'When two of our people shot Indira Gandhi, they hanged them,' he was saying. 'What was the fault of those thousands of Sikhs killed in Delhi? Nobody has been punished for that.'

I found myself in complete sympathy for once with a view over the mike that morning. After reporting the assassination of Indira Gandhi I had had the misfortune of reporting the killings in Delhi over the next couple of days. More than 3000 Sikhs were killed, but no justice followed. I filed three affidavits before the Mishra

Commission on killings and interventions by Congress leaders who at the least did nothing to stop the killers. The Mishra Commission dismissed my affidavit on the ground that I could not produce an independent witness to show that I'd been there to see what I saw, nor could I produce a log book from the *Indian Express* to establish where exactly in Delhi I was and at precisely what time. I could have added to the arguments on the mike, but the angry voice would hardly have wanted me to.

Someone else had taken over the mike now as I went upstairs to sit down in the hall. He was comparing the Delhi killings with the 3000 or so who died in the 11 September attacks. 'You see how they feel ...' he was saying—how they had honoured and remembered the dead. It sounded like a telling difference. New York had dealt with those deaths by mourning and remembering, New Delhi had dealt with its by forgetting and moving on. As had most Sikhs. Sikhs should learn from New York, he was saying. 'That is the way we should remember the thousands who had died.'

Much of the anger from behind the mikes was aimed at Sikhs in Punjab as much as the Indian government. 'We have seen how their corruption ruined Punjab. They have sold us to Delhi to fill their pockets. Now we have seen Punjab handed over to killers.' To the Congress government in Punjab, that is.

Next came anger with Sikhs in Britain. 'These people are getting grants from the British government and filling their pockets. The Home Office must be told who are the people they are giving recognition to. We have to come to some decisions and tell the government here. If they don't care about us, then we have to think about who to vote for. If they cannot think of the good of Sikhs, keep them out. So that they don't damage Sikhs any more.'

The meeting was going to make a point to local political leaders, and they had turned up to have the point made to them. Labour MP Rob Marris was called up to the mike, but not before an announcement in Punjabi and in English. In Punjabi: 'When the MPs come, give them a good impression. Don't get up and walk off in the middle. Or they'll think you're not interested.' In English, for the MP: 'We are ever so pleased to see you here.' Here was an MP, the announcer said, who has 'lived up to our expectations.'

Marris did, even if he spoke rather carefully. 'I can see Khalistan is an issue dear to your hearts,' he said from under a white handkerchief. 'Those in the Indian subcontinent who peacefully and democratically push for self-determination for that part of the Indian subcontinent, their opinion for self-determination, their right to ask for an independent Khalistan shouldn't be suppressed.' It would not be right for parties in Britain to decide whether there should be self-determination in what he called that part of the Indian subcontinent. 'But it would be right for people to democratically and peacefully express their opinions.' This was welcomed with slogans of 'Khalistan zindabad'.

More local leaders were called up, but in between Khalistanis took their turn at the mike. The speeches all began at the high end of a pitch, and then moved up from there. Everything began with 1984, the year of Operation Blue Star, the assassination of Indira Gandhi, the Delhi massacres. Everyone spoke of the injustice done to the Sikhs and many ended with a loaded demand; in Britain, they said, Sikhs should be counted as Sikhs, not as Indians.

Shadow Conservative Party minister for international development and women's issues Caroline Spelman rose to say it was 'extraordinary' (British-speak for 'outrageous') that 'the government has not cared to find out how many of you there are.' The Labour government should monitor Sikhs separately and 'if they fail, it will be a task for a Conservative administration to deliver on.'

Papers I'd picked up outside spelt out these demands in an eight-point Sikh Agenda. The agenda asked for more Sikh MPs, lords and councillors, more and better jobs in government and what not. But item number 6 wanted to 'seek action from the UK government on the continuing abuse of Sikh and other minority groups, human rights by the Indian authorities' and to 'highlight the lack of justice for Sikhs in India following the massacre in November 1984.'

Item 7 was openly about 'self-determination for the Sikh nation'. It wanted to 'make known and explain the reasons why Sikhs want to establish an independent sovereign state of Khalistan to the British public, political organizations and the UK government.'

And it challenged the British ban on Sikh organizations such as the International Sikh Youth Federation.

I left the meeting less surprised by what I'd heard from the Khalistanis than what the British leaders had said. The promise to find out 'how many of you there are' was of course far from innocent. One change in the census form could dent the figures for the Indian population in Britain significantly. It could fall sharply from around 1.2 million if Sikhs were made one category and Indians an alternative other. It would be the beginning of a political storm between India and Britain.

It was a relief to get up to leave, and not just because I'm no Khalistani. Of all the Khalistanis I'd met, this was the least friendly lot. I'd often spoken to Jagjit Singh Chauhan, an engaging enough man, and great for a chit-chat now and then. He'd made a similarly fiery speech at a Khalistan meeting I'd attended at the Sheehy Way Gurdwara in Slough, just west of London. But he saw no reason to be unpleasant to me because I didn't share his views. We always found much to joke about in Punjabi. We shared outrage over the 1984 killings and I agreed that Indira Gandhi had done more to mess up Punjab than anyone else. But with the new lot it had never been possible even to talk enough to disagree. If I wanted to talk to any of them, I must be a government agent who'd come to find out something. If I didn't, it must be because I was a government agent who therefore didn't want to hear what they had to say.

I left, almost beginning to miss some of the nicer Khalistanis, particularly Sewa Singh Lalli, that Khalistan president-in-exile among so many such presidents at one time. That's how his letterhead had described him in ornate and therefore presidential looking font. Sewa Singh Lalli had promised me a 'very big post' in Khalistan because I had given evidence against Congress leaders and the police in the Delhi killings. The last time I called him he was away delivering eggs. He did not return my call. Knowing him was the closest I ever got to picking up the phone and calling a president. With him disappeared my political career.

The Halifax girls were gone by the time I stepped out, and with them that morning's picture of innocence. Someone should have mentioned to them that the cars they wanted to insure might run

into some little matter from the past, and a chap called
Bhindranwale.

GUJARATI GOBLIN

Christina Rossetti's poem 'Goblin Market' answered some questions
for Tina about growing up a Gujarati in Leicester. She remembered
it vividly from that time years back when it had become an issue
at university; I could see that when she talked about it. She was
about to begin a job teaching English when we met her for coffee
at Bobby's restaurant on Belgrave Road; if her eloquent stream of
speech was anything to go by, teaching English was absolutely the
right thing for her to do. Not for a moment was she at a loss for
words; they came, in fact, too readily for her to get at her coffee
while it was still steaming. But she did falter a little over that
poem; really, over the time her literature class discussed 'Goblin
Market' at Leicester University.

'I remember that particular seminar. We were talking about ...
we were talking about ... a poem by Christina Rossetti. Something
about a blonde girl with a red mouth. It's about loss of virginity
or something ... this that and the other .... I'd interpret it as being
totally different. I talked about the loss of innocence, but I talked
about the loss of innocence in a non-sexual way, because that's
just how I am. And I had like ten faces staring at me.'

We were chatting about her growing up in Leicester, as a
British Indian in an Indian part of Britain, the sort of situation
when clichés start to get a little mixed up. But more than hyphenated
labels, it was the poem that told her how very different she was
from the ten faces she recalled staring at her. They would have
stared at her for all the wrong reasons, not because she was so
duskily magnetic. Thoughts had drifted into my mind as we sat
down: what if I had been young enough for her? But they drifted
out fast. After coffee, she would leave for a life of her own, I'd
leave only with some tape-assisted notes.

She was talking about the class. The teacher had called a male student to make his presentation, she said. 'He went into this very explicit explanation of the loss of virginity ... and this, and that, and you know. His interpretation. And I said, no, I don't think so, and one of the girls started laughing, and she said something like how many of us take this point of view ... who'd be for Tina basically ... and they didn't agree with me because they didn't think like that.'

The moment stayed with her. 'It suddenly occurred to me at that point that my thinking and theirs was so different. I felt stupid because of that. Also, my tutor didn't explain that you can have different interpretations based on culture and life experiences. So that opened up my eyes quite a bit. What I found difficult was that all the rest of them had a white perspective rather than an Asian cultural perspective. So my thinking in a lot of areas is different.'

As she saw it, the differences arose because of the way she grew up, even if in 1978 she was born a very recent British. I moved through some milestones of her life rapidly as she talked. The coffee had dipped into undrinkable temperature, and I left it at that because the same would happen to the next cup. As she talked, I heard labels and notions take form and flesh.

'I went to Abbey Primary, and I used to love it. My experience of going to school was my first glimpse of anything English. At home everything was in Gujarati. We didn't have a television, didn't have a video. So I had no exposure to anything English. It was really strange. I didn't speak any English at home. When I went to school I learnt English. I didn't have any friends, I just had my cousins. I talked to my grandfather in Gujarati because he didn't speak much English, and I talked to my cousins in Gujarati.

'Then when I went to school, we had teachers who were white. They were my first interaction with white people. On Saturdays, my mum would take us to the city centre for shopping. We would see white people there, but wouldn't interact with them in the same way. Also, in my class we were mainly Gujarati kids, maybe there were one or two white kids. So it didn't feel like there were other kids like white kids or black kids or people from other backgrounds.

'I was about five or six when my father bought a TV. I got glued, it used to fascinate me. You know, the early morning children's programme. And they were all English kids on TV. If there was a jingle or something, I'd be singing it in school. And people would say, no, I should be singing something else. People from my community, the Prajapati community. We used to go there quite a lot. I used to sing there, I used to sing Gujarati songs. I always thought that I was living in one world, and on TV it was another world. There was my home life, and there was my outside life.'

That could have been such a sound bite, I thought, journalistically. A disrespectful thought, disrespecting of her life as she'd lived it and tried to think it through. What I was reducing to a slogan had been for her a struggle, and I saw it in the reach of her eyes from our coffee table to those experiences she had tried to make sense of. But now she had found clarity. In that choice between the merely differently coloured Brit and the Gujarati Brit, she was very much the second kind.

'I feel very comfortable and easy being with other Gujarati and Indian people,' she was saying. 'It's not so much an issue now because I've been working for the last four or five years. I've also lived in London for a little while. I don't know what it is, but there's always a sense of ease with Indian people, I don't feel like I have to explain myself. Because culturally people understand what I am talking about.

'If I talk to a friend who is Asian, I can talk about a wedding, I can talk about my mum saying something to me about food or whatever, she or he would understand. If I say this to someone who is not Gujarati or Indian, it takes a little more explaining, I feel I'd have to apologize for myself, and I'm more happy being on the Indian than on the white side of things, you know.'

It was the easier side to be on. After Abbey Primary, Tina went to Rushymeade Secondary, where, she said, about 96 or 97 per cent of the students were Indians, Gujaratis. It was only when she went to Leicester University for three years for a combined honours degree in English literature and the history of art that she encountered overwhelmingly white people. 'It was a very lonely experience,' she said. 'I was the only Asian on the course among

200 plus.' English literature is a popular degree at Leicester University, but clearly not popular with Indians.

She took with her to university all the experience of growing up in Belgrave, and that meant she read a different 'Goblin Market' to that read by the white students in her class.

I couldn't of course wait to go back and read that poem by Christina Rossetti, the Victorian woman who had dared suggest sex in verse.

The poem begins with Laura, who can't get her eyes off a bunch of goblin men selling their 'wares'. She thinks about what she might be missing.

'How fair the vine must grow
Whose grapes are so luscious ...'

Lizzie offers a sisterly warning.

'No,' said Lizzie, 'no, no, no;
Their offers should not charm us,
Their evil gifts would harm us.'
She thrust a dimpled finger
In each ear, shut eyes and ran:
Curious Laura chose to linger
Wondering at each merchant man.'

Laura wants their wares, but has no gold to buy them with. But the goblin men have an idea.

'You have much gold upon your head,'
They answered altogether:
'Buy from us with a golden curl.'
She clipped a precious golden lock,
She dropped a tear more rare than pearl,
Then sucked their fruit globes fair or red:
Sweeter than honey from the rock,
Stronger than man-rejoicing wine,
Clearer than water flowed that juice;
She never tasted such before,

How should it cloy with length of use?
She sucked and sucked and sucked the more
Fruits which that unknown orchard bore,
She sucked until her lips were sore ...'

Later, the men

'Hugged her and kissed her;
Squeezed and caressed her;
Stretched up their dishes ...
Pluck them and suck them,
Pomegranates, figs.'

Sister Lizzie saw the temptations, but held firm, in a way. She

'Would not open lip from lip
Lest they should cram a mouthful in;
But laughed in heart to feel the drip
Of juice that syruped all her face,
And lodged in dimples of her chin,
And streaked her neck which quaked like curd.'

Back home,

'She cried "Laura", up the garden,
'Did you miss me?
Come and kiss me.
Never mind my bruises,
Hug me, kiss me, suck my juices
Squeezed from goblin fruits for you,
Goblin pulp and goblin dew.
Eat me, drink me, love me;
Laura, make much of me:
For your sake I have braved the glen
And had to do with goblin merchant men.'

Was this a poem about loss of virginity or about loss of
innocence? I'd probably vote with the white classroom against

Tina. Why did it feel like a betrayal of Tina just to have the thought? But perhaps this most basic of possible readings of the poem—most base, really—was not what the poem was really about.

It wasn't just Victorian soft porn, even if it could softly provoke pornish thoughts. Reading this as a poem about loss of innocence, as Tina did, does pretty much cover discovery of sexuality. To see this as a poem about loss of innocence could include the loss of virginity, but also much more. But finally it mattered only that Tina had read it differently from the others. And that she believed that this was because she was Indian, and they white British.

*

Hema looked more waif-like than ever under the immense cap that was housing her head this afternoon. The weather was defence enough for it, even indoors at the playhouse across from the Abbey Primary School. Christmas was coming up, and it was snowing wetly.

The playhouse was a pretty enough place; it could belong to a Christmas picture postcard if there'd been a little less rain in the snow, or if the air had smelt different. Christmas on this Leicester street came mixed with the aroma of masalas from Gelani's store across. Which meant the place smelt right, because Hema was telling a Christmas story in Gujarati.

Hema worked some days in the local library and some as a storyteller, especially for Gujarati-born English children—or English-born Gujarati children—from the Abbey Primary. This story was being told to children waiting for their parents at the Belgrave playhouse. She was going to write it on the blackboard, and part act it. They would copy the story down in their books.

CHRISTMAS NEE VARTA she wrote on the blackboard, and began to tell, and sing, the story.

Once upon a time there were three children. It was Christmas Eve and they were waiting for Santa Claus.

One child said: 'Kyan chhe Saanta Klaus? Maru present layinay kayarey a vasho?'

Another: 'Oh yes, when will he come with our presents?'

The third: 'Jaldi aavey to saaru.'

Hema sang the three children sing, *Who is coming on a Christmas night* ...

Suddenly, a child says: 'Koi aavyu! Someone's here! Kadara Saanta Klaus hosay! I hope it's him! Chalo door molisay savay joyay!'

'Yes! Let's have a look!'

They open the door.

'Aato koi Saanta Klaus nathi.'

From outside: 'Of course I'm not Saanta Klaus. I'm the Christmas tree!'

Song: O *Christmas tree* ...

'But wait! There's someone at the door! Havay to Saanta Klaus jo hosay!'

'Let's open the door!'

'Oh! It's not Saanta Klaus!'

Voice from outside: 'Hoon to ek pari chhoon! Hoon tumhare maate ek ek present lavi chhoon! Here you are, you can open them tomorrow.'

'Havey kaun kauk hoshay? Come quickly, let's open the door! Who are you?'

'Hoon to Rudolph chhoon.'

'To Saanta Klaus kyaan chhe?'

'I don't know! I'm looking for Santa too!'

Song: *Rudolph the red-nosed reindeer* ...

Rudolph: 'Aamey thaaki gaya chhe, havey am sui jayiye chheyay.'

Before he can sleep, there is a cry outside.

'Help! Bachavo! Koi mane bachavey!'

Song: *Where Santa got stuck up* ...

A figure appears at the door. 'Jo mara kapara maney bhookh lagi chhey, khaavanu aayo.'

'Hooray! It's Santa!'

'Amara present lavyo? Where are our presents?'

'Oh, pahila maney to bhookh lagi chhe, I'm so, so hungry.'

'Here's something to eat.'

'Good! And here are your presents!'

Mums had been gathering for the story to end. 'Thank you,

Hemaben,' said the first mum who walked in to collect her kid. They must hope Hemaben's stories continue to have Gujarati endings for the children much later in their lives, even if they grow up to care little about Santabhai.

FROM THE CRADLE TO ...

Leicester has learnt to keep it Indian all the way from nurseries to nursing homes.

Grow old along with the old. The best is over, but it's not so bad in one of those Indian homes in Leicester, the sort we thought were only for white people to grow old and unwanted in.

'We are now one another's family,' Sushilaben said at the Mahatma Gandhi House, just by Belgrave Road. She was one of those abandoned 'masis' of Leicester who once thought home would still be where their children are. 'Let them not come to us. We do not wait for them any more.' 'Them' was of course not just her children, but the children of others like her. And 'we' was the new family of all here who had lost theirs.

She did not look like she was waiting either. Mahatma Gandhi House had brought the beginning of a new life, even if it was near ending. Sushilaben was remarkably not depressed and she looked at home in the reception room by the front door. Almost like it was her drawing room.

'My grandchildren were growing up, they needed the rooms,' she told me, as we stood talking by the door. Like all masis, she was dressed in a simple sari under a large shawl. 'My children put me in the drawing room but it did not look nice when guests came. So they sent me here. They said they will see me every weekend. Now nobody comes but it's all right. They never looked after us but now we are here to look after each other.'

Sushilaben invited me into the reception room. A frail and very elderly man walked slowly up and joined us on the sofa. 'They didn't want me then, I don't want them now,' he said. He too had forgotten his family, as they had forgotten him.

Two other women walked up. 'You want to bring your parents here? Wait,' said the woman who had sat nearest to me. She walked down the corridor and returned with a man who looked elderly but not retired. He was the manager. 'There are no rooms just now,' he said in Gujarati-East African English. 'You will have to wait for one of us to die, and there are plenty waiting for rooms before you,' he said. But he offered reassurance. 'We keep getting vacancies.'

We moved into the common room. A portrait of Gandhi and a map of India had been hung on the wall, they must do their bit to make the inmates feel at home. A lone man was watching TV as I walked in with Sushilaben and the others. His wife had died years ago and his son went back to Kenya, Sushilaben said. Everyone was known this way—when abandoned and by whom. But he said nothing about being abandoned as we sat down together to talk. 'We all get along very well. Singhs, Muslims, Gujaratis of all castes, we are now one family here.' Finally, everyone had come together in this pre-death club. Why did I think they should be more depressed than they were?

The common room began to fill in as we chatted about life in this house. A man introduced as Bipinbhai walked up with some difficulty; he'd been partially paralysed after a stroke. Like almost everyone else, he wanted to talk about his life; most of the time nobody wanted to know. He said he'd come to Britain during the Uganda expulsions of 1972 with a brother and seven sisters. Over the last three years only one sister had bothered to call him. 'We were like one family there. Here I don't know what happened. It must be this country. What else can it be?'

The common room was not quiet any more, but the quietness of death seemed to linger in the air—unless I was seeing an imminence of death that they were not.

'We like it here because we have to,' said Sushilaben's companion, the one who had gone to call the manager. 'You don't always get what you want.'

'What do you feel about your son who sent you here?'

'No, it was not him, it was his wife. What could he do?'

'How do you spend your time here?'

'We do what we would do anywhere. Get up, make breakfast, clean, cook lunch, sleep, come to the common room for tea, watch TV, have dinner, then sleep again.' Kumudben was waiting only for days to repeat themselves, for as long as they would.

But two days in a year are different. That is when everyone is taken out in a bus on a day trip. And they had the Christmas and Diwali parties every year too, so that was two more days other than the usual. That made four days a year to wait for.

*

The road must have been named after the new nursing home it led to. Asha Marg led from Loughborough Road to the home for the elderly managed by ASRA (Asian Sheltered Residential Accommodation). The new home had answered a growing need. Unlike Mahatma Gandhi House which stood on an old street, this one provided plenty of parking space for families to visit parents. It was wasted space, mostly. A few cars on weekends was all it saw.

Inside the office of the home, with its smart new walls and sloping roof in a new style unconvincingly following the old, the manager produced a report on the need for a home like this, and for more such. The report spoke of the 'myth that Asian people in this country are able to care for their old as well as their young under one roof because of the extended family.'

The truth, it said, is that 'some Asians are treated degradingly by their children and such treatment would include granny-bashing, taking away of supplementary benefits, not giving them enough food to eat, locking them out, making them do the housework and so on.'

Children were making orphans of their parents, and these elderly orphans were being adopted by the state. 'The state is our mother, the state is our father,' said Niteshbhai, a resident assisting the manager. 'The children know this, they know their parents can stay somewhere for free and get enough money to live on. They say why should they look after us when the state can do it better.'

Ashaben, making lunch in the common kitchen told me she'd never been better off. She was nearing seventy, and said she'd moved several homes over the past three years because the next one always seemed better. She had almost too much money. 'We don't know what to do with the money we save.'

It all made sense, but why did everyone speak so quietly? 'In India the children have no choice but to be tolerant. Where will they send their parents?' someone at the door said. 'Maybe that is good, maybe not, I don't know. Here the government will cremate us. We will die on our own two feet.'

The Young and the Faithful

The stillness on Asfordby Street broke quite suddenly a few minutes to five. Doors opened, little girls all in black with only their faces visible stepped out, carrying copies of the Quran. Boys about the same age—seven, eight years old—in mosque-ready gowns and caps emerged with them from the rows of houses strung together down the street, from little lanes to the side. They scurried down to the flat red-brick building joined to the row of houses down the street—the Jam-e-Mosque, the green letters on its white board announced—and then turned into a little lane by its side to the classrooms at the back. It was 5 p.m., time for the madrassa.

At the end of the street, close to the mosque, four men in long white robes and long black beards watched protectively over the traffic of the tiny. Only a few of the children were escorted by elders; it was safe enough for the rest on their own since the kids had the streets to themselves. A white police van drove out from the police station about a hundred yards further down from the mosque, an occasional car drove by. But it was a quiet road that took only neighbourhood traffic.

A little girl in black burkha and hijab over her sports shoes walked down a side street to the corner where I stood by the Islamic bookshop, across from the mosque. 'What are you going to learn at school?' I asked. 'I'll be learning the Quran, and I'll be learning Arabic,' she said. 'But aren't the holidays on?' 'I'm going to *our* school.'

The school after school, that is. Through term time the kids come back from regular school about 3.30 p.m., and head out to school at the madrassa from five often until eight for their daily switch from secular to Islamic education. There's a switch of schoolbags too. Two little boys walked by, carrying bags with 'Madrasah Bag' printed below a sketch of a mosque. I took a quick picture.

Before I could speak to them, two of the four chaps who had been watching over the kids came up. 'You are talking to the children, you're taking photographs, you can't do that here,' one of them said angrily through his glasses. 'The children are getting intimidated.' They possibly were, but these chaps were a little intimidating too, and I gave up my roadside post along with my plans of trying to talk to the children inside the madrassa. I was expecting to meet some children at the next madrassa I was headed for on Sutherland Street in Highfields close by.

The entrance was through a side door on Sutherland Street, a fifty-yard lane that dips in from St Peter's Road. The building looked like any of the other houses on St Peter's Road or on Sutherland Street. It had served as a mosque for many years before the Muslim population in Highfields and around far outgrew it and turned to the spanking new mosque on Conduit Street near the railway station, or the many other new mosques that came up in Leicester. But the Sutherland Street mosque continues to draw the faithful, and the students at its madrassa. Abdullah Patel, who I'd been told by an Indian Muslim friend was an Islamic teacher in Leicester, welcomed me into the madrassa.

In just the style for a madrassa teacher, Patel wore a round Islamic cap, and his grey-black beard angled outward below his ears before shaping tightly down into an inverted apex under his chin. Through his glasses I saw the sharp eyes of the knowing kind of teacher. I knew a little about Patel through my friend. He drove a taxi for a living, but he was really an Islamic scholar, and education secretary of The Islamic Centre in Leicester that ran madrassas at this and other mosques. Patel and another man from the mosque invited me into the main classroom.

'Holiday season,' I said, unnecessarily. There were no kids around.

'Only for this week,' Patel said. 'Some mosques give some time off, some do not. We will be starting our classes next week.'

'And then classes every day and weekends?'

'Only from five to seven, Monday to Friday. But we are planning classes on Saturdays also for the older students.'

'But isn't it too much for the children, after their regular school?'

'Some younger girls get tired by the end of the day, that problem is definitely there, you will see them yawning. But most find the Quran very easy, because it is a miracle of Allah. And so after a long day at school it is not stressful. Children just six or seven years old recite it fluently. At times even I am surprised.'

'But does it affect their learning and their results at the main school?'

'Not at all. Their hard work is not going to waste, it helps them do the national curriculum better. It increases their talent to learn more at day school. We say it is important to earn your bread, be successful and have a decent life. You cannot rely on social security all the time. But it is important to be successful both in this life and the life after. If you neglect Islamic education, you will not be successful in the life after. The deeds of this life will mean reward by the garden or punishment by fire. So both are important, and we give this concept at the madrassa.'

'But are the kids being forced by parents to come to the madrassa?'

'The children are conditioned to the madrassa system. Parents do not have to force them, they see their brothers and sisters and other children coming, so they also come. Children have this psychology of copying.'

'What do they learn here?'

'By the time children from our madrassas are thirteen or fourteen, they will have read the Quran many times over, all 6666 sentences of it. It is obligatory for our children to read the Quran, even if they don't understand it.'

'Is that all they learn?'

'We teach Urdu as a language, but Urdu based on Islamic thinking. We teach Arabic as a language, and we teach Islamic history and jurisprudence—deeniyat—and we teach children how to offer namaaz and perform their prayers. Every year we run a mock exam and then a regular exam, and children get prizes for doing well, and certificates they can keep in a nice frame.'

'And do the boys and girls study together?'

'Until they are eight or nine years old, then we put them in separate classes.'

'Is it compulsory for the girls to wear long dresses?'

'Girls need to wear a large, loose dress that does not reveal the size of their body parts, otherwise you may look at them with the devil's eye.'

'Could a long loose dress mean also salwar kameez?'

'O no, not above the age of six or seven.'

'Do you have other events at madrassas, like sports?'

'We have football competitions. And we have races at the annual sports event. But girls have to keep their traditional dresses.'

'And do most Muslim kids go to the madrassa?'

'Some say 90 per cent. I say about 97 per cent.'

We talked a little more. Patel was kind enough to give me a copy of the Muslim Directory as I got up to leave. I saw later that it listed eighteen mosques in Leicester, almost all with madrassas attached. That was among the close to 800 mosque-madrassas across Britain and more than a hundred listed Muslim schools where the national curriculum is taught alongside Islamic studies. Ninety or ninety-seven, there is no doubt that the overwhelming majority of British Muslim kids go to a madrassa after school.

But the Muslim Directory offered other information I wasn't expecting to find. The only pictures it prints are from Kashmir. One shows Dal Lake whose 'serene surroundings are occupied by 600,000 Indian troops!' Another shows a soldier, with the caption: 'Indian soldier, weapon ready and watching high street shops!' A photograph of a funeral comes with the caption: 'Another number added to the genocide!' The directory has been produced with support from the Muslim Council of Britain, the main contact point for government dealings with British Muslims.

Another picture shows a soldier apparently searching somebody, with the caption: 'Palestine? Chechnya? Burma? Algeria? Tunisia? Iraq? ... No, Kashmir. Indian soldiers harassing the civilian population. Muslims the world over are being subjected to occupation, oppression and torture.' The directory includes one picture from Pakistani Kashmir—of a fruit seller at his stall, with the caption 'Fruits of the world!' Religious teaching was obviously leading also to some kind of political spillover.

There have been more ominous signs of this kind of extension. None of the 7 July suicide bombers in London achieved much by way of regular education. But they were regulars at the Masjid-e-Umar on Stratford Street in Beeston in Leeds, and its attached madrassa. And Leicester has had its share of terrorist leanings arising from its madrassas.

In a study of places of religious worship in Leicester, Prof. Richard Bonney from the University of Leicester points to the discovery of a small Al Qaeda cell in Leicester in 2002. 'Brahim Benmerzouga and Baghdad Mezaine were sentenced to eleven years each after conviction for using credit card fraud to raise thousands of dollars for Al Qaeda. They were accused by the Crown Prosecution Service of working together to make military equipment, false travel documents and recruitment material. The two had details of nearly 200 different bank accounts in their possession, and Benmerzouga had some sixty films covering suicide bombings and martyrdom, including videos of Osama bin Laden, the jury heard during the eight-week trial in Leicester.

'The key organizer was Algerian Djamel Beghal, who, according to the *Independent*, apparently cultivated young Muslims through a local mosque in Leicester. He also quietly built up the network of supporters among foreign émigrés, who used the local Indian and Pakistani communities as cover. Specifically, Beghal is accused of recruiting both British "shoe-bomber" Richard Reid and would-be 11 September 2001 hijacker Zacarias Mousaaoui.' Reid in turn was reported to have been in frequent attendance at a madrassa at the Finsbury Park mosque in London. As Bonney points out, 'that there is, and has always been, a connection between religion and politics is clear.'

A terrorist group searching for recruits is likely to look first among madrassa products. But any suggestion that madrassas therefore become training grounds for terrorism, even inadvertently, is of course wildly overblown. A madrassa is just a school with an Islamic syllabus.

*

'You're late,' the teacher said, like she'd said it before to the little girl who'd just walked into the classroom, and like she'd be saying it to her again.

The girl walked up to her desk, took off her pink coat and sat down. She said nothing, she had heard that from her teacher before, and she must know she'd hear it again. She didn't look like she minded being late, or then sitting down in class as the only girl without hijab. She was going to need some reclamation.

The teacher, naturally in proper black dress and hijab, continued. 'Bismillah ar-Rahman ar-Raheem ...' (In the name of God, the compassionate, the merciful—the opening phrase for all 114 Surahs in the Quran, except Surah 9). The class, of about eighteen eight to ten-year-olds repeated after her. She went line by line through the Surah she was teaching, and the class repeated each line after her. They were memorizing the lines, and they were learning to recite them right.

The two girls nearest to me at the back of the class were moving their lips, and saying very little. The teacher saw this, and perhaps she saw me see this as well from my seat at the back of the class. She walked up to their desks, and now they had to repeat after her. With the teacher away at the back, two boys in the front celebrated their new-found freedom by starting an argument, because boys will be boys even in an Islamic school. That every kid would sit immersed in the Quran equally and absolutely was only a cliché I was carrying.

The teacher heard the arguing. A sharp tap on the desk where she stood, and the boys were back to their recital. The kids all had their textbooks before them, with the selection from the Quran they were memorizing. But most were following the teacher without looking at the text. After some time, she stopped and let them continue on their own. They did, most had done a pretty good job of memorizing the Surah, and for their age they were speaking the lines pretty much as teacher did. Who would not want to, and get picked on as the black sheep of the class?

'You need to read it, you need to remember it,' the teacher said as class ended.

I took an empty seat next to a boy as class ended.

'What were you reading?' I asked.

'The Quran.'

'But what from the Quran were you reading?'

'This,' he said, pointing to the Arabic text.

'But what is it saying?'

'Are you Muslim?'

'No. But what is the text saying?'

He said nothing. He got up and left.

I learnt from the teacher before leaving the classroom that the children had been memorizing Surah Al Alaq.

The head teacher was kind enough to guide me to another classroom. I was at the Sunday school at the King Fahad Academy just across from Acton where London begins to get northwest. The Academy which runs regular school weekdays was obviously set up by the Saudis, with the Sunday school managed by the Central Mosque at Regent's Park. Its students are from all over, as I saw in the classroom I'd just left, and the one I'd walked into—black, white, Indians, Pakistani, Arabs, everyone was learning Arabic and the Quran.

A male teacher in this classroom, in mandatory gown, beard and cap, was teaching children off English letters on the blackboard how to speak the lines of the Quran right.

'For those who cannot read Arabic,' he was saying. 'When you see one "a", no stretching, when you see "aa", then stretch.'

The students, a little older here, about ten to twelve or so, followed.

'Gad aflaha maann zakkaaha,' he wrote on the board. 'And "maann" has a nasal sound you have to practise while reading the Quran. It's called the ghunna.'

He asked a boy in front to speak the line. He did just fine. 'Very good, masha-allah,' teacher said. Others got the line right too, and the next. 'Wa qad khaaba mann dassaa haa.'

We were soon into break-time, and he set memorizing the lines taught as homework for the week. The kids were out of the class fast. I stayed on with the teacher a little.

'What were they learning?'

'The Al-Shams Surah.'

'But they were reciting it, do you also teach the meaning?'

'No, we do not. It is only after they have memorized it and learnt to speak the lines correctly that we give them a general overview of the meaning. If we also start translating, it will get too much for the children.'

No teacher at an Islamic school thinks the madrassa lessons themselves might get too much for the children. But not every Muslim teacher shares Abdullah Patel's optimism on the benefits of the madrassa for mainstream education. Some Muslim teachers do say, quietly, that the heavy demands on a child's time that a second school brings, could hardly help children do well at the main school.

'Parents do not realize under what pressure they are putting their children,' a Pakistani Muslim primary school teacher in Leicester told me. 'When are children going to do the work that will give them the competitive edge? I discussed the under-achievement of a child with one father. He told me that children should have both educations, our education and your education. I talked about the time, and he said they will find the time.'

Patel Power

In-house Innings

My London A to Z was behind time. It failed to show India Gardens as I turned into that crescent off the West End Road, after leaving the A40. On the map I'd be turning into Harvey Road, with Peacock Park further up. On ground I was driving through India Gardens to the cricket fields of the Shree Kutch Leva Patel Samaj in Northolt.

I'd come to watch a cricket match, one of the first of the season in a local Middlesex league. To the *Daily Mail* a match like this had once been a scoop: a match in which every player was a Patel. It ran the story under a picture of the teams, with the caption 'Patel vs Patel'. I don't quite remember if the *Mail* reported which Patel beat which other, because the story was essentially not on cricket, but on the many-ness of Patels.

Cricket crept into the immigration debate through the Tebbit Test proposed by Lord Norman Tebbit, about the only thing he ever came to be known for. To pass that test, an Indian who migrated to Britain and then took British nationality must then not cheer India but England (since Scotland, Wales and Northern Ireland have remained miraculously immune to the game). But cricketing loyalties never did migrate. I've sat through India–England games at Lord's and never once seen anyone Indian-looking cheer the England team against India, never once thought that anyone had Tebbit on their mind at all. But at least someone had. The *Times* once front-paged the picture of a banner by Indian fans at Lord's: 'We've failed the Tebbit test and we're proud of it.'

The *Times* picture suggested disloyalty—or loyalty, depending which side of Tebbit you're on—and the *Mail* story the numbers that might be disloyal. But the *Mail* was still missing the crucial point: that the match it reported was made possible not just by the many-ness of Patels, but by many Patelnesses. There are Patelhoods within Pateldom that could make a good deal of cricket possible between one kind of Patel and another, as at this Patel ground *nee* Peacock Park.

The match of the day was between the home team, the Sri Kutch Leva Patel Samaj, SKLP as they understandably like to call themselves, and the Muktajivan Cricket Club, of another kind of Patels. Kutch Leva vs Muktajivan, Patel vs Patel—both would be right.

I drove around to the parking lot by the sports grounds, large enough for two, maybe three, cricket fields. I parked by a maroon Ford with the number SKL1PP; the number was obviously bought at that auction of number plates as nearly aligned as letters and numbers allow to what you'd like it to be. A particularly proud Kutch Leva Patel was here, and the car said so.

It was a bright day, all green and golden, as only an English summer day can be. Not the kind of day a cricketer likes to pass unpadded. A couple of padded Patels came into view as I walked around to the pavilion, thwacking away at balls in net practice, which does not always need a net. The other players were hanging around outside the pavilion. Everyone was in the usual cricket variation of off-white; it looked like the beginning of a very serious day of cricketing.

The pavilion was a small and simple block with a lunch table laid out already in the veranda outside the changing rooms for 'Home' and 'Away'. Players were walking in and out of them. The only other man as idle as I was, at least for the moment, was a player who stood by the lunch table surveying the field. Just the man for the first hello of the day.

His hello was followed by introduction as Naju Lalji from the SKLP team who would bat first. He was to come in at number five, he told me, which gave him some time as surveyor. And quite a picturesque surveyor he was too. Two gold earrings on one ear established him at least as intended cool, and dragged what might have been an approach to middle age back towards youth. His cricket cap sat lightly above his shaved head. Against that vast stretch of green and gold on the sunny field, he appeared more a profile than a person. If he played as he looked, he could be the dream of some Patel woman getting on a bit.

'So who's playing today?' I asked him.

'We are playing the Muktajivan Cricket Club.'

'And you are the SKLP?'

'Yes.'

'You are the Patels, and who are they?'

'They are also Patels.'

'So all the players today are Patels.'

'Of course.'

'And you are the home team.'

'Yes, but they are also the home team. We share the ground.'

'But how did you divide the teams? How do you decide who is Muktajivan and who is SKLP? I mean, if you are both Patels, and you are both home teams, how come you are separate teams, and one is called Muktajivan?'

'Because they go to a separate temple.'

'Which are these temples?'

'We go to the Swaminarayan temple at Harrow, they have their own.'

'So they are not Swaminarayans.'

'No, they are also Swaminarayans, but they go to a different Swaminarayan temple.'

'Why is that?'

'Everyone believes in Lord Swaminarayan, but there are different gurus, you know.'

'Are they Patels from a different part of Gujarat?'

'No, we are all Patels from Kutch. We come from a group of twenty-four villages in Kutch. They also come from the same twenty-four villages. You see, we are like different branches of a tree.'

I was being slow figuring this out. I gathered that both teams were Patels, both Swaminarayans, both from the same twenty-four villages of Kutch in Gujarat, but they were different kinds of Swaminarayan Patels and they went to different temples. That point of separation had made this match possible. Differing disciples of the original Lord Swaminarayan had formed their own societies, set up their own temples and created their own teams.

I wanted to ask more but Naju seemed to be tiring of offering these explanations. In any case, the game had now begun, but no one was scoring runs and no one was getting out. For a forty-over-a-side game, it was slow going even for just a start.

But before the game took over I had to ask Naju the obvious question: If he was a Patel, why was he called Lalji?

'Of course I am Patel,' he said. 'It's like the Singhs. There are so many Singhs who do not put Singh in their name. But they are Singhs, no?' Poor Britain still does not suspect that there are very many more Patels in its midst than people with Patel in their name. I turned to watch a second game of Patel sons now progressing in the net practice area. Naju too was watching this second game. 'Cricket is our religion,' he said, a lot happier to talk about this pleasing sight. 'We have already picked up sixty-five kids for sharp training to become proper players. They are the colts, and there are 300 more on the waitlist.' I thought he was looking at England's future, not just a Patel future. If England is nurturing 365 colts through just one kind of Patel, one of them will show up on television one day.

But now there was movement on the cricket field. The first SKLP wicket fell. Out lbw, Naju explained; he had been keeping an eye on the big game. The opener was walking back to the pavilion with that hard-done-by look batsmen out lbw always wear. 'It was high,' he said as he walked into the pavilion, tapping a point almost at hip level. 'Don't worry,' said Naju. 'No one out lbw is ever out.'

The wicket relieved Naju of further discussion. He nodded his cap in my direction and went in to pad up. He stepped away unhurriedly, out of respect no doubt to number 4. That left me as one of only two spectators. The other was a dusky Ms Whatever Patel in black jeans and blue denim jacket. She had settled down in the fenced enclosure in front of the pavilion, legs stretched out on another chair under a shawl. By her side, a chap in white was keeping track of the game on a register.

Her presence brought an odd intensity to the game. She was the only woman on the grounds. She brought a teasing suggestion that she could end up more watched than watching. I looked at her as men do when they want to look but not be seen to stare. Her long brown hair flowed straight, more or less, into a butterfly clip before they found freedom again over her denim jacket. Her profile was shaped very much by Gujarati genes, and whatever her first name, her last would surprise no one. She would be seen as nice-looking anywhere, but here she was prettier because she and she alone brought femininity to the field. It couldn't be just me who was aware of her especially; the Patels in white must all have noticed her even if they had a lot more to do than I did. She was alone, but enough to play for. Heroism is not heroism if it goes unwitnessed.

Out on the field, the Patels were playing out the usual cricket rituals—repositioning caps, pulling up gloves, waiting with arms folded between panther-like dashes, combining strength with subtlety, speed with elaboration, finding time for swing, time for poise, luxuriating in that balance of ease and energy that only cricket allows. Was that other game all in my mind then? Something told me that in all this, dusky Ms Patel played her part just sitting there doing nothing. She was doing her bit to bring out the best in twenty-two Patels. She didn't have to be eyed, she just had to be there. Some games don't need to begin, and they never end.

A couple more batsmen had walked back, and now Naju was batting. He did in style, but not for long. He too walked back, not quite the same man. It always takes something out of you when you score less than you'd like to. He resumed spectator position in the pavilion a little droopily just when the game was picking up some life because others were now busily scoring to beat the early stillness.

The last of the overs were played out, and it was soon lunch. Dusky Ms Patel was back in the pavilion too, moving sandwiches from the kitchen to the lunch table. I left the players to the pavilion, and went to sit by the scorer, where Ms Patel had been.

The scorer was Kirit Patel, a Muktajivan man; square and steady, and virtuously unflamboyant. A small scoreboard by his side carried the logo of the Muktajivan Cricket Club on top. It must be about the holiest cricket logo in the world. It was a very Hindu-looking face, with cricket ball as tilak within an elongated vertical U for the wicket. The eyes were bats, and three wickets below the U offered a toothy smile. This was temple cricket, and it was in a league of its own.

Kirit had not kept score very happily. SKLP had scored 176 runs in their forty overs and his register showed that eighteen had come in the last. He looked doubtful that the blank page on his register would record a similar figure post-lunch. From what he told me about the Muktajivan Patels, he would have good reasons for his doubts. Theirs was not a world of sixty-five colts training and 300 waiting. 'We have about thirty-six players now, and about twelve to fifteen youngsters,' he said. Not a lot to choose from. We stepped in for lunch. The match, and the future, was going the SKLP way.

Naju, who'd got over his low score by now, was preparing for their future at Match II site, handing out low catches to his colts in that familiar cricketing arc for catch practice.

'They just love it, and we love it,' Naju said as I stopped by again for a quick chat. 'Keeps them off the streets. Are they taking drugs? No. Are they eating junk food, sitting in front of TV? No, they are right here, playing cricket with us.' In the game of cricket lies the building of character and the perpetuation of Patelhood with that character thrown in. This is where they will play, and they will play as Patels, of the SKLP variety.

Over sandwiches and gathia, Naju told me that the England and Wales Cricket Board was paying to promote Patel cricket at their grounds. The ECB (since Wales plays cricket primarily in the name of the board) had provided a grant for preparing the ground and the wicket, and every now and then it hands out a little more here and there for bats and pads and the rest. The ECB was paying for Patels to play as particular Patels. Swaminarayan gurus had once gone their separate ways, taking their different Patel followings with them. In England, cricket followed those separate ways, a separation paid for in part by the ECB. The little colts were falling into teams of differing Patel kinds before they knew it.

The SKLP was doing enough for its own cricket. Company billboards, meaning sponsorship and money, lay stacked by the side of the pavilion, to be set up around the field for the bigger matches. Every Kutch Patel with a business worth the name had sponsored a board. The players' shirts were sponsored by a Kutch Patel businessman. One way or another, money from every successful Kutch Patel was doing something for SKLP cricket.

That of course is no guarantee of results, on the principle that New Zealand can beat India. The proportion of numbers to success ceases to matter past some early critical point. But if a Muktajivan club had to choose from thirty-five, and SKLP from a few hundred, it would always be advantage SKLP. By the end of the day it was an easy win for SKLP.

The fortunes of SKLP and Muktajivan on the field reflected the number of available players. Muktajivan were much the senior team, they'd had a cricket team since 1969, Kirit told me. The SKLP was set up only in 1985. But something had changed in the world of religion, and cricket followed.

Muktajivandas, the Swaminarayan swami who set up a sect of his own in the 1940s, died in Bolton on a visit to Britain in 1979, I gathered from the book *An Introduction to Swaminarayan Hinduism* by Raymond Brady Williams. Muktajivandas had left the Ahmedabad sect of the Swaminarayans, itself one of the factions that the Swaminarayans had split into. He then set up his own institutions and temples which came to be called the Swaminarayan Gadi.

'Although the group is relatively small, the devotees seem to be very loyal and lavish in their support,' Williams writes. 'In 1957 they celebrated a golden jubilee of his birth by giving him a gift of his weight in gold, ten years later they celebrated his platinum jubilee with a gift of platinum, and when he was seventy he was weighed against five types of jewels.'

Muktajivandas was among other leaders in the Swaminarayan faith who were believed by followers to be incarnations of Sahjanand Swami, the nineteenth-century preacher who came to be known as Bhagwan Swaminarayan and is believed by Swaminarayans to be god himself. He set up a separate sect in the 1940s. In October 1972, Muktajivandas proclaimed he represented the personification of Swaminarayan Gadi, and came to be treated as god by his followers.

Muktajivandas died in Bolton on a visit to Britain in 1979.

Despite the lavish adulation of his followers, the Muktajivan following has remained small as compared to the following of the temple of the Ahmedabad sect in Kingsbury in north London that the SKLP Swaminarayan Patels go to. The SKLP have grown, and have a smart new Swaminarayan temple to show for it just off Kenton Road.

The Patel vs Patel match of the day was a consequence of a transplanted religious subdivide. The difference of sects was expressed through separate teams and strengthened by it. Didn't Naju say cricket is their religion?

MILK AND MURDER

It took me a while to figure out what the two Patels were really saying. It sounded like there was a conflict between a Patel federation in Wembley in north-west London and a Patel association in Tooting in south London, and that this division was at least partly because in Gujarat in the nineteenth century one kind of Patel used to kill newly born daughters by drowning them in milk.

But Dr M.I. Patel, industrialist and former sheriff of Mumbai, had no doubts about this at all, and since my friend K.D. Patel had introduced M.I. also as a historian, I was listening carefully. We'd met at the spectacle of a house of K.D., the former councillor with a petrol station or two, and two concurrent wives.

'These Patels from six villages, they used to kill their daughters,' M.I. told me. We hadn't met to talk about this, but the conversation had naturally come round to Patels by and by. 'They always thought themselves very superior to the others. What superior, when they would kill their daughters?'

And this, he said, is affecting Patel lives in Britain here and now. 'The hangover of these things continues a long time.'

M.I. Patel was in London on way to a lecture tour in the US, and looked very much the businessman on way to a lecture tour of the US. As the industrialist part of industrialist-historian he said that his Patel Extrusion Group manufactures among other things the tubes that companies pack toothpaste into. Just as necessary as the toothpaste, when you think of it. He'd squeezed enough profit from those tubes, and now found himself time for politics and history.

'It was called the practice of doodh peeti,' Dr Patel said. 'They used to call it doodh peeti to make sure the girl would be killed quickly after she was born. When a girl child was born, they would just kill her. They would place the child's head in a pan of milk and drown her. I have seen it with my own eyes.' A countable consequence, he said, was that 'the population of girls in those villages came down so much.'

K.D.'s hospitality and the compulsions of two busy Patels came in the way of more. But of course if something like this were true it would be known to many more than two Patels.

That those six villages in the Charotar area of central Gujarat were quite different from others is evident after just a few brushes with London Patels. Back in Gujarat, the six had grouped themselves into an elite cluster called the Chha-gam. Other village clusters had formed in Charotar too—the Baavis-gam, the Sattavis-gam and so on. But the Chha-gam lot had the money and power. It was inevitable that they would resent the assumed aristocracy of the Chha-gam Patels. Gujaratis from those villages had set up shadow clusters in Britain along the same lines, and carried over the old divisions.

These memories and the clusters they had bred are around in London today. The Patel Association Centre in Tooting has long been associated mostly with the Chha-gam Patels, the Patel Federation Centre in Wembley with the rest of the Charotar Patels. But did memories of murdered infant girls stand between a Wembley Patel and a Tooting Patel?

*

Memories of a Delhi University professor provoked research by a student.

'I was born and brought up in one of the "six villages" of Patidars (another name for Patels) of central Gujarat mentioned frequently in this book as practising female infanticide,' Prof.

A.M. Shah from the Department of Sociology at the university wrote in the foreword of *Female Infanticide and Social Structure: A Socio-Historical Study in Western and Northern India* by L.S. Vishwanath published in 2000. 'Throughout my childhood I had heard about the practice of doodh peeti, the drowning of female infants in a pale of milk, in earlier generations in my village.'

The British today know almost nothing about Patel neighbours except that they are a kind of Asian who also have arranged marriages. But Vishwanath writes that the colonial Brits knew a good deal about the Patels under their noses—and in Gujarat there was dire stuff to know. The nineteenth-century Brits took occasional steps to discourage the practice but did little to stop it, at least to begin with. Vishwanath says no one knows how far back that practice went, but the British discovered it both among the Rajputs of Gujarat and the Lewa Patidars. And among the Patidars, particularly among the Chha-gam lot. In fact, the Chha-gam Patels Patidars would kill their infant girls because they were the elite.

'The middle and higher-level status groups in each of these castes tried to maintain their status and avoid substantial dowry payment which hypergamous marriage (a marriage of a girl into a family of higher or at least equal status) involved by resorting to killing of their female children,' Vishwanath writes. 'The problems of the top stratum in these castes were compounded by the fact that in addition to high dowries, the high-status lineage had to find eligible grooms in a restricted circle of elite families within their caste. Generally, therefore, the higher status groups practised female infanticide more extensively than the lower status groups.'

This happened to such an extent that the female population crashed. 'A census taken in 1872 in the British part of Kaira district revealed that the proportion of boys to girls under 12 years of age among lewa kanbis was 73 girls to 100 boys: but the 12 elite lewa patidar villages had only 39 to 53 girls to 100 boys. That the elite patidar villages had a low proportion of females was confirmed by the decenial census returns of 1891, 1901 and 1911. According to the 1891 and 1911 census of the Bombay Presidency, the proportion of females to 1000 males in seven elite patidar villages under Baroda (the seven including the six of Chha-

gam) was 707 and 717 respectively; the other Hindus in these
seven villages had 839 females, and the entire population 813
females per thousand males.'

Milk became by tradition the murder weapon for some time.
'Soon after delivery, or within a few hours of it, female infants
were killed by giving them some opium or poison with their
mother's milk,' Vishwanath writes. But there were other ways of
killing newborn girls. Why give the little things poisoned milk,
when you could give them nothing at all? 'In fact, the newly born
infants were so vulnerable, that neglect which took the form of
refusal of the mother to feed the female infant, or exposure to heat
or cold were enough to finish them off. After the passing of the
Female Infanticide Act, census officials were reporting that castes
which practised female infanticide were "resorting increasingly"
to neglect of their female children to escape detection.'

But do Vishwanath's pages of history continue into London
today in any sense? Quite obviously no Patel is killing infant girls
in London today through poisoned milk or otherwise, but memories
remain. Just about every Patel I spoke to about doodh-peeti, after
my chat with the two Patels and the dip into Vishwanath's pages,
knew about the practice. For the Patels who were not from Chha-
gam, this was the way of 'those' Chha-gam Patels. Just about
every Charotar Patel has a clear sense of being inside the Chha-
gam circle or outside of it. The Patels of London have organized
their lives along those distinctions.

The practice of doodh-peeti still only gets whispered about if it
comes up at all; but the differences between the Patels whose
families originate from Chha-gam and those who do not stand out
in separate buildings and in bold print.

The 624-page directory of the Sattavis-gam Patels in Britain, one
of the bigger non-Chha-gam clusters, recalls the story of the
separation of the rest of the Charotar Patels from Chha-gam, lest
their kind of Patels forget. The directory, which sits in the home
of every Sattavis-gam Patel, reports a historic resolution.

'A conference of Patidars from Charotar was organised under
the auspices of Mr Shepard the then Collector of Kaira and
Commissioner of Northern Region on 8 February 1888 at Dakor

with the pious objects of abolishing Dowry and Girls' Infanticide.

'Approximately 10,000 Leva Patidars of Charotar were present at the conference. Mr Shepard proposed a resolution for reforming the oppressive and expensive marriage customs and traditions. Villages which were considered of higher social status opposed it while those at the lower strata and ruined by bad customs and dowry welcomed the proposal. Not only this, those Patidars with hurt ego decided that girls should not get married in so-called high-status villages.'

That resolution came to have the sanctity of a constitution among the villages. The first clause of the constitution reproduced in the directory says, 'Those villages who have entered into this agreement and signed beneath should not get their girls married in those villages of so-called higher status, or others who did not enter into this agreement. Villages who are a party to the agreement should not keep any social relations on good or bad occasions or directly or indirectly.' Penalties of Rs 1000 to Rs 4000 rupees— a fortune in nineteenth-century India—were laid down for anyone breaking the code.

That was then. But the recall of that resolution in a London directory was a message. That message became necessary because in London too Patel rose against Patel, the other Charotar Patels against the Chha-gam Patels. The Patel association run first from Archway in north London and then Tooting in south London claimed to represent all Patels, but was seen as dominated by the Chha-gam Patels. So the rest set up a federation of almost entirely non-Chha-gam Patels. Now, for Chha-gam in London, you could read substantially the National Association of Patidar samaj in Tooting; for the rest of the Charotar Patels, the Federation of Patidar Associations in Wembley.

The newly rebuilt centre of the Federation of Patidar Associations on London Road in Wembley is a memorial to a repeated rebellion in   London. The old rebellion by the 'lesser' Patels came in British-ruled India in the late nineteenth century; a polite revolution by Patels of that 'lesser' origin was repeated in London principally through creation of this Federation on London Road. Ruling Patels at both the Association and the Federation speak of a pan-Patel unity but when a first-generation Patel hears of the 'Association' and the 'Federation', he hears Chha-gam in the first, and the other Charotar villages in the second. And they stand separately

The Association bought itself an old church building in Archway, north London. This was later sold, unfortunately for the Association it seems, for a new hall down an obscure little street in Tooting in south London. The Federation had a tacky old building off a decaying Wembley High Road. It's been rebuilt and made smarter, which says much about the new success of the 'lesser' Patels, as no doubt it was intended to. No success statement can ever beat 'mine is bigger'. London Road says that the supposedly lesser Patels have more than equalized.

'We rebelled against them,' Mr Patel, who will be known only as 'Mr Patel', told me at the Federation office. He had called me after we spoke to ask me not to use his name. I guessed that his call to withhold his name came on the advice of a young Patel shuffling papers to a side as we had sat talking.

'They think they are the super-Patels,' he said of the Association. 'The majority are from Chha-gam.' Anything Mr Patel said, he said with certainty. His face must have hardened into a look of immovable wisdom about twenty years ago, and it looked even sterner when he spoke of the Chha-gam Patels. He did not have to say the majority at the Federation are not from Chha-gam, because the Federation letterhead said so. It read like a condensed account of a migrating rebellion.

Patelbhai had given me the letterhead as a short introduction to the Federation. It was a picture also of how the non-Chha-gam village groups from Charotar had set up societies in London to shadow their old villages: Posun UK (a group of five villages); Chovis-Gam Patidar Samaj (twenty-four villages); Shree Bavis-Gam Patidar Samaj (a twenty-two-village group); Shree Bavis-Gam Patidar Samaj (a rival group of the twenty-two-village group); Shree Kadva Patidar Samaj UK; Shree Sattavis Gam Patidar Samaj, Europe; Sojitra Samaj UK; Shree Vis-Gam Patel Samaj (a twenty-village group); Matiya Patidar Samaj, London; Saurashtra Leuva Patel Samaj UK; Shree Sattar-Gam Patidar Samaj UK (a seventy-village group); Shree Kutch Leva Patel Community UK; Charotaria Leuva Patidar Samaj, London, UK; and the new member, the Vakal

Kanam Patidar Association.

Each group has its own history, its own story. The Sattavis-gam is not really twenty-seven villages now but sixty-six. Vakal Kanam is a group of Patels from around Baroda. Bavis-gam is now forty-eight villages. But what brought almost all of them together was that they are not the Chha-gam.

The odd one out on this list was the Sojitra Samaj, the sole Chha-gam representation in the camp of the other Patels. 'It is not very active in the Federation,' Mr Patel said. That name on the paper was an idea that a bridge can be built across the two worlds, but it did not appear to be a bridge much in use.

It was an idea which would have to battle against history and memory. 'One thing was clear when we rose against Chha-gam in 1896,' Patel said. 'They would kill their infant daughters. They used to exploit us a lot, demand all sorts of things from us. People finally got fed up. So we set up the Sattavis-gam federation then, and the first item in the constitution was that we would never give a daughter from our village to a Chha-gam family. Whoever did would be expelled.' To him, those three pink pages of the Sattavis-gam directory were just memory.

Marriage, then, would be the big test. That nineteenth-century divide would be real in London only if the Chha-gam families and the rest still discouraged marriages between one and the other. The nineteenth-century admonition had been sounded. But was it being followed?

The test becomes easy particularly on those five or six occasions in a year when meetings of the Lagna Sahayak Samiti are held at the Federation hall in Wembley, when Patel singles can book in to look for another Patel to marry.

'We do not distinguish,' Mr Patel said. 'All Patels are welcome.'

'Chha-gam too?'

'Yes. They have started coming.' He said that like he was saying, now they can't do without us, can they? 'There are so many Chha-gam girls who cannot find partners, so they have to come here.'

'Lot of marriages between Chha-gam and the other Patels?'

'No, no, not many.'

'Do the Chha-gam have their own marriage service?'

'They must have it. But we have our own database.'

'Do you share that with them?'

'No.'

'But still, you do keep your meetings open to them?'

'You see, because it can get much worse. You see our girls, they go off with fellows here, fellows there, makes your heart cry. Because if someone wants to marry someone these days, who can stop anyone? The only real problem is if a girl goes to a Muslim or a Punjabi. But times are changing and now we are beginning to accept Punjabis also.' And if you can accept a Punjabi, why not that other kind of Patel? The other Patel is a Patel after all.

But this was only the view of one Federation Patels, that Chha-gam women now would come because there is a disproportionate number of single women among the Chha-gam Patels. But was this truly because they could not find enough men outside the Chha-gam circle? And were Chha-gam men not enough, or not good enough?

These questions took me to Babubhai Patel, the colonizer of London's corners for Patels to set up shop. Babubhai's office is not far from the Patel Association hall in south London traditionally dominated by the Chha-gam Patels. I thought for a moment crossing Battersea Bridge on the Thames on way to south London that this must be the Wagah border of the Charotar Patels, because that old divide between south London and the rest had aligned itself with the division in the world of Charotar Patels. An overblown thought, but I had no doubt I was moving from one Patel world to another between which hostilities had not entirely ceased.

If Babubhai could set up shops for thousands, he could set up homes for them. But while he had set up shops for any Patel and even non-Patels, the homes he was working to set up were exclusively for Chha-gam Patels.

'Look, this is the application form,' he said. I'd settled down over tea in his office brought by his charming daughter-in-law who had a desk next to his. We'd talked some shop, and now we were talking marriage, though the two are not always distinct. Babubhai had produced the application form from his marriages folder at the estate office in Tooting. This was also business for him, if not for profit.

On the top left of the form sat the Chha-gam logo, a hexagon formed by six triangles, with the name of a Chha-gam village in each triangle. Babubhai read them out: Bhadran, Dharmaj, Karamsad, Nadiad, Sojitra, Vaso. 'That's my village, Vaso,' he said, very Vaso-proudly. He showed what a marriage applicant would do, since this was a proper application form. First, they would enter their village. The form then asked for 'Candidate's name, sex, marital status, legal status (UK/USA/India/Africa), birth date, birth place, country, height, education, occupation, native gam, special interest and desired education/occupation of opposite sex.'

Next he produced some A4 sheets with the title 'Chha Gam Lagna Sahayak Samiti Wedding Candidates List'. He pulled out some sheets with 'Vaso' printed on them, the list of candidates from Vaso. The eligible on that page would be on offer to the eligible from the other five villages. A marriage between a Vaso Patel and another Vaso Patel was something 'we never do', Babubhai said. It would be incest. 'You know about DNA, no?' Babubhai said, educationally. 'About same blood? Our forefathers were right, never marry within the family, I mean even the extended family. We have taught our children this. They listen.'

The list on the first page showed nine names, eight of them women, all in their thirties. I flipped through the other pages. Page after page listed a very large number of single women in their thirties and forties. Flipping through more pages showed a fairly large population of single Chha-gam women. If all pages went the way of these, it might confirm the case of the Federation Patels that many people still do not want to marry Chha-gam Patels. But that still left the question why they weren't marrying men from the other five Chha-gam villages.

I took a closer look at the Chha-gam women listed on the first page. 'BA Modern Studies in civil service', 'O levels and clerical', 'A levels and civil servant', 'BTech, computer, now a travel consultant', 'A levels with a finance planning certificate now a senior mortgage advisor', 'law degree and idle', 'BSc Honours in applied psychology now an overseas programme manager', and 'BSc applied economics a housing officer now in Harrow'. I liked the sound of 'law degree and idle', but I was no Patel, let alone a Chha-gam Patel.

'What is the proportion of single girls to boys among the Chha-gam here,' I asked Babubhai, and immediately realized that I'd innocently asked an explosive question. In that office room it felt like the lid blown off a pressure cooker. 'It varies,' Babubhai said. The reply was instruction: talk no more about this.

Babubhai wanted to tell me how much more of a life the Chha-gam Patels were building around themselves with every passing year. Since marriage to anyone whose family is from the same village would be incest, networking between the gams had to be formalized if marriages were to be made. And so registers were being filled, and 'meet and greet' events were being held, like the Lagna Sahayak Samiti meetings over on the Federation side.

'We are now about 5000 families from Chha-gam,' Babubhai said. 'Maximum migration came from these six villages. Everybody cannot know everybody.'

The meet-and-greet marriage meetings are becoming increasingly well-attended, Babubhai said. 'Last time we had 450 single people, this time we will have more.' This was my opportunity to ask again about the proportion of males and females. 'It varies,' Babubhai said. 'Never counted. But whatever marriages are taking place are taking place mostly within the group.'

I figured that Babubhai's answer to the question about the gender of the Chha-gam singles would not vary. I asked whether they would network with the Patel Federation up at Wembley for marriages. 'No, we have not joined them,' he said, and he sounded like they never would if he had his way. 'They set up separately because they thought the Chha-gam Patels were holding all the high positions in the Association.' On this side of the divide, there wasn't even lip service to a Patel togetherness.

I thought Subhashbhai Patel might tell me what Babubhai had not. He had been president of the Karamsad Samaj, and that, as any Patel will tell you, is the village that gave India Sardar Vallabhbhai Patel. Or the village, they sometimes add, that gave India India.

Subhashbhai Patel was just recovering from some medical treatment when I went over to see him in his house in Kingsbury but he still looked handsome in a Bollywood-villainish way. After some preliminaries on Patelhood, he produced the Karamsad directory of Britain, listing all of 1300 families.

'I see Karamsad is not a part of the London Road Federation,' I said. 'No, we are not a part of London Road.' Like Babubhai, his tone too added 'and never will be'. I thought the upturned Chha-gam noses at the mention of the larger Federation of the supposedly lesser Patels had a strong nineteenth-century profile.

The Association had come earlier because it was the Chha-gams who began to get together first, each among their own and increasingly now as the six, Subhashbhai said. 'The Federation came up only subsequently. Because they thought the Chha-gam are coming together, so they formed the Federation.'

I brought up the marriages question. 'But there are a large number of single Chha-gam women, aren't there?' Subhashbhai, in the trained manner of an official spokesman before journalists, offered neither explicit denial nor confirmation. But he did offer an explanation. 'The percentage of girls from Chha-gam marrying within Chha-gam is beginning to go down because they are not getting the right boys. When the parents came here they bought businesses, they bought shops, they bought sub post offices. So many of the Chha-gam boys just went into their father's business, and many more of the girls went into education. So they are not finding enough of educated boys within Chha-gam.' He certainly thought there were not enough men, or good enough men, for single Chha-gam women.

It wouldn't be a tragedy if Juliet Patel from Chha-gam were to love Romeo Patel from a 'lesser' Charotar village. The families would probably make peace because, as Mr Federation Patel had said, in Britain today think how much worse it can get. But when Patel families look, they do not look at first in the other Patel half.

Within their own, each Patel side is looking more and more busily. The Federation used to have one meeting of the Lagna Sahayak Samiti every year, now they have one every three months. The Chha-gams never had one until some years ago, now they are planning two a year. If seven of ten eligible men that a potential Chha-gam Juliet meets in a year are Chha-gam Patels, it's that much more likely that she will marry Ramanbhai from Chha-gam than Romeo from outside. A poor love story but, who knows, a happy marriage, and not necessarily loveless either.

I left Subhashbhai's house in Kingsbury trying to figure out which Patel had told me once that Sardar Patel could unite India but he'd failed to unite the Patels.

SOME THREE

A Khan or an Ahmed with two wives or more would draw polite silence on the subject, but once K.D. Patel decided on two concurrent wives, Gujarati gossip would buzz a long time. So everyone knows of the Patel, almost always in white, with two wives, one of them with him in public, the other never. And Lata, the wife you see in public, in white too.

K.D. owns Kusum petrol station (named after the first and more private of his wives), and other businesses besides. It's of course not as a petrol station owner that he is known; he would be entirely uninteresting as only the standard half of a couple. The bedroom curiosity his double marriage excites makes him so much more than just another married Patel.

I'd been to a couple of parties at his house in Wembley; every busybody of the area has. K.D. is the Great Gatsby of Wembley's Gujaratis. His is the unmissable house with three Mercs in the drive and all those white plaster lions on the wall. Some of the lions standing on their hind legs with the likes of a royal shield hiding their testicles from drivers on Harrowdene Road. Other lions sit more conventionally, and so don't need shields.

I'd looked in to see K.D. again. 'Kusum Villa' the legend above the front door said. You see the other wife's name everywhere, you never see her.

K.D. led me in through three large drawing rooms (he later said there were five more) before we settled for a fourth. I sat on a boring sofa beside a heavily carved jhoola. K.D., in his mandatory white suit, sat on a chair across. His fondness for white extended unfortunately to white leather shoes. Those rarely work, even when new, as anyone knows from watching them fail under Jeetendra and Biswajeet. The occasional trader with Pan Parag in a briefcase will still step out in a white leather shoe, but mostly they retired with a certain phase of sixties' cinema.

But white leather shoes would be about all that K.D. and Jeetendra, or even Biswajeet, could have in common. K.D. is not particularly heroic-looking. His dash comes from the lifetime of double devotion he is thought to enjoy. He must believe it said that he is a king among Patels for satisfying two wives when most can barely do the minimum with one.

'So, how two wives?' I asked.

'It just happened. I just don't know how it happened.'

'But surely you do.'

'I fell in love with Lata when she came to work in my office in Kenya.'

'What office was that?'

'Africana Towel Company.'

Everyone needs towels, maybe more in Kenya which is never short of heat or water. To others, this was nature; to a Patel businessman, it became opportunity.

'Were you married then?'

'Yes, I was married to Kusum. I told Kusum about Lata and then also married Lata with the permission of my first wife. The three of us have been happily married for more than thirty years.' I skipped the bedroom questions because I suspected the guessing would be more engaging than the facts.

K.D. had other things to show off. 'My house,' he said, as he saw me looking around. 'Built over 48,000 square feet. Eight bedrooms, eight receptions. I will ask someone to show you around.'

A young female manager visiting London from K.D.'s IT company in India became my guide. She was one of those tinsel girls in tight jeans that every man fancies, and no woman knows why. We went up what was designed to be described as a winding path through a garden to the disco at the back. A single bend in the path meant it did wind once. We crossed about a yard or two of bridge on our way over a pool fed by a fountain. The garden was landscaped with statues of peacocks and of a dog.

'There were real peacocks once, about twelve of them,' my companion in jeans told me as we crossed the bridge. 'But the dog ate some of them. And the climate here did not suit them.' So K.D. gave away the surviving peacocks to the zoo and eventually built memorials in the garden to both the peacocks and the dog. These were the gardens of the K.D. parties, it's where you could get to meet the millionaires who do not get on those rich lists because they know the taxman also reads newspapers.

Up the garden towards the rear stood a white three-in-one statue, three women in the nude in close embrace. 'From Greece,' my guide announced. It couldn't be just me thinking what I was, even if this was an all-female threesome.

We had reached a little back house, with a garden bar by the entrance watched over by a bronze figure of Cleopatra. 'Cleopatra-ben,' I said. Not a particularly clever one, and my companion wasn't impressed. We brushed past Cleopatra and entered a disco hall by the side of a pool that didn't look like anyone ever swam in it. It was there so that a party around it could be called a poolside party. Behind the pool was a little stage, because guests are served speeches too. Both K.D. and Lata have been elected councillors in Brent, and Lata was also mayor.

We returned to the main house and now K.D. showed me around the inside. He took me through bedroom after bedroom, some of them multiplied by mirrors on all sides, inspiring unprintable thoughts. I saw no sign of the other wife, the first, that is.

Back by the jhoola, K.D. handed me an eighty-page brochure on the couple (K.D. and Lata) like people hand out visiting cards. It had an albumish picture of K.D. and Lata on the cover, side by side. Under K.D.'s name were printed the words 'Flair', 'Fortune', 'Flavour' in large type; under Lata Patel's, 'Dignified', 'Devoted', 'Dedicated'. Within, just about every page carried photographs of Lata Patel and of K.D. But at last there was one of all three together, a posed photograph, with K.D. sitting in the middle in a white suit (also white shirt and white tie) flanked by the two wives in white saris (daring only a little non-white print) standing to the sides, each with a hand on K.D.'s shoulders. Now here was a real man.

The brochure packed K.D. and Lata photographed with eminent others, to let you know who they know, so you know just who they are. Lata Patel variously with the Queen, with Tony Blair, Vasant Sathe, V.C. Shukla, Prince Charles, Shankar Dayal Sharma, V. Venkatraman, Narasimha Rao, Zail Singh, Kiran Bedi, Amitabh Bachchan, Govinda. The only pictures where Lata Patel did not wear white were from the year she was mayor of Brent, when she wore the heavy red mayoral gown with that black furry collar in the style worn in the churches of the Middle Ages. Lata Patel was mayor no longer when I visited them. K.D. was now out of local political life too, so they were both back to white.

With that brochure planted in my hand, K.D. had made sure I'd know them much better as I left. I thought I was forgetting something as I got up to leave. It came to me at the door.

'Why do you always wear white?'

'I like white because it is the colour of purity and simplicity,' K.D. replied.

Who was I to argue?

HOLES

The Gujarati inclination to say 'hole' when they mean 'hall' has long been familiar, but I still wished it different when I heard Suresh Kansagra tell the bride's mother that she will like his hole, and so will her daughter. The bride's father replied in kind. 'You have a lovely hole,' he said as the couple settled down in Mr Kansagra's drawing room. 'Thank you,' Kansagra replied.

He'd heard that before, they all say that when they come into his drawing room to book the Kadwa Patidar Hall across from the Harrow Leisure Centre. Another man was waiting outside, most likely a father, soon to be father-in-law. Kansagra's status of taking bookings for that hall had turned his drawing room into a visitors' room.

Suresh Kansagra was a large and efficient man and carried the look of one long familiar with his importance. He would, as magistrate, as president of the Kadwa Patidar Samaj, as Conservative Party councillor in Brent. But his weightiness comes at least as much from the hall he takes bookings for.

It's a large and well-placed hall in northwest London, the part of London that becomes more Indian by the day. Built in 1993 by the Kadwa Patidar Samaj, a relatively small group of about 700 Patel families from Saurashtra, the hall has now become the place to celebrate marriage and Indian living itself. How often you get invited to a hall, any hall, is a sure indicator of how you live, even of how Indian an Indian is. Because halls connect people, and because that has consequences. Two or three Indians can be a pain, two or three hundred are such fun. If there's one thing Indians love, it is to just gather. Indians have never been great adventurers or wanderers, but they have always been great gatherers. In Britain it takes halls to make that happen because that's where the weather pushes you into. So when people want to meet or marry, Kansagra's name is never far from the mind.

'People tell me they first want to book the hall and then look for someone to marry,' Kansagra said to the father. 'I am taking bookings eighteen months in advance.' The father nodded reverentially.

I'd dropped in to see Kansagra to talk some Patel matters, but I sat in that room as mostly a witness to his significance, and that of his hall, and intruded when I could. Kansagra could talk to me only between fathers and bookings.

Finding a gap, I asked him why he was called Kansagra if he was a Patel. 'I used to be called Patel but I changed that to go back to my real surname. You see, in Saurashtra and in Kutch many have their own surnames, and either they do not use Patel or they use both. Outside we use Patel but inside we go back to our real surnames.'

'But do all Patels have other surnames?'

'No, in the Charotar area they have the gam (village) system. They are known by their gams, so they can only call themselves Patels.' But as seen from Kutch and Saurashtra, Patel may not be a surname at all, only the lack of one.

The bride's father paid a deposit of £550. On the wedding day he would pay £280 an hour, for a minimum hire of six hours. Not a bad day's income for the Kadwa Patidar Samaj. Income from the hall must make Kadwa Patidar Patels the envy of other Patels. But it isn't just the income they would be envying. It's what the hall can do for keeping your own together—Patel group after Patel group. Just about everyone knows that when people marry they marry in a hall but when a group has a hall of its own, they're more likely to have the kind of marriages they want. Patels, like others, have discovered the relationship between space and choice.

A hall has so much to do with the thing called love because what feels like magic needs time and space. A hall is love's best friend; it gives you space enough to move in, but not enough to move too far. And it gives you time together with your own. Patel fathers and mothers, who would be fathers-in-law and mothers-in-law to their own kind of Patel are not forcing matches, just building walls and settling ceilings around a Patel world for the magic to happen.

It's a saturation move. Take a hall and fill it with your own. On weekend parties, at weddings, on birthdays, on anniversaries, on Valentine's, Holi, Diwali, Janamashtami, a katha from a visiting saint, someone's twenty-fifth this, fortieth that, Christmas, New Year, Dussehra, even India's Republic Day. Think how many meetings that can mean with how many eligible people of your own Patel kind. Could that many years pass before you like one of your own that you see again and again? The chances that Cupidbhai Patel will deliver are excellent.

It's fine for eyes to meet, but you have to see someone first. Repeat appearances before a few hundred of your own gives love a better chance than any other circumstance you could easily think up. You have the occasional marriage melas, but they offer only one-off visibility; halls promise interaction. Given a hall, you don't need to arrange marriages; you need only to arrange introductions, or even just to turn up. An arrangement by parents can become love to the introduced; in the end, arranged love must feel like any other love.

The Kadwa Patidar Patels had institutionalized temptations, and others could rent the space at least every now and then. It might explain also why I was in Kansagra's room as a wandering bum and not some promising groom. As a non-Patel the hall had no room for me on all the interesting days. I'd always envied the Patels their hall as I envied all those I'd seen so often headed that way. They had a little world of their own, I didn't. They were in a space with their own, I was out on streets that were strangers. Who knows which lovely woman in which lovely sari headed for the hall was my lost chance. As an outsider, I'd never even make it as far as being the wrong guy. I was an outsider to Patels of every kind, and to every kind of group that ever hired that hall. I wish India had been smaller, then I might have got in as just Indian. It was in some despair that I watched how much that hall was doing for the others.

I stole a quick moment between one father and the next to ask Kansagra how many of their youngsters marry within their own.

'We are getting about 10 to 15 per cent of our youths marrying outside the community because they meet people in universities and offices,' he replied with statistical certainty. 'That is where people do meet others, what can you do?' He spoke, still focussed on the register, his eyes scanning dates and bookings.

If Kansagra was right on the numbers, halls are doing their bit to deliver one Patel to another, to recycle love within a community. The halls are weekend counter-magnets set up against the double danger from universities and offices. Every hall is a fortress resisting that modern march towards a mix of people where only individuals may matter, not where those individuals come from.

The last booking father had gone, and Kansagra was now going to fit me in between fathers and dinner. We'd been talking about Patel-to-Patel marriages, I reminded him.

'Times are changing and you are getting a lot more intermarriages,' he said. 'You have Kutch Patel marrying Charotar Patel, Saurashtra Patel marrying Kutchi Patel, Leva Patel marrying Kadwa Patel.' And I used to think of Hindu-Muslim marriages as intermarriages. In London, a marriage of a Hindu Indian Gujarati Patel to another Hindu Indian Gujarati Patel can be intermarriage, and the 'inter' part of it can be quite a serious thing.

It was different back in Kenya, Kansagra said. He was not a man to talk at length; he was more a deliverer of sound bites.

Maybe he was just hungry. 'We used to meet everyone there because we saw everyone as Indian and Hindu. But here everyone got segregated. There are so many of us that there are enough within every community. So everyone says I will go to my own.' Numbers, see. I knew we were so many that I would have to be alone. It looked like Kansagra had come to accept intermarriages of this kind. In these changing times everyone knows how much worse it can get. Other Patels have said so, and others think so. Better a compromise than a catastrophe, better embarrassment than shame, better a distant other than an outsider. He seemed resigned to the occasional Patel marrying a quite different Patel.

Kansagra looked past me, he was getting signalled to. But before his meal he had something more to say about communities and halls. 'It means you have a whole community to face. If I am alone and go bankrupt, who cares? But if I am a part of a community that meets once a week at a hall, where will I show my face if I do something wrong? These gatherings are a very great deterrent to wrongdoing.' This was the magistrate in Kansagra speaking. Marriage and morals and halls were all one.

'Look at the very small number of Indians in British prisons,' he said. 'And the very small number of Indians who go to jail are for some kind of petty fraud, not for violent crimes.'

'Is that because Indians have formed communities, or found halls of their own?'

'I think these community gatherings are keeping Indians out of prisons. They give people something worthwhile and honourable to do with their time.'

It sounded like a good theory to test: how many people who go to community functions also go to prison? It would be great for a Kadwa Patel from Saurashtra to marry a Kadwa Patel from Saurashtra because only then will an offspring be Kadwa Patel, and Kadwa Patelhood will not become history. But if Kansagra's theory stands, it would also mean a good Patel marrying a good Patel. A hall could save you from the wrong Patel, even a non-Patel, and it might also have stopped you going to jail.

*

The groom and bride had driven up in a small red Peugeot—not the usual Rolls. But you don't need a Rolls to stretch silver ribbons over from the front bumper to announce passenger matrimoniality. Mercifully it wasn't one of those embarrassingly elongated limousines that now tempt the British who've fallen in taste to marry American-style.

The lack of size of this car mattered. One of those American cars the size of a bus would never have made it into that little lane from Tooting High Street into the community centre of the National Association of the Patidar Samaj. That little lane had been too little even for the motor garage where the association hall now stands. The Patels bought the garage and turned it into a hall big enough to fit 500 people, but with parking for only three or four cars in front. The lane hardly suffices for visiting Patels, let alone marriage parties. The red lines on Tooting High Street had made it impossible to casually park outside.

Thankfully, I'd taken the tube. Pravin Amin from the Association was waiting for me at the entrance, along with the wedding guests. We made way for a dholak player, heralding the bride and groom from the car into the hall. The bridegroom was white, and that made this an unusual wedding. 'You don't have this sort of thing happening very often,' Pravinbhai assured me.

The bridegroom wore a white bandhgala suit, the very Gujarati bride a mauve lehenga-choli with a good deal of mango-shaped shine on it. This was obviously not an arranged marriage, and just as obviously not a fresh love marriage. They had only finally married.

Unnoticed by the dholak player, a notice board on the wall by the side carried a warning about noise levels. It was from the local council addressed to the management of the hall 'requiring you to stop causing a nuisance'. Next time the fine could be £5000, it warned. The hall stood amidst houses at the back, and any wedding here would have to be a quiet wedding. Parking problems and complaints about loud music compete to top social problems in Britain today. This hall had enough of both.

For the chap with the dholak this was a matter between him and his skill, not the hall and its neighbours. He was getting more and more carried away with his wedding kind of beat, and danced on into the hall leaving the couple well behind.

'Slowly,' the man who seemed the bride's father said to him. 'Slowly.'

'Can't beat this thing slow, you know.'

'No, I mean walk slowly.'

The little procession of six or seven led by the dholak player made its way through the dinner tables up to the top table. A manager quickly shut the glass doors behind them, with the look of a man who was not prepared to write out a £5000 cheque. The DJ playing *Hum tumhare hain, tumhare sanam* ... followed by *Mubarak ho tum ko ye shaadi tumhari* ... was adding to the dholak decibels.

The only white people in the hall (other than the groom) was a couple with a little baby. If the groom had family and friends happy about the marriage, they hadn't shown up. Or maybe it is Indians far more than white Brits who always know people who'll turn up for special occasions. There never was a Smith Samaj to match a Patel association.

The loss of this particular bride to an out and out non-Patel was not a loss to the Patel association that owned the hall, Pravinbhai told me as we queued for dinner though we were not quite wedding guests. The association that owned the hall included Patels of all kinds, but was Chha-gam heavy, and many of the Chha-gam have always thought of themselves as something of the aristocracy of Charotar Patels. But this was not even some lesser Charotar Patel group that had rented the hall, only a Kutch Patel family. A blessed marriage, no doubt, but it was the Kutch Patels' loss.

'Very few people marry whites,' Pravinbhai said to me as we dubiously joined other guests at a dinner table. 'People draw their own circle. Some say it must be within their own Patel circle. Some will accept another Patel, and some will accept another Gujarati, and some will even accept another Indian. But the vast majority of marriages happen within the same community.'

The wedding brought in some rent, as other events here must do. But I doubt this particular hall was working for members of the association. If they wanted to come, where would they park? For a marriage to happen, the two must meet, their eyes must meet, then their hearts and minds, their families, and not least then the meeting of practical interests. But first they must park.

Who knows, a woman from an Association family, most likely a Chha-gam woman, never married because she never got to this hall often enough to meet others, because she and that possible someone couldn't find anywhere to park.

*

The spaceship appeared unexpectedly as I rounded the corner on Forty Avenue, driving west past the Brent town hall. That's what the Sattavis-gam Patel Samaj had built by way of their hall, not the roadside rectangle I'd expected to see. Its façade of glass panels leaned outwards above the roadside under a wavy ceiling supported by curving white beams. Its shape announced the twenty-first-century Sattavis-gam Patel.

Off Forty Avenue I found The Avenue and then space in the ample parking lot. Through my friend Harshadbhai Patel, a local Conservative councillor, I met Raj Patel who took me on a walkabout. 'It can take 150 cars,' Raj said, pointing to the parking before turning to what was within. He was bursting with fabulous facts about this building and he couldn't wait to share them. I remembered such Patel-proud statistics as 3400 square metres of covered area—'maybe even more'—at a cost of £8.1 million.

The building was designed to provoke exclamations like 'futuristic' and a wide-eyed 'state of the art'. All sorts of angles and curves were relieved by occasional straight lines and squares. In the foyer, pink lighting marked the border of a large square on the wall in ways an observer should only be able to describe as 'somehow'. Raj and I strolled through two large halls around the foyer, all sorts of rooms upstairs and up to the third floor auditorium whose 'cascading chairs' had yet to be installed. The centre was opened in April 2005 and was still being given its last additions.

'We have arrangements to lift a car into the auditorium in case anyone wants to display it,' Raj said. I couldn't figure at first why anyone would want to display a car on the third floor of a Sattavis-gam Patel building. But Raj explained that the space was intended also for commercial use. Round the corner from Wembley Stadium and its business complex, and close to new hotels in the area, the Sattavis-gam centre was being promoted as a conference centre. Much of the £8.1 million it had cost was a loan that would have to be repaid. Renting out conference facilities would pay for the hall; it would also be a centre for other communities to hire. And it was always there for the Sattavis-gam Patels to gather to perpetuate themselves.

Every community dreams of a hall of its own. Dreams turn to plans, plans to funds, funds to buildings. This hall was still a plan when I'd dropped in to see Harshadbhai Patel at his place by Preston Road, not that far from where the structure was to come up.

Harshadbhai must be about the busiest of the Sattavis-gam Patels. The home office he invited me into was a mess, and I felt immediately at home. Harshadbhai took position behind piles of all sorts of papers and reference books; he looked like he knew where to unscramble the mess for what, so that was all right. Even on that first meeting he seemed very familiar, like I'd seen him before. He was very much the moustached hero on an Indian campus in the seventies, and those chaps always knew what they were doing. Harshadbhai was going to show me his plan, and he knew just where that one was in the papers. It was a pamphlet called the '27-gam Patidar Building Project'. This was the project that would get Patels from the original twenty-seven, and now sixty-six, villages in Gujarat's Charotar a hall of their own.

A list of 'Priorities' sat on the pamphlet by the side of a picture of the model.

A HUNDRED YEARS FROM NOW IT WILL NOT MATTER WHAT MY BANK ACCOUNT WAS, THE SORT OF HOUSE I LIVE IN, OR THE KIND OF CAR I DRIVE ... BUT THE WORLD MAY BE DIFFERENT BECAUSE I WAS IMPORTANT IN THE LIFE OF A CHILD.

Below that attention hook came the collective plea of the Sattavis-gam Patel leaders to cough up for Patelhood of the Sattavis-gam kind:

How easy it is to forget. Time moves on. Circumstances

change. Families multiply. Houses get bigger. What car do you drive? Is it still about survival or is it about wanting more? Perhaps wanting more and sometimes wanting just for the sake of it?

The biggest oak tree perhaps over 100 feet tall and standing up to the tests of nature for more than a hundred or two hundred years. We've all seen them. The oak tree cannot forget its roots as only by its roots does it survive. The nutrients in the soil are washed in by the rain entering through the roots and thereafter the tree is fed and grows and once grown survives all nature throws at it. Unless a rare disease hits the oak tree it outlives man, unless man itself destroys the tree.

Do you remember your roots? From whence you came? Are you better today than you were then? Better fed. Better off. That's as may be but what keeps us all together is the protection of our roots. Call it our culture. In a world where culture is dying and modern fashion dictates a modern style of culture and not always for the better.

We are all about to plant an oak tree in Wembley.

Planning permission has been granted. In East Africa we had our roots, our cultural places to visit, to meet, to discuss. Now we are about to embark on an oak tree that could last 100 years or more. This is bigger than any one of us. It is a chance to come together, to work together for the benefit of us all.

As somebody once said, let us come together now to work today, for all our tomorrows, and the tomorrows of generations to come. Without your support it will not be as good as it will be with your support. Please!

As an elected leader, Harshadbhai knew just what to say to journalist types, and he was answering the 'why' question before I could ask it.

'We need it to keep the young with us in our ways. I have three daughters. Culturally they are not under the influence of the West at all. They speak fluent Gujarati. If they didn't tell you they were born here, you would think they are born in Gujarat.' That, he meant, shows how good they are.

'Once you have lost your language then ultimately you have lost your culture,' he said.

'But can you force Gujarati down the throats of the young these days?'

'It is not question of down the throat, it is question of education. We do not find a lot of youngsters rebelling against our ways. When it happens it is the fault of parents, they do not educate them properly. If shown right direction, they will follow. We do not have to tell our young to celebrate Navratri. They are ready before we are. We want our culture preserved. Our culture gives better life, it gives more secure life. In every way. Socially, financially, in achieving their goals.'

'But how will the building of a hall help the young achieve their goals in life?'

'Because that happens when you are a close community. Then what happens, you see this person, let us call him or her X, who is a doctor. Then I also want to be a doctor. When you are close like this, it brings more and more competition. So then greater and greater good results come.'

He could defend every statement he made. Gujarati students do have some of the best results in schools and universities. Is that because they go to community events where they are under watch, and will get talked about? So that the more of your own that watch you, the better you will do, and the more regularly you go to a community hall, the higher your marks? This theory too needs testing.

Harshadbhai's list of the virtues of a hall was a long one. If you need an anchor in your life, you need a community. And when you have a community, you need a hall for it—you can't talk long in the rain. Community means communication. The hall would do its bit to keep the young in their cultural ways, but it didn't have to feel that heavily driven. It would also be just a place to meet one another. These days community works when you turn it into a club, somewhere nice to go to with your own. A hall can be a hole after all.

CORNERED

Why don't Indians ever play football?

Because every time they get a corner they put up a shop.

That old joke tired out some time back. Behind the till of every corner shop, it was thought, was an Indian. Mostly true. It was also true that behind many Indians and certainly most Patels at the corner shops was Babubhai Patel.

If you can allow an exchange of a Mars bar for small change across a shop till to produce a legend, it would have to be Babubhai. He alone did much to change the face of London: he turned Britain into a nation of Patel shopkeepers, a few thousand of them. In the world behind those shop tills he's known as the 'guru of CTN' (Confectionary, Tobacco, Newspapers). Tucked into these stores, the corner stores, was often the post office. Babubhai mastered the business of shop leading into post office, and of turning post office visitor into shopper.

Babubhai told me his rags-to-riches story in the office of his company BA Finance, on Garratt Lane near Tooting Broadway Station in south London. Rags-to-riches for immigrants usually means 'significant to substantial'. But he was not just the subject of the story, he was a multiplier of it into a few thousand others.

Babubhai's office didn't show that success, and what it didn't show advertised his style. He played himself down as he played down his office. You wouldn't suspect he was guru to anyone unless you were in the CTN business yourself. His balding, smiling looks made him the kindest of uncles. And kindness is good for business. 'My father always used to say, help others and others will help you. Because they will come back to get your help.' For a fee, naturally.

Babubhai had worked out ways to cut costs and improve the productivity of pennies, the known recipe for a shop's success. But first he would have to arrange the capital to do all that with. He had begun to channel loans the Patel way and even the Asian way in Nairobi through Standard Bank, now Standard Chartered Bank.

When a Patel off the boat from India wanted capital, it was Bababhai he'd turn to. When he wanted investment advice, it was Bababhai again.

It worked well in East Africa of the sixties, but did not last. 'My post got Africanized,' he said. So he sent his wife and children to London, and followed two years later in 1970. He landed with two assets: he knew banking, and Patels knew him. Off-the-boat Patels had needed him in Kenya, now off the second boat in Britain they would need him again.

Within a month of arriving in Britain, Bababhai told me, he set up a small finance company at Trafalgar Square. It would be easy for arriving Patels to find him there. At the same time, he got together with two other Patels to buy a sub post office on the far less spectacular Trafalgar Road in Greenwich in south London. The lesser Trafalgar was going to show what to sell at the real Trafalgar address. It was a business waiting for Patels.

'The three of us bought it on a goodwill of 5500 pounds,' he said. 'The income was 5000 pounds a year from the post office for selling its stamps and what not. The rent for the sub post office in that old church property was £70 a year.' With the goodwill paid, there was steady income for the three Patels when weekly wages could often be as low as £15 a week. Plus—and it was the discovery of this plus that changed the face of London—Bababhai found that real income came from sale of newspapers, chocolates and drinks at the post office. The post office became only the hook to get customers in, and very soon what the chocolates brought in made post office fees only extra income. *Lots of chocolates for me to sell, lots of pennies for me to make.*

'The margin for the sales was a minimum of 20 per cent,' Bababhai said. 'The volume was good.' Bababhai looked pleased even in retrospect. When a Patel says volume was good, he is usually taking in a fair bit of money, though all money is small in relation to what could be.

The partners rapidly bought three other sub post offices. In 1973 they disbanded the partnership, and each Patel set up his own business to run. Bababhai entered the business of getting others into this business. He wouldn't buy shops; he would make it possible for others to buy theirs. He became the corner shop consultant and financier.

'So many people came to see me. I used to give them advice—how to buy, how to get finance, who to approach. I used to do all this for them and after that I used to give them training in my own sub post office.' He would teach budding Patel shopkeepers how to restrict pennies going out and invite more to come in. A training college unlisted in London's records had come to exist for the spread of Patel corner shops.

'My office became like a doctor's waiting room,' he said. A 'those-were-the-days' look came over him, and I could see the lightest of smiles in the eyes behind those financier glasses. In that rush of the seventies Babubhai got more than 2000 CTNs going and at least another thousand later, after the immigration wave from East Africa had subsided. 'Once these people set up, they told their friends and relatives. Then they train, then we again finance, see, that is how it goes on.' The Patels advanced rapidly into London's corners, and changed life around them.

Babubhai offered consultation without a consultation fee. 'First I would find out a good business for a client in a good location. Then I would negotiate for them. I would always bring the price down more than they would ever pay me in commission. Then I would arrange for the solicitor, the accountant and the stock-taker. Then I would arrange the finance and then the insurance. I would only take commission from the client on completion.' It didn't end there. 'I would monitor the business for the next six months to make sure it was going well.' And to top all this, 'I used to give them courage.' When had pre-Patel London ever provided service to match this?

The banks came to know Babubhai Patel, and that money given through him was money for the bank. Natwest presented him an award 'as one market leader to another'. Babubhai likes to think banks were competing to be his best friends. 'Other branches of Natwest, other banks also began to come to me. I never had to go to a bank, the managers would always come here.' He tapped on his modest table to make the point.

'But if business was so good, why were white British people selling?' I asked.

'You see, they used to employ staff and close at five.' Babubhai saw that as answer enough. How much more backward could anyone get than to run a business, employ staff and close at five? A Smith employing a Jones could never beat the advantage of a Patel couple's togetherness at the till.

Other weaknesses in the British character showed up. 'Those were the days of the recession, and they thought everything was going to fall apart. So they sold everything and went to live by the sea.' Babubhai pointed in the general direction of the English Channel.

When white Brits see a recession, they look at figures that don't add up, they look at the headlines, and head for the sea. A Gujarati comes into his own when margins shrink. With their backs to the shop wall, and loans to repay, the Patels did away with staff and with downing shutters at five, and with not raising them on weekends. They made pennies add, from customer after customer, day after day. The surrender of London's corners to Patels was soon complete.

This K.D. Patel was a fair bit taller than the K.D. with the two wives; he could be such a thing as the athletic shopkeeper. I was talking about Babubhai with him at his shop near Clapham Junction station. He had had a fateful conversation with Babubhai Patel years back. This is what he remembers:

'Babu kaka, I want to borrow 550,000 pounds for this shop I have seen.'

'How much money do you have?'

'10,000 pounds.'

'You have ten thousand and you want to borrow 550,000?'

'Yes.'

'No problem.'

Memory condenses such exchanges nicely, and makes neat stories of them. Like most Indian stories, they improve in the telling. But whatever got said between the two, K.D. got the money. His shop at Clapham Junction today has an annual turnover of a few million pounds.

'I have never seen a banker, I never want to see a banker,' K.D. told me. 'For us there is only Babu kaka.'

K.D.'s shop has cornered a good deal of business in that area though he was getting besieged by Goliaths. 'I have a Marks & Spencer store third door from me. Walking distance I have twenty-four-hour Asda, I have Somerfield, there is Woolworth, there is Superdrugs and now a Sainsbury's is opening up. They are all my neighbours.' He spoke with the grim lightness of a man set to conquer adversity through just everyday work.

The Goliaths have the economy of scale on their side to price several products lower than most Patels can, but K.D. was not David for nothing. 'Main thing I have is location.' It could hardly be better, just across from the station. 'You have 3000 trains a day passing through here. All of them do not stop, but many trains stop.' The ones that just hurtle through must sound like so many missed pennies.

Without scale on his side, K.D. still undercuts the big guys. 'We also make some products cheap, and keep some others not so cheap. These are just tricks of the trade, everybody does it.' When his shop was nearer, people wouldn't cross the road to save a penny or two. By the station, clients need to save seconds, not pennies. So he'd tailored his services accordingly. 'We give really fast service at the till. If you come into our shop, you do not have to wait. Because we need your money fast.' Everyone who walked into his store was a till to tap, and he was going to do this efficiently.

As a Patel, he knew the British well. 'I know they love chocolates.' So he stocks about 250 varieties. K.D. is taking on the Goliaths with all sorts of other extras. Like an offer to accept gas and electricity bills. 'If I process bills of 15,000 pounds a week, I get only 100 pounds commission. But that is still 5200 pounds a year.' If you multiply every recurring income and expense into an annual sum, all income is good, and no expense too little. Penny wise, pound very wise.

K.D. had started off with one shop in Streatham bought with his three brothers through Babubhai Patel. 'Then also he arranged the finance for us—no security, nothing. Then we got another shop on the same road and then a supermarket in Dulwich.' Then, as usual, each Patel brother set out on his own. Now the three brothers have a shop each, and their sister three. Each has invested the profits in several properties to rent out, and the value of each has risen. It pays to look after every person-penny.

K.D. works twelve to fourteen hours a day, and says he likes it. 'People in this country, they don't want to work, that is why they are depressed.' But he is working away only because it's working out for him. Not every Patel has a shop nicely across from a railway station. And not every David Patel has triumphed in the face of the expanding Goliath chain stores.

'The Patels can stop London,' Vinod Nakarja had said as we were gup-shupping somewhere. When he left that line hanging in the air and invited me to his shop to find out how, I was always going to.

Some days later, we were talking behind the locked doors in the little post office at the back of his shop in Gerards Cross, just off the road to Oxford as you leave London. We were in the post office because the wife was handling the corner shop part of the business, and business must go on; Vinodbhai was happy to talk to me but not if he had to lose money in the bargain. And we had locked ourselves in because there's money in the post office, this is London these days, and you never know.

Vinodbhai, dark and tough-looking, could have had a future in Gujarati cinema as a menacing hero. The lines he was delivering now would match the role. London wakes up. And what's in the papers? Can't buy one, the Patel shops are all closed. Yes, the *Metro* is free, but those would all have been taken by now. There is that non-Patel store but the *Sun* would have sold out. What a way to start a day. These Patels.

No morning milk, no tea. How long can milk last even in the fridge? Can't buy the train ticket at the store either. Buy at the station, then. But what a queue. What if you miss the train? Those few minutes in the morning make all the difference. And the Patels had to do this on a Monday when everyone buys their weekly pass. If this is happening to Londoners, what would London be like ...

Face after face appeared outside the toughened glass as we talked, they wanted stamps and the usual at a post office. They saw two Asian men talking inside. Who'd have guessed that one of them was painting scenarios of bringing their city to a halt?

They were lucky Nakarja's thoughts hadn't touched their lives.

No, the Patels won't stop London. But in the imagined discomfort Patels can bring to Londoners, Nakarja (another of those Kutch Patels who find it fashionable to drop 'Patel' and take up the village name) saw the power of the Patels. If only the Patels would see it, and be prepared to use it.

But why would he want to treat London so? 'I will tell you.' I waited while he sold some more stamps to some dear old ladies. 'Nice day for a walk,' he said. 'Yes, not bad at all,' one replied. These things need to be said to dear old ladies; they visit post offices more than anyone else.

Nakarja would tell me all, but only by and by. Customer is king, and I was only a reporter.

'The *Sun*,' he said. 'The newspaper *Sun*.' I was from India, and he had to make sure, because what do people from India know. 'The *Sun* carried an article that was so abusive of Hindu gods, so abusive. I told them that day that I would not sell the newspaper.' Not only not sell, he would show the *Sun*, and show London, through his Newsagents Action Group, NAG, that others would not sell it any more either.

'A few Patels, they agreed, but the rest, they did not want to know. You see, our people, they have never been united, that is our problem.' The *Sun* got away with it and London was let off because Patels would not unite. Indian history was repeating itself through shops that remained open as usual.

NAG tried to get Patels to unite for the sake of business if not for Hindu gods.

'Look at this.' He held up a packet of Bombay mix. 'Do you see?'

'Yes,' I replied. 'Bombay mix. Why they call it Bombay mix I don't know.' I was missing the point here.

'You see the price, 35p, printed on the packet. So they are telling me at what price I should sell, they are fixing my margins for me. More and more, these fellows, this is what they are beginning to do.'

The Bombay mix was eating into pricing strategies, Vinodbhai explained. Pricing every product to the penny is a carefully considered calculation, depending on competition, location, volume, the preferences of the area, and that balancing act of what you will price low to keep them coming and what you can mark up to swell profits. Those decisions have to be taken over each of a few thousand products. When manufacturers stamp a price, they limit the shopkeeping genius of a Patel. These decisions were abusing their business choices, not just their gods, and still Patels were doing nothing.

NAG never did become an effective group. It ran into what Nakarja thought were Indian cultural fault-lines that had stayed so long they'd become genetic. And it failed because customers who walk into closed doors may have memories, and no one is in the business of counting how much money you could lose from each displeased customer, certainly not over something silly in the *Sun*. NAG failed because Patels were in the business of keeping shops open, not closed.

Nakarja was holding up the view that Indians were divided and therefore they played too easily into the hands of the divide-and-rule game the British had started so long back. These two taken together, and they usually are, must add up to one of the oldest Indian moans. It's migrated quite smoothly to Britain. Every time a Britisher does something that does not please all equally, they are dividing and ruling. You think you see it, and then enjoy the wisdom of observing how little things ever change.

So Patels thrived, or survived, in their corners by themselves. When business was going, it looked after itself. When it failed, it failed alone.

Several Patel businesses have failed before the advancing Goliaths who've begun to scatter little Patel-like outlets around the country.

The race does reach an end point. The first Patel shops started opening late, and then the supermarkets began to open late. The Patels opened weekends, and laws were changed to let the big guys open weekends. Then the Goliaths began to be open twenty-four hours, and now a few Patels are beginning to open twenty-four hours. The Patel was likely to be nearer you, but now watch the signs: a biggie is coming to a corner near you.

Babubhai figures that CTNs with a turnover of less than £7000 a week are beginning to close. One small-shop Patel after another has been telling him about the pinch. Tightening margins need higher volumes to redeem them. When sale volumes fall below a level, the fewer pennies that margins leave don't add up. Cost price needs volumes to sink it sufficiently before sale price. If you can't buy enough, you can't buy cheap enough.

On the other hand, overheads are beginning to take too big a bite from gross income. Local taxes have doubled in some areas. Electricity bills are higher, and everyone needs twenty-four-hour freezers. Banks are beginning to charge now for small-level commercial transactions, and the cost of credit for bulk buying is now higher. More competition means you need to spend more on getting your store to look good. More crime means the cost of security has gone up, along with insurance premiums. The days are long gone when some customer could walk in and ring a bell just to pay.

But, as with most things Indian, the moan is greater than the loss. 'Our people grumble, but they survive,' Babubhai had said. They even flourish.

I ran into Nakarja at a swank hotel party a week after we spoke. He came in an expensive car, wearing a black bandhgala with golden embroidery on the collar. Not the picture of a man whose business is falling apart. In any case, by now a CTN Patel has a career of profit behind him, a house to live in, and rent from another two, with mortgage mostly paid off. About the worst that can happen to him now is comfortable retirement.

As the biggies come in, more and more Patels are selling. And who is buying those shops? 'Sri Lankans,' K.D. said. 'You see, when they compare in Sri Lankan rupees, a pound is a big thing. And they work day and night. They keep their shops open till twelve at night. There is no family life.' Sound familiar? But unlike the Brits who had retreated before the Indian invasion into their corners, sea breeze is not for Patels. Property in London is far more invigorating. The Patels began to buy property in the seventies. Since then, house prices have shot up as much as fifty-fold.

The Goliaths pulling down Patel shutters are getting some help from the younger Patels. One survey among Gujarati retailers showed that only 6 per cent of the children of first generation shopkeepers want to run their parents' business. 'My children see me working fourteen hours a day,' Nakarja said. 'I have never had a holiday. But they want those holidays. They want proper jobs.'

K.D. Patel's son has studied to be a pharmacist. At shop after shop, the same story is repeated. These Patels went one way, their children are going down about three or four—pharmacists, computer programmers, accountants, solicitors. Younger Patels are stepping out of their parents' corners. No, the Patels cannot stop London. But London is not going to be able to stop the Patels either.

Circles

NINE NIGHTS

'You are not, please, you are not going to matchmake for me,' Kalpana was saying from the edge of the back seat after we finally made it to the car. The edge of the seat was all she had because we were giving her friends a ride to the first garba evening of Navratri. Her mauve lehenga-choli deserved more space, but lehenga management in a crowded car is an art all Gujarati girls learn in time. Happy little problems, these, that white Brit families rarely run into.

It was the time of the year when everyone deserves to be a Gujarati. After tonight there would be all of eight more Navratri nights to come. Nine if you add the poornima night (of the full moon), even ten more if you were a spectacular enough garba and dandia dancer to go on to the competition at the end. I figured there must be a quarter of a million Gujus and some others like me crowding into cars headed for Navratri dancing in Britain this evening. This is when you wish cars were bigger than they are.

My friend Harshad wasn't coming, which meant he was not being a good Guju. He was tired, he said tiredly, after driving trains all week. His seventeen-year-old son Ashwin wasn't Navratri-ready either. Blame the parents, since 'blame' it is in the Gujarati world, that he'd grown up more a Londoner than a Gujarati. His hair was long, he played football, and he played in a rock band. We would look at him and ask if England was going to claim him forever, or Gujarat recover him at least a little.

That left Harshad's wife Vijaya, his brother Ashok, their daughter Kalpana, who had just turned twenty-one, her two friends and I. Vijaya had shown all the signs of readying her daughter for a future husband. Kalpana had been dressed with almost the fuss due to a bride. That had delayed us at the Harshad home in Edgware, as had the mandatory rounds of 'why don't you' and 'I told you' when an Indian family steps out. These too had been flying mostly around poor Kalpana.

Mum was determined to prevail over the unwise confidence of her daughter that she could do her own thing; and daughter was determined to grow out of the controlling ways of parents. A global kind of conversation which gets amplified for Gujaratis with marriageable daughters at this time of the year. Nothing would push away that constant doubt from the back of mum's mind: did the daughter have a hidden boyfriend? If she did, maybe the right guy at Navratri could out-magnet him. Over these nine nights they'd all see she was single, and they'd see how very nice she looked. She should have proposals enough, properly routed through 'community leaders' and parents, well before the ninth night was done. To the 'settled', Navratri brings more of a reassuring sameness, but for an unattached Gujarati girl just over twenty-one these nine nights are like no other. Husbands are in the air. The future dances circles around her.

Parking at the Harrow Leisure Centre was full, always a sure sign of an Indian event. We found a slot eventually, and headed for the hall. The women raised their lehengas just that bit above their shimmering sandals as they stepped past puddles from the afternoon rain. I found myself stealing more than a look or two at those light payals circling Gujaratan ankles, such a world above the soaked grit of the parking lot.

We were late. The garba within was in full flow, to the swing of *Pankhida, tu urhi ja*, that theme song of Navratri. We excused our way through the babble to the stepped seating to a side, originally intended for spectators of some game of basketball and now adapted to Indian requirements. We joined the outer ring of spectators, five or six circles deep. The garba circles were going round in another five or six rings on the floor. They could have inspired the painter Raza to yet another series of his Bindu paintings if he'd stepped out of his Paris studio and made his way to the Harrow Leisure Centre. He'd also have found more colour here than his palette could hold. This hall must have packed more colour than all of white Harrow.

The fascination of the garba lies in the forward movement within the circle that keeps turning back on itself as it moves along. Arms swing back as you move forward, then they go forward just as the circle changes its mind and decides to go the other way, before moving forward again. The circle keeps going one way when it looks like it's going the other way. It's an optical illusion to a beat of five steps that travel anticlockwise, but bend clockwise back upon themselves along the way within every set of five.

Vijaya and Kalpana didn't belong to the spectators' circle, and they weren't there long. Together they walked up to join the swing of the circle, husband to-be or not-to-be forgotten. Everyone was doing their own thing, and everyone was doing just one thing. That can happen with most couple dances, pairs can move so very differently to the same beat. But the garba is peculiarly inclusive. A masi would take the minimal steps to some limp claps to mark the beat, and her neighbour could be swirling along with a grace that defies you to look away. You could do that little, or that much, all within the same circle.

The tempo increased, and the speeding circles began to shed dancers, leaving only the young to build their eddying circles up to the finale. After a breather of a dance where groups linked arms for forward-and-backward steps, we gathered around the little temple in the middle of the floor for arti. A small figure of Durga rotated slowly on a round pillar, about five feet high and two feet across. The *Pankhida* singers onstage at the far end began the arti, and everyone joined in. Not the *Om jai Jagdish Hare* that I was used to, but its Gujarati incarnation to the refrain of *Om jayo jayo ma Jagadambey*.

And finally it was time for the dandia raas everyone was waiting for, the men particularly. While the flowing circles of the garba are best left to women, this stick dance was a little more suited to male energy—at least the men thought so. All of us, who had been spectators at the garba with pairs of dandias waiting impatiently in our hands, were now on the floor.

The large garba circles had broken down into smaller circles, pairs of rows really, where one row stood facing the other. We must have been about twenty pairs in our lot. We would each play dandia with our facing partner to a count of five, and then step left to come up with the next set of five with the next facing partner. Your opposite number did the same, which meant that every set of five that followed was always with your opposite number's neighbour's neighbour. At the end of the row we would simply cross over to the opposite one.

A man in glasses with 'community leader' written all over him took a stand behind the mike onstage to start us off with a count of five. An athletic-looking chap by his side with a dholak strung down from his shoulder, clearly a Punjabi even if he hadn't worn his karha, underlined each 'one, two, three, ...' with a sharp smack on the dholak. We closed in on one another, and away we went.

To Gujaratis, dandia steps come with mother's milk. On 'one' you make contact with the opposite number's dandia with the dandia in your right hand swinging right to left, on 'two' it's the same with the other dandia swinging the other way. Both are forward movements. On 'three' you step back to tap your two dandias against one another. On 'four' it's forward again, right dandia moving back to tap the opposite, right to left. 'Five' is the step sideways, with a swivel thrown in if you can. Dancers launch all sorts of variations, but around this basic pattern.

We were a pair of facing rows, not a geometric circle. But we moved within the circle principle because we were only going around one another. Two or three rounds on, I spotted Kalpana in the next circle. I stole a look at her circle every time I turned around to switch rows. I counted up to four chaps in there worthy of further investigation by Vijaya.

Many things happened during the circling through the dandia raas that meant Kalpana was where she should be. It made the roving eye unnecessary because the circle itself was moving. Every alternate person simply kept appearing face-to-face for the dandia rituals. Now and then, two deft dancers who were next to each other would swap places, so each could face the set that had been skipped before. We were in a real-life slide show.

It's the nature of a circle that nobody in it disappears from sight of the other. The outsider may be visible, but is not, is not meant to be, in the first line of sight. The circle is for its duration a closed world by the agreement of those in it. The group, and only the group, has been thrown together for everyone in it to share rhythm and ritual and to open themselves to awareness of one another.

Holding one another in sight is the first step to developing eye contact, should two people want it of course. In a circle you either look or you meaningfully don't, it does not leave the third option of not engaging at all. And, in a Gujarati circle, when you look, you can't too obviously be seen looking. Eye contact here means corner-of-the-eye contact, followed by networking later to take it further. Add to this eye movement the change of direction that the circling rows make possible, and you can begin to eye other circles, as I had Kalpana's. As you go round and round, early research can be fine-tuned into re-search, and that can invite migration to other circles. Over an hour or a little more of dandia, anyone looking for a change can simply leave a circle, and not always do it the courtesy of leaving in a pair.

Vijaya and Ashok quit after some time and headed for the spectator stands. I joined them. From here, every moving circle appeared a rotating catwalk. Everyone in all the circles nearest you could be counted on to be quite close to you at some time. They appeared as close-ups within the larger picture. You could take a good long look at a good many as they approached and receded, and I had no doubt Vijaya was doing just that. She'd probably forgotten that she'd even heard her daughter's protests; that was just standard youngster noise you step past. Kalpana didn't have a boyfriend, not at least that anyone knew, and if someone suitable was presented to her, he wouldn't be less suitable because the manoeuvring came from a parent off a dandia floor.

The evening had concentrated that search. Long before anyone joined circles on that floor or abandoned them, we were all part of the loose circle that was headed for that particular hall. Like all circles, this one drew to it those it was meant to and kept the rest out, because circles are also remorseless separators; they are society's oldest device to establish inclusion and exclusion. But many circles are drawn far tighter than ours was at this hall this evening. Through Navratri, thousands and thousands of Gujaratis head for halls hired only for members of their own caste. So anyone who goes dancing to a hall had joined that outermost circle to begin with, and that circle kept the rest out. Few can match Gujaratis in drawing circles on an evening so closely in line with the structuring of little worlds.

No one knows better than a Gujarati at Navratri that you can go round in circles, and still get somewhere; get someone, that is. But not everyone was here looking. For the rest of us, the appeal of the evening lay in the annual sameness it brought. So many faces appeared from Navratri of the year before. We moved to the same steps, often to the same music, and with many of the same people. The dance was yesterday once more; it would be more of the same the next day, and next year. It was the time for the year to come round full-circle, and slow down for a week or so.

If Vijaya had made some mental notings, she kept them to herself. She had garba-ed, dandia-ed, prayed and gossiped, and wouldn't find it a failed evening if she left without a son-in-law in the bag. We were just a lot of sweaty, happy people by the end of it. A few quick steps round that old path was always going to be a fulfilling enough end in itself.

Harshad was waiting when we got home. He'd seen it all; what might have been the pull of sameness had staled in his mind into boredom. He was the dancer who wouldn't dance because he knew the steps. He didn't want the colours because he knew the hall would be colourful. He didn't want to see and be seen because he had seen some, and they him, and the rest didn't matter. When a Gujarati gets tired of Navratri, that Gujarati is tired of life.

Behind the window with the saffron-coloured 'Om' is the engine room that makes so many circles go round. It's the office of the Brent Hindu Council, and when it gets going at this time of the year, it can handle more people in a day than the grand new Wembley Stadium across from its window.

The usual amazing numbers had been circulated for the new stadium: enough to fit 90,000 spectators, or 25,000 double-deckers and what not. You wouldn't have thought Venilal Vaghela could look at the stadium past that 'Om' and hope to rival it in any way—until you realized that Brent means Wembley, Wembley

Gujaratis, and what Navratri means to them.

Venilal's office didn't need a board, not with that 'Om' there. And within it, everything Hindu you could think of. Shiv and Ganesh watched over the desks, phones and filing cabinets. Copies of a magazine, *Hinduism Today*, sat on the shelves. In a mini-auditorium to the side, an 'Om' painted on a golden sheet took up a whole side wall; a map of India hid most of the wall on the other side.

Britain found a place too in this Hindu scheme of things. A portrait showed Durga sitting on a globe floating on the sea, with Indian flags in evolutionary stages rising above her—a 'Vande Mataram' slogan in 1906, the charkha in 1931, the Ashoke chakra in 1947. The Union Jack lay at Durga's feet. No game of cricket could produce so spectacular a failure of the Tebbit test.

Had bhajans played in the background, they would have been just the right audio accompaniment to this picture, but Venilal Vaghela was listening to Schubert on BBC Radio. I've always found Venilal, who has found a way of growing and greying and still looking young, to be a Hindu more of the cerebral than the bhajan kind; the karam yogi, as he said, who would rather think and act than pray and meditate. 'Four Ps rule my life,' is another of his lines I remember. 'Propagate, Preserve, Practice and Protect.' Which meant, he said, that he is always up to one P or another. His passion, mission maybe, is to push Hindus into British politics, and Hinduism as far towards centre stage in Britain as possible. He managed the first ever Diwali celebrations at the House of Commons, and he worked with Ken Livingstone, the willing mayor of London, to help set up annual Diwali celebrations at Trafalgar Square.

More routinely, he is the man behind the Navratri celebrations, still the biggest event the Brent Hindu Council organizes. The local council pays the Brent Hindu Council, which then pays different groups to hold their Navratri celebrations. Brent is less than half white; the majority of the rest are Gujarati and they've made sure the council uses some of their local taxes to pay for Navratri.

Venilal Vaghela had Africa somewhere in his Gujarati-Hindu hyphen, like most Gujaratis you run into in Wembley. He grew up in what he knew as Northern Rhodesia before it evolved into Zambia. He left for the US in 1964 because 'the apartheid was really bad,' he'd told me in the course of one of our many chats. The US offered him a green card, but the offer was accompanied by a letter telling him he was to be drafted. 'I became a draft dodger like Bill Clinton.' He was moving Gujarati circles in Wembley because he just managed to save himself becoming a Vietnam War veteran—or a name on a casualty list. The British passport he had in Rhodesia brought him to Britain. After this job and that, he came to spend most of his time working with the Brent Hindu Council.

Venilal's office is usefully located right next to an Indian pub, and it supplied the beer and bhajia for our chat about this Navratri. It was right to speak of Navratri in celebratory style. It's the time when religion becomes fun, when praying merges into dressing up and dancing.

Vaghela brought out the Brent borough guide to Navratri celebrations that listed details of who was celebrating where. 'Everything is here,' Vaghela said, showing me the list. Thirty-eight halls had been booked in Brent for Navratri. I found myself looking more at the who than the where. The list read like a guide to the Gujarati caste system in London. Most of the dancing, the dressing and the praying would happen within a caste, and halls had been allocated accordingly.

I made some calls the following day, more or less alphabetically and, in less than an hour, I discovered more about the Gujarati caste system than I had in years.

Ashaben Desai from the Anavil Samaj of which she was president told me they are a group of very special Brahmins from Surat.

'You have heard of Morarji Desai?' she asked.

She waited, and I said, yes, I had.

'He was prime minister of India. He was from our samaj.'

'But, as a Desai, wasn't he a deluxe sort of Patel?'

'No, no, nothing like that. He was brahmin, from our community.'

The community was booked for their Navratri in the gym of Wembley High School. 'Not every day,' Mrs Desai said. 'Our community is not that big here, so we take the hall only on weekends.'

So, on two consecutive weekends a year, the likes of Morarji Desai go round in their own circles in London to be among their own.

The brahmkshatriya Mandal UK sounded like a mix of brahmins and kshatriyas.

'That is exactly what we are,' Ramanbhai Chhatbar from the mandal said.

'How did you come to be brahmins and kshatriyas?'

'Because there was an evil man, I forget his name, he decided to destroy all kshatriyas. So some of them put on the janau that brahmins wear, and so they were saved. So we became the brahmkshatriyas.'

'So do you think of yourself more as brahmins or as kshatriyas?'

'Originally we were like kshatriyas, now we are more like brahmins.'

'When did this thing happen?'

'Oh, long time back, because we are the descendants of the Kauravas and Pandavas.'

'Which ones, Kauravas or Pandavas?'

'Same thing, one was the other's chacha ka ladka.'

'What was the profession of the brahmkshatriyas?'

'Colouring and printing of cloth, especially saris and ladies' clothes.'

'And here?'

'Lot of people are still in cloth business. But not everybody.'

'But the Mahabharata is very old, and printing is quite recent, no?'

'No, our people have been doing this for long, long time. You see, in our Jedhpur village in Gujarat, many are from our caste. They have been expert in bandhini prints and they are expert in printing on ghagras. They used to do printing using wooden blocks long back, and some still do it. But now some have come into modern printing methods also.'

'So this goes back to old Mahabharata days?'

'Yes.'

'Your samaj has come together here in Britain for Navratri?'

'O yes, for many years now.'

'Do most people still marry within the brahmakshatriyas?'

'It used to be 100 per cent. Now 10 to 20 per cent are going out.'

Somchand M. Parmar, listed as president of the Gujarat Arya Association, introduced his lot simply.

'We are mochis,' he said.

'Does that mean shoemakers, or generally leather workers?'

'Originally shoemakers. But that is not the case now. That was the case thousand years ago. That business has died down now, these days shoes get readymade in factories and all.'

'But why do you need to get together as mochis now?'

'Because we are one community. We are a very big organization. We have bought property and we are setting up our own hall, cost of £1.2 million.'

'Will that help to keep the community together?'

'That is the purpose of it, isn't it? We have to keep the community closer together.'

'Is it working? Are most people marrying within the community?'

'About 90 per cent.'

It was not a question I would stop asking, and the 90 per cent figure or thereabouts was the answer I would always get. It may not be accurate, but it did at least say something about the dreams of caste leaders and the efforts they were making to see them come true.

The Kshatriya Association was a bit of a surprise on the list. I didn't know there were kshatriya warriors among Gujaratis.

'We are a very large community actually, you see,' said Bharat Vakharia from the association. 'From Navsari, Balsar in Gujarat, now we are in Britain, Fiji, United States, Canada, Australia, New Zealand.'

'But you are all kshatriyas?'

'Actually kshatriya is a modern way of saying it. We are all khatris actually.'

'So what does that mean?'

'We are in the tailoring business. Sewing and stitching was our profession originally.'

'Isn't that more the profession of the wanzas?'

'Tailoring has so many communities.'

'Are people doing that business here in London too?'

'In London there were quite a few factories, and after coming here many of our people worked in these factories. There was big demand here, and lot of people made a lot of money also. But now nothing is left in stitching—so many cheap imports from India. So people are taking up associated business like dry-cleaning, they have even opened sweets shops, started travel agencies, property business. But still quite a few work as sample machinists, cutters, do repairs at dry-cleaning shops.'

'And you?'

'I have a dry-cleaning business.'

'You have help from the family?'

'My wife is in tailoring, my father-in-law is an expert tailor. He could see a show on stage, even a photograph, and do a cut to match.'

'How do you compare with the wanzas?'

'They are also very good at tailoring. They are good with made-to-measure and up to date styles. We are also expert in many things, like Punjabi churidar.'

The Vanza Society London were holding their Navratri separately from the Wanza Samaj UK. The spellings announced a difference that must have resulted from 'organizational issues'. I could not find Vinod Tailor, listed as secretary of the Vanza Society London, so I asked Mahesh Sonigra from the Vanza Society UK about an elderly Wanza I'd met some time earlier.

'He is a founding father,' I said.

'You see, we have quite a few founding fathers.'

'But are they different to those from the Kshatriya Association?'

'We and kshatriyas, we are same profession, but different clans. Originally we are also kshatriyas. But now there are different classes. But we also have some surnames in common, like Visawadia and Parmar.'

'What's the point of difference?'

'We have different beliefs.'

'Like what?'

'Our deity is Hingaraj Mata. Her shrine is now in Pakistan.'

'Who is she?'

'Like any mata, Jai Mata Di, she was our protector. And also Gopal Lal Maharaj.'

'Are you a tailor?'

'Yes.'

I hadn't expected that many tailors down the list. Certainly not separate tailoring circuits, each arranging their Navratris, and through that marriages within circles of their own kind of tailoring families. Venilal Vaghela was listed in the Wanza Samaj UK. I called him again about the list.

'You see, they took these caste issues with them to Africa in the thirties and forties, and they kept them there. And then they brought the same thing to Britain.'

But couldn't it have changed, couldn't everyone have come together, at least as Gujaratis?

'If we could find a hall that can take 10,000 people, we would bring many into one hall,' Vaghela said.

The caste system continues because London has only caste-sized halls. In finding halls for the caste groups, Brent Council is paying to keep the caste system going. But if everyone could get together for the Navratri dancing at Wembley Stadium, would caste issues disappear?

STITCHES

I was driving down East Lane amidst cars full of tailors. I knew they were tailors, or at least born into families of those known as tailors, because those nine Navratri nights begin to announce a car's caste content within a mile or so of its destination. These cars were carrying Gujaratis dressed for garba, and the school they were headed for was one that a wanza group had booked for their Navratri. Tailors, then.

I'd spoken to many tailors over the phone off the list I'd picked up at the Brent Hindu Council. I'd now come to the East Lane school in pursuit of them, and particularly their children, to get a sense of their 'tailorhood'. A teenaged lad at the eats corner just outside the garba hall had taken a break from talking to a girl, so I asked him who the wanzas are.

'We were darjis, you know, tailors,' he said. He must have been eighteen; he'd begun to find that post-adolescence confidence.

I asked him why he would rather be here.

'You come here, you play garba, you are a part of something, something more than individuals. Tony Blair himself has been talking about tradition.'

'What does the word wanza mean?'

'I don't know the real meaning. Something with darjis, something to do with stitching and things, our grandfathers and others, they used to do tailoring.'

'So wanza must mean tailoring or something.'

'It means our community. It probably meant something before, but it just carried on. We all have sewing machines at home.'

'Is it nice to come together as wanzas?'

'It's good fun. You meet new people and stuff.'

'Why don't you go to some other garba?'

The girl he'd been talking to before I intruded, explained. 'Because there's lots of people here our age. And it's safe and comfortable, you know who you're playing with.' Just the kind of stuff parents love to hear, and these teenagers were saying it on their own.

Through the evening I spoke to several wanza youngsters. Every one of them knew their tailoring origins. I was tempted immediately to settle to a neat conclusion: that a sense of caste continues among the young. But I tried to argue with myself against this conclusion. What did I expect to hear from youngsters at the wanza garba? And what of all the wanza youngsters who had gone to non-caste garbas, or not gone to garba at all?

A quick wanza test showed there couldn't be that many of those. Garba evenings were being held by the Wanza Samaj (UK), the Vanza Mandal (East London), the Vanza Community of South London, and there are Vanza communities in Leicester and in other towns. Hundreds of families had gone to any one of these halls. Given just a few thousand families in Britain, most wanza families would turn up at some garba or other of their own, the young very visibly with them.

This hall was filled with youngsters. I'd been to the wanza Navratri at the John Kelly School, and the young were all over, even if their per capita noise always suggests there are more of them than there are. Taking the broad population and visible numbers, most of the wanza young must be where their parents wanted them to be.

This didn't surprise me. I'd learnt long back to discard the suggestion offered lazily as perception that the young today are very British, that Indian ways will pass away with the older generation. Why does everyone say that like they are the first to say it, and for the first time, and then not right? I see far less an abandonment of parents' ways among Indians in Britain than in families in India. Standard wisdom can sometimes stand quite far from truth.

Perhaps this traditionalism in the young shouldn't surprise anyone. It is also true that the overwhelming proximity of a wide species of alien colours and cultures brings you closer to parents than you might otherwise have been, or that when you're surrounded by so many so very unlike your own, parents work that much harder to seduce the young to come their way. Why else would so many young wanzas take such pride in the tailoring skills of their forefathers?

And why the 'but' in 'but the young . . . ' that precedes a dismissal of parents' ways? The older ones are not exactly extinct, and their ways not temporary aberrations because the young do not follow them exactly. We'd run into a great deal of silence if we were not to talk about some people because they seem closer to passing away than some others.

The parents in this hall had a keen sense of their past, and they'd been working at passing it on to their young. They were the smart next generation now in the frontline of parenting in difficult new London. That their families came to Britain from India via East Africa was to others a pattern; to them it was their life story, told and retold, it only needs a new audience or a willing older one. One spoke of Hira Lal Parmar as their wise old man. I knew immediately he was the founding father I'd forgotten, the one who's memories had been tapped for a narrated history of the community. He and his lot had told them what they were telling their children, and just about everyone thought it was important to know. I picked up a condensed history of the wanza flight to Britain from conversations here and there outside the garba circles, there was plenty of ready memory around. Here's a chattering history of some London wanzas:

'The wanzas began to sail out from India to East Africa in dhows from the 1890s onwards. Nobody remembers the first wanza to step off a dhow on East African soil, but he must have called in others. And there were agents around in Gujarat offering three-year tailoring contracts in East Africa for a fee of Rs 300 over three years, plus housing and other needs.

'The wanzas made a place for themselves sewing khanzos for native East Africans, in the style of the long gown that Arabs wear. There were no machines, the wanzas did it by hand, and their fine work meant they were in demand. It was not until the 1930s that local Africans turned to wearing trousers and suits. The wanzas then learnt to do those, and they were in demand again; that fashion revolution too passed through their hands.

'But there wasn't that much money. The desire to work in East Africa was a measure of how much worse it was in Indian villages. The tailors worked first under German rule in East Africa. The British came to rule after the First World War. The wanzas seem to have had no problems with either, both needed to wear tailored clothes.

'The wanzas took fast to sewing machines when they came along, but money still wasn't good. The railway line the British began to construct between Mombassa and Nairobi in what they carved out as Kenya brought jobs, but it also brought dangers. Many died from malaria, typhoid and other diseases. Lions often attacked workers on the railway line. Some wanzas had to take on work amid such dangers, and many were killed. A lot of them took the dhows back, or the steamer later.

'Money came finally after the end of the Second World War, in the period of British rule in East Africa into the early sixties. Manufacturing was in demand, and the wanzas, strengthened by new arrivals mostly from Saurashtra, and by their new generation, began to prosper. But local African rule later brought complaints that wanzas, like other Indians, were exploiting local people. They began to migrate to Britain in the early sixties, leading up to the exodus from Uganda in 1972.

'Clothes and manufacturing was still a big and going business in the Britain of the sixties and seventies. The wanzas soon found enough to do and a new prosperity that even Africa under the British could not give them. Quite a few wanzas still work in garments factories, and in the tailoring and associated businesses one way or another. Many have of course gone into other businesses—they are solicitors, pharmacists, professionals of one kind or another—but wanza homes still have sewing machines, if only for sentimental reasons.

'Wanza groups in Britain began to take shape from the mid-seventies. In East Africa everyone knew everyone but here people got scattered, so societies were set up to keep wanzas in touch, to socialize, to come to know one another, for marriages really. About 80 to 90 per cent of wanzas marry wanzas. They come together for the welfare of their children, so that their children know their religion, their culture, their language, and one another, so that all this can continue. And they get together so that the young may know who a wanza is. Because you are no one if you don't know where you come from.

'Everybody is related to everyone going back generations, and that means people develop a lot of respect for one another. Or try to. It doesn't always work, there have been differences among elders, and whole wanza societies have split. But you still look around in one another's groups to find the right wanza for marriage.

'It is working, because the children now want to know their origins. In the seventies, youngsters didn't want to be known as Indians, now they are proud to be called Indian, and wanza is after all only one kind of Indian. Their origins, their ways are their identity. Together you support one another, you know who you are, how you came to be who you are. Among the wanzas fewer marriages break down because so many take place within the community. This Navratri too a few marriages were fixed up and that was by just the fourth of the nine evenings.'

Wanza societies had formed around these common memories. Navratri was going to make sure their commonness goes down the generation line.

I remember our dhobi in Delhi like I last saw him yesterday. His bushy, winged moustache, in the style of the late Veerappan, was unforgettable. He always wore spotless white cotton, a simple advertisement no doubt of his skills. He came back to mind in London after I ran into Indians who all called themselves dhobi, though none washed clothes for a living.

The Rajput Dhobi Samaj was one of the Navratri groups on Venilal's list. They would be at the Park Lane Primary School, the list showed. I missed the hall twice down Park Lane, a short and winding road that leads into unexpected English greenery from crowded Wembley High Road before reconnecting with the Indian world towards Preston on the other side. The third time, Paresh Modasia from the dhobi samaj guided me by mobile, and I found at last the little side road that dips suddenly down to Park Lane Primary School.

I couldn't step far into the crowded little hall, and found myself stuck next to a handsome young dhobi fellow watching the garba, waiting for the dandia to begin. He was studying something in computers, he said though some this-and-that kind of talk we got into. I said that studying computers in Britain, and coming to this hall for dandia because his ancestors may once have washed clothes, did not go together.

'But that is where our families come from, and our parents have taught us to respect our elders. If we have opportunities in this country it is because they worked hard and took risks and took their chances.'

'But would you marry a dhobi girl?'

'Oh yes, absolutely.'

'Why does it matter that her forefathers should have been washermen?'

'No, it's nothing to do with that. It's just that our families all know one another, you aren't just marrying someone out of the blue, and life becomes a lot easier in similar families.'

'You mean this is not just about washing clothes, which was just the origin, it's about families knowing one another.'

'Of course.'

Pareshbhai came up and called me in to a side room, away from the music. We sat down for prasad in a corner 'We obtained funding for the Queen's Jubilee celebrations,' he said, very dhobi-proud. 'We used the money to hold a cultural programme, with bhajans and film songs. We organized a havan at the Westminster University Sports Hall, and we held an exhibition of people's experiences since they came to the UK.' The dhobis were doing fine with some help from Her Majesty the Queen.

Far from fading, the dhobis now had a society that was coming into its own. The Dhobi Samaj had begun to take shape only towards the end of the eighties, Pareshbhai said. 'We've been around a long time, we used to meet around Diwali and Navratri. But we felt the need to come together, because we started encouraging the young to participate in what we do.' To add to togetherness at Navratri, he said, the dhobis now have a cricket team, and they hire a cricket ground in Hounslow, near Heathrow that brings them together through the summer.

Pareshbhai's reasons for getting the dhobi samaj going sounded familiar—it could be the same community leader talking everywhere. 'Now the children come, meet each other. They know who the parents are, they trace back different connections. When you find your extended families, the whole samaj becomes a family. You have togetherness, unity, support. You don't get isolated. If you have a problem, you can call one another, there's always help and support available. In a new country, the extended family can be very helpful.'

And marriages? The real question, the old question, the old reply. 'You can count on your hands the number of our youngsters who have married outside the community,' Pareshbhai said, holding up one hand. 'Our kids know us, they know one another.'

Work as a computer programmer if you like, but when you marry it will be to another dhobi. The caste itself which drew forefathers to wash clothes in Gujarat once doesn't matter any more; it's a memory link for a group to gather around. Gathering brings familiarity, and that becomes a reason to gather more, and then to marry within the gathering. In England, you need your own islands to live on, with your own for company, and eventually as family.

What if my Delhi dhobi with the Veerappan moustache had chanced his future on a dhow to East Africa? What if he had become a British subject in an East African colony, then found himself in Britain where he did not have to wash clothes for a living any more, because there were other things to do. What if he then found other people of dhobi origin. Would he rather be alone in Britain or join them?

I thought the dhobi computer programmer a good match for Kalpana. But he wanted a dhobi girl, and since he was doing the dhobi circles, Navratri wasn't going to bring those two together.

~

HAIR TOGETHER

Someone had tried to gatecrash the hairdressers' dance party, and precautions had been taken. The hairdresser caste, the limbachias, were at their favourite hall at the community school in Queen's Park, one of those in-between zones cities have between centre and suburb.

Two bouncers and their Alsatian at the gates looked on high alert. A third chap flashed a torch in my face. Non-limbachia, the light must have told him. Not only did I not belong to the hairdresser caste, I wasn't even Gujarati.

'I've come through the Brent Hindu Council,' I told him.

'We don't have any information about you.' He was one of those smart lads with a quick manner that made him a natural for dealing with outsiders. He had a mobile phone in one hand and a walkie-talkie in the other, and who but the very responsible get to hold both.

'Could you check with the Brent Hindu Council?'

'Park outside and I'll see.'

He got on to the walkie-talkie and I went back to park round the corner. By the time I returned to the gate, he was ready to let me in.

'Sorry, we've had trouble, we have to be careful.'

'What trouble?'

'Oh, just some trouble. We took care of it.' Cool lads take care of these things and don't talk about them much.

Inside, about a dozen men were hanging around the foyer, very visibly in charge. Behind them it was garba time, and lots of women had joined those swaying circles. A few men had joined them, just to show that men never should. To my embarrassment, I found myself noticing everyone's haircut. But at a party where a haircutting origin is the only thing that has brought everyone together, how could I not, I told myself.

The word 'hairdresser' didn't quite describe it. It sounds too falsely high-streetish. 'Barber' would be a little closer to the Hindi or Gujarati word 'nai' that more usually describes the traditional profession of the limbachias. But 'barber' is too value-neutral it's merely descriptive of a profession, and therefore no translation of 'nai'. To think of the limbachias as 'nai' sounded disrespectful even in thought, because attitudes dripped from that word. The Gujarati nai was caste apart long before hairstyles became acceptable social art and the profession of the nai evolved into hairdressing, even hairstyling.

I wandered across to the garba hall and back to the foyer, determined to get hair off my mind. Everyone at the hall had come together as people of nai origin, but I wanted to erase the thought because they were not living off other people's hair any longer.

A manager in off-white kurta-pyjama was ticking off names on a list at the front desk. The checklist looked well marked, and the hall was pretty full. But again, before I knew it, I was staring at his hair. Every single one, black in the company of some streaky greys, was in the directed place. Was that because he was limbachia? Silly thought. Their hair was far more on my mind than theirs. Hairdressing had brought them together, but it was not a commonality they noticed. It just worked as some invisible, even unmentionable, glue.

It was a glue they had sought out. Many of the men in the foyer had worked at nai bonding for years, some most of their adult lives, to make sure the Shree Limbachi Gnathi Mandal would not weaken with time.

A young, slightly stocky limbachia, Jitendra as he introduced himself, led me away from the foyer to the school office. Mary the caretaker, elderly, frail and bustling with corridor common sense, brought us chairs.

Jitendra sat where he could watch a video monitor supplied by security cameras. He had reason to, he said. A group of youngsters had turned up at the school gates. They wanted to join in the dandia. But they were not limbachias and so were turned away. One hurled a stone at the building and this led to a near scuffle at the gates. They left abusing the guards and threatening to come back in a bigger group. Jitendra was staring at the screen for signs of a fresh attack.

'Do you get a lot of trouble?' I asked.

'Sometimes. These were just some yobbers who wanted to make trouble. They wanted to come in, and we told them it is not open to all.'

'They wanted to join the garba and dandia?'

'Yes.'

'You don't let others in?'

'No. They said they will buy tickets to come in but we said we are not selling any tickets.'

'But why not let them in? It's only dandia.'

'But this is a limbachia event.'

'There are some groups that sell tickets ...'

'They have become greedy. They even advertise their Navratri celebrations.'

'But why are you so firm on keeping others out?'

'We want to preserve our roots, preserve our traditions. Like the Jews. Look at the Jewish example.'

'But is it happening?'

'It will take another generation for us to know if we've been successful. But our young are all with us.'

'Would you say other youngsters are being kept out because you want your young with you?'

'Yes, you could say that.'

'How many marry within the limbachia community?'

'The last one who married outside was eighteen marriages ago.'

'And who did she marry? A Gujarati?'

'Of course. But not from our community.'

Jitendra was beginning to not like this, particularly not memories of that loss of a limbachia girl to a non-limbachia. He seemed more taken by the screen. '25 per cent of our costs are on security,' he said. 'The Hindu Council helps us with some money. The rest we have to do ourselves.'

A young fellow walked in, followed by another.

'Who were they?' he asked. 'Were they Hindus?' And the other, 'Who were they? Were they Gujarati?' I figured that if they were non-limbachias it would be an intrusion, if they were non-Gujarati, it would be an attack.

The two security guards now walked in. This was becoming like the control room of Fortress Limbachia. Their duty hours were over; this evening they had earned their fee.

'Can we get more security?' Jitendra asked.

'Not now, man, it's too late,' the bigger of the white guards said. 'But they'll be back. I know the type.' He was the type who always knows the type.

'Shall we alert the police?'

'Yeah, maybe we should. But I gotta go.'

So did Jitendra, and so, he made it clear, must I.

I was the outsider who had been let in, and now I had to go back outside where I belonged; I had come far enough, the others hadn't got as far as the foyer, never mind the hall. As I left, I saw through the door the circles still going round and round in limbachia purity.

Mahendra Solanki is famous in London's world of limbachias as the man whose grandfather went to jail with Gandhi. That made him one of the natural founding fathers of the limbachias in Britain. He spoke of his family history with a good deal of pride when I looked in to see him at his house in Hayes, not far from Southall.

Mahendrabhai had just returned from Luton, about 40 miles north of London, from an assignment with a computer firm. His wife would join us soon, he said. I asked if she was a limbachia. Yes, he said, a little surprised at the question. Mahendrabhai could hardly have become a leader at the Shree Limbachia Gnathi Mandal without that qualification. Now he wanted marriage to work for other limbachias, as it had for him.

'That is why we arrange so many occasions to get together,' he said, settling back on his sofa. 'The primary purpose is to make it easy for the boys and girls.'

'It's not just Navratri, then?'

'No, no. We have something happening every month. Letters are going out every month. We have cooking competitions, sponsored walks, picnics, and of course Navratri and Diwali, so many occasions in the year. Last year we had 1200 people at our Diwali celebration.'

'That means most limbachias in London.'

'Yes.'

'Is it all really just to arrange marriages?'

'We are not for arranged marriages, we are for arranged introductions.'

'What's the difference?'

'We only see that the young are introduced. It's up to them and their families to take it from there.'

'How many youngsters are there to introduce to one another?'

'There are about 200 teenagers in London.'

'All this for 200 teenagers?'

'Well, they are our future.'

'Why is it so important that they should marry among limbachias?'

'We want our girls accepted in the family they are going into. We are concerned about our daughter, for her safety. We do not give the girl away just to the boy, she has to be accepted by the family also.'

'But what if a limbachia girl were to marry a lohanna boy?' I asked that one with daringly, even if lohannas were also Gujarati and Hindu.

'Our traditions are very different from the lohannas, it would not be very easy to be accepted. So also for my sons I want limbachia girls because it would be easy for them to adapt.'

'You mean the young are listening, they don't want to do their own thing?'

'The last marriage to a non-limbachia was eighteen marriages ago.' Not just Mahendrabhai, not just Jitendra, the community was counting, and counting carefully.

We had paused a bit. Mrs Solanki who had a little earlier brought us some masala tea and some sweets that are always on offer in Indian homes around Southall, had come to join us.

'The young, you know, they just love these events,' she said. 'My daughter has lots of friends at school, but she gives priority to the community. If there's a function, she doesn't want to miss out.'

'What does she like about it?'

'From childhood she has met so many children at these events. She has come to know them, they are such old friends now.'

'So for her it is not a caste issue, just meeting friends she grew up with.'

'Oh, yes.'

'But does she know that this is really a caste, that this is a caste of haircutters?'

'Yes, I have told my children that originally our people were haircutters.'

'And what did she say?'

'She said, oh how nice, because I want to be a beautician.'

'Are there others from the limbachias who are still hairdressers?'

'Oh yes, we have quite a few.'

Children of Gujarati nais are now London hairdressers. The rest have gone other ways, but they don't want to forget where they came from.

The Navratri spirit was spilling over into Diwali; it comes only some days later, and festival moods have a way of lasting. The auditorium that had served as the garba hall was filled in with chairs for the Diwali fashion show of young limbachias. There were plenty of vacant chairs. I took one at the back, and saw that Mahendrabhai and some others, limbachia leaders naturally, were onstage.

They were discussing some differences between community leaders. There had been splits and disputes within the limbachias, as there are in every Indian group. Indian founding fathers are a particularly quarrelsome lot. It sounded much the old story, with a new set of names.

I was getting more interested in speaking to the two young limbachia girls sitting to my left, chattering quite speedily about others in the hall. I intruded into a pause in that gossip to get the attention of the one next to me.

'You going to be onstage?' She seemed dressed for it in bright red and gold.

'No, just watching,' she said.

'This is the limbachia fashion show, isn't it? What exactly is limbachia?'

'Our whole families, no, they believe in Limbachia Mata. There.' She pointed to the figure of Limbachia Mata in the corner of the hall by the stage. The goddess figure was in a mini-temple, with little bulbs lighting up a winding path to her feet.

'Yes, but who is she?'

'Our goddess.'

'And who are the limbachias, the limbachia people, like you all?'

'We come from Gujarat, and our families were hairdressers,' said the other girl, the one in a blue lehenga-choli, 'lenga-cholley' as she would say. It was a taught reply she had obviously grown up with.

'So you are all here because your families were hairdressers?'

'Yes, that's what our forefathers did back in Gujarat. Not everyone but, like, most. And there's some people here still do it.'

'Would you do it?'

'I like doing hair, but I wouldn't do it for a living.' We were talking right across the girl in the red.

'Isn't it funny you all should meet because your forefathers were hairdressers?'

'I suppose, if you think of it like that.'

'You don't think of it like that?'

'Everyone here's like friends, and we've been together, like, years. This hairdresser thing, right, that was in the villages in Gujarat.'

The conversation was ended by a few words in Gujarati from someone mum-like who had walked sternly up from their side.

The girls left. Young girls were never going to be allowed to talk to a male stranger for long, rightly of course.

On stage, the founding fathers had had their say and left and their chairs removed. A hero-looking host and a hostess suitably demure in a sari had replaced them and were now saying DJ-like things. From my seat at the back I began to survey hairstyles again. They looked no different from hair at any other gathering; for some reason I was disappointed that hair, which had brought everyone together, was not announcing itself in some way. That extra bit had been done to hair here or there, but that, I noted with disappointment, happens everywhere. I saw only my eagerness to believe that all hair is special but limbachia hair is more special than others.

The compere pair combine began to announce items, something Bollywood after something else Bollywood. Someone did kathak of sorts to the instrumental of *Dil to Pagal Hai*, others appeared in impersonations of Jackie Shroff and Hrithik Roshan. A young girl stepped on to the catwalk, working hard to get her waist to gyrate to *Shakalaka baby* from *Bombay Dreams*. Her version went down well, it couldn't have anywhere else. The limbachia caste offered her a world to shine in. A little pull from Bollywood, and a little push from parents had made stars of young limbachias.

The parents had begun to catch them really young. Six to eight-year-olds walked up and down the catwalk, starrily dressed by mums. Three performed a dance to *Chura liya hai tum ne jo dil ko*. They'd been pulled into caste long before they'd ever hear that word. One day it would more than likely become a world to live in and marry into. The parents were keeping watch, and keeping count.

Hindu Ways

HEN-DO

The tree came crashing down just yards in front of the lady in the mauve salwar kameez. She was just ahead of me, so I suppose we were both lucky. You'd have thought a tree that tall would give reasonable notice before turning horizontal; it was down before we knew it. It was a stormy day, a proper storm, the kind Londoners love to complain about but can't get enough of. Brits love disasters, and nothing makes their day quite like a crisis to act cool in.

The lady had parked her car in the same parking lot I had picked at the bottom of the little hill below Alexandra Palace, the huge exhibition and conference centre that towers over north London. It gives you quite a view of north London, should you ever want a view of that many more rows of red-tiled roofs squeezing buses down narrow roads.

This morning it would have offered a different view. Fallen branches and trees had blocked many roads, and extended my half-hour drive to two hours. The tree that came down in front of the mauve lady was quite the closest I had got to a falling tree. She and I were now fellow survivors, and that made conversation mandatory.

'Thank god, my children are there already,' she said. We were headed to Get Connected, an educational mela for children to celebrate Diwali and to learn about Hinduism. But not enough trees had fallen on London roads: the parking lots were packed. Hers would not be the only children to have got to Alexandra Palace and got there in good time; many parents had braved the storm to give their children a peek into Hinduism. It's not every day that London sets up a magnet like this for Hindu children.

Mauve lady and I stood by the tree for a bit, talking about the close shave we'd just had. We counted the yards between us and the tree; these would reduce no doubt in our stories later. We finally continued up the hill. Closer to the top, we joined others who had stopped to look back at the tree; there would be other escape stories, that would improve with every telling. By now we were a little Hindu procession walking uphill, always a good Hindu thing to do—a suburban London offering of the Vaishno Devi experience.

Our minds moved to the mela ahead. 'When you tell the children there is a Hindu mela, they don't want to stay at home,' my fellow survivor said as we walked up the last steps of our pilgrimage. 'We never forced them, they wanted to come.'

The storm was still in whistling mode as we entered Alexandra Palace. The desi babble within, the inevitable product of families, kids and more kids hanging around, sounded so much better. The hall had been partitioned many times over, and people were wandering around the sections, each of which was advertising a Hindu experience of some kind. This is where they would get connected to Hinduism, maybe even converted to what they'd been born into. It was an attempt to convert born Hindus into believing Hindus.

I strolled up to a section marked by a handwritten poster as the 'Chill-Out Zone'. Someone was making Hinduism cool. By the side of the poster was a large photograph of a swami with two smiling children on either side, one of them cutting a birthday cake. Words had been put in the mouth of a little girl and the swami, comic-strip style.

Girl: 'Swamiji! When vasanas get exhausted, then the ego is not there. Then who realizes?'

Swamiji: 'There is an ant fallen inside this cake. He looks to the right and finds there is cake. On top of him and below him is cake; it is all cake-o-cake. The intellect is like the ant.'

Below the picture sat the slogan: 'Like the salt doll dropped into the ocean disappears to become the ocean, so also the ego realizes that "I do not exist" and disappears to become the self.'

This was worrying. If this sort of stuff lay within a chill-out zone, who'd get connected to what? I had no idea what an ant besieged by cake should think. If this poster was anything to go by, it looked more like a recipe for getting disconnected. Maybe it was just me that Hindu wisdom had escaped, but I certainly wasn't able to keep track of the kind of Hindu thought that mixed ego with ants and cake. And for kids, smart as they are, this kind of thing might just become harder than homework. But the great thing about Hinduism is that you can shop around, no one thing is *the* thing, and I walked on in search of something simpler.

The music coming from one end of the hall sounded less intellectually challenging. *Dola re dola re dola ...*, I heard. After swamiji and his ant, I needed this. Down at that end, chairs had been laid out before a stage in a makeshift auditorium. I wasn't the only one headed that way. Parents and kids were all gathering there.

It wasn't long before the auditorium filled up. *Dola re* wasn't very Hindu, but it had got us connected. Other songs followed, but in a while the music stopped and a rather nice-looking woman in a sari and large red bindi appeared onstage, mike in hand. Her hair, left loose, framed her darkly as it dropped down to her hip past her whisked-almond midriff. She'd have been a strong candidate for a Miss Vedic contest in some forest clearing back in 1500 BC.

Miss Vedic made teams out of the left and the right in the make-do auditorium. 'This team is called Radha,' she said, waving her hand over the left side of the auditorium. 'And this is called Krishna. And now, guess what, everyone, we are going to have a contest.' No more *Dola re.*

'Okay,' Miss Vedic announced. 'Who can name a Hindu god?'

Silence, and then more silence, from both Radha and Krishna. Too easy a question, who wants to answer it?

'Come on, you can tell the names of girlfriends and boyfriends, and not of your gods? Come on, who can name a Hindu god?'

One little hand went up, and a mike found him.

'David Beckham.'

'No, not David Beckham, he is not a god. Well, he is to some, but not to us here, he isn't. So who can name a Hindu god?'

More silence. The Hindu quiz was not working very well.

She gave up, and listed them herself. 'Ram, Krishna, Ganesh ...

Okay, what did Lord Chaitanya make famous?'

It was a tough one and she wasn't waiting for an answer. 'He made famous the Mahamantra: Hare Krishna, Hare Krishna, Krishna Krishna, Hare Hare! Hare Rama, Hare Rama, Rama Rama, Hare Hare! Okay, now, loud as you can. Here you go.' She pointed her mike at the Radha team. More silence.

'Listen guys, if Lord Chaitanya came down, he'd be like, you know ...'

She turned to the Krishna team. This worked, and Krishna took up the chant.

'Great, this group is going to god. And this group,' she said, turning to Radha, 'this group, is going back home.'

Miss Vedic decided to keep it simple. 'So tell me, both of you, who was Radha and who was Krishna?'

Silence.

'Hello, Hindu youth. Okay, what is Hinduism? It is a religion going back to India. And okay, and what's a Hindu?'

'It lays eggs,' said a kid. Like he'd heard, 'What's a hen do?'

It was time for Miss Vedic to move on from the quiz, it had gone on long enough and got nowhere. She was joined by a handsome chap wearing a sherwani over a dhoti, female attention written all over him. She introduced him as DJ Technics, a student from King's College and also a member of the Pandav Sena, the Hindu youth movement of the Hare Krishna Hindus. He looked a dream Hindu DJ.

'Okay, we are going to the Bengali part of India,' Miss Vedic announced. 'It is very famous. It is very cultural. Most classical music comes from Bengal. Also Lord Chaitanya. But first, we will go to the Bollywood part of Bengal, then we will go to the classical side.' Bengalis would be pleased to hear that she thought that's where the classical music comes from, though they wouldn't be too glad if they had to admit to anything Bollywoodish. But here in this auditorium bare facts were for outdated bores like me.

Miss Vedic stepped aside, and a chap in a transparent red shirt and dark trousers walked up to centre stage. He coiled himself into a stillness that said it was about to unleash something. Two statuesque women dressed in heavily zaried lehenga-cholis glided up behind. And then DJ Technics switched the stage alive.

'Muqabala, muqabala, Laila ...' the song blasted. Red Shirt became Hrithik Roshan, the women his skilled shadows. The dancing was good enough for a real Bollywood set. Now both Radha and Krishna came alive. They were competing now at dancing around their chairs. Lord Chaitanya was no muqabala for this. Next came *Yeh duniya dil ko darati hai, Ye dil rab se nahin darta*. And then something like *Oye Baby chum chum* and, yes, DJ Technics would not keep the hall waiting long, *Dola re dola re dola* ...

Dola done, Miss Vedic returned with the mike. DJ Technics went back to at-ease at his control centre. Miss Vedic had still not given up on the quizzing. 'Okay, so now, who was the first Asian to win the Nobel Prize?'

A quick hand went up this time. 'V.S. Naipaul.'

'No, it was Rabindranath Tagore. And speak up, people, so the gods can hear.'

The classical quiz was stopped right there with a 'VIP announcement' from DJ Technics: Simon Hughes, MP from the Liberal Democrats, was here. An MP is always a candidate in waiting, and to a candidate these are rare crowds to address. On the other side, for Hindu groups this was the time to let British leaders know they are enough to make a difference between quite a few winners and losers. The festival was not just an event for parents and their hopefully Hindu children, but also a political matter between community leaders and political leaders. It was an advertisement and a warning.

Hughes was not about to overstay what he knew must be a lukewarm welcome. 'There are three reasons I am here,' he said quickly. 'One, as an MP in London who represents many Hindus and who has been to India, I have come to show my solidarity. Two, I used to be a youth leader and was so frustrated with the older leaders. It is good to see young people taking to public life. Three, I came here to see future Asian politicians and leaders, possibly a future prime minister.' The lines were scripted to draw applause, and they did.

'The Hindu community is very good at business,' Hughes continued. 'They are great with fashion, art, with their culinary skills and so much more, but they have still not fulfilled their potential in terms of political leadership.' He wound up his speech now. 'Thank you for your pride in your culture. Come back next year bigger and better because we love you.' Applause again. British MPs can give these short, sharp speeches almost in one breath. And, unlike their Indian counterparts, they know when to leave a mike.

Miss Vedic now decided it was time to call off the quiz. She came down among the Radhas and Krishnas. She aimed the mike at a teenage girl on the Radha side of the aisle.

'What have you learnt about Hinduism today that you didn't know before?'

'I just got here ten minutes ago.'

'What is the song you liked best?' she asked someone on the Krishna side.

'*Vande Mataram.*' This was going to be the Krishna team's day.

'And you?'

'I liked everything.'

'And you?'

'I liked the food.'

'Yes, we Indians, we all like our Indian food, don't we? And what did you like?'

'I liked the dances.'

'And what did you come here to see?'

'To see what exactly the Hindu youth are doing.' A reply at last that she must have wanted to hear.

'Yes, that is exactly what this festival is about. Our aim is to promote Hinduism.'

Miss Vedic was done and, onstage, DJ Technics was getting busy again. The beat came on. Three dancers carrying huge Indian tricolour flags came dancing to a basic beat, then put the flags aside.

DJ Technics was handing action to the audience now. He hit the domes of Alexandra Palace with *Apana sangeet vajey, Apana sangeet* ... No more silence now, not from Krishna, not even from Radha.

I headed back for the challenge of the Chill-Out Zone to look for something more comprehensible than cakes and ants. This time I ventured past the poster. Cool blue screens had split the area into four sections labelled Air, Earth, Fire and Water. I entered Earth. A timetable by the entrance announced the programme for the afternoon: stress elimination workshop, meditation, Vedic chanting.

'We call it Chill-Out Zone because it sounds like a cool name,' said a girl at the entrance, there to say these things. 'You can sit here, meditate and reflect, gather your thoughts.' She was one of the volunteers in black T-shirts that said 'Get Connected' in yellow.

'We need that, not just entertainment,' a chap standing by her side said. Apana Sangeet had only just faded away, and he wanted some visitors here now.

'Why are you doing all this?' I asked them. That must have been the first question they prepared for, the first they asked themselves.

Between them, they bullet-pointed the reasons pretty fast. 'A lot of the young are beginning to take a new interest in India, in Hinduism,' the guy said. 'I think it's driven by the new British interest in India. There are so many things Indian now on British television, they have so much interest in Indian music, Indian food, fashion, you name it. And so many of our own youth now, you know, want to know about their customs and their religion.'

He was repeating wisdom that sounded like it had surfaced at about three preparatory meetings for the mela. Some of the volunteers had been trained with all the answers, and they were waiting to be asked. The chap and his companion no doubt believed what they said, but between them they spouted what sounded like prepared wisdom pretty rapidly.

'This is not about providing all the answers,' the chap said. 'But we do learn a lot from our parents and we want to give something back to the youth. You see, we've been born into this amazing, amazing culture. We have so many traditions in the house, but we don't know what they symbolize, we don't know the meaning. The young now want so much to know what's going on. These things go back thousands of years. I have started to learn, I am adopting them in my daily life, and it helps so much.'

'A lot of this stuff has been in languages we don't understand,' the girl said. 'It's in high-level Sanskrit, and now there are translations available in English. A lot of this stuff is on the

Internet and that is one reason everyone's getting so interested.' Once people got interested, they would get connected, as these two no doubt were. They believed quite firmly in the connections they were promoting.

But the Chill-Out Zone was for those possibly connected already, and I stepped to the kids' zone next door, which appeared a good deal busier. This is where they wanted to catch 'em young, and this festival was really more for Hindu kids.

I ran into my fellow survivor in the kids' zone. Her children were colouring Ramayana books on a table close to a huge flag of India pinned up on a screen. A painting exhibition had been put up over partition screens, the produce of kids trying to be Hindu and be good, which they must be told was the same thing.

Beneath a multi-coloured 'Satyam Shivam Sundaram', correctly spelled with some assistance no doubt, a kid had written: 'You should tell the truth not a lie you should tell the truth so you dont get told off you should always tell the truth.' Another had drawn a figure of Ganesh under the banner 'Help Ever Hurt Never'.

A poster exhibition raised the questions the kids might ask. A boy on a poster asked: 'What is Hinduism all about? Why so many gods? It's all so confusing.' Another boy on another poster asked: 'Do I have to come on pilgrimage to India? I'm going to miss the Cup final! What makes India so special?' A girl poster asked: 'Today in school we learnt about evolution. What do Hindus believe? What happens at death? Does this affect how we treat others, including animals?' Another offered advice on 'How 2 respect your parents'.

A partition screen listed the seven matas we all need to respect. 'Desa Meta is where you live as a citizen, so your desa mata is UK.' And there is Bharat Mata, 'the ancestral country, in this case it might be India.' And there is Bhoomi Mata (Earth), Deha Mata (mother), Matru Mata (mother tongue 'never to be abandoned'), Veda Mata (spiritual heritage) and Go Mata (sacred cow). If any kid could remember even a fair fraction of all this, that kid would go back a more knowing Hindu than I've been all these years.

But perhaps the kids were learning something they were not being taught. It seemed like a message that hundreds of kids were here, and as Hindu kids. They didn't have to make sense of cakes and ants and learn all seven matas by heart. And it didn't matter that what got them going was Bollywood. The fun was the hook, the Hindu message could have been what clever people call subliminal.

Bollywood now followed the kids right into their zone. My tree-spared companion's kids must have seen it coming. They'd filled colours enough into Ramayana pictures, and were leaving the books to join a girl in a Get Connected T-shirt gathering some kids around her. With a flourish she switched on *Laija Laija* on a CD player and launched into a dance. The other kids quickly abandoned their colouring books to follow her. Now this was fun, and it seemed okay by the Indian flag and all seven matas.

Priti had such a striking presence the second time I met her that I was surprised all I could remember of her from our first meeting at the Oadby racecourse in Leicester was her blue leather shoes. A passing shoe fetish, who knows?

We'd agreed to meet at a bhelpuri stall, but if two people can meet exactly as planned at a mela, either something's not right with them or the mela's not doing its thing. Priti had done a great deal to get the Get Connected mela together in Leicester. After Alexandra Palace, Leicester wanted to Get Connected too, and Priti and her gang obliged. It can't be easy to get a mela, or Hindus, together, and if she didn't turn up she must have had more momentous matters on hand than a chat with me.

We met later at the Sanatan Mandir in Leicester. The venue was about as clear a statement as anyone could make that this would be a business meeting, not a date. That date business was neither on my mind nor hers, but in Leicester a lot more males and females meet in people's minds than they do in their own lives. Pack thousands of Indian families into houses strung together around a central street, and people will come to know people; residents will become that rare thing in modern cities—a community. And what's a community without an expanse of sustaining gossip?

Priti led me to a prayer hall next to the mandir. Some masis and kakas, the not entirely respectful Gujarati words for the elderly, had just vacated the hall. We sat ourselves on a bench for kakas who can't sit cross-legged on the floor, because masis invariably can.

Priti looked confident and radiant. She had all the grit and grace of an Indian woman who spends an efficient day at work and then floors men with her effervescence in an evening sari. This evening she wore a black jacket and trousers because she'd come straight from work.

'Your email says "nhs",' I said. 'Is that National Hindu Students?'

'No, it's the National Health Service,' she said. 'I work for NHS.'

That was in her non-Hindu mode. But why would she have a Hindu mode at all? It must be the Indian-from-India in me, but I couldn't figure out why a hip, accented British Indian girl and others like her would spend months fixing a mela at a racecourse to connect young Hindus to Hinduism, and to one another. There was always so much else to do, with or without boyfriends or girlfriends.

'So just what did you do to make this event happen?' I asked.

'We are a committee of young professionals. We have site managers, architects, all under the age of thirty, and we did professional high-quality presentations on the Get Connected agenda at all the temples. The feedback we got from the temples at first was, these young people, what are they going to do, what do they actually know. We were looking for temples to sponsor us, to help us financially. The temples gave us a very small fraction of our overall budget. We struggled to raise the money.'

'And what was your total budget?'

'All in all 45,000 pounds.'

'Where did the rest come from?'

'Some businessmen sponsored us.'

'So what did the temples say?'

'I found it very annoying when I had to go and say at different temples that you don't see what these youngsters have in them, why can't you see these are the people of tomorrow. It's all very well to have these massive big buildings and these extensions done to them, but what is the point when young people will not attend these temples? You're here today but you're not tomorrow. The youngsters are not just going to come and take their shoes off and come into the mandir, because they don't know what it's all about.'

'What makes you think your event made a difference?'

'I've got living examples of what was happening after our event. After the two days of the event we asked for some volunteers to stay behind. So many young people came to help out. Then a few of us said that to thank god let's all go for the arti. And then all these young people, who didn't know the first thing about doing an arti were all here at this temple. We said, wow, this is so good. It was all just amazing. So if there was one religious person there, it almost started to become a mentoring, peer education kind of thing. And they were saying to one another, you go hang around in bars, why don't you come to the mandir. It wasn't coming from me. It was young people networking. And they were talking amongst themselves.'

'You mean if you can talk Hinduism in their language, they're waiting to come.'

'Oh, absolutely, absolutely. They were doing it on their own, it wasn't coming from the displays, it wasn't coming from the workshops.'

'And you, have you always been a pucca Hindu?'

'I picked this up later. I was born and brought up in this country. I didn't even see India till I was eighteen. But I've always had this thing that India is where I originate from, I am always Indian. I was Indian because I knew I was different to all the other white kids in my class. Being Indian made me special. I was Indian when I came home. And then I was Hindu because I would go to the mandir on a Sunday.'

'How did you become so much of a Hindu?'

'I think I was fifteen. It was 1988, and I went along to a recital by Morari Bapu. That was the first time he came to do a Ram katha for the youngsters. A lot of young people went along, because it was summer holidays, no one had anything to do, and they were targeting young people. Lots of young people, in fact most kids from my school went along. I went along just because I had nothing better to do. It was on our school grounds. That Ram katha changed our lives, it opened us up to Hinduism. It was in

Gujarati. Lots of people didn't understand it, I didn't understand it fully. The funny thing is that on the last day of the katha, young kids of the age of four, five, six, who didn't understand a word of what Morari Bapu was saying, they were all crying, saying, Oh my god, the katha is now finished. So many people still talk about that katha. Something had happened to make them want to progress in the Hindu way of life.'

'Did you get picked on by others, that Hinduism is this and that, that you worship a monkey god and things like that?'

'Oh yes, all the time when I was at school. I still get it. I get it at work. I was organizing this Get Connected, and we were exposed to a lot of media. My work people would say what is this you're doing, what's all this about idol worshipping. Last week I'd gone for my cousin's wedding, I had mehendi on my hands, and they said, what's all that, have you been writing with orange pen on your hands? No, I said, this is traditional. You know, there are people out there who still lack knowledge. And I know from the white people who attended this event, because we were asking for feedback. I know some people said they learnt a lot about Hinduism: that we have only one god, really, when they thought we had thousands of gods. We said, yes, we have thousands of different roops of god—forms of god—but there is only one god. They started to relate to that.'

'Was there a lot of this when you were growing up?'

'Oh, yes, sure. When we first moved to Leicester, and I was a kid, we were living in the area of Rushymead. And when we moved there, Rushymead was predominantly all white. So when we used to go out and play, all the kids were all white. And we used to be called Pakis and all kinds of names. That you smell of curry, and why are you coming out, and all kinds of racist remarks. Then, as time passed, Rushymead and Belgrave and Leicester all became predominantly Hindu. Now there are only two white families living in my street. Everybody else is Indian. So we kind of took over.'

'Feels better now?'

'I feel at home. These two white families on our street are actually very friendly, they are very accommodating, they are very pleasant to meet in the street and say hello, good morning, how are you. They don't have no problems. Like, for example, when it's Diwali, every house has diyas lit up, and these white families, they don't say anything to us, they help us celebrate, and we take food to their house. And they enjoy it.'

I could hardly claim that in listening to Priti I was listening also to so many others. But skipping details, this is the kind of thing I heard from a lot of youngsters again and again, in Leicester, in London, everywhere. Not from all, though. There's a partition among the Indian young. There are some who'll go out to immerse themselves into the English way, won't speak their parents' language, won't even eat Indian food. Maybe I'm biased because of my own irredeemable immersion in ways Indian, but I could argue that Indians who present themselves as differently coloured cultural Brits are a minority. Just count the youngsters at Navratri, and there can't be that many others left.

I doubt that many who came to these events—and there have been others—got connected to Hinduism through a great deal that was presented. What mattered is that they came, as Hindus that's what made the connection.

~

KRISHNA'S ARMY

We were an army, of a couple of thousand or so, and we had a general of our own. 'He's the senapati,' a chap by my side said as our army began to march out from Russell Square, just beside the School for Oriental and African Studies.

The chap, another busybody from Wembley like me, had not joined the march yet, he seemed to be lost between joining and watching. We were just watching the force emerge on to Southampton Row. The senapati was also watching from our pavement, a slim and very busy guy under a red baseball cap that his followers wouldn't miss. 'Great turnout,' I said to the senapati. 'Could have been better,' he replied. He introduced himself as Arjun Ruparelia. He had taken a moment off from shouting commands over his hand-held hailer and walkie-talkie to talk to me, and I was pleased with the attention from the leader.

But the senapati was more the manager of the procession than its leader. The real leaders were Krishna, Ram and Hanuman, and they had just taken position at the head of the procession. We were all straining to get a glimpse of them. Hanuman, I saw carried a mighty mace—his gada, and Krishna was blue all over. The tourists—Japanese, who else—on the open double-decker bus from The Original London Sightseeing Tour now stranded on Russel Square must have had a better view of the gods on the street than most others. This was the first bus the police had stopped for the procession, and the tourists were clicking busily away at a sight no London promotional pamphlet had promised.

I squeezed through to the start of the procession for my darshan of Ram, Hanuman and Krishna. Underneath the blue paint on her face, Krishna I saw was a petite girl of sixteen or so. She'd taken care to do her arms in blue. Her legs down to her feet below her knee-length red and yellow half-sari were also Krishna-blue. She wore a shining crown held in place by a firm rubber band, and she'd done her face up with bright bridal dots around her eyes; not what anybody said the original Krishna did, but girls must have their privileges. In her left hand she held a one-foot tall brass Hanuman with a long red tail.

To her left was the plumpish Hanuman himself. He had not attached a tail, but rounded lines around his mouth and the bright silver gada he carried over his shoulder said it all. To Krishna's right marched Ram, wearing mostly red, with a long bow wrapped in silver foil over his shoulder. He was a tall chap, and wore his crown with becoming ease over a shoulder-length wig that came curling down in the accepted style of the Vedic forests Ram had inhabited for fourteen years.

I shadowed the three gods down the pavement on Southampton Row as they began to lead the procession, walking alongside an elderly man with very youthful vigour. We stopped near a crossing to look back at the tail of the procession, still hidden in Russell Square. 'This is wonderful, just wonderful,' he said. 'I am eighty-four. I never thought I would live to see this day.'

It was the day of the big protest against an order to stop public worship at the Hare Krishna Mandir in Letchmore Heath village, just north of London. Some residents of the village had complained against the many people the public worship brought through here, and their complaint had been upheld by the local Hertsmere County council. They were always going to get a sympathetic hearing. The English get particularly passionate about saving the way of life of the English village, because the village defines England more than London ever could.

Letchmore Heath is a nice quiet village and the village pub is its heart. It's the place to gather for the village gossip underneath the mock wooden beams pretending to hold up that old roof. There must have been months of it when ex-Beatle George Harrison bought the estate next door; it was a story that outlasted barrels of lager. The trouble did not arise until long after George Harrison donated the estate to the Hare Krishna sect. Bhaktivedanta Manor, as it then came to be known, became a local pilgrimage centre, particularly on Janamashtami. Thousands of cars brought tens of thousands of Hindus through the little village all of Janamashtami night.

What was pilgrimage to Hindus was traffic to the village. But it did more than ruffle the English way of life for that night of the year, it divided the village. Some people thought traffic on a few nights a year, especially where no one touched a horn, was okay. Other thought not, and they took a stand for old England against post-immigration Britain. They complained to the local Hertsmere council, and prevailed. The council ordered a halt to public worship at the temple.

The council ruled that Bhaktivedanta Manor had been approved as a centre for religious learning, not a place for public worship. But that ruling did nothing to stop the Hindu cars on Janamashtami; of all birthdays, no one was going to miss Krishna's. They still came in thousands to the blue god's birthday bash, and they came to make a point about themselves in today's Britain. It became that oxygen of every conflict—a prestige issue.

Now the Hindus were protesting. My fellow walker, Bal Mukund Parikh as I learnt his name was, thought it wonderful that so many Hindus had found something to complain about, something to fight for. What else would have brought a couple of thousand young Hindus out together on the streets of London?

The youngsters had decided to do more than grumble in dad's car. They set up an 'army', and called it the Pandav Sena. The army behind the senapati on Southampton Row was that Pandav Sena, backed by irregular forces. It was a local village matter no more. If some residents of Letchmore Heath had gone beyond village matter to raise the spirit of old England, then the Pandav Sena was making this the place to mark a Hindu foothold in Britain.

Had the temple been left alone, the young Hindus would likely never have thought much of it, or of any other temple. This was no metaphysical awakening, no recent rediscovery of Vedic texts. This affirmation was born in denial. The longer the council maintained its ban, the more Hindu became the youngsters determined to break the ban. No parent could, without a reference to context, just for the sake of Hinduism, have persuaded a Ram, Krishna and Hanuman on to Southampton Row, and then convinced a couple of thousand others to follow. Young Hindus had mobilized their own army, a senapati, and the gods themselves to lead it. No more was Hanuman the 'monkey god', a strange figure to be hidden from white friends, no more a secret between you and your parents. This Hanuman appeared to be leading everyone through the heart of London.

For all of one silly moment I thought it would be sacrilegious to go talk to the gods. Then, to erase my embarrassment over that thought, I had to. So I said hi to Krishna, and she said hi; her name was Anita Halai. She went to school in London as Anita; as Krishna, she was having a great day out. Her parents follow the Swaminarayan sect, she said. But she had strong enough convictions at sixteen, or whatever, to follow Krishna and not Swaminarayan. It was a bold decision. The Swaminarayans make Krishna a lesser predecessor of the nineteenth-century Sahjanand Swami, who they consider god himself, Bhagwan Swaminarayan. At the celebrated Swaminarayan temple in Neasden, Krishna is only a small figure to the side of Sahjanand Swami. So Anita was no ordinary Krishna, she had triumphed on the side of Krishna in domestic battles. For a daughter in a Swaminarayan family to follow Krishna, and now to become Krishna, was a religious coup of sorts for the Hare Krishna temple.

The Neasden temple had not worked for her. 'They separate males and females there,' she said. 'And that's a lot of Gujarati which I don't understand.' If they have a beautiful temple, the Hare Krishna people have a lovely estate—and they talk English. 'But I'm not against the Swaminarayans. I think Hindus should get together, right.' She wanted the two as cousins, not rivals. She had some pretty firm views on religion.

We were walking now through the red lights by Holborn tube station, the police were making sure we had right of way. I could hardly have dreamt that I could one day walk past that tube station with a real blue Krishna by my side, as the police halted traffic to make way for us. Krishna looked remarkably unselfconscious. Her mind was on the battle, not the traffic. 'We must fight for the temple, everybody only goes to the temple, they don't really do anything.'

Hanuman on my left walked quietly, looking a little bored. After a bit, I told him that. 'I came because this other guy couldn't come,' he said. 'Then this other guy called me, and he was like desperate because this other guy couldn't come. But to tell you the truth, I'd rather be home right now.' After a pause, he said, 'Maybe it's not so bad because at least everybody's taking pictures of me.'

I asked if the gada he was carrying was heavy. 'No, not really,' he said, and offered it to me. I suggested it would be more appropriate for him to keep carrying it.

We were approaching Bush House at the end of Kingsway, with India House next door. They were going to loop around behind Australia House on to the Strand. I decided on the shortcut. I said bye to the gods and stepped aside to watch this re-public day parade.

Right behind the gods two lads were carrying a large six foot by four picture of Radha and Krishna at Bhaktivedanta Manor. Then came the rest, marching, singing, waving banners. 'RAPE of Religion' said one banner, with 'rape' in bold red letters. The slogan sat above the picture of a woman being dragged away by policemen outside Parliament House, an Om flag in her hand. That had happened at another demonstration in support of the temple. Below her picture sat the caption: 'She's not your mother ... but she could be. This is what they're doing to Hinduism. What are you doing about it? If you're not on our side, you're on theirs.' 'IT'S TIME TO RUMBLE! RISE & WAKE UP BEFORE IT'S TOO LATE!' cried another banner held up by two girls making fists every now and then of their little Gujarati hands. The banner warned also of a 'future proposal to ban wearing of turbans.' The closure of the temple was 'the final twist in our backs, while we stand and watch!' Another poster carried a call from the original Krishna: '*Mam anusmara yudh ca* ... Remember me and fight— Bhagvad Gita 8.7'.

I'd never have thought this lot would ever be seen in anything like a Krishna army if I'd seen them somewhere else. Not the chap in the deep blue sweatshirt with 'Armani Jeans' printed on it, with a saffron sash around his waist, under the placard BRITISH HINDUS FEEL RAPED. Or the girl in glasses in maroon salwar-kameez with UNOFFICIAL APARTHEID ALIVE IN UK. Not the tall guy in the loose T-shirt with BRITISH BORN, BRITISH RIGHTS on his placard. Or the tall girl in the green T-shirt that was never going to descend to belt level with REMEMBER ME AND FIGHT. The chap with gold ear rings and denim jacket with a coke bottle in one pocket, with WHEREVER THERE IS KRISHNA, THERE IS VICTORY, and NO TEMPLE NO VOTE above the girl in the flimsy white dress approaching transparency.

A bunch of about thirty girls came by shouting louder than most. 'We-want-jus-tice, when-do-we-want-it, NAAOW!' The sena was marching to different songs. *Ram ji ki sena chaleee* ...—that was a bunch of gym-going guys. Two girls holding a banner 'Ram Sena, Woolwych' came leading another lot. One of them was dressed in tight jeans, suede shoes and a loose orange T-shirt, the other in a long blue skirt and particularly high-heeled leather boots, her hair tied back with a saffron scarf. 'Hari bol, Hari bol ... Hare Rama Hare Krishna, Krishna Krishna Hare Hare ...' they chanted. This was a very Londoner-looking Ram sena.

Up before Bush House where I was standing, the senapati had detached himself from the army and walked right back, so had Krishna. 'We have to tell India something,' Senapati told me as I walked up to him. 'We're going to present a petition.' They crossed the road to head for India House, and I walked along. Ram and Hanuman were leading the march round the corner.

Krishna, her pocket Hanuman still in hand, Senapati and I walked up to the front door of India House. We came up against a glass door, locked, with another glass door behind which also looked very locked. Behind the doors three men were sitting around in gup-shup mode, obviously security staff who had the place to themselves on a Sunday. They would have seen Krishna under her golden crown call out to them with a wave of her blue hand. If they were surprised to see a visitor like her, they didn't show it.

One man walked up behind a glass panel. He looked too annoyed by the intrusion to bother with the shape and colour of the intruder. Years of government service had come to sit on his face, and they would never leave. To me he was bhai sahib, to Krishna and Senapati he was Mr India.

'Yes. What you want?' bhai sahib said. Why do you want anything here, that is.

'Open the door. We want to give you something,' Senapati said.

'What you want to give?'

'Open the door, we'll give it to you.'

'We cannot open door just like that.'

'Listen, man. Just open the door, we want to give you something. We want to give it to India, you know, to In-dia.'

'That is all right but we cannot open the door.'

'Oh please, come on man, we have something for In-dia.'

Mr India was now joined by another member of the Sunday gup-shup society. A tall chap in a green sleeveless sweater, he knew what to do with this as I presumed he did with all situations.

'First you tell me how have you come in here,' he said to Krishna. It surprised me that he too seemed not to notice Krishna's colour and crown.

Krishna looked at us, then back at the chaps behind the glass. She was losing her cool. 'Come on, you silly idiots,' she said in a low voice. Not for them to hear.

'Look, can you take this for India.' Senapati was trying again.

'How we can just take anything?' The man in green was now going to do the talking.

'I don't know how, but you'd better do it.'

'But who are you?'

'Look, we're British citizens, right, but we're Indian, you know what I mean. We feel Indian. We're, like, with the Indian government.'

'But how you have come in here?'

Krishna produced a little camera from somewhere and started to take a picture.

'No! No camera! How you have brought camera here? Leave it out.'

Now Krishna spoke. 'Look, we want to give you this petition, right. We want a picture giving it to you, okay?'

'No, not okay. No camera. You just go out.'

'But you've got to help us.'

'This is Gorment of India office. Anyone can take pictures?'

'What is your name?'

'Why I should tell my name?'

By now the third man had appeared behind the glass. He had been staring suspiciously at the Hanuman in Krishna's hands.

Senapati saw where the third man was looking. 'We are not going to give you Him.'

'All right, but what do you want to give?' Third man wanted to end all this.

Senapati waved a black folder. The petition was inside.

'All right, you can pass it from here.' He pointed to a slot in the glass.

Senapati tried, but the folder was too big. It wouldn't go in straight and it wouldn't go in folded either.

'All right, you can leave it outside. We will pick it up afterwards.'

'But what is your name?' Senapati said.

'Why do you want to know my name?'

'Because I'd like to know who I've given it to.'

'You can say you gave it to duty officer.'

'But can you come to the door? We want a picture of us handing it over. We told them we would take a picture of handing it over.'

'No! No camera!' The man in green was angry again.

And so now was Senapati. 'India is messed up, man. Better get your government sorted out.'

'You just leave this and go.'

'Look, we're Indians. You are Indians. You're not respecting we Indians, man. You know, you're really not respecting us.'

Bhai sahib, the first to approach, had been staring at me as I took notes.

'What you are writing? Why you are writing?'

Before I could say something, Krishna raised her camera.

'Look!' bhai sahib said. 'Inside Gorment of India office, never take picture. Never do it.'

'Where are your Vedic principles?' said Senapati.

'All right. You just leave it outside and go.'

'I'm not giving this in, man,' Senapati said. 'I'm not giving this here.'

Senapati walked out, carrying the undelivered folder. 'Bloody mad,' Senapati said. 'They're in no way representative of our culture. I'm going to give this directly to India.' Krishna and I followed him out. India of all countries had snubbed Krishna of all gods.

I looked at the petition as we caught up with the procession on the Strand. It was printed in ornate type:

To the Most Revered Governors of Bharatbhumi,
Namaste, Jai Sri Krishna.

We the undersigned, hereby wish to petition the government of Bharatbhumi, India, that as residents of Great Britain, we are in need of your assistance to maintain our cultural heritage. We feel that not only is it your duty but also an obligation which you must fulfil. You hold the position of representing our Saintly Raj Rishis who ruled according to our traditional Vedic principles. In order to uphold our rich heritage of 5000 years we insist that you take the necessary action to assist our plea.

We may not be responsible for our heritage but we are responsible for the future. Our future depends on our past — our heritage. The British government have taken plans to ban us from all worship at the home of our cultural heritage —the Hare Krishna temple outside London. We call upon

*you to preserve our culture and act as the responsible heads
of the state that you are and uphold Sanatan Dharma.*
    We hope that due consideration of our plea is taken
    Yours in the service of Sanatan Dharma,
    *British Hindu Students Movement, Pandav Sena, Ram
Sena, National Hindu Students Forum and all other British
Hindus*

I completed the march up to Trafalgar Square almost guiltily.
I wished India had received the senapati better. But the march
ended happily enough and victory balloons went up before everyone
went their way. Hanuman finally laid the gada aside and went
home as Nitin Patel. Krishna was Anita Hilai again.

Victory was theirs, later. Step by step the message went home
to the government. A national Hindu uprising could not be handled
by local zoning wisdom any more, the government decided. The
dispute over public worship being allowed at Bhaktivedanta Manor
was taken out of the hands of the local council and referred to the
Department of the Environment. The Hare Krishna lot offered a
solution to the department. They would build a new access road
to the temple from the opposite side of Letchmore Heath. The plan
was finally approved. Money poured in, the new access road was
built. The Hindu way, the English way—both had been vindicated.

SHAKHA

Hounslow was Hounslow Nagar because this was the day of the
big shakha. The Hindu Swayamsevak Sangh, the British cousin of
the RSS in India, was celebrating the birth anniversary of the RSS
founder Dr Keshav Baliram Hedgewar, and swayamsevaks and
sevikas from many of the weekly shakhas held around London
would be here at the Heathland School.

I'd been looking forward particularly to meeting the sevikas.
The thought of encountering a few hundred British Indian RSS

women was funnily exciting, I'm not sure why. As it happened, I got to park right by the ground taken up by the sevikas, and I saw exactly what I'd expected to.

A group of girls in white salwar kameezes were lifting dumbbells to commands from their leader's whistle. The leader had the tangy good looks you associate with a heightened awareness of males. Her dupatta descended in a disciplined diagonal line to lock itself into a tight waistband over her kameez. It signalled modesty with a mission. Besides, loose dupattas and lifting dumbbells don't go together. I watched her a while from the car. She was in complete charge of herself and the other sevikas. She became a little more interesting for being a little intimidating, the kind of appeal a good-looking policewoman carries.

Not everyone in the group lifting dumbbells was in white. Some were in their Sunday usual, more like everyone's idea of young Asian women in London. This would change if and when they saw the light.

Behind the dumbbell girls, a group was twirling six-foot lathis to commands from their leader. Not a skill a London woman can use much, but no doubt they were told it was meaningful for the mind. Further up, another group was playing the more acceptably girlish kho-kho. Everyone looked like they were playing with a purpose other than the playing of the game.

I walked past the girls' ground to the sevaks who had the ground further up. 'Move on, maite,' a chap in the middle of a bunch was shouting, a very Londoner 'maite' from a very Londoner sevak. He was making room for himself in a chain of six. They linked arms, called in a seventh teammate, and closed themselves in a circle around him, facing outward. The other team of six charged at the circle, yelling 'Har Har Mahadev' that unmistakable slogan of Hindu muscle. 'Jai Bajrang ki,' the chaps in the circle of six shouted. The Mahadevs were charging to get the chap the Bajrangs were protecting.

The teams clashed. The maite, a thin chap, and probably quite gentle outside the circle, was kicking and pushing wildly at the Mahadevs. After some grabbing and pulling—just the kind of thing good Hindu boys are taught never to do—the circle collapsed. The Mahadev team dragged their prey away. Next round they would close a circle around him to face the charge of the Bajrangs.

'It's a game called sher-bakri (lion-goat),' said a man who had walked up to my side. He was elderly, but in youthful white trousers and white T-shirt with a saffron lion printed over the pocket. 'It is a very good game for developing the character.' He smiled approvingly at the boys, moving his head in turn from the sher to the bakri side. 'It is so difficult to stop myself from joining them.' But he was there to show others the way. Many of these teams were one shakha versus another, he said. So there were teams from the Harrow weekly shakha, from Slough, from Wembley and other places in the 'south-west zone' of Britain's shakhas.

The boys charged at one another for a bit and then my companion decided to call the games to a close. 'Come on, we are going to start our meeting now,' he said. His words guillotined the game where it was. The boys disappeared to their changing rooms, and he and I walked to an indoor basketball court, picked up our blue mats from a side and headed for the discussion circle on the floor. We were still waiting for some others, and there was time for a few introductions.

Someone announced Narain Swaroop Sharma, elected Jan Sangh MP in 1967, long before the Jan Sangh grew into a government-ready BJP. The pioneer had turned NRI; and here he would always be a star. I wandered into another group and ran into Ramanbhai Khatru whom I'd met at several BJP events. He was looking around the basketball court, pleased with the turnout. 'One day we will win,' he said. Ramanbhai had retired some years ago after repairing watches in north London. He has been a shakha regular for years, he said. Like Dina Nath Bahl, a vaid who was seventy-two but looked hardly fifty. He told me he'd been a Sangh member since his days in Rawalpindi before the partition. He was also a pandit. 'But I don't do marriages any more. So many marriages break up, it is so sad.'

We sat down on our blue mat circle, and the meeting began. 'We are not useless,' a member was saying to his neighbour as he moved into cross-legged position on his mat. 'We are just used less.' Through some talk of this and that, my guide at sher-bakri made his point a little louder than the rest. 'You see, even after the domraja dinner they do not realize what has happened.'

'Domraja dinner?' I asked. 'What is this domraja dinner?' I had given away my ignorance too early, announced myself as alien among my own.

But RSS men have disciplined themselves to be patient with the ignorant Hindu. 'Of course you will not know,' he replied. 'Even in India the English language press has not reported it.'

A man in the circle brought a copy of *Panchjanya*, the RSS newspaper. The banner headline in Hindi called that dinner the 'revolution of the century'. He explained the revolution. Brahmin sadhus and sants from Varanasi had gone to dinner with the low-caste Sanjit Chaudhry, the 'domraja' who manages the cremation ghats of Varanasi. *Panchjanya* had a picture of the dinner with the caption 'unbelievable sight'. The caption named Mahant Avaidhya Nath of Gorakhpur, Vishwa Hindu Parishad leader Ashok Singhal and former police chief of Uttar Pradesh Sri Chand Dixit among the dinner guests. This was the first time that the sadhus and sants of Varanasi had visited the ghat, where the cremation and management of the recently dead was handled by low-caste Hindus. Thousands of people had lined the roads of Varanasi to witness their journey. Long-haired sadhus in saffron would sit on the floor of a harijan's house in Varanasi in dinner diplomacy that would transform Hindu society. The dinner had been proposed at a 'religion parliament' by Vinay Katyaar, head of the militant Bajrang Dal, and everyone else agreed to join.

At the dinner, *Panchjanya* reported, the domraja's mother handed out gulab jamuns to the sants, and the sants ate them happily. Given those doing the serving and those doing the eating, this was news. It was revolutionary that Hindus were having dinner with Hindus, that some Hindu leaders had their gulab jamuns that evening where they had never had gulab jamuns before. With them were dissolving the differences across a caste divide that spanned centuries.

I sat unexcited over this revolution. Because if this was revolution, it was not the first. Now and then, here and there, some upper-caste sadhu has shared a symbolic meal with some lower-caste people. It was going to take more than gulab jamuns to change Hindu society.

The meal had answered half the bonding test of roti–beti (literally, dinner–daughter). But this was the far easier half. The revolution had achieved all of one meal by way of roti. But beti? Would any of the sants be happy to hand over their daughter, or the daughter of a less celibate associate, in marriage to the domraja's son? Or to another of those low-caste workers who make a living off corpses and their remains at the cremation ghats? That would be revolutionary, but that will take some time coming. Society must respect the difference between a gulab jamun and a girl.

My lack of enthusiasm over that caste-bridging dinner must have showed. 'You people from the English language press of India, you are worse than the English language press of England.' This was aimed at me, it came from a sombre-looking man in wide glasses set within a thick frame. Those glasses always add weight to words, and I felt the accusation that much more. He looked at me piercingly, like he was looking through me, and not liking what he saw. 'You do what you want, don't do what you don't want, but we will win.'

Someone who'd been introduced as an arrival from a Birmingham shakha defused the hostility. Because why pick on me, he said, look at others around you, see how little the Sangh, Hindus in fact, are recognized in Britain. 'We are the largest community here and we are the least understood. Just Asians, that is what we are. How many Hindus are in jail? Less than fifty. How many Muslims? Go and count, go and ask the Home Office. And for these people, everybody is an Asian. We are not Asians, we are British Hindus. We must tell them that.'

More such views arose from the circle and grew into a chorus. 'We are one in six in the world, we have tremendous assets, but when we have problems we are marginalized,' said one. 'What is wrong?' another member asked. 'Are Hindus too mild, are they not sufficiently empowered?' And another: 'We cannot consolidate our position as a powerful, influential community because we are divided. That is the main cause of our undoing. Hegdewar said we must meet regularly to overcome this. The days are not very far when the youth can take up techniques we have learnt here.' Anger relieved by occasional hope flowed on for another half hour or so.

By then the elders had talked, the young had done their exercises.

The sevikas were now walking into our basketball court to one side, the sevaks to another. Our circle made way for them.

A sharp whistle ended the chatter. It came from Maite. He was standing at one end of the court, facing the gathering. Very captain-looking. Chest out, stomach in, arms straight to the sides, hands tightened into fist, stern profile, crew cut. He could have been on the cover of a regimental magazine, the new recruit bristling with promise. I pitied the enemy who ran into him.

Some of the elders took their chairs onstage, by the side of the chief guest, police officer Alan Hamilton. Once they were settled, Maite launched those moves that are to the Sangh the stuff of discipline, and to outsiders military stuff. He marched to a side of the basketball court, stopped, spun around, clicked his heels, and blew the whistle again. Five sevaks and two sevikas ran up to take positions facing the RSS flag on stage. Maite took two smart steps to the flag and halted. He moved on, and one of the seven took position where he had halted. Six halts later, all seven were in place behind him. The whistle sounded again, and everyone fell in place behind the top seven. A few hundred babbling youths had been ordered within minutes into seven neat rows.

Another sevak marched up to Maite's side, very earnest behind his glasses, very much the thinking lieutenant type. He asked Maite's permission to unfurl the RSS flag. Permission granted, the flag was unfurled. On another command, a few hundred hands went into namaste and heads were bowed simultaneously. To more commands, prayers were recited. Maite ordered everyone to attention, then stand-at-ease, then into cross-legged sitting on the floor to listen to the chief guest.

'I have never, never, and I absolutely mean that, I have never, never seen such discipline among the youth in Britain,' Hamilton said. As a police officer he must know youth in Britain as a world of football louts, of bullying gangs, neighbourhood quarrels, fights in the pub, teenage sex as common as blue jeans, pregnancies, hordes of one kind against bunches of another, of helpless parents watching all this if they hadn't already turned away. Where else would Hamilton find this kind of London youth?

Discipline was ordered relaxed after the meeting, and it was a relief to see everyone doing such normal things as eating samosas. The HSS crowd began to look a little more Indian.

I saw little Bharati by an eats table; she had taken position in her straight line some minutes back with a push from her parents. Her father was a member of the Sangh parivar. But she seemed pleased, not just pushed to be there.

'I've been going to the shakha since I was three,' she said. That gave her eight years experience as a sevika.

'Is that because you are a Hindu?' I asked. 'Can you be Hindu without going to the shakha?'

'Hinduism is, right, like different things, and there are so many gods and in the end only one god. There's not like only one way to worship that one god.'

'Is that why you come to the shakha?'

'I find the games fun, I make friends.'

'Do you know anything about India?'

'There has to be, like, a Ram Mandir. That was the birthplace of Ram and building a mosque over it was not very clever. Then they broke it down, and then arresting the leaders was a bit stupid. It was done only to please Muslims.'

'So you would like a BJP government?'

'The BJP should win elections but the Muslims, they vote all together, and there are some Congress Hindus who are traitors. The Hindus are scared because the Muslims are rough and do these bombings. The Muslims are scared because the BJP is powerful.'

A cup of tea later, I wandered over to Brijesh. He was nineteen, and he'd just started to study law at King's College. We got talking about growing up a Hindu in Britain. Like the time he was twelve, he said.

'It was really hard then. It was so hard to say what Hinduism is, who you are. A twelve-year-old in India may not understand either but he does not have to explain.'

Brijesh recalled the many 'points of attack'—idol worship, the caste system, the many and strange gods. 'You can't try to answer all this, you can only tell the other chap to get lost, if you have the confidence.' And confidence in being a Hindu was something he didn't have. 'I was very confused at the time. There was so much that was strange and wishy-washy, it was so hard to explain. It was all so incomprehensible, it genuinely was.'

But Brijesh had now found some ready answers. 'I can tell people today that we do not worship the idol, it is only a point of focus, a symbol to enable concentration, to bring out ideas of devotion. An idol is like the pole in pole-vault jumping, you use it to get to the top, then dispense with it.' And he had found answers for questions from other religions—the Christians have their cross, the Muslims their Kaba. 'Ours is a more elaborate, more complex symbolism. When we worship Ganesh, obviously it does not mean god has an elephant head. It is symbolic.'

'But you don't sound very confident about your own answers.'

'There are so many twists and turns, there are no direct answers. That intellectual reasoning is not there. I feel I want to give reasoned answers to all those questions, but it's frustrating. If only it had been a monolithic faith. Too many rituals, too few answers, that's where Hinduism has come unstuck.'

He had run into everyone's problem. You can tell children they're Hindu, you can try to tell them they must be proud to be Hindu, but nobody can quite tell them what it is to be Hindu.

He knew he couldn't talk to a red-cheeked teenager in England about some deeply philosophical, wonderfully diverse, all-embracing faith. Red Cheeks had no time for a Christian soul, never mind a Hindu one. Ganesh was to him a god with an elephant's head, and that was just odd. A Durga with many arms riding a tiger is bizarre, a god who is a blue-coloured baby who grows up to acquire many girlfriends is a holy playboy, and that makes no sense. And if these are the figures Brijesh would pray to, how much more un-British could he get? A twelve-year-old Hindu in Britain can be quite a loser. He's the British Hindu who doesn't know how British he is, and who doesn't know what Hindu is.

But it was okay at the shakha. You didn't have to explain yourself to anyone. There were things to do, and the others, who were like you, did not ask questions. And the parents were all there, and so many grown-ups around couldn't all be wrong. The Sangh had recognized the pangs of growing up Hindu in Britain, and reproduced the shakhas at least partly as a way out. It offered collective routine as an answer to complexity, at least for now. The philosophy at London's suburban shakhas was not to be too philosophic. Respect Hindu philosophy, leave it alone, and get on with a togetherness bound by discipline and common purpose. Those questions and answers can go on for ever.

Just being together was enough. These bonds would strengthen Hindu society, and a whining immigrant minority badly needed that strength. The rest could come privately. Pray to god personally, but be protected while you pray. You can't abandon yourself to meditation if you're under attack. Hindus have been attacked too often, they have lost for too long. Hinduism needs muscle to protect Hindus, and its own metaphysics. Here you don't sit around interpreting symbols, you play kho-kho. You do the bodh pranam to the saffron flag. You do what you must when the whistle blows. That was Hindu enough, for now.

Maite turned out to be Rajesh. He had much to do at the super shakha, but we caught up later for a cup of coffee at an Italian place on Kingsway, just across from India House. Rajesh had only to step around the corner from the London School of Economics where he was studying.

Over cappuccinos, as usual never hot enough, he told me what the shakha meant to him.

'I was taken to the shakha by my father,' he said. He was just a kid then. 'I have been going ever since, on weekends. I just can't think of life without the shakha.'

'And why not?'

Rajesh stirred his cappuccino, and made a little clearing between the foam and his young moustache. 'Because that is me, a Hindu. My Hindu identity is for me a matter of self-preservation.'

'But why do you have to be Hindu to preserve yourself? And if Hindu is what you want to be, why a shakha?'

'Because a shakha is where you meet others like yourself. For many of them it's a sense of rejection that brings them in. In a temple, at a shakha, you may not know the meaning of the Sanskrit words, but at least you don't get rejected.'

Shakha began to sound like a club for besieged Hindu boys. You didn't have to be fired by ideology, just attracted by a desire for normalcy. Aliens within a cocoon are not alien to one another. The shakha was the weekend Hindu hideaway. Hegdewar's ideas were working in Britain in ways he never could have anticipated. Because you don't even have to be very Hindu to want to be there. At a shakha boys can be boys. Outside they might just be brown Asians worshipping strange gods.

Rajesh told me he had set up a Hindu society at LSE. He spoke of it as among the more useful things he's ever done, almost like setting up a shadow shakha.

'But why set up a Hindu society at LSE?'

'It really gets to you when you get to the university. That's when you get your choices, that's when you make your decisions about who you're with and where and when. You can go to a rock 'n' roll club, you can go to a white pub, and it can be a bit awkward, you can come away thinking this is not the place for me. Or you can think the disco is the place for you on Saturday night and a shakha the place to be on Sunday morning.'

Rajesh told me he goes dancing almost as often as he goes to the shakha. 'You have to, if you want to be with the girls.' But he will not give up the shakha, he said. 'Going to the shakha gives me confidence. You go once a week and charge your batteries. It really makes you feel assertive. It's the entire programme, the bodh pranam, the queues, all the exercises to the commands of your leader, singing together, playing together. They all work for me, at different times in different areas. It's so magnetic, I can't describe it. It's an experience you have to feel, and you want it again and again. It's a nasha, real intoxication.'

Rajesh was silent for some time, looking into the rain outside. We were by ourselves near the window; it was quiet in the cafe. The waitresses had taken up a table not far from us; ours was a world very far from theirs.

Rajesh looked at them too. 'I have many white friends and Muslim friends but there are some things they just don't understand.'

'Like what?'

'Like marriage, and I don't mean just arranged marriages and love marriages. At my age you start thinking about marriage, what you think the wife should be like. I can talk to a few friends at the shakha, I can't talk to anyone else.'

'So what do you think about marriage. Don't you want to marry some sexy sevika? Maybe all sevaks should marry sevikas.'

'No, no, each should marry someone else, that way you can bring more people into the parivar.'

But he also knew that these things don't always work that well. 'So many sevaks, you know, their wives are fed up because the men put everything into the Sangh. One sevak from Leicester went to Paris to help set up a shakha, and his wife didn't even know he'd gone. Now that can be a problem.'

Some Sundays later I drove up to my nearest shakha. The HSS tool hire shop on Kenton Road couldn't have been better placed for giving directions. 'Just take the turning opposite HSS,' Anil Pota who heads the Overseas Friends of the BJP told me. That road would take me a couple of hundred yards down to St Gregor's School, and this was where the Sunday shakha was held.

Pota had been very welcoming, and sounded very shakha-proud when I ran into him at a temple in Kenton some days earlier. 'We have about sixty to seventy shakhas every weekend in Britain,' he had told me as we sat chatting in his BMW—one of those new things more squat than sleek. 'We have an attendance of about 1200 every week, and most of them are youngsters.' He suggested I should come and see for myself.

His directions were precise, and he seemed right about the youngsters. I saw a small and happy group on a golden Sunday morning on the paved basketball court in the school grounds. The twenty or so chaps had split into kho-kho teams, it looked like a great way to begin a day like that.

It was a while before I spotted the older sevaks. They were walking around the periphery of the basketball court in threes and fours. For that relatively tame tour, their pace was rather purposeful. They walked very straight and wore a focussed look. This was disciplined patrolling, no Sunday stroll.

Quite suddenly a whistle stopped the kho-kho. A team leader in blue T-shirt issued orders in Sanskrit. The teams launched now into kabaddi. The switch came like a badly done cut from one film scene to another. It made the kho-kho and now kabaddi players look like some wound-up toy.

The kabaddi ended as abruptly as the kho-kho on another command from the leader, the sanghchalak. A football was brought out from the boot of a sevak's Ford. Not standard at a RSS shakha in India, but the HSS was adapting to local conditions since football is what gets young boys going. There were other signs of respect to local conditions; no one wore khaki shorts.

One group of the elderly who had completed their clockwise parikrama of the basketball court had stopped, and I walked up to join them.

'You must have seen the new book,' an elderly sevak was saying. 'Hindus will become a minority in India in 200 years.' He paused, seemed to approve of the silence around him, and added, 'The Muslims will become the majority.'

The silence was never going to last after this remark. Many-sided wisdom sprouted.

'But it may not happen. You see as education spreads among the Muslims, they will stop having so many children.'

'Arrey, what education, bhai. What education they will get from the madrassas?'

'But really, in 200 years they will be majority?'

'Yes, the book explains this. I forget the name, but you must read it. It has explained very nicely.'

'But you know you cannot say about 200 years. These people, they just draw a graph, and they just show a line going up. But graphs do not go like that. They go up and down, and then again up and down.' The sevak holding out this hope made his point waving a finger up and down in the direction of Kenton Road.

'And really, Hindus. Who will convert now to Islam?'

'Arrey bhai, it is not a matter of Hindus converting, you just see how many children the Muslims have. That is the problem.'

'But one thing I tell you. Indian Muslims are not for Pakistan. They have seen what has happened to Indian Muslims who went to Karachi.'

'Arrey bhai, you tell me this. When these killings happen in Kashmir, how many of these Muslim leaders speak out? They keep talking about this moderate leadership. Why doesn't the moderate leadership speak out?'

'Do you know about the Christians? Have you heard about the

Christians in Kashmir? They are saying the hair at Hazratbal belonged to Christ.'

'Yes, Christ went to Kashmir. Those twelve years when he went missing, he was in Kashmir.'

'But they are not able to convert anybody in Kashmir.'

'These British are such fools. But how did they manage to rule us?'

'Because we are bigger fools.'

'You know, they said, Sir, Sir, Sir, and they took over the country.'

'And even now in India people say Sir, Sir, Sir.'

'You see, between Muslims and Christians it's a different matter. But the Muslim leadership never speaks out about killing of Hindus in Kashmir.'

'They are scared, that is why. I don't know why they are scared.'

'But you see how America will deal with them now.'

'Oh, I am not sure at all about America's way of dealing with these things.'

'Next they will go for Syria, then Libya, then Iran. But why they never talk about Pakistan.'

'They will go for North Korea.' But no one seemed very interested in North Korea, even if Americans went after it.

This was more or less standard shakha-speak, and it continued a while. The other sevaks had by now stopped and were talking in their own circles. And again, suddenly, the sanghchalak issued an order in Sanskrit, and conversation halted. He gave commands, and those brought us all into a circle. More commands followed, all in Sanskrit, and we did as commanded. 'Attention! Stand at ease! Attention! Right turn! Left turn!'

Another order, and we all sat down in the circle. An assistant of the sanghchalak distributed a sheet with the words of a song written on it in Hindi, English and Gujarati, with a translation in English.

He began to sing it. He sang well, and everyone repeated quite in tune; the notes sounded comfortably few as not to challenge a non-singer.

Jai Bhavani, Jai Shivarai ...
Raksha kee is bhoomi ki,
Nyaya, neeti, adarshon ke ...

The translation read:

Victory to Bhavani (Durga), Victory to Shivaji!
Shivaji protected this land as well as law, order and ideals.
He awakened the spirit of Dharma.
You are the inspirer of the youths.
You are the icon of humanity.
You were a man of sterling character.
Let us hail victory to Shivaji.
Let us hail in Jija Mata.
Let us hail victory to valour.

Not everyone repeated the lines on cue, simple as the tune was. The sanghchalak had a word to say about this. Get it right next time, he warned, and gave further precise instructions.

The shakha was drawing to a close. We formed two straight rows. Again we were called to attention a couple of times. On order, the two men right at the back took a step to their right, and marched past us to the front. Another side step to the left and they were at the head of the rows. On order, they about-turned and inspected the rows. The chap in front in my row was considered to be a couple of inches too far out to the left, and he was ordered in line. I couldn't see the chap giving the orders for our row, so I must have been all right. Another order from the sanghchalak, and they marched back to the back of the rows. It was their job to straighten us out, and they had.

They about-turned again. A good deal of brisk marching followed. The leaders marched towards one another, away from one another, towards us, away from us. Another order, and we brought our hands together in a namaskar. Very different from the laid-back namaskars I'd been brought up on.

A second group song began. I stood a little embarrassed by my silence. I'd never heard this song before. In my silence, I figured I heard the approval of Indian secularists. On that basketball court at St Gregor's School in Kenton, I heard the choice that had divided India. There were two kinds of Indians, at least two kinds of Hindu Indians. Those in our lines and those outside of it. Whether you stand in line or outside decides what kind of Indian you are, even what kind of country India will be. This basketball court is not where I'd expected to encounter that question.

Summer Gurus

GROUNDED BAPU

Morari Bapu is something India produces and Britain never, a holy celebrity.

The long queue of devotees I was overtaking on the lawns of the Grimms Dyke Hotel just north of London under propulsion from a busy volunteer, proved it. Morari Bapu was giving darshan to devotees at the far end of the lawn; I was jumping the queue, guiltily, because I was going to interview him. But perhaps the queue itself fed the devotion of those in it. Just walking up to him and touching his feet would have been too easy. Difficulties in access always feed true devotion, just as the numbers negotiating the difficulties multiply conviction. So I swallowed my guilt as I navigated the shortcut right up to him.

It was never going to be easy to get him to talk to me after I asked just the wrong question.

'Why did you do a katha on board a Jumbo jet?'

A businessman had told me that he and some of his friends had chartered a Boeing 747 for Morari Bapu's katha, with the seating rearranged in katha-friendly style. The katha would usually begin when the aircraft reached 35,000 feet or so. It was an unusually moving location for a katha, and I had to ask Morari Bapu why he'd done it.

Sitting on a jhoola, quite his favourite kind of perch, Morari Bapu continued to nod to bowing devotees before answering. I must have asked his least favourite question, and he did not look pleased. The question meant, among other things, that I was not particularly devoted to him.

'It is our ancient Hindu tradition to do parikrama of holy

places,' he replied. 'Where you find a holy place, you will see people will walk around it many times. What is more holy than our Dharti Maa? So when we did our katha on the aeroplane, we were doing a parikrama of our Mother Earth.'

'And is that the reason you did a katha also on a ship?' Because another summer his devotees had hired a ship for the katha.

'Yes. But then I simply go wherever my devotees make arrangements. My only interest is to do my katha, and to explain the Ramayana to anyone who comes to listen.'

The look he sent past me made sure the minder ended the conversation. What might have been an interview was reduced to a two-question intrusion. The queuing and bowing fans must have presented a far more pleasing sight to Bapu.

I made it back past them, unescorted this time, but even that quick chat had given me a new status among Gujaratis. When an Indian jumps a queue, he isn't rude, he's just important. And I'd not only had darshan of Bapu, I'd spoken to him.

The devotees in the queue never got as far as a close-up darshan of the man when they got to sight him. They were bowing more to the wooden khuraon placed on the ground than to Bapu on the jhoola. Wooden footwear is the surest I-card of gurudom, but there was tradition behind bowing to those. Everyone knows that Ram's khuraons sat on his throne for fourteen years, symbolizing the absent king, because Bharat could not bear to occupy the throne instead of Ram. Living up to that tradition, khuraons would never be normal footwear for a guru, they would be an announcement of godliness.

I felt privileged to have gotten as far as an aborted interview with Bapu. At kathas he was only a slight figure in the distance, blown up on screen. For the first time I'd seen his familiar good looks up close, the squarish, well-formed face sanctified by a red tilak, still black if receding hair and a very white beard. A folded black shawl made a shelf of his right shoulder, as usual, above his customary white vest. That look never changed.

Devotees were still pouring out of cars to join the queue as I headed back to the parking lot. Some crusty white folk were making their way to the bar within the hotel, but they were far outnumbered by the Gujus headed for Bapu's darshan. Grimms

Dyke had adapted very well, as they say, to Indian conditions. It had made possible the jhoola under a tree Morari Bapu is so known to love, and it provided pleasing pathways for those long queues around its castle-like walls wrapped in ivy below red-topped turrets. The hotel was built deliberately in the style of something out of a Grimm's fairy tale. But old England has faded under new Britain, and Gujaratis have done their bit to speed up that change.

In a land where nobody listens to almost anybody any more, Morari Bapu manages to draw tens of thousands. When people go to a holy celebrity for darshan, it's hard to know what to call them—fans or devotees, but in whatever capacity they attend such kathas, they listen all day, day after day, ten days at a time. A fair bit of the summer vacation can be spent doing just that in huge tents set up in parks, or the 11,000-seat Wembley arena. Those numbers can be multiplied many times to include those watching kathas broadcast live on local Indian channels. The phenomenal numbers must sting every priest into wondering where good Christians have gone.

Certainly, no British leader of one kind or another has talked in mid-air as Morari Bapu has, which is what led to the question that began and ended my interview. What if the Archbishop of Canterbury were to deliver some sermons similarly? I found myself thinking of headlines for that story. 'All in the Air'. 'For Christ's Sake'. Compared to headlines in the *Sun*, no doubt these would be polite.

I left Grimms Dyke with headlines that never were and an interview that almost wasn't. But before those queues my questions meant nothing. They didn't question him, and that's all that mattered to them, and to him.

We were all going to hear Morari Bapu at katha, and Manubhai Madhwani was going to tell us all about it. Manubhai Madhwani, or Moneybhai Madhwani as some like to call him, is one of those businessmen who made Morari kathas happen. He'd invited the media to a press conference on the katha.

We were invited to the Edwardian I Room at St James's Court Hotel, later renamed Crowne Plaza St James, a close neighbour

of Buckingham Palace. Moneybhai, balding, portly and a little
sage in that successful way, was receiving us at the door. By his
side was Mayur Madhwani, the one who had walked off, legally,
with the charming actress Mumtaz, every man's love of the seventies.
But at least Mayur had celebrity-looking hair with those grey
streaks that always look distinguished for some reason, unless it's
an eye-of-the-beholder hang-up. Behind the hosts stood posters
slightly taller than them, announcing a 'Festival of Spiritual Unity'
named 'Samabhav', to be held at Roundwood Park. It would be
a festival to highlight the unity of the spiritual essence of all
religions. The Indian businessman seems always at worrying ease
with things spiritual.

The Madhwani byline was a rather prominent feature of the
announcement. Two video monitors of the forty-inch plasma kind
were installed high in Edwardian I. One flashed pictures of the
Kakira Sugar Works in Uganda, reworked into success by the
Madhwanis after the wasting days of Idi Amin since the 1972
expulsions. It showed fields, factories, happy workers, cared for
workers, workers who said 'Kakira, we salute you!' The second
monitor featured Morari Bapu doing a Ram katha. This would be
a festival of spiritual unity, with Morari Bapu as hero, seen as
held up by Madhwani.

A young lady was handing out copies of the group brochure.
Kakira was obviously the star of the Madhwani success. A
presumably happy worker—Hira Singh, almost certainly a
Punjabi—had written an ode to Kakira, prominently printed in the
brochure:

'Ah! Kakira sugar is ever so sweet
So say one and all whoever we meet
As we merrily walk down the street.'

But everything that fed the success story was not so sweet. The
magazine told us about the Nile Breweries that the family lost
during the Idi Amin exodus, and got back in 1992. Now 'a full
rehabilitation has been implemented to improve the production
and quality of beer'. And the company had launched a new brand
of beer in Tanzania with 'a higher alcohol content to cater for the
specific group of people who love to have a strong beer'. No one
would serve beer at the katha, but beer could help serve a katha.

Manubhai took over from the monitors. 'We are businessmen,' he said in his halting but weighty way. 'And increasingly it falls to us to be responsible for the kind of world we live in and the kind of world we leave to our children. Without unity, without finding the way to allow all of us to live in peace and understanding, the legacy we leave our children will be a world of polarized peoples. Far from uniting today we see more than ever a world divided, a world divided by dogma. Our faiths must now unite us, not continue to divide us. My family give thanks for once more having the opportunity and the resources to serve our fellow human beings.'

If a festival like this can at all bring spiritual unity, why not have it in Uganda or India where it is needed more, someone asked. 'It is needed more here,' Madhwani said. 'We have made this country our home, but what have we done for our children? We will reserve a special area for the youth at this katha.' More noble aims were announced. I was a little surprised that monitor one and the brochure had accompanied this talk of spiritual unity so closely. I found myself unable to forget that the stuff of one monitor would pay for the content of the other, and that the blessings of the other would further the success of the first. Spirit sometimes can supply spiritualism.

With Harlesden and Neasden as neighbours, Roundwood Park could not have sat in a more nondescript location. Among those who value these things, Harlesden and Neasden present the sort of address that takes courage to admit to. But anything that is gettable to from north-west London in fifteen minutes is fine for gathering Indians.

With Indian-carrying cars to front and back for company, I crawled along Harlesden Road and then Longstone Avenue down to Roundwood Park, which now stood out for its huge white marquee. The parking lot in the park was packed. This was in any case the VIP parking, you could tell from the number of Mercedes Benzes with 'RAM' featuring in number plates bought at auctions. At a few hundreds or even thousands of pounds each, those number plates complete an Indian statement by way of a Merc.

I drove past the privileged parking to plain London roads. Where would Londoners go if the city did not allow roadside parking? After the usual spot-the-space contest, I found a slot, and walked down to the marquee through that Mercedes car park. A Merc is the clearest statement of wealth there is, and Indian businessmen like to make some things very clear. But there were some Jaguars, BMWs and a couple of Rolls around too—some had dared to be different. At this festival of spiritual unity, the one unifying factor in the parking lot was the price tags of those cars. Out in the forests Ram had presumably led a hard life; here in this English park he could command a pretty expensive fleet of cars. I didn't need to step into the marquee to figure that well-tyred bhagats would have all the front seats.

They looked dressed for devotion as they stepped out of the cars and into the marquee through the VIP entrance. The preferred wardrobe for the day was silk kurta-pyjamas for the men, boutique saffron for women. I crossed the catwalk from VIP parking to the VIP marquee to walk round to the other entrance.

The katha marquee had been announced to be 500 feet long and 90 feet wide. It wasn't enough. On this side, the outside of the marquee was taken too, by perhaps a few thousand. Within, the thousands of chairs were all taken, and so was the entire floor space by still more people. The latecomers outside were lucky that rain had not been forecast.

The katha had begun. Morari Bapu sat on what had been done up as a spiritual throne. It was a much satined and cushioned podium, with a halo done in silver arching high up behind him. The throne was in the middle of the marquee, lengthways, and had height of place among smaller podiums on either side. Preachers from other religions—Christians, Muslims, Jains, Sikhs, Buddhists— took these equally lower positions on the sides. They had no silver halos either. The architecture didn't seem encouraging of spiritual unity, but the others sat comfortably in their seats below him, and if they didn't like it, they didn't show it.

Morari Bapu began to sing in his low, somewhat husky voice: 'Sita Ram, Sita Ram ...' The thousands sang after him. Gently he took the pitch higher. The rest followed as far up as they could. He speeded up, and so did the rest.

He could sing of course, but the marquee was not overflowing with devotees to hear him sing. Everyone was waiting to listen to his views on the Ramayana and on the world. He must have something to say if so many had turned up.

It was at a later Ram katha, this one held at Wembley arena, that I caught up with some of his crowd-pulling magnets. And figured also why the Merc number plates said Ram and not Krishna. He is known for his Ram kathas. Other businessmen import summer kathas on the Gita, but it wouldn't be Morari Bapu doing those. Businessmen are happy for blessings from any god, but they do have their favourites.

It was the last of ten or eleven days of the katha, and Morari Bapu was making quite a point of that separation between the Ramayana and the Mahabharata, between Ram and Krishna, that is. 'Ram' was written decoratively and prominently in Hindi below the throne on which he sat. It was a word of worship, but also a statement on the exclusion of Krishna.

'I don't criticize, but I don't accept,' he was saying in Hindi, with a good deal of Gujarati thrown in. 'The Pandavs, they left their home and ran, leaving the adivasis cleaning the utensils to die?' He paused in recalled shock, because Krishna had saved Arjun but not the adivasis. 'Of course Krishna must have done this, but a sadhu's heart cannot accept it. Did only Arjun have a soul? Do the poor have no soul? The brothers just ran, leaving the poor to die?' He was not exactly dividing Hinduism between Ram and Krishna, but he spoke as a devotee of Ram who was at the least a very doubting fan of Krishna.

'So much happens, the Pandavs lose one thing after another, and they just don't give up gambling. Maybe I don't understand. But what can I do, I just cannot accept this.' Arjun, Krishna's beloved Pandav, was Morari Bapu's least favourite. 'What did Arjun say? That if anyone insults my bow, I will kill him. Kill! When some people take vows, it is to do nothing less than to kill. And what had the Kauravs said? That I don't care about your bow! Just one word of insult! And he wanted to kill him! Kankariya maar ke jagaya, aur tu mere sapne mein aya, balama tu barha vo hai.' Morari Bapu never goes on long before breaking into a film song. The transition can sometimes be incomprehensibly subtle. The congregation of 11,000 began to sing with him. 'Kankariya maar ke jagaya ...'

Morari Bapu returned to Arjun. A man of word, wasn't he? 'But the word is not so important. Krishna broke his word so many times during the Mahabharata. You see, he did not get trapped by verbal truth. True religion is beyond verbal truths. Once it happened that a patient could not get sleep. He went to a doctor, who gave him some medicine. Then the doctor asked him the next day, did the goddess of sleep come to you? And he replied, Oh, I was fast asleep, I do not know if she came or not. So you see, verbal truths mean nothing.'

Morari Bapu came up with another story about truth. 'You see, this holy man, he went to live with the adivasis in the jungles of Africa. But there they said they want to eat him. So he thought of a way of saving himself. He said, why don't you cut my foot off and eat it. If you like the taste, you can eat the rest of me, otherwise why waste your time and my life? Then by a trick he gave them a false wooden foot. They cooked it and ate it and did not like it. So they let him go. He survived, but he knows he lied. He knows he did not give them the real foot to eat.'

Stories and songs will always be crowd-pullers, but he was not drawing crowds just as a religious storyteller or singer. He was making us feel good about ourselves. 'It is not so bad to sin,' he was saying. 'People are good, it's just that sometimes the times are bad. So we do what we do. We make mistakes. And who does not go wrong now and then? Do you know, I once got a Diwali card from J. Krishnamurthi, you know the famous philosopher. In that he had written to me, "Please sin a lot, and best wishes for Diwali". So you see, we all sin. But it is not good to do the same sin again and again.'

It would, he said, be a sin not to sin. 'If you take the name of god, your sins will be wiped out, even if you have committed many. And if you don't, then god will ask, why did you do no wrong? Did you doubt my power to forgive you? At least you should have tested my compassion, my ability to forgive you.' I would be doing god a favour by sinning because god's powers to forgive would otherwise be doubted and wasted. We could all believe this and go back from this katha quite happy with ourselves. It was a dip in a verbal Ganga.

Morari Bapu offered evidence from the Ramayana of the need to sin in order to establish god's power to forgive. 'You know the story of Ahalya, the woman who sinned. She was turned into stone. But she would come back to life again if Ram were to touch her and bless her. Ram came and blessed her, and she became human again. Yuhin koi mil gaya tha, sarey raah chaltey chaltey ...' Everyone who knew the song joined in, and many did.

'But don't forget, it was not just she who was waiting for Ram to come and forgive her. Ram too was waiting to bless her and redeem her. Don't worry about karma. Think about kripa. Karma is the prime minister, karma is president. Only the president has the right to pardon a condemned man. If you accept you have sinned, it will all go away. Say to god, we are your children. If children go wrong, it is the mother's fault. If we go wrong, then god has gone wrong, we can say god, you are responsible. But if you believe, you will be redeemed, like Ahalya.

'So if you go wrong, don't be angry with yourself, don't feel guilty. Say I am human, I have gone wrong, so what? And if anyone says anything, say you have this from god and from your guru. Koi meri aankhon se dekhe to samjhe, ke tum mere kya ho, ke tum mere kya ho, tumhi mere mandir, tumhi meri pooja, tumhi devta ho, tumhi devta ho ...' he sang and added a twist of his own: 'Bahut ayu beeti, chalo main jaga doon ...'

What next? It could be anything. 'I was in Vancouver, and getting bored at my friend's house. So I said drop me in the forest on your way to work, and pick me up on the way back. Then in the forest I sang and I cried. Basti basti parbat parbat gata jaye banjara, le kar dil ka iktara ... You see, society chains us: do not laugh or cry, it says. If we have no freedom to laugh or cry, we are not a religious society. You must cry once every twenty-four hours to be healthy. Women cry a lot, so they remain healthy, they have fewer heart attacks.'

And then the Bapu had this to say: 'What does a donkey eat? A donkey eats only paper. No donkey ever gets diabetic even if he eats jalebi. And Sufis ride donkeys. Once a horse said to a donkey, I can go faster than you. The horse got to the crossroads first, and then told the donkey later he got there one hour earlier. So the donkey said, look, your sardar is coming to ride you. He will take you to war. But me, I will go to bhajans, I will get satsangh, you will die. So go slow, there is no need to go too fast.'

Morari Bapu was coming to the end of the katha. He took the shawl off his shoulder and wrapped it around his head, turban-like. 'Ye gharhi na jaye beet, tujhe mere geet bulatey hain, aa laut ke aa ja mere meet ...' About 11,000 pairs of hands provided the beat.

Day after day, all day, this had gone on, but still ended too soon. Whatever Morari Bapu is, he's not boring. The English katha season will bring him back, thank god, even if that means more Ram than Krishna.

~

DIVINE AMBASSADOR

On his throne-like sofa chair installed many heads above head height at Piccadilly Circus, Parmukh Swami Maharaj was a manifestation of god to the thousands marching past him; god, not just guru. For this sect of the Swaminarayan faith, Sahjanand Swami, a Hindu leader in Gujarat in the nineteenth century always maintains a living ambassador in this world, currently Parmukh Swami Maharaj. So he was god's man, really, and a man of the ultimate god. Godliness to them culminated in Sahjanand Swami, or Bhagwan Swaminarayan as he came to be called. Lord Krishna was only a far earlier and much lesser incarnation of Swaminarayan, many milestones back now in the holy evolutionary process.

That faith determined Parmukh Swami's elevation inside Piccadilly Circus. It meant he could survey his followers below and they could look up to him, as they should. But for someone so tied into celibacy that he must not look at women, or even think of them, his only company at eye level was Eros, London's dubious god of erotic love. The companionship could hardly have been on the mind of the Swaminarayan followers. This was a procession to celebrate the opening of the spectacular temple at Neasden, and Parmukh Swami would bless it from the heart of London, and to be seen there doing so. Eros just happened to be the figure nearest him.

A Rolls had brought Parmukh Swami into Piccadilly Circus and was parked right inside, by the base of the Eros statue. It's the only time I've seen a car in there, or a throne with someone on it for that matter. Some negotiations with Westminster council and the police, and perhaps persuasion from higher-ups must have gone into the parking of the car and the installation of its occupant at that height.

The men bowed deep towards the throne as they marched past this high point of the procession. Parmukh Swami, elderly, portly and gentle, was everything you'd want to look up to in a holy Hindu figure. The round face with the round red tilak over a sparse white beard could have walked out of any Hindu calendar.

From his perch, Parmukh Swami would have seen the long march all the way down Piccadilly. The men who had been marching ahead of the women had almost moved on, and now the women came marching by. The male–female division of the procession, as at the Neasden temple, was as strict as any Islamic division in such matters could be. The women too in turn bowed their heads and looked up to him, hands folded. It was all right for women to look at the swami and the male sadhus, but not at all right for him and his sadhus to look at the women. I watched particularly to see if Parmukh Swami would look at the women. He did, more than once. But who can say whether he looked at women, or just made himself aware that the procession had turned female.

It was a victory march. London's Swaminarayan temple had come long before the Delhi temple that Parmukh Swami inaugurated in November 2005. The Neasden temple had added Vedic architecture to the London skyline and Hindu history to Britain. The Hindu image in Britain was being lifted by architecture and edifice as never before, and London should know.

Bands led the procession, playing Western and victorious sounding marching tunes. A pick-up van dressed like a lion carried a life-size image of Sahjanand Swami. Figures of his associates accompanied him. Other floats dressed like birds mostly, carried images of Parmukh Swami's predecessors; they had been living incarnations of Sahjanand Swami in their time. I thought London was being given a darshan of the gods. A devotee corrected me: The gods were being shown the city they were moving into. They would see London, and bless it.

Parmukh Swami later went to greater heights than Eros level at Piccadilly Circus to bless London. He showered petals on London from a helicopter, and never mind that Londoners had no idea they were so blessed. The white helicopter had taken off from the grounds of the Swaminarayan school next to the mandir, and brought him back there. The Rolls that had taken him inside Piccadilly Circus now took him from the school grounds to the temple and the thousands waiting for him inside. He entered over a rangoli of fresh flowers, blessed to be scattered by his feet. As far as the worshippers can work it, Parmukh Swami's visits to London get the protocol of visitation from god.

And did Parmukh Swami think he is god's messenger on earth? He has never said so. He speaks of himself only as the servant of Bhagwan Swaminarayan. A miniature figure of Bhagwan Swaminarayan cast in spiritual-looking splendour, is carried by a sadhu before him wherever he goes. The two go together; you do not worship one without the other.

Parmukh Swami has been far from uncooperative with the eagerness to treat him as god. He's unassuming in his manner and in his language, but he assumes treatment as though he were god. On his birthday he was sat in a chariot pulled by devotees dressed in orange bridegroom-like uniforms. Other volunteers in blue and yellow ceremonial dress and turbans did the garba before the advancing chariot. Parmukh Swami did not appear an unwilling passenger at all.

His followers believe he is in exclusive communion with god. The deities at the Neasden temple, as at the Delhi temple later, were consecrated by him. Which meant he whispered words that only he could, to summon deities out of stone, to turn a building into a temple. With a brush dipped in honey he had opened the eyes of the images to the devotees before them. He and he alone could talk to both god and man. To women too, as long as they sat behind the men and he could speak without looking.

Parmukh Swami does not tell anyone to follow him, but from a peacock-blue stage-throne done in an overpainted idea of magnificence on a recent visit, he told stories about faith and spirituality. Sukh Swami was Sahjanand Swami's constant companion, he said. 'He would accompany Maharaj everywhere, and never leave his side despite all discomforts. Even when Maharaj appeared to everyone as though he was just a human being, Sukh Swami never doubted that he was god.'

Sukh Swami won blessings for this. 'Maharaj praised him. You know we all have our "ups and downs"—and let me say that in English because I am here. I went in a plane, in a helicopter, you go up and down in those. In the world, in business, in work also ups and downs come. But in religion, in faith, there should be no ups and downs, it should always be up.'

Parmukh Swami had other stories to tell. 'You know Bharat raja, after whom Bharat was named. Rushab Dev was an avatar of god. He had 100 children. Bharat was the eldest of them, he was the ruler then. Rushab Dev called his children and told them that this royal rule will bring you no peace. If you want peace, go to some great sant mahatma, and learn about atma and paramatma. You will get joy and your soul will find peace.

'Rushab Dev did well to give this teaching to his children. You have to learn seriously from this kind of teaching. Parents teach their children, guide them. If the child listens to them, the child does well. If the child does not follow their advice, the child becomes unhappy. But these days nobody likes to be told what to do. Today's children will say "nonsense". But our culture was that of the children of Rushab Dev. On his advice Bharat gave up his rule.' It didn't really matter what he said, his words became divine in the listening if not the speaking.

That godliness makes this a Hinduism with almost nothing in it of Ram or Krishna. At the temples in Neasden, Gandhinagar and Delhi, the sanctum sanctorum reveals the godly hierarchy of this sect more eloquently, and probably more accurately, than all the speeches and literature the group produces. Once you've admired the stone carvings on the walls and pillars, it's hard not to pick up what the placement of the deities says.

As you enter the sanctum sanctorum at the Neasden temple, a small figure of Ganesha stands to one side, with Hanuman opposite, each in tiny shrines of their own. Further ahead, and to a side again, Ram and Sita stand fairly small to the left, with Shankar and Parvati facing them from the wall opposite. All this is only the sideshow.

The middle of the temple, which you would face as you enter, announces what this temple is primarily about. The main figures sit in three central shrines. First, to the left, Sahjanand Swami stands in the company of Krishna and Radha, all three still small figures. In the middle stands the life-sized deity of Sahjanand Swami along with figures of the first close followers. To the right, Sahjanand Swami stands alone as Ghanshyam, as he was called in his younger days. Looking left to right, Sahjanand rises from the company of Krishna to come into his own, in the company of those who were the first to recognize him as god, and finally, he stands alone because as god he would. The three sets of figures tell the evolution story.

In a corridor behind these figures, created to make a parikrama of these Swaminarayan images possible, sit the figures of earlier living carriers of Bhagwan Swaminarayan's godliness since his time, leading up to the figure of Parmukh Swami to the extreme right. A successor to Parmukh Swami has probably been agreed on, but this is the big Swaminarayan secret, a secret that matters to this particular sect of the Swaminarayans, that is. Because many others believe in Bhagwan Swaminarayan, but not through the Parmukh Swami path. The Neasden temple stands as a triumph of Hinduism in London, but also as a picture of schisms within Hinduism, and within the S./aminarayan sect itself. The divisions that grew around Sahjanand Swami in Gujarat in the late eighteenth and nineteenth centuries were brought to London and set in stone.

In his book *An Introduction to Swaminarayan Hinduism*, Raymond Brady describes where Sahjanand Swami came from and how the divisions within the sect came about.

Sahjanand Swami was born near Ayodhya, but it was in Gujarat that he became established as a preacher and reformer in the early nineteenth century, before his death in 1830. His followers changed his childhood name to Ghanshyam, which was also one of the childhood names Krishna was known by. According to reported legend he led the life of a wandering sadhu. Devotees began to gather around him, and in time began to look upon him as god. But many others did not, and he was made leader of his group only in the face of strong opposition and many desertions.

Sahjanand found many followers and was said to have built six large temples. He also wrote out a text (the *Lekh*) to spread the faith. India was divided in two for the purpose, the Amdavad group for the north and the Vadtal group for the south. A split in the Vadtal group led to the creation of the Akshar Purushottam Sanstha, the group that has built the talked about temples in London, Gandhinagar and Delhi.

The split came when Swami Yagnapurushdas (1865–1951), Shastri Maharaj as his followers called him, broke away from the Vadtal temple in 1906. Shastri Maharaj believed that Swaminarayan had appointed his close follower Gunatitanand Swami (1785–1867) as his spiritual successor, and that Swaminarayan would always be manifest in the world through his chief devotee. This was the beginning of the sect that believed in a living personification of Swaminarayan, god to them, that is. The Vadtal sadhus feared Shastri Maharaj would place images of Gunatitanand Swami in temples, and opposed Shastri Maharaj. And so Shastri Maharaj left Vadtal with his supporters, and the Akshar Purushottam Sanstha was born.

The Akshar Purushottam Sanstha believed Pragji Bhakta to be a successor of Gunatitanand Swami, followed by Shastri Maharaj himself, then Yogiji Maharaj (1891–1971) and now Parmukh Swami. Legal disputes between this and other groups have continued since the separation.

London is home to several other Swaminarayan splinters, since Parmukh Swami personifies Swaminarayan only to some Swaminarayans. Muktajivandas Swami left the Amdavad section in the 1940s and started his own sect that came to be called the Swaminarayan Gadi. He came to London in 1970 and led a procession from Hyde Park to Trafalgar Square, much the route taken by the procession to mark the Neasden temple. The route taken by the Parmukh Swami group was no doubt a statement on how much farther the Parmukh Swami people have gone down that path, how many more they are, how much more they have, and have built.

The Muktajivan group bought a church hall in Golders Green in 1981 but only a relatively small group meets there regularly. The Amdavad group back in India have their own temple in Willesden Green, through the autonomous Swaminarayan temple in Bhuj in Gujarat. This is not very far from the Neasden temple. Swaminarayan followers from Kutch have their separate temple just off Kenton Road in north-west London.

At these other temples they worship Swaminarayan directly. They believe Swaminarayan left no living lineage through which he may be manifest. But those who believe in that special spiritual relationship between Swaminarayan and Parmukh Swami have the more spectacular address. A good deal more money has gone into a belief that admits a god by your side who can talk to you. It helps dissolve the distinction between god and guru.

An Indian abroad is far more ready to receive god than the average Indian in India, Swami Satyanandmitra was saying. 'I could never have imagined this kind of popularity of our religion when I came here first in 1976,' he told me. He was on his annual visit to London, the visits have been at least annual since he set up his own centre in Harrow where the driving test centre used to be just behind the civic centre.

Like Swami Hariprasad, Satyanandmitraji had a follower sitting on the floor by his side. Satyanandmitraji and I chatted at sofa level in the American-size house of a devotee in Pinner, just north of Harrow. 'In 1976 I did not even think I would come here again and again,' he said. 'But people just began to say you must come every year.' Britain may or may not get an Indian summer, but it gets a more and more Hindu summer every year.

Swami Satyanandmitra, a comfortably elderly sadhu, lives mostly in Hardwar but has charitable institutions all around India and abroad. He had a devoted following in East Africa, and as they migrated to Britain, his summer flights changed path too. He likes this moneyed flock, he was saying, because their money makes them more religion-ready. 'This happens everywhere. As people progress economically, they begin to believe more and more in religion. In 1976 people had just come from Uganda and from other countries in Africa. They were busy just trying to get settled. In poverty, you see, people turn to religion out of fear. When you are well off, then you make a proper choice. So it becomes important for good people to come here and give them direction.'

'So is proper Hinduism also an NRI thing?'

'It may be, because the conditions are such. People here are more dedicated. Either they don't want to know. If they do, they want to take something good from it, they want some knowledge. Who was Ram, who was Krishna, who was Rana Pratap? Why do we keep pigtails, why do we ring bells, why do we go to a temple, why do we say "Om"? There's a lot of reasoning. In India nobody cares. Others are going, so we are going. It is herd instinct.'

'But is there such a difference between practising Hinduism in Britain and in India?'

'You see people here have fewer practical difficulties. Here you don't hear of corruption. You do not need to pay a bribe for a train reservation, for going to a hospital. This whole problem of bribes, this has really shaken the belief of people. As long as there is poverty and corruption in India, India cannot become a truly religious country. How much can you expect from a poor man? That he should be honest? When ministers get caught in corruption, he asks why should I alone remain honest?'

'So you need money and comforts for true religion.'

'Absolutely, you cannot do without that. You cannot be religious on an empty stomach. Bhhokhey bhajan na hoey Gopala/Ye lo apni kanthi mala. Ram and roti must go together.'

'But there are so many religious preachers in India, aren't they making some difference?'

'So many of those people who do kathas, give religious lectures and talks, what they do is so often different from what they say. When they see that, people despair. They don't know what to believe in any more. So they lose faith.'

'But what is getting so many of the youngsters here so involved with Hinduism?'

'When people of other religions get aggressive about their religion, then the youths of other religions say we should also get assertive about our religion. So this is psychological. Christianity and Islam are spreading very fast on the basis of their money and their strength. So youths from other religions will want their own utsav, their garba, their raas, Janamashtami, Ram Navmi, anniversaries of their mahatmas. This is good, because it keeps the festivals going, and preserves our traditions.'

'So do we have other religions to thank for this new interest in Hinduism?'

'Youths see other religions. But when they see Hindu philosophy it touches their hearts more. I do not criticize the philosophical background of other religions, but they do not have anything like yoga and meditation. When our youths sit for meditation, when they go for yoga, for vegetarianism, they find it is of great benefit. These things calm our minds, clear away our tensions. When we express faith in our god, in our religion, it cuts down our depression as well. So one says to another it has helped. These days no one will follow religion just for moksha, they want to see it doing some good for them here and now.'

The resurgence in faith led Satyanandmitraji to set up his own centre in London; halls here and there had served enough as part-time temples. Everyone's comfortable enough now to receive religion—once summer sets in.

BEDROOM

And then there was the case of this guru.

The police were among the first to know, and only the police can respond in much the same way to so many different cases. Clearly, to the policewoman who took notes as the Gujarati woman spoke, this was just another case, even if it was recorded as a case of rape by a holy Indian.

This is most of what the policewoman recorded at the Leicester police headquarters, barring the names:

I am the above named person. I am a Hindu woman. I have been married for 23 years. We have three sons, aged 22, 15 and 13. We have another property on the same street and live within extended family.

Last year I came into contact with Gulabnath Bapu. I chose to have him as my Guru. He has other followers in England. It is an honour to have Bapu stay at the house. He moves at various addresses during his stay in the UK. As Guru he expects his followers to observe certain rules and they are as follows: (1) to be vegetarian, (2) not to drink alcohol, (3) not to see a person of opposite sex with bad intentions (commit adultery), (4) not to tell lies or steal.

Since meeting him for the first time around spring time last year I had met him personally again, worshipped him and abided by the rules set by him.

Around the beginning of May 2002 he had been staying somewhere in Leicester when my brother-in-law invited him to stay at our house which was considered a great honour for our family. Bapu accepted the invitation and came over to stay with us on 13 May 2002. During this time I acted as his sevak, which means taking care of his requirements— washing his clothes, preparing food for him. During his stay he had his own bedroom with one double bed, chest of drawers, a computer and a coffee table.

The house we live in is a three-storey house. On the first floor there is a bathroom and three bedrooms and one bedroom on the second floor. The bedroom I share with my husband is at the end of the hallway, next to it is a children's bedroom, next to that was Bapu's bedroom and adjacent to that was the bathroom.

I usually get up at about 6 o'clock in the morning and normally I am the first person to get up.

On Friday 17 May I got up and had a bath at around 6 a.m. When I came out of the bathroom Bapu opened his bedroom door, he was wearing a saffron coloured linen dhoti, and a tunic top, also in saffron colour. It is quite common for Bapu to wear saffron coloured clothing. I was wearing a full-length night-dress, a bra and no knickers, I was on my way back into my bedroom when Bapu's door opened. He put his arm around me and guided me back into his bedroom.

Once inside the bedroom he embraced me and kissed me on the lips, he did not use any force. I was very shocked at what he was doing. He sat me down on the edge of the bed and pushed me backwards so I was lying across the bed. My legs were hanging down beside the bed. He pulled my night-dress up using one of his hands and with the other he inserted his penis into my vagina. To do that he did not have to remove any of his clothes. He would have to just pull his clothes (dhoti) to either side to enable him to expose his genitals.

I felt like I had gone into a sort of trance. I felt I was not able to do anything. He was on top of me for about a minute. He then ejaculated inside me. He did not use any protection. Whilst he was on top of me with his penis inside me, he spoke quietly. He said the children must not wake up. He seemed anxious that I might make a noise and wake up other people in the house.

While this was happening I remained still and silent, I had my eyes closed, and I did not attempt to push him away. I was so shocked at what was happening.

The other people in the house at that time were my husband and two sons who were sleeping in our bedroom. In the bedroom next to Bapu's were two other boys. Upstairs on the second floor was my other son.

After Bapu had ejaculated, he withdrew his penis. I got up from the bed. I then straightened my night-dress and said to Bapu, 'I will get your coffee.' I went downstairs and cleaned my teeth in the kitchen as normal. I got Bapu's coffee and returned to his bedroom. I left the door open. Bapu was sitting on the bed. I put his coffee on the coffee table, I sat on the floor opposite Bapu about six feet away from him, I stared at him. He did not speak. I said, 'Who do I call my guru now?'

He replied that he was still my guru because when I chose him as my guru it meant I pledged my 'body', 'soul' and 'wealth' to him. I told him that my guru should not have done what you have just done. He further said that I should keep him in my heart and look upon him as being my guru.

We sat there for about 15 minutes whilst he had his coffee. I got up and went into the bathroom, washed myself and went into my bedroom where my husband and children were still asleep.

I felt a little bit discomfort on the outside of my vagina area where I applied Sudacrem. I got dressed for work and woke my husband up. By now it was about 7.30 a.m. My husband went into the bathroom and I went downstairs and had a cup of tea whilst he got ready. We left the house at around 7.45 a.m., my husband drove me to work on Leicester Street, which is only about five minutes drive from my home address. As soon as I left the house I broke down and it was as if I had suddenly realized what had happened. I started crying. I could not stop and continued to cry throughout the journey to work. My husband asked me a number of times what the matter was, but I was not able to say anything.

Throughout the day I continued to cry at work and my colleagues asked me what was wrong. I did not tell anybody what had happened.

At about 5 p.m. on the same day my husband picked me up from work. He again asked me why I had been crying in the morning. I asked him to take me to the park near Waitrose, I believe is called Evington Park. I did not want to go back to the house because there would be too many people there. My husband parked the car in the car park opposite the nursery. I told my husband that Bapu had raped me that morning, my husband did not believe me initially. I think the reason for not believing was because it was unbelievable that Bapu would do something like this. I suggested that we should inform my husband's elder brother.

I went back to my home address with my husband, he went into the house and returned with his brother. We all then went to the park. My husband informed him what had happened, he was very shocked and said now it had happened anyway, we shall have to deal with it as best we can handle. I was crying. It was decided that I would not be alone with Bapu at any time.

My husband's brother was concerned about other female members of the family and how they can be protected from

Bapu. It was decided that my sister-in-law will attend to Bapu's needs along with her mother. By this time it was getting late and we were expecting a lot of people to arrive at our house at 9 p.m. The people were coming to our house to honour Bapu, pray and sing. During the evening we were all very busy with the guests and nothing more was discussed about the incident for the rest of the evening.

On Saturday I went to work at 8 a.m. At around 2 p.m. I telephoned a family friend. I asked him how I could get Bapu to leave without upsetting him as I was worried that he would curse me and the family. He assured me that Bapu would not do anything like that and nothing bad would happen if I asked him to leave. He did not ask what my reasons were for wanting him to leave.

I finished work at 4 p.m. and returned home. On the same day, Saturday, early evening, my sister-in-law asked me what the matter was as she felt something was not quite right. I told her what had happened on Friday morning with Bapu.

On Friday and Saturday night I slept at the other house a few doors away, so that I was away from Bapu.

On Sunday Bapu said he was going to stay at other follower's house where he wanted to be dropped off. He asked my husband and brother-in-law where he wanted to be dropped off in Leicester. He asked that his clothes he had taken off that morning to be washed and forwarded to him at the address where he was staying.

After Sunday morning I did not see him or speak to him again. Sometime during the following week he telephoned our house and spoke to my sister-in-law. He asked why myself and my husband had been cold towards him. She pretended to know nothing about the reason. Bapu told her that my husband and I had asked him for £1000 and that he had refused. He also told her not to mention that telephone conversation to anyone including her husband. She went straight to her husband and told him about the telephone call. I can say that neither my husband nor I have ever asked for any money from Bapu.

On 26 May 2002 a friend came to visit someone we know

in Leicester. He informed that friend about what had happened to me with Bapu. At that time it was disclosed that his twelve-year-old daughter had made an allegation that Bapu had sexually assaulted her. We discussed everything and my husband and I decided that Bapu must not get away with what he was doing, that is the reason for us to come to the police station today to report it.

Since the rape I have had sexual intercourse with my husband every night since Monday 20 May to 26 May 2002. This is normal sexual activities for me and my husband. I did not have sex on Friday 17 May and Saturday 18 May and Sunday 19 May 2002 because Friday was the day of rape and Saturday I slept at the other house. On Sunday I chose not to have sex. Since the rape I have not experienced any discomfort during sexual intercourse with my husband. We do not use any protection when I have sexual intercourse with my husband as I have had a coil fitted.

After the rape I have washed all the clothing I was wearing and the bedding from Bapu's bed has been washed too.

I would describe Bapu as an Asian male, 72 years old, 5ft 6in. tall, medium build, shoulder blade length greying hair, a very long (chest length) beard and a moustache. He wears gold earrings on both ears through the middle part of his ears. He wears glasses. He has two front teeth missing. He wears a long large brown beads necklace and a similar beaded bracelet. He also wears a white bead bracelet. He always wears saffron-coloured clothing.

It has been over a week since the rape but I still feel anger within. If he came in front of me I feel like killing him. I will attend court to give evidence if required.

She did. The trial was held at the Leicester Crown Court in July.

Her statement to the court read: 'Bapu is a spiritual leader of Hindu religion. I do not believe him now. He was teaching Hindu religion. I had visited his ashram in India with my husband and children in 2000. I do not know whether it has existed for 200 years. I do not know how many disciples he has. I do not know he has written books on religion. He comes to the UK every year, his followers provide all the expenses.

My husband at present has no job. He is trained as a tailor and a musician. He plays the tabla. We are very close to the others in the joint family. All of them play music.

I first met Bapu in 2000. He was regularly coming to Leicester. Everyone was following him, therefore I made him my guru. There was no other particular reason.'

There was of course a cross-examination. Bapu was defended by the celebrated Gujarati solicitor Shantoo Ruparell. The woman made her statement and then ran into a barrage of questions, put to her by a half-white, half-Punjabi woman barrister.

Q: In September 2000 were there any difficulties in your marriage?
A: No.
Q: Did you visit Bapu crying?
A: No.
Q: When he was at your house or the house of your husband's brother, did you visit him?
A: Yes.
Q: Did you visit him with another lady being present?
A: No.
Q: A special visit to him?
A: No.
Q: I suggest that you visited him with another lady when you were upset and crying.
A: No I was not upset or crying.
Q: Do you remember before taking vows an occasion, was there any time when you and another lady went to visit the guru?
A: There was someone with the guru.
Q: Did you go alone?
A: No I did not go alone.
Q: Have you ever met him with your husband prior to taking the vow?
A: No.
Q: I am suggesting that you visited him with another lady. And that time you were crying and upset.

A: No.

Q: The reason you were crying and upset was that you told him that your husband suspected you of having a relationship with your boss.

A: No.

Q: Did you ever speak to Guru about this?

A: No.

Q: Were you not present when Guru spoke to your husband about the suspicion?

A: No.

Q: The reason why you became followers of Guru in September 2000 was not to stop or put an end to your husband's suspicions?

A: No.

Q: Guru suggested that by jointly taking the vows, in particular regarding the adultery, there will be trust between you.

A: No, not like that.

Q: Nothing like that happened?

A: Yes.

Q: You agree that you both took vows on the same day?

A: Yes.

Q: It was your intention to follow teachings together?

A: Yes.

Q: Were you alone when you took the vows?

A: No.

Q: Were there about ten people?

A: The house was full.

Q: Following your taking the vows, you visited the ashram in December 2000?

A: Yes.

Q: Did you spend six days?

A: Yes.

Q: Time spent listening to speeches?

A: We used to.

Q: Did you borrow money from him?

A: No.

Q: Did you not borrow 5000 rupees from him?

A: Yes, to spend money in India.

Q: Borrowed money, 5000 rupees in India, and paid in UK?

A: Yes.

Q: I want to turn to 2002. Help me with some dates. Guru arrived in UK on 13.4.02 before he visited your husband's brother.

A: Yes.

Q: He visited him for prayers also on 13.4.02.

A: No.

Q: Did you live with your husband's brother?

A: Yes.

Q: April and May, did you live with him?

A: Yes. Still we are together as a joint family. He and his wife. There are three sons and one daughter. Myself and my husband we live at 128 and 122, we have one kitchen. I have three children, three boys aged twenty-two, sixteen and fourteen.

Q: And they all live at the same address.

A: Yes, his sons stay with us.

Q: Concentrate on April and May 2002, was anyone else staying there?

A: No one else was staying with us.

Q: On 13.4.02, Bapu's visit. You said Bapu was in your house on 16.4.02.

A: Yes.

Q: Would you agree he was in your house on 16.4.02?

A: Yes.

Q: Would you agree that he started to stay on 5.5.02?

A: Yes.

Q: Was he supposed to stay for two weeks?

A: I do not know but he was not supposed to stay for two weeks. In-between he would visit other places.

Q: But he stayed nights at your place?

A: Yes.

Q: On 19.5.02, he left. It was at the end of two weeks on the nineteenth.

A: Agreed.

Q: Bapu stayed with you, did you speak to him on 15.5.02 and asked him to be relieved of your vows?

A: No.

Q: Are you sure?

A: Yes.

Q: You were at that time looking after him?

A: Yes.

Q: Were you working or had taken time off?

A: I was working.

Q: All the time? Did you go to work as normal when he was there?

A: Yes.

Q: During the stay were you alone with him?

A: No.

Q: Who cooked the food for him?

A: Other ladies.

Q: On 15 May, you went alone in his room and asked to be relieved of your vows?

A: No.

Q: He told you that if you wanted to be relieved, then it needed to be discussed with your husband?

A: I did not go to ask him.

Q: Did you have any discussion about the vows?

A: No.

Q: You did not want your husband to know about the request.

A: This has not happened.

Q: You asked him to speak to your husband?

A: No, never happened.

Q: He insisted that your husband be told about this.

A: No.

Q: He scolded you?

A: No.

Q: Were you angry with him because of this?

A: No.

Q: During the time he stayed with you, did your boss ever visit your house?

A: Yes.

Q: Were you working in May 2002?

A: Yes.

Q: Is it a garment business?

A: Yes.

Q: Machinist?

A: Yes.

Q: Have you a male boss?

A: Yes.

Q: What is his name?

A: (name given).

Q: Did he visit you the time Bapu was with you?

A: Yes, (boss) stayed outside the house and asked me whether I would work. My husband came out of the car then. I do not remember, I did not go to work Monday and Tuesday, on Wednesday he came. I went to work because I had urgent work to do. He went from outside.

Q: How long were you outside with him?

A: He was outside talking to me at that time Bapu and my husband were coming out of the car.

Q: What was the time?

A: About 6 p.m.

Q: Did your husband ask you about (boss)?

A: (Boss) was outside, my husband saw him, and asked me why he came to inform me about work.

Q: Was your husband upset because your boss visited the house?

A: No.

Q: Was it because of (boss) that you asked Guru to be relieved of your vows?

A: No.

Q: I want to turn to 16.5.02. The day before the morning of the allegation on 16 May, did your husband take Bapu to Dudley?

A: Yes.

Q: Was it right that they were going to Dudley for a religious function?

A: Yes.

Q: Did your husband's brother also attend this function?

A: Yes.

Q: What time did they get back?

A: About 3 a.m.

Q: Who was present in the house?

A: Two boys were sleeping with me, my bedroom is opposite.

Q: Was the wife of your husband's brother there?

A: No, but his sons were there.

Q: In the second room on the same floor, anyone else?

A: My other son in another room.

Q: You went to take a shower and were going to the bedroom.

A: Yes, at that time I was caught and he pulled me in the bedroom.

Q: You told that other people were close by.

A: Yes.

Q: Did you shout?

A: No.

Q: Did you struggle?

A: I was scared, he had strong hands.

Q: Did you try to get away?

A: He started kissing me, I was shocked, I was scared, I did not move.

Q: Was he kissing you in the room or corridor?

A: In his room he pulled me.

Q: You told that he never kissed you like this before.

A: I could not speak. I have never said that.

Q: Has he kissed you like this before 17.5.02?

A: No.

Q: When he kissed you did you think of shouting out?

A: I could not speak, I was scared, I could not do anything.

Q: You said he pushed you on the bed?

A: Yes.

Q: When he did that, what did you think was going to happen?

A: He pushed me and ...

Q: Did you try to get up?

A: I tried but I could not.

Q: Did you try to push him?

A: Yes, he tried to scare me.

Q: How ... scare?

A: He was saying, you should not wake up the children.

Q: But you wanted the children to get up?

A: I was very scared.

Q: Did you try to make any noise?

A: I was not knowing what he was doing.

Q: When he put his penis in you, it hurt, did you shout?

A: I could not talk, I was in shock, I was not able to do

anything.

Q: No noise?

A: No.

Q: I put it to you it never happened.

A: No, he raped me.

Q: After the rape what was the first thing you told him?

A: I went out of the room.

Q: Before you left the room what did you say?

A: I am going to get you coffee.

Q: Look at your statement on 27.05.02. I will get you coffee.

A: I was scared. I left the room. I told him that I will get him coffee, then I went downstairs, I made coffee and came upstairs. I went in the bedroom. I went to make coffee, I made coffee and stayed with him for 15 minutes.

Q: When in the house, you did not cry?

A: I was crying.

Q: Have you discussed about the Sudacrem with your husband?

A: I asked my husband to put the Sudacrem on me. I asked him to put.

Q: It does not say in your statement, remember this day.

A: It was not written, I remember now.

Q: You have been discussing your evidence with your husband?

A: No.

Q: Are you sure you were crying?

A: When he was putting the Sudacrem.

Q: Did the husband tell you about (boss)?

A: No, I was crying because of what the guru had done.

Q: Were you crying the whole day?

A: Yes.

Q: You did not tell anyone?

A: Yes.

Q: Anything to do with the boss?

A: No.

Q: Did work colleagues ask you?

A: They were asking why I was crying but I did not say anything.

Q: Every day husband drops you and collects?

A: Yes.

Q: Did the husband ask you why you were crying?

A: Yes.

Q: Did your husband ask why you were crying?

A: Yes, we went to a park.

Q: Have you invented this against Guru because of your relationship with the boss?

A: No relationship with boss. I am working there, I have no relationship with him.

Q: When you returned home, that was the first time you saw Bapu on that day?

A: I have not seen him after coming to my room.

Q: You took part in prayers?

A: I did not take part.

Q: Were you looking after guests?

A: No.

Q: There was a ceremony a couple of days later on 19.5.02 at the residence of a dentist?

A: I do not know.

Q: Isn't he the brother of your sister-in-law?

A: Yes.

Q: When Bapu came to your house, did he give you money for safe keeping?

A: No.

Q: He gave you 1032 ponds.

A: No.

Q: Money which people had given him.

A: No.

Q: He gave it to you and your husband for safe keeping.

A: No.

Q: He asked for it before leaving and you said you will return it later.

A: He has not given me any money.

Q: On 18 May on telephone from someone you said 'evil snake'.

A: He asked me what I was talking about. I told him he has power, I do not know how to remove him and protect the family.

Q: Did 'evil snake' appear in your statement?

A: I have not said that. I was in great anger, if he would have been in my presence I would have killed him.

Q: Have you discussed this matter with your family friend?

A: No.

Q: You went to the police on 26.5.02.

A: Yes we went to his house, another friend was there. His wife had asked me what had happened. We discussed this matter, then he told me that this means I was in law raped. He pushed me to go to the police. I was worried about family and community. Afterwards I went.

Q: From 17.5.02 to 24.5.02 were there a lot of meetings? You, your husband and the other family?

A: No, I was not well, I was not eating, all the time my sons were feeding me.

Q: Why were you not eating?

A: After the incident, I was shocked, I was thinking why was he doing this? Outside he was different.

Q: On 17 May evening, there were a lot of people in your house for religious ceremony. Where were you?

A: I was in my bedroom.

Q: When you took vows, were these for life?

A: Yes.

Q: Did you have another guru?

A: No.

Q: When you took vows, other people were there?

A: Yes.

Q: Other couples?

A: Yes.

Q: You promised four things when you took the vows.

A: Yes.

Q: Do you follow them now?

A: No.

Q: Why?

A: Because I do not believe in these any more.

The jury ruled that Bapu was not guilty of rape. All eyes in the court room were on him as he walked up to his solicitor Shantoo Ruparell. He took off his mala and put it around Ruparell. Who could have done more for him?

London Leather

RED CAPS

The minute I stepped into Gurdev Das Luggah's threads-and-buttons store on Katherine Road in East London I knew it had been a struggle for him. No shop looks like it can sell a new religion, but Ravi Trimmings was about the unlikeliest of the lot.

Luggah, tall, dark and with suggestions of a handsome past, looked the failed fighter. He was talking thread with a customer in a hijab as I entered. He nodded in my direction, and I waited. We would not be discussing cloth or thread, but the new holy book he had put together that he wanted all Ravidassias to adopt.

Some recent conversations had opened up that new name to me—Ravidassias. The Ravidassias, many of them Punjabis, were from families considered caste-bound to work with leather and animal hides, which meant a profession either of shoemaking or other work with animal carcasses. It was seen as 'dirty' work, and those who did it were themselves seen as unclean; they became untouchable to Hindus who would never handle leather this way. For that work with chamra, leather, they had come through abusive association over centuries to be called the chamaars.

That this was neither right nor decent is beyond doubt, but, over years, those marked by society as the chamaars struggled to find another name for themselves that didn't carry abusive associations. A consensus formed over the name Ravidassias, deriving from Ravi Das, a fourteenth-century preacher who was a shoemaker by profession, and so also derided as a chamaar. Guru Ravi Das, as he has come to be revered, was from this caste but in being acknowledged as exalted by the castes 'above' he'd become the model of acceptance. In naming themselves after him, they would be chamaars no more; they would now be defined self-respectfully by their own, not abusively by others.

One shloka and about forty shabads written by Guru Ravi Das are included among thousands in the Guru Granth Sahib, the holy book of the Sikhs. His verses were included in the Guru Granth Sahib for their excellence and as symbolic of a cross-caste embrace. On that inclusion those abused as chamaars hung hopes of their own elevation or at least acceptability. If the Guru Granth Sahib could find room for those verses from Guru Ravi Das, surely Sikh society too could find a place as Ravidassias for those they have stigmatized as chamaars. Or so the Ravidassias thought.

Trouble arose at first with the very title: was he 'Guru' Ravi Das or not? To his followers he was, but he is not counted among the ten Sikh gurus. The Sikhs therefore consider him among the bhagats, the devotees of the ten gurus who figure in the Guru Granth Sahib, and don't like anyone calling Ravi Das a guru.

Luggah had decided to do something about this. The verses included in the Guru Granth Sahib were not the only ones Guru Ravi Das had written. Rather than place a magnifying lens over the verses in the Guru Granth Sahib, Luggah had taken those verses, searched out more, and compiled them into a separate holy book for the Ravidassias. He had introduced it at the Ravidassia centre on Carlyle Road in East London, and got its followers to worship it wearing red caps, to mark themselves as followers of the new book. Luggah was building up the exclusiveness of the excluded, and he wanted it to show. It was this new religious practice that I'd dropped in to see him about.

Once he was customer-free, Luggah led me to the office at the back of the shop, a darkish retreat from the front counter. Luggah positioned himself to keep an eye out for customers and I took a small, straight chair across from a mountain of buttons. They were of a pink that made me nervous. I was thinking what London might look like if these buttons attached themselves to cloth and went public.

Luggah had been watching me survey the button mountain. 'I was the first cloth manufacturer in this whole area,' he said after taking a phone call in Punjabi untouched by Britain. 'I was also the first wholesaler in this whole area.' But the first decent turnover of buttons in a certain part of London, and a deceased manufacturing business were not the firsts he really wanted to boast. Anyone can sell buttons, not everyone can put together a brand new holy book for a new religion.

'It took me twenty-two years to put the new holy book together,' he said. 'I began work on it in 1965 after coming here from Jalandhar in 1963.' He paused to let the significance of this sink in. He then reached out to a filing cabinet by the table to pull out the result of his efforts, a Bible-sized book wrapped in red cloth within a polythene wrap. Luggah removed the wrapping reverentially. The title read: *Shri Guru Sikhya Sahib.*

'The Guru Granth Sahib has only forty shlokas of Guru Ravi Das ji Maharaj. This one,' he said, raising it a respectful few inches towards his forehead, 'has more than 1200.'

'Where did you get the material?'

'Every year I went back to India to collect material. Every time I found new books on Guru Ravi Das ji Maharaj, new literature. I wrote letters, I was interviewing people. If I found material I wanted it all.'

'And how did you find the time?'

'I did most of the work when I was working in a rubber factory in London, in my first fifteen years in London.'

'But did no one else try to do this in India?'

'Yes, Sant Hira Das, he is from Phagwara, he has made a place there. He wrote *Ravi Das Deep*, that is pure history. I got that, then I researched it and put it into the form of shlokas. Then I developed it into bani, in the ragas, in the way of the bani of the Guru Granth Sahib.'

'You took the material and turned it into verse in Punjabi?'

'Yes, that is what I did. In the same style as the bani of Guru Granth Sahib.'

'And you have read the Guru Granth Sahib?'

'Oh yes, for thirty-four years I used to read from Guru Granth Sahib as a priest. It is a great work. We have no quarrel with it. All we are saying is that now we have our own separate book of the teachings of Guru Ravi Das ji Maharaj. Let them follow their book, we will follow our book.'

'But you did find other shlokas, other than those forty in the

Guru Granth Sahib?'

'Yes, a great scholar, Prithvi Singh Acharya, had already found 300 shlokas.'

'And when did you publish the book?'

'I completed the study in 1987. Then I placed it before the committee at the temple on Carlyle Road. I mean the good ones among them. We had the Ravidassia Sartaj Committee UK at the temple—all sensible people, intellectuals, thinkers. So the committee had the book printed in 1991-92. So now we have a book.'

'What will you do with it?'

'Our people will know now that they are Ravidassias.'

'But they were Ravidassias before.'

'But because they believed in the Guru Granth Sahib they were seen as Sikhs.'

'Why do Ravidassias want to be separate at all?'

'You must hear sometimes what they call us. They call us chamaar, choora, bhangi, nai.'

'Why does your group always wear red caps?'

'Guru Ravi Das himself had said that our colour must be majeethia—red—and so we had the red caps.'

I'd seen some followers of the new book in red caps at the Ravidassia centre on Carlyle Road. They were the more colourful part of a whole new set of rituals. The *Shri Guru Sikhya Sahib* compiled by Luggah was placed alongside the Guru Granth Sahib in the prayer hall. The priest who read from the *Sikhya Sahib* wore a red airman-style Gandhi cap. Many Ravidassia followers of the new book sat and listened, also wearing bright red Gandhi caps. Kirtans had been composed and recorded for the new religion. The tapes were being played out loud in the prayer hall, some to the tune of familiar film songs.

But this was only at this Ravidassia centre among the many in Britain. Enough Ravidassias had migrated to Britain from Punjab, and done well enough to set up several centres of their own. The biggest by far is in Birmingham, down Soho Road in Handsworth. Another big centre is the one down Western Avenue in Southall. The Ravidassias have twenty-three centres all over Europe, one now in Rome, and another in Paris, built with the help of donations from Ravidassias in Britain. Wherever Ravidassias went, they needed a place of worship of their own. But those centres all had the Guru Granth Sahib as their only holy book, though some rituals and sayings were introduced distinct from Sikh rituals. In place of the Sikh greeting 'Jo boley, so nihal, Sat Sri Akal', Ravidassias commonly used the greeting 'Jo boley so nirbhay, Shri Guru Ravi Das Maharaj ki jai.' Some Ravidassias use both that greeting and the Sikh greeting.

The Carlyle Road rituals marked a break from the breakaway rituals at those other centres. Luggah's lot eliminated the Sikh greeting and added two others: 'Jo boley so nirbhay, Ravidassia dharam ki jai' and 'Jo boley so nirbhay, Sadh sangat ki jai.' For more casual use, they were to greet one another with 'Jai Gurudev'. Ravidassia men were to be called 'Chaudhary' and the women 'Chaudharain'. Red caps were desirable but it would not be binding to cover the head or to sit on the floor in the prayer hall. The congregation at Carlyle Road was required to adopt *Shri Guru Sikhya Sahib* as their holy book and to place a statue of Guru Ravi Das at the head of the hall. There wasn't a statue there at Carlyle Road yet, and they were using a portrait of Guru Ravi Das instead.

Prayers in this form continued for some time at the Carlyle Road centre. But a religion that required you to walk around in red caps did not go down very well in that part of East London, even if most followers would take their caps off before stepping on to Carlyle Road itself or on to the busy Romford Road to the side. Attendance at the centre declined. Many Ravidassias who were regulars at the centre took up other premises to meet and pray, with the Guru Granth Sahib as the holy book. Opposition to the Red Cap religion led to legal challenges. Eventually the Luggah group lost control of the centre as a result of a court order.

Luggah made enemies at least partly because he held himself up as the harbinger of a new religion. In a booklet circulated to promote his new religion, he spoke of himself as 'Sant Gurudev Dass Luggah'.

'How did you come to call yourself a sant?'

'You see "sant" is not a proper word. We don't have a proper word so far for people who conduct the prayers. Hindus say pujari, Sikhs say giani. I am just a simple man. I am not here to sit on chairs and have my picture taken. But who is a sant? Sometimes a sant was just a beggar. Sometimes they were people who were worshipped. Some were sants because they were lost in their own world. There are different types of sants. We say sant because we have no real name yet for a preacher.'

Luggah was a stopgap sant, heretical to Sikhs, unacceptable to most Ravidassias. More than the Sikhs, Luggah felt betrayed by the other Ravidassias. 'They know nothing about the Ravidassia mission. They follow a different type of policy, and they made themselves the majority. They wanted to have the Guru Granth Sahib back in the prayer hall. They did a propaganda against us. They wanted committee by election. We said we will have committee by selection because that is our constitution. You tell me, religion is always by preaching by the learned. It is not by vote. Religion is not a parliament. We said we will not allow vote. They took us to court.' That ended the Red Cap reign at the Carlyle Road centre. Now Luggah's group meets at rented premises in the neighbourhood.

*

Carlyle Road was blocked up ahead by a white limousine. This one went on beyond the usual elongation: it hyphenated those 'stretch' letters all the way into yards of car in a bid to add to that dubious American list of the 'awesome'. I've always found it hard to admire a car just because it stretches itself to the size of a bus, but on a road on which mere life-size cars get squeezed by parking on both sides, the driver of that limo was certainly impressive.

The limo had stopped outside the Shri Guru Ravidassia hall and released a very Bangladeshi bride in the company of bridesmaids who shone only a few sequins less than her in the bright afternoon sun. The wedding guests were headed for the Ravidassia hall, to the right of the Ravidassia centre. The centre rents out the hall for weddings and such.

The Ravidassia centre stood a distinct pink among the usual red-brick look of a British suburban street. It was the pink of one of Luggah's buttons format-painted over the facade. Maybe it was done during his days of the Red Caps.

I weaved past groups of young Bangladeshis who had taken hands-in-pocket position outside; if you're male, young and cool, you don't walk into wedding halls with your family. I was going to the centre to meet Bali, a member of the new committee at the Carlyle Road centre. The Luggah group had by now been ousted. The Guru Granth Sahib had replaced the *Sikhya Sahib* in the prayer hall.

I ran into Bali at the entrance. 'These are Bangladeshis, you know,' gesturing towards the gathering. 'Most of the people who rent our hall are Bangladeshis. We hardly have Indians hiring our hall.' He was balding in a sporty sort of way and said everything with passion. After a pause he said, 'They have too much money.' The pause might have meant something else. For too many Indians, this was 'chamaaran da hall'.

I followed Bali into a musty room at the back of the centre. 'You should hear the way some of them say Ravidassia,' Bali said as we sat down. 'They say it like we are chamaars.' That of course was always going to be the problem; people would just translate. You'd be Ravidassia to yourself, but chamaar to too many others.

'Look at us here. We are the Ravidassia gurdwara. Isn't it strange that believing in the same book, reading from the same book, we should have separate gurdwaras? These white people, they may be English or Welsh or Irish, who cares, they can go to the same church. But we people, we unravel identities like you peel onions.'

Bali ran his mind over all the gurdwaras in the neighbourhood he does not go to. 'There is the one in Barking, 95 per cent jats, there is Rosebury gurdwara, one at Goodmayes, the Santan da gurdwara, the one on Neville Road—they are the carpenters, you know—and the Upton Lane gurdwara, the namdharis. But you see if you have caste-based gurdwaras, then Sikhism is not the same any more. The spirit of Guru Nanak's message, it is all gone.'

The Ravidassias were separate from the Sikhs, but that didn't make the Sikhs all one. The jats from the farming background traditionally go to their chosen gurdwaras. The ramgarhias, mainly carpenters but also others like blacksmiths and masons, have their separate gurdwaras. So do the namdharis, who believe Guru Gobind

Singh was not the last of the Sikh gurus but was followed by a succession of living gurus.

Bali doesn't go to their gurdwaras and they certainly will not come to this one. Something, he was saying, has gone badly wrong between what Guru Nanak preached and what too many Sikhs practice. And not just in East London.

'If all are equal, why do you have community-based gurdwaras? The Ravidassias, the people in the leather trade were a depressed, downtrodden people in India. We were looked down upon by the jat Sikhs. And here same thing goes on. When they need donations to set up a gurdwara, they take from all of us. When it is established, they say, why are you here?'

He was sounding a little like Luggah here. They had both seen and suffered the same things but they believed in different ways of dealing with them. For Bali, the problem with the Sikhs was no reason to distance himself from the Guru Granth Sahib.

'The Guru Granth Sahib has been around for 400, 500 years. And our guru is also in it. We could not have the book written by Luggah in its place. So we got hold of the Guru Granth and we removed the other book. You see, whatever the logic of the new book, there was never any spiritual attraction to it. A religious book, it needs large numbers of people with it. It needs time. It needs history. And what did we have? One book published by one man with some approval from a few more. But most people were not interested, they just did not want to bow before it. You see, it had no roots.'

But it did have roots, I argued. It had the forty shabads and one shloka from Guru Ravi Das, it had brought together other compilations, it had brought together other teachings of Guru Ravi Das. So that was the book that had so many more teachings of their guru. Why was that not good enough?

'Because there is no suffering behind it,' Bali said. 'A religion needs suffering. Think of the suffering of the fifth Guru. Sikhism really picked up only after that. And after that also it took a few centuries to develop. You cannot win respect, you cannot win following unless you have suffered. You cannot just make a religion in a drawing room.'

Luggah had laboured for twenty-three years, but he had not

suffered. An annual British Airways flight to Delhi did not add up to suffering. Or even the painstaking compilation of teachings, and trying to adapt them to the style of the Guru Granth Sahib. If this was scholarship, then scholarship can still only produce a book, not a holy book.

'I have never seen that other book anywhere,' Bali said. 'They are not crazy. Nobody wears red caps at any centre. We do not say that is a bad book. But read that book at home, read it from another platform. Not where Guru Granth Sahib is kept. He wanted it here. Tell me, could you replace the Ramayana by just something else? It is most difficult to get people together over something like this.' So now there is one holy book, only, separated followers.

PARTITION

Gianiji ran into the old divisions soon after he arrived in Britain. Enough Sikhs had arrived before him to set up a gurdwara at Shepherd's Bush just west of Central London. A Sikh Cultural Society was also in place at the gurdwara. Everyone went there, and so did Gianiji—for a while. 'Then some things started happening that were not right. The same old things. We did not think they would happen in London.'

We were sitting, six or seven of us, around Gianiji in the little library-office at the Ravidassia Bhavan in Southall to listen to those stories. The others around the table were all Ravidassias; they knew the stories, they'd heard them, told them, over years. Now everyone was gathered to listen, and tell, again.

The darshan upstairs was done, we'd had our tea and pakoras in the langar hall next door. Home and lunch were far, and a bore, and this was talk-time. The library was just the place for Ravidassias to sit and look in on themselves, a cheerful, many-sided little room with windows on all sides. The sun shone in on us, and there could hardly be a better time and place to talk of how everyone came to be there at all, or even how the bhavan we sat in came to be there.

'What we wanted did not happen, what we did not want started to happen,' Gianiji repeated. As Gianiji, his beard was necessarily long and pointed, but it stood out the more because he was otherwise a diminutive man. He had just begun to speak but others joined in, like many voices with one memory. Everyone had much to say, because what did happen was not one thing but one thing after another. The past came crowding in on us around the table.

The togetherness at Shepherd's Bush did not last long. That gurdwara was quite far from Southall, it was the place to go when Southall Sikhs had no gurdwara of their own. But in the early sixties, they began to meet at a home gurdwara at 11 Beaconsfield Road in Southall. Then they built a small gurdwara at The Green. And then, finally, the gurdwara at Havelock Road, now rebuilt at a cost of millions of pounds into a spectacular structure.

'We all used to go to Beaconsfield Road, then The Green, then Havelock Road.' This was the stocky man who sat to my right. He ran a shop in Southall. Getting everyone's name was not necessary, I'd been told, and I didn't push. Names were a sensitive matter here. 'But you see, in the prabandhak committee of that gurdwara, they started developing an attitude. When anyone from the Ravidassia community would have a wedding, they would make one kind of arrangement. When it was someone from the jat community, it would be another kind of arrangement. And it was something else for the ramgarhias.

'Those members from the prabandhak committee, they told us if you are not satisfied, go and build your own gurdwara. They told ramgarhias same thing. So the ramgarhias bought a laundry on Oswald Road and made their own gurdwara there. We were also being treated badly. And that is why the other gurdwaras came up. That is why you have now separate gurdwara for jats in Southall, separate for ramgarhias, and now we have our own.'

It was the jats, said the frail and elderly man from the far end of the table. It couldn't be me reading these experiences into his face; he did seem to wear a long creased bitterness. The jats controlled the Havelock Road gurdwara. 'You see, they would not let any of us join the executive committee. They would just find some excuse. So we felt the need for something of our own, where we could do this or that, see, but they kept ignoring us.'

Rebellion rose within the Sikh Cultural Society, with Gianiji in the forefront. 'I said to so many of our people, if they cannot include us with any honour and respect, then let us quit. So this is what I started to do. Some people stopped going to the gurdwara. If they wanted help to do a wedding, I was there for them; we used to do it somewhere else. If someone wanted to do Akhand Path, I would do it with some others.'

'You see, let us get to the bottom of this,' said a man sitting opposite me, he couldn't not have looked the picture of a gentleman if he tried, and it wasn't just the tie and the good-doctor manner. 'When our numbers were small, our difficulties were less. We had small jobs, we had very little money. When more and more people came, the numbers grew, the needs became greater. People, their thinking expanded, they started thinking of other things now. That was the problem, when you come from one society, one country, and still people are not treated like equal.'

They were never equal in India, and the time had come to be not equal in Britain. It had to happen, the shopkeeper said. 'We came from the same land, from the same culture, how could we change suddenly? Today so many years later we are still there, if you ask me. You think it is any different now? Where are they sitting and where are we sitting? We always think of background, this one here, that one there, nothing can stop it. Same thing is happening today, never mind if people are educated and living in England.'

I asked if it was any particular incident that had turned them away from the gurdwara at Havelock Road. 'Oh yes,' he said, speaking in a low voice that sounded like it had just receded some years. We could hardly all hear him around that table. 'I remember that day, it was so cold. There was so much snow. I had taken my family to the gurdwara at Havelock Road, it was the birthday of Guru Ravi Das ji Maharaj. But what did I see in the gurdwara? Nothing. They had done nothing for our guru's birthday.

'That was the day that ignited everything for us, that was the day that we said we have to have our own separate organization, our own separate place. We raised money and we bought 25 Park Avenue, which is a bungalow. There were some restrictions, but it was all right, it was a stepping stone to this place we have now.'

There was silence. Everyone thought of that turning point, that turning away point. It was the beginning of a coming together, away from the others. At the bungalow meetings they raised funds to buy a scouts' hut, which they built into this Bhavan.

But it seemed obvious to me that their assertion of independence had brought confirmation of the very separateness they had been fighting and, who knows, fleeing. They weren't now being edged out of the mainstream of Punjabi life, they were edging away on their own. Guru Ravi Das had moved towards inclusion, his followers were now inviting exclusion. Surely, the minute you turned into the Ravidassia Bhavan from Western Avenue, you marked yourself by your caste. Ravidassia was after all only a thin and very transparent imprint over that heavy old label, chamaar.

I made these suggestions with some hesitation. Didn't they want to be included in the larger society rather than stand away as Ravidassias?

'Let me tell you,' said the gentleman across the table. 'Yes, that is how it should be. But we have not reached that point yet. We don't know when we will reach it. That may come, that may come, that may come, but we don't see it yet, it is far beyond our sight.' He didn't sound like he thought it would come, ever.

'I will tell you how this happened,' he continued. 'It was thrust upon us. It is still thrust upon us. You ask me about my caste, I tell you I don't give a damn about the caste system. I don't know why people cling to it. But what to do? We said, all right, if this is going to be thrust upon us, then let us become somebody. Let us get united, let us show these people, that all right, you have thrown us on the scrap heap, now we are going to show you that we are human beings, we have the brains, we have the education, we have the organizational skills, we can promote our society in such a way that it can stand up, you know, in the whole system of this country.'

'But when you set up as a different group, you only stand out,' I repeated.

'It has given us a sense of pride, of achievement. Because we are telling our brothers that, look, you cannot just throw us on the scrap heap, you cannot just throw us on the rubbish heap. We are human beings, we are a part of your society, we want to have the same honour, same respect, same place in the society, and we are trying to become capable of it.'

'You mean 600 years after Guru Ravi Das, you are fighting the same battle, here in London?'

'This is what I call enigma. See? Enigma. Even after proven things, even after Guru Ravi Das proved this wrong, our society clings to it. Why? I don't know.'

The youngest member of our group, so far about the quietest, now loosened his scarf and spoke up. 'It is like being British,' he said. 'You think just having a British passport makes me British? No matter if you are first generation or third generation, whatever generation, you can have a British passport, European passport, but that does not make you British, it does not make you European.' That too was a caste-like system, he was saying, that no Indian could change. This caste system, that caste system, they were just facts of life.

'You see, here I have my brown colour. And discrimination is here just like there is in the caste system. You will always be portrayed under this Asian banner. But when I am Ravidassia, I am not just Asian. At least I know who I am. And my children, born here, they all have British passports, but they do not think they are British. And I do not expect some British person, some English person to classify me as British just because I have a British passport. So I have to know who I am because I cannot be British and I cannot only be Asian. I must know where I belong, where my ancestors come from.'

'And have you told your children this?'

'Basically I bring them to the gurdwara, I have educated them who their guru is, what our guru's teachings are, what caste we are, it is very important to be a member of this community, so that I know which community and which caste I belong to, so that I can portray the same benefit and the same identity to my children. So I have told them where they belong and which is their caste.'

'But what is all this about which caste anyone comes from? Can't you just forget it and move on? Just be, you know, just people.'

The shopkeeper to my right spoke to me with the deliberate

kindness reserved for the naive. 'You know something, if we had let them put us where they wanted, if we had been scared of them, if we had agreed to some of the things they wanted, our identity would have been finished. From being in a situation where we were told you can't do this and can't do that, we are in a stage where we can stay in our own sabha, our strength is intact. They respect strength, I tell you. Now those very people who never used to care about us, now they come and consult us on some things. Because we are come to foreign land, they say we can deal with some things if we are one. So today we have own voice, own strength. Why? You think their thinking has changed? No. Because we have maintained our identity. If we had remained the way we were, we would not have been valued.'

The others might hear in Ravidassia only a new name for the old. But the Ravidassias were recreating themselves to themselves, overwriting stigma with a new religion. Their breaking away from the old Southall gurdwara to set up their own bhavan became for them an opportunity for a new pride, or at the least a new self-acceptance.

Thoughts on this were piling on to the table fast now. A turbaned Ravidassia—he must think himself Sikh as well—who had joined us a little later, said separateness was wonderful, because memories of proximity were painful. 'You know, I was a student of DAV College, Jalandhar. And what did I see? At the shop they would leave the change on the counter. They would not give it to me because he might touch my hand, because I am untouchable.' From being untouchable in the wider world, as the chamaars were thought to be, it was far better to have a world of your own where no one was untouchable to anyone else. I was a little surprised at figuring out this late that I was sitting with people who were considered by so many to be untouchables.

'Nobody says we will not touch you because you are untouchable, but the attitude, it just showed in their attitude,' the sober and grandfatherly looking man, a loader at Heathrow, joined in to say. 'They thought they were the highest, they show it, you can feel it, you can go anywhere but you feel it, the attitude is there, that they are the untouchables.'

A solicitor, the youngest in the group, young enough for denims and a hint of the Southall sense of a Jamaican accent, brought up memories of growing up in his village in Punjab. 'The shopkeeper in our village, he was a brahmin, and when I went to give him ten paisa, he would move his hand away if we ever tried to put it in his hand. There was a tin next to him, we would have to put the money on the tin, and he used to pick up the money from the tin, and then he used to wipe the tin because it had been touched by a shudra, because I am of the lowest caste, you see. That's something that really sticks in my mind.'

The turbaned Ravidassia recalled those days like they were yesterday. 'The difficulties I faced in society, I do not forget. I only used to ask a question, I am human being like any other, I belong to same society, brought up in same environment, in the same place, why the hell I am looked down upon? Why hurdles are put in my way for human achievements in society. I have right to education, I have right to form an association, I have rights which are rights declared fundamental rights of human being. Why those rights are denied to me? It is a funny old world.

'And when I came here same things happened. Now by inventing our organization we have achieved one thing. We move freely with one another, nobody looks down on anyone. And we have removed that inferiority complex, we have placed our people at par with others. We should not have to do this. But this is the way the world is, the way it works, our society works.'

The solicitor narrated a story of a Sikh woman and her Ravidassia husband who split up after twenty years of marriage. 'After all this time she turns around and tells him to get lost, she says I don't want anything to do with a Ravidassia, I don't want anything to do with a chamaar, to put it bluntly. This is after twenty odd years or so. And her son, her son refuses to accept him as the father because he says I cannot possibly be a chamaar's son.'

These stories were about what had happened, but in the retelling they became stories that could well happen again, that are in fact happening now in variations. And there was power in these stories because the characters seemed interchangeable with the self—he today, me tomorrow, it was him, it could have been me. Every individual's story became the story of a community, a collective experience lodged into group memory.

The accuracy of the divorce story, or of any other, was not the issue here, the telling of it was, because it spoke of a way of living where the distant and the merely possible begin to feel actual. At meeting after meeting, in conversation after conversation with Ravidassias in Southall, in Bedford, in East London, Birmingham, the same stories were repeated with only the particulars different.

'Tell me, do you know who your father is?' Gianiji, who had been quiet for a while asked me. He was answering my question about forgetting Ravidassia roots and moving on. 'Every child grows up and asks, who is my father? The mother will have to tell the child who the father is. Because children, when they play, they talk of their father. If a child is not told about father, he will ask who is father. So in our birth we know who we are. For all of us together, who is our father? Always somebody from one caste. And you know when they always ask, when the children have grown up. They always ask when it is time to marry. Who is the father.'

It had to be this, finally. That you don't have the option to stop being Ravidassia. You might just get away with it at a school among very different others. But marriages between Ravidassias and jats or ramgarhias were never going to be easy to arrange. Take away the odd love story between Ravidassia and non-Ravidassia, and the rest just had to look to marry within the caste. Whether this group, any group, exists at all, will depend on how many marriages take place within it.

'But are most marriages taking place within the community?'

'Yes, at least 80 per cent,' someone at the table said.

'It must be 99 per cent,' came another voice.

'No it is 100 per cent,' said the gentleman-looking gentleman. 'You see, that is why we need the centre, that is why we need the hall here. It is not just for birthdays and festivals, all our weddings take place here.'

'You should have seen the weddings at the Havelock Road gurdwara,' the shop owner said. 'If we could not celebrate the birthday of Guru Ravi Dasji there, you think they would let us have the wedding the way we like? There was one, I remember, and they were in such a hurry, and they spoke so fast that no one could understand what they were saying. Tell me, marriage is a big thing, you would like someone in your family to be married like that?'

'If they had not treated us badly, maybe this guru's home would never have come up,' the gentleman said. 'We would not have felt the need to build one, the ramgarhias would not have felt the need to build their own gurdwara. But now we have a centre point, for all our gatherings, for our weddings. And now this place, this hall here, is just not enough for our needs. And you know, that attitude of theirs, that attitude was the foundation stone for our gurdwara.'

It was uneasy triumph. Because everyone at the table knew it was a pity that it had been necessary in the first place. The final triumph could only be the demolition of what they had created because one day nobody would notice a need for such separation.

When fifty Sikhs meet, they are fifty Sikhs. When 500 meet, they are jats and bhapas and ramgarhias, and yes, Ravidassias. The different, and differing, gurdwaras in Southall are each a house of god and the gurus; together they are, at the very least, also a monument to locally failed Sikhism.

BARKER SHOES

A shoe can carry so much more than the person above it. Just about everything the Ravidassias were facing really came down to shoes that everyone's happy to wear, but only they would unhappily make. Only Indians get that way about shoes, leather shoes anyway. It's a metaphor for hurting by humiliating.

When Sikh religious leaders at the Akal Takht have wanted to punish a Sikh for straying from the Sikh path, they have ordered him to clean shoes, and to be seen to do so before cameras to heap on the humiliation. Punjabi abuse is rich with shoes. The contempt for chamaars must go back at least as far as that tradition of leaving shoes outside temples, and later gurdwaras.

England looks at its shoes differently. That is partly why I was headed for a friend's house in Northampton on my way to a meeting with a group of Ravidassias in Bedford.

I'd just turned off the M1 motorway two junctions further from the exit to Bedford to see my Punjabi friend who was now managing the factory for Barker Shoes in Earls Barton village. He was no Ravidassia, this was a modern-day acquisition. An Indian company had taken over the old British shoe firm. The factory was closed for the day, but he took me through their website.

Guru Ravi Das had one thing in common with the nineteenth-century Englishman Arthur Barker; they both began as shoemakers. Their written stories too began somewhat the same way. 'Guru Ravi Das was born in a humble family . . . ' And from Barker Shoes, 'The foundation stone of the Barker brand was laid in a humble cottage in the heart of England's shoe manufacturing industry in 1880, by an enterprising Northamptonshire bootmaker.' The similarities ended of course at the beginning. It was possible in England not to be ashamed of the leather link. I read through the Barker boast.

Arthur Barker was a skilled craftsman and natural innovator, whose boots were highly sought after. Unable to satisfy increasing demands, he employed other craftsmen in surrounding villages to fulfil his growing order book. With a keen eye on the future and a shrewd sense of timing, Barker invested in factory premises at the turn of the century, later securing contracts to supply the British army with boots during the First World War.

Throughout the interwar years, the Barker brand went from strength to strength as Arthur's three sons joined the family business, taking the brand into new markets and territories. In 1947, a new factory was built in Earls Barton to house the women's shoe production, and in 1950 the brand established a separate sales company to sell direct to retailers.

For over a century, the Barker brand name has epitomised fine quality English footwear. Barker have been making high quality shoes for almost 120 years, every one a masterpiece, created by the finest craftsmen, from the finest leathers on the finest lasts, in time-honoured tradition. Every Barker shoe still passes through 165 stages of production; the traditional skills of hand cutting, stitching and lasting are still used; and every pair still takes some six weeks to create ... with each pair individually hand-cut and matched from the finest leathers. In every country of the world, every time a pair of Barker shoes is worn, another step in distinctive English shoemaking is made.

Arthur's three sons were born into the leather business and proudly took it further, but an inheritance that could be a matter of pride in one country was cause for shame in the other. Most Ravidassias who migrated to Britain have nothing to do with leather, but they are still fighting off that 'chamaar' label. Indians and Brits are alike in their obsession with the past, but that obsession can take rather different ways.

I'd driven on to Earls Barton after an evening with Des Raj Mehmi's family in Bedford. Des Raj had been active in Ravidassia matters, and I'd wanted to see him for some time. I wanted to see also whether Bedford had seen the Southall kind of partition between the Ravidassias and the Sikhs, because the Southall split might just have been another of those quarrels mandatory in Indian organizations, though I thought that unlikely.

But Des Raj Mehmi had other matters on his mind when I called him. The Ravidassias were angry, he said, over the incident at Talhan in Punjab where a portrait of Guru Ravi Das was said to have been torn down by some jat Sikhs during a quarrel. The groups had fought, the police were called in, and a Ravidassia, Vijay Kumar, died in police firing. Mehmi led a Ravidassia protest outside the Indian High Commission in London. A memorandum was handed over to the Indian High Commission, and that's about the first thing he showed me when we met in Bedford.

'The jats refused to sell milk to them, engage them for work in their fields, prevent them from easing in the fields, normal practice in villages, and forcing them to defecate in public by the side of the village roads,' the protest letter said. The attitude, the attack and then the protest were another round of events that made sure the past never becomes history for the Ravidassias.

Des Raj Mehmi was the man for just such a protest. He'd

launched the Sri Guru Ravi Das International Organisation for Human Rights in 2002, a year earlier, he told me when we got to his house near Bedford. Mehmi, a handsome Punjabi in a big sort of way, lives in Kempston, a small and once industrial town. We'd met at a petrol station by the outskirts of the town and I'd followed his gold-coloured Mercedes to his house. Another car carrying his friends and relatives followed me, and our little Ravidassia motorcade made it home soon enough despite the unexpectedly heavy traffic tiny Kempston had managed to produce.

We added up to quite a meeting in the drawing room, largely on the strength of a joint family. 'The Mehmi family, you see,' Mehmi said, 'is quite something.' Through the evening the Mehmi wives brought us Coke, biscuits, tea, pakoras, Bombay mix, salad, beer, whisky, dal, roti, pulao, alu, raita, chicken curry. Nothing special. In a Punjabi household all this is the gastronomic equivalent of breathing normally.

Only, the conversation did not sound normal. Talhan was the trigger. It linked past with present, and Jalandhar with London and Bedford. The Talhan incident had become only a more extreme extension of the experiences of British Ravidassias with jat Sikhs in Britain. Exclusion was the painful commonality. The story of Guru Ravi Das himself, those memories of growing up in India as marked people, the disputes with the Sikh gurdwara management in London in the sixties, now the tearing down of a portrait of Guru Ravi Das by jats in Talhan, it all felt like a single unbroken experience, always waiting to happen before it actually did.

Before anyone knew it, we'd moved from the troubles in Talhan to those in Bedford. The divisions Gianiji and the others had spoken of in Southall were a part of something much more. Different stories with a sameness came pouring out, but with fresh pain in their happening, and retelling.

Life changed, a young turbaned Ravidassia said, after his Sikh mates at the Lucas factory in Bedford got to know his caste one day. 'So they started calling me a chamaar. I asked them who were the panj pyare? They were our people. When that time came to give your heads, where were you? They said this was just a joke, but I say this was not a joke.' The panj pyare were the five who offered their heads when Guru Gobind Singh called for volunteers to sacrifice their lives for him at Anandpur Sahib in 1699. The five had come from different backgrounds, including the 'lower' caste, but the Lucas worker had apparently argued that only those seen as low had risen before the call of Guru Gobind Singh.

A lady in a green salwar kameez was not hiding who she was. She wore a gold chain with a portrait of Guru Ravi Das in the pendant. But she said she had to answer for it in the factory in Hazelwood where she worked. 'It is a food factory. They make sandwiches, pizzas and all that, and a lot of Asian people work there. When I talk of celebrating the birthday of Guru Ravi Das, they tell us, why do you call him a guru? He was a bhagat. I say he was our father, we can call him what we like. But it just goes on, this kind of thing, just always going on.'

The Lucas worker said his son has come home with stories, so it was not just the elders. 'These boys were getting together, they had made some kebabs, and the sauce was in one plate. Then someone said he is a chamaar's son, get him another plate for the sauce. But good thing the host said no, he said we are all one, either we eat from the same plate or we don't eat.'

The parents around the room all said their children brought home similar stories. 'The children come home and say they are teased, they are called chamaars, they are humiliated,' Des Raj said. 'What do we explain, what do we say? They ask us that we believe in the same book, why we go to separate gurdwaras? What do we tell them? They ask us, who are we? My kids have asked me that. They say, daddy, what's wrong with us? Why are we untouchable? My boy, he says to me, I am smart, I am young, I am well-spoken, I have a smart car. Why am I untouchable? He says the whites never say that to us. What do I tell him?'

Here in Bedford, as in Southall, no one thought it would come to this when they landed. The early migrants all got together to set up a single gurdwara at Queen's Way. And then came the attitudes, and the inevitable split: the Ravidassias their way, the ramgarhias theirs, away from the jats.

'We wrote a letter to the ramgarhia gurdwara and to the Queens Park gurdwara that we are taking out a Nagar Kirtan on the birthday of Guru Ravi Das ji,' Mehmi said. 'The ramgarhia people said all right, no problem. Queens Park also said welcome. When we took out the procession they gave us respect.' This sounded fine, but there had to be a but. 'They wrote back to us, and they called us "Ravi Das Bhavan". You see, they never write to us with the proper name of our bhavan, which is Shri Guru Ravi Das Bhavan. They will not speak of Guru Ravi Das ji as guru, or even as a bhagat. They just wrote, Ravi Das Bhavan. There is no respect in this.'

The Ravidassias decided to write back. 'We wrote to them to say there is no such institution of the kind they are describing. We wrote to them to say that there is a Shri Guru Ravi Das Bhavan, and next time will you please write to us correctly?' Some days later Mehmi says he ran into a member of the gurdwara committee. 'He is my friend, and he apologized to me. I thought that is the end of the matter. But the next letter we got from them again said only "Ravi Das Bhavan".'

Dinner was now being served, but with bitterness in the air. 'Do you see what this means?' said Mehmi. 'They have accepted white people, they have accepted black people, but not their own people. To white people they will say "Mister", they will say "Sir", but they cannot show respect to a guru of their own people, whose teachings are included in their holy book. We fought against the British, Shaheed Bhagat Singh was from our same land, Shaheed Udham Singh was from our land. And they can show respect to those people who our people fought against, but not to us.'

Sikhs accept white people more than fellow Punjabis even when it comes to marriage, Mehmi said. 'It is all right for a girl from a jat family to marry a white person but not one of us.'

Sikh–Ravidassia marriages were said to have had hellish consequences. 'It happened recently,' said Mehmi's wife who had come in to take a break from the demands of the kitchen. 'This boy, one of our boys, such a good job in the railways, he married this jat Sikh girl who was already divorced and had a child also. But the girl's bua refused to come for the marriage, and so no other member from the family came. And the girl's side never gave a party for the marriage, the boy side had to do the party.'

The marriages that have taken place between the two communities have rarely succeeded, Mehmi said. 'The couple have always suffered, because the other family can never stop thinking of the boy or girl as a chamaar. And this is England in the twenty-first century. This is what we are dealing with.'

Disputes continue in Bedford over the Guru Granth Sahib. 'They insist that people who read from it should have beard and turban, but that is nowhere written in the book. They think it is their book but we too believe in it. We also want to honour our sants, but they say we cannot do that in the presence of the book. The Guru Granth Sahib is a great book that teaches equality. And so we also worship the same book as them, but this is not good enough. They think everything has to be in a certain way, and we are not showing proper respect to the holy book, which is not true. And though they worship the same book that teaches equality, so many of them still call us untouchables.'

'Will you consider Luggah's solution of worshipping a separate book with Guru Ravi Das's teachings?' I asked.

'I have some sympathy with his basic premise. But it was not acceptable for Luggah to declare himself a sant and make his own rules and regulations. And it will never be easy to get away from such a great and holy book as the Guru Granth Sahib. We keep a portrait of Guru Nanak at our bhavan. But do they keep a portrait of Guru Ravi Das?'

❧

NAME AND SHAME

'What is a chamaar?' I asked a fifteen-year-old girl at the Ravidassia Bhavan in Southall.

'Some people who are Sikh,' she said, 'they classify chamaar as a very low caste. But I don't believe that, because if you're in Britain everyone's the same caste, unless you're rich or whatever.'

'Has anyone called you a chamaar?'

'At our school we had a fight, they were saying to me that Oh, you are a low caste or whatever. It happened a year ago. It's still going on now.'

'Who said that to you?'

'I go to a girls' school, there's that bitchiness, that Oh, you are low caste. Because their parents haven't taught them, that's what I believe, their parents haven't taught them about our religion. If they don't want to know, they can think their own thing. But they should learn.'

'And what's going on now?'

'Just the same thing. They keep saying it.'

'But how do they know who is who?'

'They can always tell from the surnames.'

I asked a seventeen-year-old boy the same thing.

'They always say you are a chamaar, you are this, you are that.'

'Give me an example.'

'One time is like, you know, you're all going out with a group and you meet someone and they started talking, chamaar, low caste, he shouldn't hang around with us because he is a chamaar, low-caste like. I tell them, mate, I'm a chamaar, what's wrong with that? I said, I'm a human being, what's the difference? And they didn't say nothing. They just shut up, like.'

'Did that happen once or more than once?'

'Then you think it won't, then it does. I was with a group of friends once and you know this Hindu boy, he had his car, and you know those orange jhanday, he had them on his car but he was a Hindu, and this girl said, bloody chamaar, what's he got one for? He said, oy, I'm a chamaar, so what's wrong with that? She didn't say nothing.'

The surname left nowhere to hide. 'In India surnames are like a language,' I remembered a Ravidassia saying. 'You just pick up a language.'

So one way to escape the stigma would be to change the name. This was common, a Ravidassia solicitor I'd met earlier told me (many Ravidassias spoke to me only after I agreed not to use their names). 'The Ravidassias, those who lived where the majority of people were Sikhs, they would have names which say Singh. Where the majority were Hindus, they would have names like Ram Rakha, Rakha Ram, you know, Ram would appear. Where there were Muslims it would be names like Allah Rakha, you see, so Ravidassia community, they did not have an identity themselves because they were not able to have one.'

A change of name would help find a job. 'Those days if you were a Ravidassia it was not easy to join the army, and most of them adopted the name Singh and, you know, kept long hair and wore a turban. My uncle was one of those, so by keeping the name Singh he was able to join the army. So many have the name Das, and Das means slave, and so, as people realized they could change, they began to change names.'

'Ravidassia' is itself a name only now in the making. Gandhi had called them Harijans. 'Why Harijans?' a Ravidassia had argued. 'It means children of god, right? Why do I have to be a child of god? Why can't I be the child of my parents, like everyone else? How did Gandhi dare to call us Harijans?' Whoever wanted to be called kindly by another name so you could be saved from your own?

At the Ravidassia Bhavan in Birmingham, the biggest British centre of the Ravidassias by far, a member of the management said he had pushed hard for 'Ravidassia' to be adopted as the official name. 'Our community in the past was given many names by politicians, like Gandhi said Harijans, some others and so on, I said, so, enough of this rubbish, we are all educated now, let's simplify this one to Ravidassia community.'

That meant circulating new literature about Guru Ravi Das, even if it did not come formally from some new red book. Everyone tells the story of how the brahmins made fun of Ravi Das once because he did not wear a janau, the brahminical thread around the torso. So Guru Ravi Das ripped open his heart and revealed a shining janau within. Everyone tells the story like they believe it and like you would be showing caste prejudice if you didn't. The story made Ravi Das more brahmin than the brahmins; no one was arguing yet that he did not have to be brahmin-like at all. The Ravidassias were finding stories of triumph because those were the stories they needed.

Independence meant the establishment of their own little world in which a new collective memory could be created. The unhappy story with the Sikhs and their gurdwara was being replaced by happy stories involving only their own, told to themselves. It had become necessary to wrap old legends in new wonder, to 'touch up' the actual past in much the same way as individuals 'improve' their biographies. As with therapy for an individual, friendly authority sought to build a new life story for the group.

A Ravidassia song I heard at the Southall bhavan spoke of the 'Amrit Bani' of Guru Ravi Das, the expression used by Sikhs for their holy scriptures. Another song presented Guru Ravi Das as Krishna. Yet another was composed to the tune of *Raghupati Raghav Raja Ram*. The new narrative was the therapy. A shared label had made them a community to others; shared narrative is seeking to build them into a community for themselves. But Ravidassia research into a new narrative for themselves is as yet only looking within. Collecting thoughts do not always immediately add up to collective thought.

'I see that you are proud of Guru Ravi Das and you are fighting for your rights,' I said to a Ravidassia businessman. 'But is there also sometimes a feeling of embarrassment, maybe even shame over these origins, and all those experiences of rejection?'

The question was certain to make him furious, and it did. 'Ashamed? Why should we be ashamed? Those people who have been doing this to us, they should be ashamed of what they are doing. What wrong have we done?' I apologized for the hurt caused and hoped he would drop the matter and move on. But he never did forgive or forget, and we did not meet again.

The apology did not sweep aside the question. There was an overlap in that little exchange, between ideas of guilt and ideas of shame. One is so often disguised as the other, but the two are not the same. People who would drop decency with someone they saw as a chamaar were of course guilty, and of course they should be ashamed of themselves. The one so judged, or so seen, would have done nothing to be guilty about; but that does not by itself wipe out feelings of shame. You don't have to do anything to be ashamed of in order to feel shame. It's like rape. The rapist ought to feel the guilt, but whether he does or not, the victim feels the shame. Thousands of prisoners have lived with feelings of shame in concentration camps, having done nothing to be guilty about or be ashamed of. Guilt over causing hurt is rarely a problem; getting hurt always is.

Think of Tolstoy's Levin: 'There had been in his past, as in every man's, actions recognized by him as bad, for which his conscience ought to have tormented him; but the memory of these evil actions was far from causing him so much suffering as these trivial humiliating reminiscences. These wounds never healed.' J. Alfred Prufrock too could have been a Ravidassia.

'And I have known the eyes already, known them all—
The eyes that fix you in a formulated phrase ...'

Every time I met Ravidassias, the one thing I felt I could never talk about was leather. It would be like kicking into a wound that never heals, particularly when they were making such efforts to cover up that wound.

Ravi Das himself seems to have handled prejudices in others a good deal better than many of his followers, I gathered from a book by Dr K.N. Upadhyaya, former professor and chairman of the Department of Philosophy at the University of Hawaii, in the 'Mystics of the East' series, published by the Radha Soami Satsang Beas.

A verse from Guru Ravi Das included in the Guru Granth Sahib is translated in this book as:

O fellow gentry, I am renowned for belonging
To the caste of cobbler ...
My subcaste is Kutabandhala,
And men of my caste still carry cattle carcasses
On the outskirts of Banares.

That made him a member of the 'lower' end even of the chamaars of the time, and his engagement in shoemaking a 'step up' within the caste. But Ravidassias themselves rarely refer to Guru Ravi Das as a shoemaker, let alone someone who worked with animal carcasses. Much of the recent elevation of Guru Ravi Das denies the experiences that defined a life and became the source of the teachings.

In one of his verses in the Guru Granth Sahib, Guru Ram Das, one of the ten Sikh gurus, is quoted as saying of Guru Ravi Das:

Ravi Das the cobbler offereth prayer;
By singing such a prayer to God
For a single moment

He has turned from a lowly caste
Into an exalted one,
And all the four castes come
To bow down at his feet.

There is no precisely documented biography of Guru Ravi Das. Upadhyaya offers only 'an approximate outline of Ravi Das's life', and so what is said or shown of Guru Ravi Das by his followers today—and what is left unsaid—probably says more about those doing the believing than about the guru they believe in. The portraits of Guru Ravi Das at the bhavans across British towns, and in all the literature around him, are only portraits of an agreed idea of an appearance. One thing stands out in these portraits—there's hardly a hint of leather in them.

The commonest portrait of Guru Ravi Das shows a pair of wooden khuraons by his side; the man who worked with leather footwear is not presented as wearing it himself. Wooden sandals have a stronger association with most Hindu gurus. The portraits of Ravi Das with the wooden footwear by his side, very deliberately not leather, seem to lift him into a 'pure' domain beyond history, in which leather seems unknown, and places him in the company of brahminical saints. One portrait shows him seated on a leopard skin; but this is suggestive more of an ascetic guru and certainly not of a professional association with the hide business.

Denials of Ravi Das's 'chamaar' origins came early. The preachers Priyadas and Anantdas are cited by Upadhyaya as writing that Ravi Das was really a brahmin disciple of Guru Ramanand in his previous life.

'The Bhaktirasbodhini by Priyadas (an eighteenth-century text) relates a story accounting for his birth in a cobbler's family,' Upadhyaya writes. 'It is said that Ravi Das had to be born in a cobbler's family on account of accepting alms in his previous life from a businessman who had dealings with cobblers, generally regarded as a low profession.' Anantdas is cited as saying in his text *Bhakta Ratnavali* that Ravi Das was born in a cobbler's family because he had eaten meat.

'These stories seem to have no factual basis and are probably just attempts on the part of later caste-minded devotees to "exalt" the status of Ravi Das by associating him with a high Brahmin caste in his previous life,' Upadhyaya writes. But this could be a touch of shame over the origins of the one they worship as a god, who would lift them out of their own chains of shame. The Ravidassias are denying that Ravi Das could have been a chamaar, so how bad did they think being chamaar could be? The condemning other will look away some time; the continuing pain is from that look that gets locked within the self, and which you learn to hold close because you know that's how the world is for you. So much of the Ravidassia difficulty is embedded within the Ravidassias.

Aunt and Agony

LIFELINE

That Punjabi countess look, if there is such a thing, sat rather well with Kailash Puri's status as possibly the most writing and written-to woman in Britain. She looked the range from impressive to imposing every time I looked at her over the days I spent at her flat by Ealing Broadway Park in London. She was the writer turned character; the controlled look of a character on a set never left her. Her black and grey hair would always blend unflinchingly all the way into a tight bun at the back. Her eyes, with a hint of blue somewhere, looked at me like they could see through me, but kindly. The blue in them introduced a woman who could have been Countess Kaur in a Barbara Cartland novel set in Chandigarh; their kindness made her a natural agony aunt.

I asked her on one of those days how many letters she'd received all her life. 'Thousands,' she said. 'Thousands.' She said it with a rotation of her wrist that suggested I should make a liberal multiplication in thousands. I knew this of course through years of knowing her. She's been the only Indian agony aunt to be around for two generations, getting to be three. For more than fifty years she's been the one to turn to when no one else was around. I knew of other couplings of 'most' and 'Indian', or even 'only' and 'Indian', that she had made in Britain and that no one would challenge. The most prolific Indian columnist. The most productive novelist. Certainly, the only Indian woman who has published so much on sex.

For some reason we never talked in her sitting room. The flowery red of her upholstery hemmed in by curving wooden gloss gave the room a period parlour look just right for a Punjabi countess. But it was too much the standard Sikh setting for 'aao-ji-haan-ji' kind of talk. Kailash Puri and I chatted in her kitchen. Tea would be nearer, and kitchen conversations are so much more honest.

I'd done a feature on her many years back, of the kind that journalists do because they must. Now as I spent more time with her, I saw just how much she had taken on, all her life, and I saw that the aunt isn't done because the agony isn't over. The letters still come, with new pain written into every one, every time. They speak of the insides of lives agonizingly different from the usual picture of Indians as the carriers of some subcontinental culture, or as producers—more than other migrants—of some variation of the rags-to-riches script. Through those thousands of letters only she saw so much of the misery in the lives of migrants who became minorities with time, and their children, born into a bit of both.

Kailash Puri was a lifeline particularly for Punjabis in distress—there's more to Punjabi living than parantha breaks between bhangra and snoring. Milk and honey are remarkably cheap in Britain, but it never became the land of milk and honey of so many Punjabi dreams. When it didn't, they—women more than men—turned to Kailash Puri. Unseen behind the agony column in the local Punjabi newspapers, she was there to hold their hand.

If the British High Commission had wanted to limit immigration from Punjab, it might just have circulated some of her columns. Or copies of the thirty-five novels she wrote in Punjabi, besides hundreds of short stories, many of which drew from lives that unfolded themselves to her. She's lived a life of stories, stories that came to her, stories she told.

Many of them were bedroom stories. Not erotic and exciting—real bedroom stories rarely are—but stories of fear and failure, of some of the darkest of difficulties that rarely get talked about. Kailash Puri lifted that silence over sex through column after column in the Punjabi weekly *Des Pardes*.

I read many of these agony columns, on sex and lovelessness, on betrayal and suspicion, greed and control, misery after misery. I could see what opened people to Kailash Puri. She was always the person on the page, and never one to dilute honesty with politeness. What is the soul of Punjabi expression if not straight talk? She was the family aunt who'd wandered into a column, and family aunts can be counted on to talk tough.

I first met Kailash Puri at her quite spectacular house in Liverpool with its even more impressive garden landscaped by her husband Gopal Singh. Neatly laid turf spread into a manicured mini-meadow around mock rocks and a fountain that worked. That garden was an important statement for a migrant house to make in their fancy Blundellsands neighbourhood. The Puris had moved here back in 1969; they were the first Sikhs in Liverpool. That arrival, after centuries of white suburban history, created quite a stir, Gopal Singh told me on a walk around the garden. They needed to be seen as okay, and one sure way into England's social heart is through the garden. It was their green card to neighbourly acceptability.

That was their second coming to England. The first was before 1947, and it was only now in her kitchen that I got to follow her through her days in London before India became independent. This I did conveniently through a copy of her lecture at a meeting hosted by the Oxford University students' union. She had dug out the copy from underneath hills of paper in another room; her bookkeeping was hardly as good as her housekeeping. The lecture told of an Indian couple in London in the days of British India.

'When I arrived in 1946 there were very few Indians in the UK. I joined my husband, a Ph.D from Lucknow University who came to England as a Government of India research fellow in the University of London. There were five or six students. One from UP, one from Delhi, one from Bengal, one from Colombo.

'Accommodation was hard to find due to air-raid destruction during the Second World War and labour difficulties. Residential places were scarce for visitors and hardly obtainable even for British people. The question of discrimination against Indians and the oft-repeated accusations that the landlady would close the door after seeing a person of black-coloured skin, hair or eyes is not difficult to understand. My husband and his friends had with difficulty and with their exceptionally good friendly relations acquired four rooms in one building near Paddington in Cleveland

Gardens. This was, as far as I know, the first "little India" in England.

'There was one Indian restaurant, Shafi's in Piccadilly and another, Veeraswamy. There were however two or three dhaba-like places in the East End, where a plate of chicken curry and dal with paranthas was offered at five shillings per person (twenty shillings then to a pound). The food was heavenly but ten shillings was big money. My husband was getting 350 pounds a year for his fellowship, of which ten pounds to twelve pounds was spent on rent, gas and electricity every month. This was a big chunk out of our resources.

'Almost every item of food, clothing and other necessities was rationed. Everyone had a ration book. One egg per person per week, a quarter of a pound of bacon, a pound of meat, a pound of sugar, a pint of milk, a quarter of a pound of butter was on our shopping list and these had to last us for quite a time. Potatoes, dried eggs and fish were not rationed but were costly. A guinea for a fowl was a costly treat.

'There was only one Asian food store, Bombay emporium, where dal was available for ten shillings a pound. In the beginning therefore all we Indians would cook and eat together.

'I travelled thirteen days on SS *Princess of Scotland*. We brought some foodstuff, rice, poppadums, chutney, pickles, which went a long way. We met with British people everywhere we went, we were treated as princely. My husband used to be addressed as "maharaja". It was most flattering to be addressed by the shop assistants, "What can we do for the maharaja?"

'As cloth was rationed, three yards was the quota per person, per year, sufficient for a three-piece man's suit or a ladies dress. We became short of turbans and went to the rationing officer for extra coupons, and asked for twenty-four yards for four turbans. I still remember the officer turning pale at this request, and getting the first cultural shock from the Sikh maharaja. But it did not take us long to convince the officer that the turban or a sari was six yards in length. So we received extra coupons.

'There were other problems of a similar nature, but nothing damaging to our culture, religion or nationality. We were still a part of the British Empire and respected as such in the proper quarters. We had easy access to India House and officials had to look after us in many ways, although efficiency had a great deal to be desired.

'There was only one Sikh temple, Bhupendra Dharamsala on Sinclair Road in Shepherd's Bush. It was difficult to get even a dozen Hindus and Sikhs together for a Sunday gathering. Community meals were not easy because food was rationed. But I must give credit to the people living in East End who would like magic produce dal, milk, butter, and everything you needed for a meal for twenty persons. There were two other Sikhs living in London, and a Sikh doctor who used to come from Birmingham, and one or two from India House who would come off and on.

'We were invited frequently to India House meetings and functions. As negotiations for independence and transfer of power were in progress we used to see our Indian leaders—Pandit Jawaharlal Nehru, Mr Jinnah, Mr Liaquat Ali, Sardar Baldev Singh, and Mr Krishna Menon who was the life and spirit of the Indian community.

'It was only after early fifties and sixties when people came in groups with work permits and vouchers that problems started. Many came from rural backgrounds. Many had a university degree, but got work in factories or in shifts to earn extra money. Some of them had to get a loan to get here, and nearly all of them had to support families back home. They had a habit of multiplying a pound with twenty-five or even thirty to get a figure of thousands of rupees. They felt themselves rich overnight.

'Such was the attraction of coming to this financial paradise that people used all sorts of methods and means that later became scandals, to be here. Factory work was not difficult to get, but it was hard, and coupled with the desire to find suitable accommodation near the place of work, it created social problems with the native population. The British objected to the smell of curry. See, how the problems of yesterday became today's assets.'

I asked her if she remembered anything about 15 August 1947. 'I know that the India House people announced something, did some flag-hoisting to celebrate independence. But we wanted to know something about our family because families were being uprooted. We used to get some news at the gurdwara, communication was absolutely nil. The only way was to write letters, and then those too stopped. Wireless was there at gurdwara, we used to listen, but would not get much news, but we got to know of killings on both sides.'

I pressed her to tell me about the Indians she knew in London then. 'There was a Sikh grocery shop owner by the name of Chhatwal, who had come to be called Chat-a-While because his wife was English. Only three to four persons were there. It was all very painful. We then got a radio in our bedsit, for which we paid two and a half pounds a week. But we used to hear in London about Krishna Menon, they said he lives in one room and drinks tea all day. And the Indian students, they used to eat roti with knife and fork. So odd.'

Kailash Puri had spoken in her lecture about discrimination, but she had other memories too. 'We used to get tired of hearing praise. They would say lovely eyes, lovely hair. When we came we were like lords, it was a very different England for us.'

The Puris returned to India in 1950 after Gopal Singh's fellowship ran out. He took up a job at the Forest Research Institute in Dehra Dun and later with the Botanical Survey of India in Pune. It was in Pune that Kailash Puri first began to write, for the newspapers *Preet Larhi* from Amritsar and *Punj Dariya* from Jalandhar. And then she wrote in *Subhagwati*, a women's monthly in Punjabi launched by Gopal Singh.

The couple migrated to Nigeria in 1962 where Gopal Singh launched a botany department at Ibadan University. After that they spent two years in Ghana. Kailash Puri kept up her columns in Punjabi newspapers across those distances. They returned to Britain in 1967. After struggling to find work for a while, Gopal Singh found a job in Liverpool in 1969. He went to work, and Kailash Puri began to write her way into lives through Punjabi newspapers, principally *Des Pardes* and *Punjab Times*.

'So what did you see?' I asked. She looked at me like I'd asked her to read out her 500-page autobiography. The stuff of fifty years of a column and thirty-five novels doesn't get told over a few cups of tea. But she is never short of words, and I followed her with my notes.

'What have I seen? What I have seen of our men here in this society, what shall I tell you?'

'Why, what is it about Indian men?'

'The man, you see, is very insecure, very cowardly, and very jealous. They are so afraid all the time that the woman will easily become friendly with someone. And they are very competitive. If she is beautiful and intelligent, and a good conversationalist, she has had it. The men mellow down a bit with age. But this happens with most men. This is the result of a modern multicultural society. A woman meets all sorts of people, she is free to leave home whenever she likes, she can be housed in a refuge home, no one will know where she is, she will be protected by law. And they all say it is because of Margaret Thatcher.'

'You mean our men are insecure and they blame Margaret Thatcher?'

'Of course, of course. They say that this sali Margaret Thatcher ruined our women, she gave them so much protection. Men are very unhappy about it. They say woman should just do what the man says. They say it is okay also if a woman is beaten up, it is good for her.'

'But there's not a lot of that, is there?'

'You'd be surprised.' She looked at me with some surprise that I didn't know better.

'But so many women are so independent, they are doing so well.'

'You don't know, that can be a big problem. A real big problem. Girls get promotions quickly, man does not get so much. Then he cannot stand a woman's earning power and her status. Then communication fails, meetings end, then marriage ends. Success for a woman is a big problem, a very big problem. If a woman succeeds, man is so jealous, then he cannot stand her beauty, he cannot stand her success.'

'Everyone in India thinks this is such a modern, such a progressive society, people have money, and comforts, they are doing so well ...'

'Let me tell you, this lovely woman, she is married into the family of such wealthy jewellers, and she is beaten up. They lock all the rooms of the house when they leave for their business. She has access only to her own room. She sits there alone and cries, she says to me, tell him to behave or I will leave him.'

'But what do you do when something like this happens?'

'I can only talk to the woman, who has approached me.'

'But why do they keep her locked up?'

'Indians, you know are very, very suspicious people. I know this other family. The man, he used to follow her to the market, he would tell her you are going out to meet boyfriends. One day he beat her up right in the shopping area. It was his own inferiority complex, he tried to cover his shortcomings by beating her.'

'But some of all this happens everywhere, doesn't it?'

'A lot of men who come from India to marry girls here, they beat up their wives a lot, they cannot stand the refinement of the wife. One man, he used to beat her up, and then he would tell her to tell her father that he beats her up. He said he wants her to tell the father, so that the father suffers. He used to tell her she is sleeping with white men. And this other man from India who married a girl here. He told her you are not virgin, you are used to sleeping with so many men, so why not become a prostitute. The things they say, they are crazy.'

'But the men are having affairs.'

'When a boy from here marries a girl there, again and again I see that there is another woman, he never stops seeing this other woman. That is all right, but the women can't do anything like this. You know, I know this woman in Derby. She worked in a factory on machines, she was very good. Then she started her own clothes business with her husband. They employed this Pakistani girl. The man became very friendly with her, and he just stopped talking to his wife. He used to have such intense love for his wife, then they stopped talking. No conversations. Nights he would stay out. But she felt she must go on, because he had a lot of money.'

'And then what happened?'

'I don't know, she stopped staying in touch with me.'

'Do you see this kind of thing a lot?'

'All the time. All the time. I have seen one thing. You know, these leaders of our societies, these presidents and these general secretaries here and there, they are terrible at home, terrible. This man, he is a big leader in a gurdwara. He leaves home at eleven in the night and comes home at four, five in the morning. She (wife) says when I ask him where he goes, he fights with me. The woman is always at fault when it is a man's fault. This girl had been married two years, they never had sex because he would immediately have premature ejaculation. But the girl was blamed that the two had no relations. If the boy is lacking something, the girl is blamed, that is how marriages break.'

'Are extra-marital relations a serious problem?'

'Who is not having them? Another thing I tell you. Our men, they are very fond of white women. This girl who lives in Kent approached me, lovely girl. Her husband has a white girlfriend. And you know what, this Indian couple's daughters and the white girlfriend's daughters, they would go to the same school, same class, and they gave the same man's name as father. This woman, she says to me, how do you think I feel?'

'Everyone says men want affairs with white women, but they don't want to marry them.'

'Sometimes it is a genuine liking also. This man got transferred from London to the Midlands. There he began to have an affair with a white woman, divorced. He then came back to London. He told me he keeps thinking of her. He says he enjoys sex with the wife but can't get the other woman off his mind. So I said to him, the relationship you had with this woman, create that kind of relationship with your wife.'

One after the other these stories rolled off her memory.

'And there was this man, forty-two years old, company director, 40,000 salary, company car, everything. He was living with his wife up north, married for nineteen years. Two boys and one girl, all going to public school. Then he came to London, took house here, family also came. But he had been having an affair with a white woman there. She was divorced and had two children. He made her his secretary, gave her the company car, took her on holidays to Bermuda, St Lopez, he would not be with his family for Christmas and New Year. He told his wife, you marry someone else, I do not love you. And she said he is very English now, and he would say to her, you are very backward. I want a smart woman, I want to enjoy life. He told his children their mother behaves like a middle-aged woman, I cannot enjoy life with her.

Later on, he divorced her and he married the white woman.'

'It can't all be men.'

'Oh no, it isn't. This woman wrote to me, she is having an affair with a white man in her office. And then something happened, he left the office. She was so depressed, she was unwell after that, crying all the time. She would say, how can I get him back to me. This other girl, she got married in India. And she would keep delaying him from coming to UK. Her parents said she should bring him here but she kept making excuses. At last her mother called me. I said let her daughter talk to me. Let her tell me what is on her mind. She said she was in love with her class-fellow since she was seventeen, they had been sleeping together, she wants to marry him. She does not love her husband, she does not want to be with him, she said she wants to be with her boyfriend. So there was no way but divorce, and this is what they did. Then she married her boyfriend.'

'You really don't see a lot of happy families.'

'Happy families? Do you know how much incest there is in our society here?'

'Incest? You mean incest within a single family?'

'No, no, I am not talking about cousins. I'm not talking about men having affairs with their salis. Oh that is so common here, I cannot tell you. I mean father and daughter. Brother and sister. I have seen quite a few such cases.'

'Among Indians here?'

'Oh yes, lot of cases involving father and daughter. Among Punjabis, Gujaratis, and even more among Pakistanis. Very often it is the wife who complains. There have been cases of girls as young as fifteen being raped by the father. I wrote a story based on one real case. She was young and beautiful, and the man was getting no satisfaction from his wife. The daughter, you see, she is young and beautiful. And she is around.'

'And brothers and sisters too?'

'Yes, but cases of father and daughter seem to be more common.'

'Sex seems to be creating a lot of issues, it always does, doesn't it?'

'But good sex between husband and wife should not. Here there are so many families, they do not know what to do because someone is gay or lesbian. There is this boy in a bank, very nice boy, very nice wife. Father is a doctor. But the boy, he would never talk to her after marriage, he would just stay away from her all the time, be with friends, just always move away from her. So the girl said she bought these new panties and went to him wearing them, and he said, you wear a dressing gown because you will catch cold. Can you believe it? He was gay. She came to me, she told me he had never really wanted to marry her. The marriage was forced. Then it ended, and she married someone else.'

'And do you see a lot of lesbians?'

'Not that many. This woman who is lesbian came to me. Her husband brought her. She would refuse to have sex with him. But her parents had forced it. She was in a very bad way. That marriage also ended.'

'You've been writing a lot about problems when people marry outside their communities. Like about Sikh girls going with Pakistani men.' This was the hidden explosive in Sikh society. Whatever the number of cases, the fear this would happen was far greater.

'What can I tell you about this? I have been writing about this for thirty years now, you don't know what this is doing to our society.'

'You see this as a problem that has been going on for thirty years, and you say it still goes on.'

'O, there is now even more of this. Nobody wants to talk about it. Girls, they are being ruined. So many have told me of being raped, of being gang-raped. And there is no future for them. And nobody wants to talk about this.' Other than Kailash Puri.

PAKISTANI THREAT

This wasn't the first time Kailash Puri had written about relations between Sikh girls and Pakistani men, and it might not be the last. But this time she found herself confronting two Khalistanis who came to Pakistanis' defence.

The trouble with being a migrant was that too many unlike your own had also migrated. So when Sikhs from Jalandhar and Hoshiarpur migrated to Britain, so did Muslims from Mirpur and blacks from Jamaica. Migration multiplied the danger that the family daughter would take off with the wrong kind of guy, wrong being of course anyone who was 'other'. Among the wrongs, nothing quite like a Muslim girl going to bed with a Hindu or a Sikh, or a Hindu or Sikh girl with a Pakistani Muslim. Kailash Puri has been writing for years that too many Sikh girls are getting seduced by Pakistani men. This was another round in that writing, except for the Khalistani intervention.

The first article followed some brief editorial comments in the *Punjab Times* published from Birmingham, that Sikh society should be alert to the dangers of such liaisons. Kailash Puri wrote the following piece in the 15 October 2003 issue under the title, 'Why the conspiracies to ruin Sikh women?'

> In the *Punjab Times* Oct. 1, 2003, Rajinder Singh Purewal's editorial 'Sachi Dastaan' is really a true account. This has not just started happening now, this agony, this destruction, this shame on Sikh society. I have been writing about this for thirty-five years. I have written about all this in 'Qaumi Ekta', and I have written about it so many times in my monthly column 'Sejh Uljhanan', which I wrote for twenty years. I've had many letters from India about this. But while all this is going on, our society here has been silent about it. No gurdwara or organisation ever talks about this, the injustice that is being done to Sikhs by Pakistanis. Why are they out to destroy our daughters?
>
> This began at the end of the sixties, when Indian and Pakistani immigrants came here in waves. I wrote about this openly in *Des Pardes* in the early seventies, that our innocent girls are being misled by Pakistanis and ruined. I have met many such girls and asked them, could you not find some boys other than Pakistanis? Why did you let your lives be ruined by these 'lovers'? The replies I got threw me in deep anxiety.

There is one thing I have been losing sleep over. I was so shocked, and so agonised by it. I was very unhappy, because this question is very serious. It made my insides tremble. It was hard to tolerate what I was told. I was told that our boys are so rude, so crude, so lacking in character, so badtameez. I cannot understand how they can tolerate what is going on with the women. They have no shame at all. They do not know how to respect their sisters and daughters. They are so cut off from Sikh religion. They are so stone-hearted and so selfish, they have brought such a fate upon Sikh girls that they are now left good enough only for Pakistanis.

These youths of ours, they tell girls in universities that 'if you break up with me, I will blackmail you and ruin you. I will send your pictures to your husband-to-be and your in-laws, you will be ruined for ever.' My spine trembled to hear of such abuse of love and of innocent girls. Is this what a sardar has become? Where are Sikh principles? Are these not the Sikhs of Guru Gobind Singh? No one will ever forgive them.

In schools and colleges, even where there is no co-education, girls and boys will meet. Meeting leads to friendships, friendship leads to love. Such friendships can also lead to marriage. But 95 per cent friendships are made and also broken. No one seems to have any problems about that. Raat gayi, baat gayi. Then they live their life as they please. But some boys, they will not marry, and they will also not leave the friendship, and then they will see that the girl loses her reputation. What kind of injustice is this, to a friend and to a girl?

To escape all this, girls have left friendship with Hindus and Sikhs. And for Pakistanis, the doors to heaven have opened. For the girls this heaven of a few days then turns into hell. And there is then no way out of that. Poisonous letters about the Khilafa are tempting girls, and the Sikhs have taken no steps about this. All this is being done because Sikhs are doing nothing to stop it. There is no scheme in schools or colleges to prevent this. Pakistanis know what is happening, and they have become encouraged by this indifference from Sikhs.

If even now Sikhs do not take heed, then no one will ever forgive them. Destruction is upon us.

Kailash Puri followed this up with another article in *Des Pardes* a week later.

It has become a misfortune for the Sikh community that Sikh men take so much interest in religious life. They do not just take part, there are strong contests, fights, quarrels, arguments. There have been murders even. This is not just in Britain. In all cities in Europe, there is a flood of the yellow turban, the Babbar Khalsa and all. They give lectures, they talk about their greatness everywhere.

These are not just verbal disputes. People write to newspapers with their arguments, they write speeches that run into full pages. They abuse one another, they call one another thieves, cheats, crooks. All their life they will not get tired of fighting with each other and running one another down.

Every week the newspapers are full of complaints that they make. From Brussels to France, Germany, Spain, Italy, Canada, and in America this is the same situation. For the last forty years these people are busy throwing dirt at one another.

I have just one question. These 'servants' of the Sikh panth have taken out so many processions, they have held meetings, they have made speeches, they have burnt so many flags. This goes on all the time. On the other side, Pakistanis are misleading and cheating young Sikh women. What is going on? Why are these Sikh men not thinking of doing something when Pakistani men are tempting away, destroying, torturing their sisters and daughters? These girls will cry all their lives, and there is no one who will listen to them.

What good are these processions and meetings to the Sikh panth? Or to sisters and daughters in this panth? It is surprising that in the face of this cruelty, these custodians of the Sikh faith watch all this so silently, say nothing, do nothing. I know these so-called leaders whose daughters have left home because they were miserable because of their fathers, and the fathers did not say a word. They put purdah over all this, so that no one comes to know what is going on.

In one live TV debate, one Sikh councillor was also called to speak. His own daughter had disappeared from home. And despite this, he kept saying that our daughters never step out of the house. That we are joint families, we believe in arranged marriages for our daughters. I was talking about the situation these days, how so many women have to suffer, how they are tortured, how parents force them to marry against their will. And this is what the Sikh leader was saying. How could I expose the hypocrisy of a Sikh brother on television?

This face is so false, the facts are something else. Is this the way to build a strong society?

With tan, man and dhan Pakistanis are destroying, humiliating the girls of Sikh society. Their plan is to use all their resources to get Sikh girls to convert to Islam. They hold meetings regularly in universities. And where are our gurdwara leaders, these leaders of the panth? Are they asleep? Do they not know that panth is not just shaken, it is becoming hollow.

There is still time to wake up, to protect our sisters and daughters, to explain to them, to persuade them not to follow just anyone with eyes closed. Think, understand, talk to someone, discuss these things, read Gurbani, please do not destroy yourself, save the panth from collapse. I am shocked, where is the conscience of Sikhs sleeping?

In prayer for the happiness of Punjabis,
KP

Two letters from Khalistanis appeared the following week in *Des Pardes*, the first by Rajpal Singh Dhillon.

She is a well-known writer, but it is not right to take a dig at us over our kesri turbans. Since she does not use the name

Kaur, people may be right to think she is a Hindu. So how can anyone tell whether she is targeting Sikhs or helping them? She may be a good writer, but what she has written is something unfortunate.

We see the problem before us. If Sikh women are going with Pakistanis, being led astray, leaving home, this is very worrying. Only families who have had to endure this pain will understand their problem.

It is not good to have said that she knows the Sikh leader whose daughter ran away. She did not spare the Sikh leader. What is his fault that a daughter was born to them? She must have been properly educated. They have already faced this unfortunate experience, so why did Kailash Puri call his words hypocrisy, and dismiss his words like that? The people she calls the champions of kesri turbans do not target people like this. They just want to fight against Hindutva in India, because they are a minority. Has everyone forgotten the oppressive regime during 1984 in the Delhi riots when the daughters of this community were raped?

She should give some proper suggestions to help these girls, not just criticise us. Suggestions for our children, in universities, what kind of vigil we should keep. How we should influence them with our culture, to help our society. We will help in every way.

The second letter was from Parminder Singh Bal.

She has talked about the issue of defending Sikh women. In this she has made all Pakistanis enemies of Sikhs, by saying that our innocent girls are being misled, and led astray by them.

But not all Muslims are enemies of Sikhs. The teachings of Sheikh Farid and Kabir are in the Guru Granth Sahib. And if Ahmed Shah Abdali destroyed Darbar Sahib, Indira Gandhi did no less with us in 1984. She says our girls are being married to Pakistani Muslims, or have friendship with them. But when girls go with black men, white men or Hindus, it is the same thing. But she is quiet about the rest, why is she writing only against Muslims.

It is not her fault, because in 1947 the Patwar biradari in Pakistan faced a lot of atrocities. The honour, the property of sisters and daughters was looted. This is why Muslims were butchered in East Punjab.

In our village a Muslim baba said that we all believe in the same god, he begged us to let them stay, he said they will all become Sikhs. He said take our daughters. But some of our crooks, like there are among Muslims too, they wanted the Muslims uprooted, and promised to take them to refugee camps safely. But they killed the men on the way and brought the young girls back. They looted all their money and jewellery. There are crooks in every community but no community is all crooked.

It is not just the daughters or boys of our community, we are all living in a multicultural country. According to the law, after age sixteen anyone can have a physical relationship with someone, and marry someone. People do have relationships, these are the times we live in.

If, as you say, our daughters are being forced to live in Pakistan, then tell the police and home office. If you don't want to do that, tell us. We will take some strong steps. This is a matter of law here. If there are excesses being committed against us, we know how to defend ourselves, history is witness to this.

Yes, we Khalsas do burn flags, because the Indian Union is occupying our land illegally. We want the Nishan Sahib everywhere there are Khalsas. 'Raj karega Khalsa'. We will keep demanding this, according to our wisdom and our capacity. You should be happy about this, not unhappy.

The Indian government has been trying to get Sikhs to fight Muslims, so that this has an effect on the people of Punjab and of Kashmir. Forget these weak positions, remember that slogan 'Pagri sambhal jatta, Pagri sambhal jatta, Lut laya maal tera lut laya maal oye'. The wealth of the Khalsa Samaj is declining. You must use the power you have for the independence of the Khalsa.

To this, Puri wrote back:

On Oct. 24 I wrote in *Des Pardes*, and on Nov. 7 Rajpal Singh Dhillon and Parminder Singh Bal's letters were published. No doubt these are both very capable and very wise people, and now they have shared their wisdom with readers. I salute this wisdom.

When a researcher speaks of certain findings in society, they are not talking about every individual in that society. All people are not crooks and killers and thieves, or alcoholics or rapists, they do not all beat their wives. Everyone knows that we are only pointing to the irresponsible and those really at fault.

They say that when a woman loves, she gives tan, man and dhan. She does not hold anything back. Like Heer, or Sita who was ready to sink into the earth but not speak a word against Ram. She kept wishing well for Ram.

Hardly anyone would know the tragedy of women better than me. Whatever I said about Sikh girls is the truth today. The parents of such girls need to be alert. When I said this I did not know that I would run into the likes of Parminder Singh ('mennu nahin si pata mera sar Parminder Singh naal vajjega').

What kind of Sikh culture are you talking about? And what kind of panthic leaders are you? I have been writing for forty years, I have written books in Hindi, Punjabi, Urdu and English, I have attended hundreds of conferences, and won so many international and national awards. My research, my views are honest, pure and revealing. My research has always been, and with the blessing of Guru Maharaj, and of my sahiban, with their guidance, it will always be honest.

Everyone knows that I have devoted my life to studying these issues. I have been able to be a support to thousands, to the daughters, the daughters-in-law of our qaum. And so I will continue to do until my last breath.

LIVES AND LETTERS

I saw what Kailash Puri had meant by 'thousands and thousands' of letters. They sat in boxes, piles, folders in her cupboard. She picked one here, one there, and read them out to me at the kitchen table, taking care to leave the names out. Most letters were in Punjabi, but some from the younger ones in English. I listened like an intruder into anonymous lives.

How much of that agony came from personal relations or the lack of them and how much was a result of migration is hard to tell. Pain doesn't offer distinctions for the benefit of anyone pretending sociological insights, but the letters Kailash picked up to read were all from women. When in trouble in Britain, the women behind the letters were alone; Britain had provided comforts without warmth.

From those thousands, these are just a handful of the ones in English.

I have been reading your column for four years, you are so good at solving people's problems.

In my four years here, I have not seen one day of peace and joy. I have two children, one boy and one girl. For a long time I thought that in our [Indian] society once you are married, the woman should respect her husband. That is the way happiness lies. But when the husband is not a husband, if he does not believe in his wife and gives more importance to what others say, then it is the limit. Everything is wrong outside its limits.

After living with my husband for three years, I gave birth to two children. I used to work on a sewing machine at home. Then we bought a house, but he cheated me and bought it in his sister's name. He would take my whole pay packet from me straightaway because I would be paid at home. He would take it and then beat me up. Forgive me, I must say I did my BA from India. But now I find that I am just like dirt out here. My husband used to beat me up and push me out of the house at night. He used to say that I cannot take a penny from his earnings. I was not allowed to use the phone or write letters.

In the end I realized that divorce would be better than this. The case has been going on for a year and is about to come through. I filed for expenses because if everything is in his sister's name, what will I get? At this time I have no place to live. For a year I have been living my days and nights in agony and fear. My eyes hurt, I cry so much. I have no place to stay, so I have left my children with my husband. Can you help me?

All I get is £24 a week from social security. I do not even have money for a newspaper. Can you help me, guide me? I am from district Ludhiana. Do you know anyone I could marry? Even if he has children, I love children, I like to look after children. I am thirty. If you have better advice, please tell me, so that my life can become a little happier.

I am jat Sikh and I want to marry a jat Sikh. I believe in the Guru Granth Sahib. Please help me ... I have no one to talk to, no one can give me counsel. They just want me out of their houses, I don't know where to go and I have no money to rent a room. Only marriage can save me, life has become hell. I hope you will tell me what to do. I am sending a self-addressed envelope.

Kailash Puri said she wrote back, she couldn't remember what she wrote back to say. Some days later the woman called to say that the landlady had read Kailash's reply. The landlady seemed to have some involvement in the matter, and the woman said the landlady had ordered her never to write again. Kailash never heard from the woman after that.

*

I hope you will not dump my letter, you write back with so much affection to all. Please do not publish my name, or my family will come to know.

I work in a clothes factory. A man gives me a lift to work. He works with me, he is handsome and single. I have become friends with him. But one day, suddenly, he took me home instead. I said, aren't we going to work? He said there is work at home. He carried me into his bedroom. I do not know what happened to me, I could not say no to him, and he began to have sex with me. I said nothing. Later he dropped me home.

Next day I went to work again but on way back I wanted to go to his house and then come home. So we have sex every day. I am married. I am afraid that my husband will come to know or that I will become pregnant. But I can't do without him either. When he touches my body I forget everything else, I forget I am married to someone else. Now I do not know what to do and what not to do. Should I leave work? I have no idea what to do. Tell me what I should do.

*

I am a sixteen-year-old girl, I am finishing my last year at school. The problem is that last year I went on a French exchange. I could not help but notice how good-looking the foreign men were, and was especially attracted to a young guy.

We became good friends which then gradually led to a close friendship. There's no one else I'd rather be with. He is coming to England to visit me, but my family does not know anything about this and would be horrified if they found out.

I need to tell them quickly as they are arranging for me to view some young Asian men with the intention of getting me married once I've turned eighteen. What can I do?

*

I have a problem. I had an affair before I was married and we used to make love. Now I have been married for seven years but I still enjoy sex with other men. I enjoy drinking and the company of men. I must have sex every day. Maybe this habit is like my mother's, who has been having affairs all her life. But please tell me, is it all right to have so much sex? I can't sleep unless I have had sex. I can tell you another thing. My husband also enjoys sex with other women. I consider it just a pleasant pastime. Is this okay?

*

I am not happy with my husband because his family will not leave us alone. We can't do anything without them being there. It wouldn't be too bad if my husband was talking to me. He just sits there watching TV all the time, even when we have just a few minutes together. If I say anything to him or just simply put my arm around him he shouts his head off and goes off to the other room. It makes me very upset and I just want to die. We don't even sleep in the same room now, though we have only been married two years last week.

I had a very difficult school life. Everyone used to tease me because I was the only Asian in the class. Then college was the same. I just wanted to leave everything, just run away from it all. I wanted to get married since I was thirteen years old. I could not wait to see what it was going to be like. Now look where it's got me.

I don't know why I changed so much since the second year at secondary school. I guess it was because at school everyone put me down. I mean, they always laughed at me, the way I talked, the way I dressed, etc. It made me feel very shy and insecure and hate myself. Now I always feel scared and unsafe. I feel people are watching me all the time and talking about me. My husband treating me this way just brings back all those bad memories. But then I think to myself, if only I had the courage to stand up for myself it might have been different. For instance, if they called me 'Paki' I should have answered back instead of just sitting there and burning inside with anger. Even now if someone says anything to me that offends me I don't answer back, I just keep it inside myself and pretend it never happened.

I try to please others even if it means hurting myself. I have told my husband many times how much I miss him not sleeping in our bedroom but he just doesn't seem to care.

*

I'm twenty-one, Indian and unhappy about my life. I don't want the same things as my parents want. I don't agree with arranged marriage and I'm far more independent than my mum. My parents are very stuck in their ways, very traditional. I can't go on like this. It hurts too much. I hate all the arguments and fighting.

There is no way on this earth they would ever let me do the things that are important to me, like studying and making a go of a career in teaching and, more importantly, moving in with my boyfriend of two years. They don't know about him. I love him to bits. He understands me completely.

I want to run away. It's not a decision I have taken lightly. I've actually left twice before. Once when I was eighteen and again when I was nearly twenty. Both times I was brought home against my will. The second time this happened, they threatened me. I was told that if I tried to leave again, I'd be found and killed. I felt awful. Since then I have tried really hard to be the obedient daughter they want but it's simply not me. I don't think I can carry on like this ...

They sent me to India for several weeks because they felt I needed to clear my head and needed a heavy dose of Indian culture. [My boyfriend] and I kept in touch via email. It hurt so much. In my head we were still together. When I came back from India, I wasn't allowed to keep my mobile phone, and I wasn't allowed to use the Internet. I'd also thought a lot. I thought I'd give it one more try. To be the obedient daughter my family wanted. I didn't call or write to him. I decided it would be best if we both got on with our lives. But I still thought about him a lot.

I worked my bum off in the shop, my parents' business, to keep busy. I did a lot of house work too. I tried so much to fit in. I went to all the weddings and birthdays I was invited to ... Slowly, I realized that I'm far too Westernized.

I didn't want all the rules and protocol of Indian society. I really tried but I just don't fit in, I'm not happy. I'm twenty-one and soon they'll be pressuring me to agree to marriage. I know people who are happy to have an arranged marriage. But it's not me. I'm too strong-willed to be 'ruled over' for ever. Right now, I do what I have to, to have an easy life. I avoid arguments and confrontations.

Around six to eight months ago, I logged on to my email and online pager. He is on my buddy list and we got talking. It felt wrong, like I was just looking for trouble. We chatted for a while online. He gave me his work number and told me to call him. I did, maybe around two weeks later. I still tried to keep it platonic. Then he asked me if I'd elope with him. I was blown away. I didn't say yes or no. I told him I'd think about it. I was so shocked. I let the dust settle for a couple of days. I thought and I thought and I thought. He told me he'd support any decision I made and that he loved me.

It became clearer that I could only carry on like this for so long till I implode with all the crap I don't agree with and false cheer I use to keep my family out so they don't see how much I hurt. I also realized just how much I love [my boyfriend]. He's the most beautiful person I know. If you met him you'd say the same. I don't care that he's black. I'm not bothered what people have to say. So I decided that I would elope. But I'm going to do it right. I can't afford for my family to find me. I hope you can see exactly what I'm doing now. I've not made an impulsive decision. I want a life of my own, and I know he will stick by me whatever happens. If that means my studying or working or whatever, he'll be there and I want to be with him forever.

So maybe you can advise me how I could go about changing my national insurance number. I don't want to leave any trail.

*

I hope you are well. I am very confused with my life since

I got engaged. It's really a long story and I'll start from the beginning. I was sixteen last April when me and my dad went to Pakistan along with a few of my aunties. I knew I was going to see this boy. Well this boy is my dad's sister's son and my aunt has been after me since I was twelve. I knew that because we used to get letters of them asking for my rishta.

So last year I went to Pakistan but I didn't like the boy. My parents gave me no choice. My dad said he would lose his respect even though I told him many times that I didn't like the boy. My parents were very selfish with me. I found out that many other people had asked my dad for my rishta but my dad had refused without even asking me.

I don't like the boy they want me to marry. He lives in a village in Pakistan, he's unqualified and can't speak English. He's very shy, and his looks, I think I'd better not write about them. He's not my type at all. All my cousins said to me do it for your dad's sake. And I thought and thought and no one would leave me alone till I said yes. So I had the engagement for my parents' sake.

Now I am back in England, engaged to the same boy I don't like. My parents are happy but they still won't let me go out where I want to or dress how I want. My background is excellent I haven't been out with any lads and I'm a virgin. I wear salwar kameez and I haven't cut my hair even once. I have to wear a dupatta on my head and I can't even talk to a boy even if it's my brother's friend. I'm sick of living like this in England. My parents still think they're in Pakistan and life at this moment is bad for me. I feel like running away or killing myself and solving the problem all together.

I have no one to share my problems with and I am dying from inside. No one has ever complained to my parents that your daughter is bad. Every one thinks I am good which I know I am. I am Muslim and I'm tied up into two cultures. Which way shall I go? The only way I can think is to kill myself so my parents can find out what it was like for me. My parents are applying for my fiancé this week. I hope the law says he should stay there. It's no use telling my parents. They don't care how I feel. All they care about is my fiancé getting here and then he will send money to Pakistan to support his poor family.

Thank you very much for reading my letter, at least you're taking some notice of my problems. I'm sending you an envelope with my work address and I hope you'll reply. I'll die but at least I won't cry.

Kailash said she always wrote back. But at some point the correspondence would drop, and she had no way of knowing what happened next. What stayed in her mind, and in mine as I listened and recorded, were only snapshots from an unhappy album.

❧

QUESTIONS AND QUESTIONS

What's an aunt who doesn't scold? And why shouldn't she, even if it's from the pages of *Des Pardes*? Kailash Puri was showing me some of the letters she'd received in Punjabi, and her replies to them. But this one appeared in English, just as it was written, in Kailash Puri's agony column 'Apna Aap Karey Deedar' (Look Within Yourself).

Question: I am Makhan. I have been in the UK for 7 years. I am 29 years of age. I have a shop with off licence. When I was my qualifications MA History of D.A.V. College Jallandhar. I work 15 hours a day 7 days a week. I have no demands or needs and I still can't get fixed up with a girl. All my family is in UK. Girls have more demands than boys. If they want marry their girl to a discent boy keep girls under control. Girls do not want to work, but want everything. Girls go to clubs and get drunk and get there virginity broken. We need a answer by next week. We want for your answer. We know you can't give a answer to this one. Give answer in Punjabi or English.

The aunt wrote back in Punjabi.

Reply: According to you, you went to D.A.V College. It is surprising that despite an MA you have made so many mistakes in your letter. In Jalandhar, Ludhiana and Amritsar, even children in the fifth grade do not make so many mistakes.

Then you say you have been in business for seven years. In seven years of working in a shop, you have not learnt a few basic things about how to conduct yourself and how to speak. But I can see from your letter what you are. When you say you cannot get fixed up with a girl, you blame girls and their parents. What you have said about 'decent' girls, keeping 'under control' and about virginity is very unfortunate. You say that you have no demands and still you have no relationship. That girls have more desires than boys. That parents do not control their daughters, that girls do not want to work but want everything, that they go to clubs and lose their virginity.

Well, relationships do not just happen on the street. Decent conduct and so many other things are important to girls. Such as the boy's abilities, his personality, his family, all these things are very important. Parents cannot give a girl away without inquiring about all these things. You must ask yourself why you are not fixed up if you have passed MA, you are young and in good business. If your demands are valid, why are the demands of girls not valid?

I agree that parents need to look after girls to make them act in a moral way. But girls too must control themselves, both girls and boys must. Books, TV, the whole atmosphere, and not just the parents, have an influence on girls and boys. Parents always warn girls against sexy kind of clothes, high skirts and dresses and all that. But how much knowledge children pick up from their parents, I cannot say. And, as for working, which world are you living in? Which woman does not work? Some may not go out to work, but they work at home. If women had not worked along with their husbands after everyone came here, the community would not have been so prosperous. The success is more than 50 per cent that of women. Even at age sixty and seventy they work to help their husbands.

Also, every club is not a maikhana. It is not just a place to drink, it is not decadent merely to go to a club. Western people go routinely to clubs. They go to play table tennis, cards, squash, they go for karaoke, they go to have a drink, to socialize. You cannot stop them. So why these rules only for our girls? They should apply equally to men. Men can go to women, they can change their partners, that never becomes a blot on their character. When they marry, they suspect a girl, that she is not a virgin. They do it because they have lived like that. If she does not bleed they get angry, they forget what they have been doing in their own lives. Let me tell these so-called Romeos that the hymen can be broken without sex too. During sports like tennis and badminton. Use of tampax can also remove the hymen, and there may not be much bleeding during the first time. The girl is not at fault. Of course, this should also not become an excuse for girls.

But see, at least I did not throw your letter in the bin.

*

Question: Only a few days ago I came back from hospital. I had to undergo an operation. Since I have come back, I can't stop crying. I can't sleep at night. I am in such a bad state that I cannot speak to anyone. I am not a young woman, and have grown-up children. We are a happy family. But I cannot understand what has happened to me.

In the hospital, a black doctor operated on me. He used to come to see me daily. The moment he came near me, I would come alive. I would blossom like a flower. I would wish he would just keep sitting by my side. When he held my hand I felt I have found god. My whole body, my soul felt alive. Ever since I have come home, I cannot get him off my mind. I want to run back to the hospital, look at him, listen to his voice. God knows what has happened to me, all the time I think only about him. But then I think I have everything at home. My husband and kids are all so good. Please do something for me. I am miserable. How can I go to that lovely black man?

Reply: How suddenly the spark of love appears sometimes. It is a mystery how someone can just appear and set off lightning in another person from head to toe. Like Heer–Ranjha, Soni–Mahiwal, Romeo–Juliet ... these are very beautiful moments. Heer took the name of Ranjha so much that she felt she had become Ranjha. It feels like a meeting of the souls. There is no experience to match it. But now you are back home. And that lovely man is back in his home. He has no idea that a woman is longing for him like this. Remember, time is a great healer, many things resolve themselves with the passage of time. Maintain your daily routine to calm yourself down. Go for pranayam and yoga. That will calm the mind and bring stability. We recommend such remedies for psychologically disturbed patients. Take daily walks, keep yourself busy. Enjoy the company of your husband and children. Slowly, thoughts of this man will become a distant fragrance, just a sweet memory.

*

Question: Sat Sri Akal. I have a big problem, please help me. I have four children. My son aged twenty-three was always a good and obedient boy. He has a good degree and I have had no problems with him. But when I told him about marriage, then his reply shook my soul. He said, 'Mum I am gay. I cannot be happy with any woman.' I am not prepared to believe that my son, who has never gone beyond home and university, could be like this. I talked to a GP too. He said it is in his mind, but there are no defects. If he tries, he can get okay. Can you help this miserable mother? Can my son be cured? I can't talk to anyone about this. Our society, our Sikh religion does not accept this. How did my child end up this way? He now has a white friend, he says he is very happy with that white boy. He talks of leaving home and going to live with him. Please tell me how I can save my son from this wrong path. He has no good future in this.

You must know what I am saying, you are like a doctor. Don't tear up this letter, please. Waiting for your reply this week. I am not giving my address, I am afraid that everyone will come to know. I just want my son to be okay. I pray to god every day, Oh god, show my son the right path. I ask with folded hands, please write to me. I came to know from my son that not only he, a lot of our Sikh children are going down this path.

Signed: An unhappy mother.

Reply: Yes, I can see there is pain, much pain, deep pain. Forget treatment; no hakim, doctor or psychologist has been able to answer some of the questions you have raised. From Japan, Germany, Ludhiana, Lahore, Los Angeles, London, Arab countries, even in all Islamic countries, there have been men practising such ways for thousands of years, quietly. In Britain, such people can now live together legally. Before it came out in the open, people like this were ashamed of what they did, they used to practise their ways in hidden ways. I agree with your doctor that it is coming from his mind, and that there is nothing wrong with him. If he tries to control himself, he can be okay. But while agreeing with the doctor, I find myself disagreeing with him as well, because I have tried to understand and solve this problem among countless Asian boys and girls. There has been some success, but some people become so set in these ways that they cannot change. They don't even want to think about changing.

There is a particular reason for this. Since this community is now accepted by law and society, they do not feel the need to change. The government has lifted any shame from being gay and lesbian and this has multiplied this problem immensely. At least your son has told you this openly, but there are hundreds of Sikh children like him out there.

I feel deeply sympathetic with your unhappiness. As a mother, I can feel your pain from within. How can a mother accept something like this? These kinds of liaisons have brought hell to the home of so many white people as well, because parents naturally want their children to marry and produce grandchildren. Do not make yourself unhappy on this count any more. It will hurt, but there is so much that is unbearable which we have to bear. It is not easy to calm the mind, the heart. So, keep your routine, do your prayers. Love your son so that he keeps his relationship with you, and so you can enjoy the relationship with your son. Just to accept this defeat will be your victory.

*

Question: My sisters and relatives are all fair and lovely but I am dark. I don't like it, I'm ashamed of it. They all look white, and I am ugly and dark. No salwar kameez colour suits me. I have been to many hakims for medicine to make myself fair but all of them are crooks. I have spent so many pounds but still I look the same. I am very sad and unhappy. I think you alone can help me. Please tell me how I can make myself fair. Please write to me.

Reply: What is the measure of beauty? Judges of beauty do not look just at complexion. They look at personality, height, the figure, the features, your ability at conversation, your intelligence, and so many other criteria. The colour of the skin is meaningless. Naomi Campbell is a world-famous model. Just for a few minutes of modelling she gets up to £50,000. People happily give that kind of money.

Modelling apart, this is an illusion in our society that fairness is considered beautiful, even if the features and personality are hopeless. This is just foolishness. Don't compare yourself to anyone. If someone else does, say you do not need to compare yourself to anyone else. Take this out of your mind that white is beautiful.

*

Question: I am a twenty-seven-year-old English Catholic woman. For three and a half years I have been seeing a Sikh man. He loves me very much and I cannot live without him. We are true soulmates. When my parents came to know, they were furious. They pressured me to leave him but this was impossible for me. They are not angry any more, but they don't want it either. My boyfriend's parents do not know about us. He said he would convince them a few weeks before we got married. I kept believing what he said but now it is a different question.

I am five and a half months pregnant and I am worried. He does not try to understand my situation. I cannot give birth to an illegitimate child. I have told him we should marry soon but now he says his parents will never accept us. They will not be able to bear this shock. If I insist, they will disown me. He does not care about my worries, he still meets me to have a good time, but he doesn't want to accept this reality. I am writing to you on the advice of my Indian friends. Please help me.

Reply: What could be the right thing to say? I have been seeing this kind of problem for ages now. What does one do? Only the two people concerned can do something.

Sometimes people come and meet me, they come a few times, and I hear complaints from both sides. I try to help in achieving family unity, love and respect. But the rules and ways of Victorian times are no longer valid in this country. Those values are buried in the past. Forget Victorian values, now you have divorce, you have one-parent families, illegitimate children. These things are happening all the time. Because boys go out with English girls, it is causing difficulties and divorces within Asian society.

The question of your Sikh boyfriend, the pregnancy, your love, his indifference, the fact that he does not have the guts to tell his parents ... these are such complicated questions. On the one hand you have this irresponsible man, who enjoys the woman and then does not care about her future. And this is not just an affair, here you have soulmates. He made you pregnant after all, so the man is equally involved in it. You will have to think about the future very seriously.

One more thing. Every woman must know that a man can always run away from a physical relationship. But if a woman has an illegitimate child, it can destroy her life, her future. An Asian unmarried mother can never marry again; her parents, society, everyone curses her. I know the situation has made you unhappy. But if there is a marriage against the wishes of the family, without family and society on your side, how long will it last? Single women should know that whether a woman has friendship or a physical relationship, the woman gets a bad name. For centuries women have been told this is a mistake, a characterless thing to do. Women with illegitimate children have always been looked down upon. This is true even today.

Young women ask today, why is a woman alone held responsible? Equality exists only on paper. How many men have accepted it? This problem is not just with Indian families. Young English males also behave like this. You must uphold your self-respect, your character, your principles. Your respect is in your hands. A bad mark on your name always sticks. These things can never be washed away. Once you have got a bad name it sticks to you.

*

Question: Dowry demands are ruining Punjabi society here. Boys are becoming too greedy. All their life people work in factories, save money for their daughters' wedding, we do as much as we can, we don't say no. But when they hand a list, I want to die. Nor can we keep daughters at home. In this country the greed is so much that they do not hesitate to ask for details of the girl's bank account. They want thirty tolas of gold, electrical goods, sets and pairs, Scotch whisky and brandy at receptions, these things are so common. We have had to let go three rishtas for our daughter because of these demands. But we are worried that we are not going to find a good family, a family that does not want dowry. Only people like you can save us from this problem. Please save society from this hell.

Reply: For the last thirty years I have been writing about dowry in newspapers here. I have delivered so many lectures on the rising demands for dowry. No one has been able to stop this problem from growing, like divorce cases or alcoholism which are on the rise. People do not address their shortcomings, they do not look critically at themselves. People do not hold any discussions or seminars on this and therefore the problem is never tackled.

Jnanpeeth Award winner Mahasweta Devi has a suggestion for escaping from this evil. She says women have to raise their voice, so why not campaign jointly against dowry? Just laws will not help. We have to put our own houses in order, and that is not happening anywhere. It does not help to condemn all men either. If you compete with men, and abuse them without any basis, the way some lesbians do, it will not help. Women must deal with this issue strongly and sensibly. Neither can live without the other. It does not help to abuse people and criticize them, that can never be the basis of a solution.

Don't forget how feminists began to influence young women during the sixties. They began to live in communes, where charas, ganja and LSD destroyed thousands of youths.

*

Question: I am a divorced woman of twenty-nine, and a mother of three children. I read your 'Apna Aap Karey Deedar' with great interest, and my friends read it too. But you are so grandmotherly in your replies. This will not do in England. Women will have to face up to men. Tit-for-tat is the only way. Think about this. This letter is from six women working in the same office in London.

Reply: Well, yes, I am your grandmother's age, but fortunately that means I can look back half a century and also see the pitfalls in the future. I have a deep connection with society, with its pains and its troubles. I see people in pain, those who cannot talk to anyone or share anything with others. They trust me, they talk to me. Many have found a new life after consulting me and they bless me for it.

I have never found tit-for-tat to be a solution to any problem, and it can never be a solution. Look at the way children fight with parents, and husbands and wives with one another. Good behaviour has gone to hell. People do not act human any more, they throw dirt at one another. They shut their doors on their own, they threaten to leave home and sometimes, before you know it, a married couple are talking divorce.

Our society too will soon begin to face the same insurmountable problems that English society faces. People with views similar to yours also come to me. Their situation is getting worse than that of the English. Is tit-for-tat all that is left to learn? Or do we need to know how to explain things to husbands and to mothers-in-law? This tit-for-tat attitude is going to destroy the traditions and culture of Punjabi society.

Kailash Puri has taken many more such letters and published them in books, naturally leaving out names. Those published letters are only a small fraction of all she received, directly or through the Punjabi newspapers.

~

AUNT AND SEX

It was back in 1970 that the article appeared telling people how they should do it. It was the print equivalent of opening a nudist camp in Southall.

'People were shocked, they were shaken to the roots,' Kailash Puri said. 'They began to think, is there something we don't know? We want everything explained. Because, you see, without knowing people can remain unsatisfied all their lives. People said, you know, birds and bees are fine but we want Kailash Puri.'

'Yes, but were people getting a kick out of it? This was what so many will call dirty stuff coming from a woman.'

'Oh, not at all. There was a stir in community, that someone has the courage and the knowledge, she can teach us. And those people who like to be holier-than-thou, they would keep the newspapers and books under their pillows and read them. Everyone said this is the first time we have been given any knowledge about sex. And we can read this in presence of parents and brothers and sisters, and not feel dirty, not read like thieves.'

'What did you write in that first article?'

A cutting of the article wasn't hard to find. It had appeared in *Des Pardes* on 14 June 1970 under the title 'Eternal Longing'. It read:

Human beings, animal life, plants, are all incomplete in their own ways, each is searching for fulfilment. For fulfilment you need the romantic and the physical touch, material needs are not enough. To find these, you begin to knock at doors.

We need this like we need food and sleep. Just as that

longing is eternal, this longing is equally important for man and woman. Without this fulfilment, life is unbalanced.

You must understand nature. The laws of nature are pukka. This is clear, no one can doubt it. Science and psychology confirm this day after day.

Two thousand years back, during the course of religious learning, Vatsyayana wrote a book in Banaras that became the book of sex not only in India but across Greece, Egypt, Europe and in other civilisations of that time. Vatsyayana gave a deep and true account of sanjog, of love-making.

Many scholars say you need books to learn about things like finance, but sex is natural, you don't need to take a course in sex. But Vatsyayana says no. Proper sex takes two people in a real sense. Too often the need of a man is believed to be more than that of a woman. But women must be understood. Women have their ups and downs with sexual demands and feelings, even seasons can have an effect on them. So women need sex at the time it suits them, in the way that suits them.

People all over the world think that love-making is a very straightforward thing. There is no problem, they say. But I can tell you that many a time this can put people through a lot of problems. This urge, it comes to a man's head like a flood. But if you think it's only a man's obsession, then it is not a true union. Only if this brings the right kind of response do you become two bodies and one flame. And that is a divine feeling.

This joy of merging into one another, of losing yourself in your partner, you can find only when there is sweetness and love for one another running through your veins. Both need to be mutually loving and caring, and then each can give joy to the other. Think of this as divine union, something pure and pious, not something to be stolen in a dirty way.

When two people are together and their physical and psychological needs are met, then they begin to enjoy themselves, then all hurdles in life can be crossed. Life can be a bed of flowers.

People think that it is easy for a man to satisfy himself.

The truth is the opposite. It is never just release, it is equal giving and taking that can satisfy him.

For the sake of this love, this togetherness, this joy, and to achieve this satisfaction, a man has to proceed delicately and work hard. He should engage in foreplay with his wife, and learn to keep some control over himself. Only a man who cares for his wife's pleasure can control himself and wait until she has her orgasm.

The Masters and Johnson survey shows after looking at the case history of thousands that 50 to 75 per cent married people crave satisfaction they never get. East or West, wives and husbands hesitate about these things and they build barriers. They do not share their fantasies and desires, and so distance grows, imbalance grows.

After this article, there was no stopping. Week after week she wrote more and more on sex for more than twenty years. Much of it was about matters sexual. The readers, mostly from the Doaba, the land of two rivers (rather than five) within Punjab where Jalandhar and Hoshiarpur stand between the Ravi and the Beas, had never known anything like this in village, town or district. And she was talking women's sexuality to them. Both *Punjab Times* and *Des Pardes* carried her column, it would have been disastrous for either not to. She was obviously getting circulation going in all sorts of ways.

She invented a new vocabulary for her Punjabi readers. Like 'madan chhatri' (the umbrella of joy) for the clitoris. Or 'hath rassi' for masturbation, 'sumlangi' (gay or lesbian), 'sikhar santok' (orgasm). She wrote, and people wrote in week after week for years. And how could she not have addressed that size question, the one concern that keeps the schoolboy alive in every man. A surprising lot of letters came in along the lines of one that suggested that aubergines get sold out because men are 'gentle'men.

'I have had so many letters on this subject, so many I cannot say. People are smitten with this problem, smitten, I tell you. This bak-bak-bak about size, it used to go on and on. Men, you see, they are very strange people. And another thing I will tell you. They are not very nice. It is not very nice to think like this. After all, what are you thinking, what are you saying?'

She proceeded to set matters straight, with precision, in an article, 'Lingam: Savaalan da Savaal' (Penis: That Ultimate Question).

The average man takes great pride in his height and looks, a good body and shining good health. He does not just want it, he is obsessed by it.

From age four or five, a growing up boy will say to his mother, 'Next birthday I will be as big as daddy.' The thought of growing up and being strong is a source of great joy. This is a particular difference between boys and girls. Every man dreams of body strength and virility. As the body grows and the height grows, the man begins to get a sense of his strength.

This is especially so before his fathers or elder males in the family. But seeing them, he also begins to have doubts, he begins to think something is lacking in him. Forgetting age difference, he thinks only of one thing and starts worrying. 'Why is their thing bigger than mine?'

But you cannot really ask anyone this kind of question. Whenever he gets the opportunity, like when someone is having a bath etc. he will look at the other's thing out of the corner of his eye, and what he sees may throw him into deep anxiety. These fears that get embedded deep in the mind become even more frightening when he can compare himself with friends in school. There is nobody to advise him, nobody who can guide him what the facts are.

The strength of the penis is of tremendous importance to the male. If you think there is a problem here, it can create deep psychological problems. This fear takes over his conscious and unconscious mind. He does not have the courage to share this anxiety with anyone. But within himself he is miserable, he fears that if his penis is small, thin or weak, he may never be able to have sex. And if he does, then he fears he may not be able to get his wife pregnant. This doubt and anxiety can create psychological illness.

This is not just among Indians, the whole world is gripped by fears about sex. This is misleading males all over the world.

Writings in ancient India, in the Arab world and in China talk about this anxiety of a male comparing his penis to others he might see. He thinks the other is longer, thicker and stronger, and he asks why is his own so small and thin. But while comparing himself with others like this, men forget that everyone's height, and body are unique and different, and so also will be other parts of the body.

Also, when a man looks at his own erect penis, then it is natural that from that angle he cannot get a full idea of its size. And so it begins to look small compared to that of others. To remove such doubts from one's mind, it is good to look at the erect penis in a mirror, it gives a better idea of its size. But even so, the height, the looks, the clothes of others always looks better than one's own. This is common in the world.

Perhaps it is because of this that there are many full-size mirrors inside the toilets of many restaurants in London, so that a man can look at himself and his size in the mirror and find some satisfaction. This is very encouraging to many people.

The normal size of a penis is three inches, or slightly more. Maybe about four inches. Normally, three and three-quarters of an inch is the average. But weather conditions and the state of the mind can have an effect on this. In cold weather for example, or after a cold water bath, it shrinks by an inch or maybe more. These things vary from body to body. Nothing unusual here, no need to worry.

Usually a man will look at a tall and strong man, and estimate the size of his penis accordingly. But Dr David Delvin says this is not necessarily so. He examined the size of 300 penises. One man's length in normal conditions was 5.5 inches even though he was only 5ft 7 in. And a big healthy man was only 2.25 inches although he was 5ft 11 inches.

Many people believe that the penises of African people and those from tropical countries are bigger than those of Europeans, even though a European may never have seen the penis of an African. According to the statistics collected by Dr Delvin, it can be said that people of different races are all of different shapes and sizes all over the world, but so far as penis is concerned, the final difference is no greater than 19-21. But because of the diet in hot countries, a better climate, and also some restriction on sexual relationships, sexual relationships in these countries are healthier than those in European countries.

The well-known Masters and Johnson survey examined thousands of African men over a period of two years. Their report says: 'There were no structural differences between their genitalia and those of Europeans. Indeed, by far the largest male organ we saw during that time belonged to an Irish engineer. It may have been of significance that X-rays showed that he had abnormally dilated and tortuous blood vessels in the lower part of his body.

Dr Rolf Bennett, a famous sexologist says that ordinarily a penis may be three or four inches, but when erect its length can increase 100 per cent. But when it is big even under ordinary circumstances, it may extend only 75 per cent and no more. It is clear from this that when erect, the size varies from six to seven inches.

By the blessings of nature, however small and shrunken it may seem ordinarily, when aroused by a partner, it comes into its own. So there is no need to compare or copy. Because under those circumstances, no male ever gets a chance to see a male friend, unless they are homosexuals. So why do men nurse the illusion that someone else's penis is bigger than theirs? This is just suspicion coming from one's own mind. It arises from irresponsible talk, and from the advertisements of quacks that can throw a normal man into a deep well of anxiety.

The other thing that worries men is that women like men who have a big penis. But thanks to nature the length of the vaginal passage is so elastic that it can easily adjust to the size of a man's penis. That is why it is pointless to think that a small penis cannot please a partner. The vaginal passage of a married woman is only three inches before childbirth.

After childbirth, there is not that much difference ...

Writers Phyllis and Eberhard Kronhausen narrate an ancient Chinese story. A Chinese king had relations with a young and beautiful woman. But he had questions about size, and so he said to her, 'Tell me what kind of penis women like. Very big? Medium? Or is it hard erection that gives a woman joy?'

The girl became shy, but how could she turn down the demand of a king? So she told him what she really thinks. She said, 'Size and erection are god's gifts to man, they are outside the body main, you can see it all. But the real question is how much satisfaction a man can give a woman during intercourse. How much does he love her? How much does he look after her? A woman is not particularly concerned whether penis is long or small, thick or thin.'

The story goes that the king then asked, 'What is difference between a hard and a soft penis?' She was a simple girl, but she replied very sensibly: 'A long penis with good circumference but which is weak and soft is inferior to a small and thin penis. But at the same time, a strong and hard one that is pushed roughly is inferior to one that is soft but moved delicately.'

I wish I could say how far the doubts of my brothers from Punjab were laid to rest by this article. But this was one article to which the response could not be measured by the number of letters. I suspect that some male readers felt silently reassured.

There were naturally going to be times when she would be attacked for her writing. As with her article on the 'Madan Chhatri'.

Men have always explored woman's body and given all sorts of names for both the hidden and exposed parts.

Between the two thighs, there is like a jungle of hair. The Mansarovar of life is hidden here. But this also has many parts. You can see here the labia minor, or the inner lips. These are of a length of about 1.5 inches. If you look where the top lips meet, then just there is a hidden and tiny sex organ. This is the Madan Chhatri. Greeks called it the key.

Clitoris is a Greek word; in Greek 'cles' means key.

Sexologists say that this is very important in orgasm. You can't see it because it is hidden under those lips, and there are glands above it, of about a quarter of an inch. The clitoris can be from one-eighth of an inch to half an inch in diameter.

Since ancient times, this has been considered the female equivalent of the penis. In some parts of Africa they practice female circumcision. The upper part is cut off. They say that only after circumcision does a woman become complete. But this is rubbish, she is still a woman. The Madan Chhatri is not obvious like the penis. But it does transform during sex. When it is stimulated, there is a lot of blood flow, and it increases slightly in size. When this happens, it sends a very sharp message to the brain ...

One angry reader did not think this should be the stuff of newspapers. He wrote to the editor:

Your newspaper is good in all respects, it takes up important matters and issues. But I cannot understand why such a sensible person like you is publishing articles like 'Madan Chhatri'. This article is a shame upon the community.

You are a Sikh person, you are sensible. Have you forgotten what you are, to sink into such disgusting articles, which are a shame also on you as the editor? I suggest that you better stop this column straightaway.

Fan mail came in to defend Kailash, but she is good at defending herself. She countered with a letter of her own.

My works are never written only for women. This knowledge is bright like the afternoon sun. It is not one-sided, and never will be. The basis of your complaint is physical and psychological. I will write about this another time. But this subject I have written about is universal. This has always been a very important part of everyone's life. Many people are still marrying very young. Young men start imagining a woman's breasts, her thighs. Men have longed for this kind of beauty, even ignoring the needs of their wives.

A man's private part feels excited just thinking of the beauty of a woman. When a man wakes his wife, he is ready but she is not. The woman is sleeping, unaware of her husband's feelings until he is upon her. And afterwards the man simply turns to the other side and does not care for her. Therefore foreplay is necessary for joy, it is necessary to be on the same wavelength. Otherwise it all becomes one-sided and selfish and just a way to treat heat. There is no togetherness, the breath of love is missing. And then the woman is blamed for everything. This is the custom.

After years of such writing, and after publishing ten books in Punjabi on sex, Kailash Puri said she did stop writing on sex, even though Punjabi editors begged her to continue. 'I did not want my epitaph to say I have written only on this', she said. But when she did write, 'there was not one aspect of sexual relations that I did not write about'. Kailash counts that as an achievement to treasure. 'I wrote to inform people in decent and plain language, never using the kind of four-letter words and cheap language so many Punjabi writers of today use. I wanted to keep the respectability of man–woman relationship that was respected by my husband and myself and by our children.'

She would like readers to see her writing on sex the way Punjabi writer Kartar Singh Duggal saw it: '[Kailash Puri] never wrote about sex with feelings of shame. And she made sure no one would read her with feelings of shame either.'

Illegally Yours

FRESHY

He was Kashmir Singh, he said, which meant that was the one name his mother had not given him. But I had to call him something, and Kashmir seemed best since that's what he was calling himself now.

Over the years he said he'd spent unnoticed by authorities in Britain after arriving unobserved through East Europe and Italy, he was never going to carry with him the name on his school certificate in Punjab. Or the one he got from university, because he said he had done his masters in Punjabi before disregarding the British High Commission in Delhi and moving into Britain without the knowledge of Her Majesty's customs, coast guard, immigration and whatnot.

It's an old convention that when you travel illegally, you never travel as yourself or even looking like yourself. Like his fellow passengers, Kashmir too had cut his hair and shaved off his beard. I 're-Sikhed' him in my mind as we walked down Broadway in Southall in search of tea and pakoras, and decided Kashmir would look much better as the turbaned Sikh. I saw him in Punjab in a maroon turban, and a substantial but controlled beard, and I saw in him the confidence that goes with that kind of look. Not as he was now under a self-effacing crew cut and a furtive look in his light brown and otherwise interesting eyes. But even without that Sikh look, he must be interesting to women, maybe even irresistible. Or, who knows, because of that non-Sikh look, because even Sikh women have definite views on the turban one way or another.

Never mind the Sikhnis, Kashmir would never have made that long a journey from Patiala to London under a turban, nor would many thousands of others whom British ministers and newspapers call 'illegal immigrants', who see themselves more as informal guests making themselves at home. On a trip like that you don't want to stand out in a crowd.

I'd accidentally spotted such guests before, while taking pictures in Southall. A fair population of males ducked every time I aimed my camera at them. Maybe a lot of them just happened to have become camera shy at the same time and place, but I thought it more likely that every head that vanished was one that didn't have its mug on a proper passport.

We stepped into the Chandni Chowk restaurant on Broadway. It was a cold and damp day, and you must never let one of those pass without pakoras if you were born in north India. They arrived quickly on our table, with the usual accompaniment of puddles of yellow oil and cups of tea creased over with the brown film that you had to blow gently aside to access the tea below.

'How did you come to England?' I asked. Naturally, we were speaking in Punjabi. He'd said he would tell me because we'd met through common friends and because he believed I wasn't a 'plainclothesman'.

'I just could not find a job,' he said. 'I used to look for jobs in newspapers. I used to read about agents who can get you to England. I found out an agent, I paid him four lakh rupees.'

'That easy?'

'Yes. The agent took us by air to Moscow. We were a big group, about fourteen or fifteen of us. The agent was there in Moscow to meet us. He had arranged all the passports and visas and everything. But in Moscow he asked us to throw away our passports. We gave them to him.'

From Moscow they had travelled on bus and train for a month, halting for the night at tiny places where everyone slept on the floor. At one stage they had to walk long distances in the snow under the eyes of two white agents.

One day, he said, one of the group fell ill and couldn't walk any more. 'One of the agents shot him. He died. I saw that. One more fell ill on the way. He disappeared. None of us came to know what happened to him.'

I had no means of knowing, of course, whether all this was

true. The route through Moscow and overland through Eastern Europe has been popular for illegal migration for a long time. No one who fell ill on the way could be taken to a hospital, and agents wouldn't want to leave people behind with tales to tell, but he could just as well be inventing these stories. His earnest manner meant nothing, he must have produced plenty of fiction in that manner whenever required.

Eventually, he said, they reached the Austria border. 'I managed to get through. Ten of us got through. It is a matter of luck, how they check and where you can hide. The agents told us this is going to be a big gamble. Two of our fellows got caught, but there was no big checking on that train. We were happy.' The train took them to Milan. He wandered about a bit, lost, at the station, but a man sought him out and took him away.

'The man who met me took me to a room. I saw many of our own people there. They all lived together. It was so good to meet Punjabis there, I could speak to them in Punjabi and I felt good. For two days I had lot of food and whisky with them. Then they told me where to go to work.' He joined the rest packing tomatoes and fruits into little boxes, for E5.50 an hour. 'But we worked more hours than we were paid for,' he said. 'We were all like that. If there was work, we would do it, nobody used to count the hours. My friend told them one day we are not like Italians.' At the end of the day there was 'good whisky, very good whisky'.

He worked like this for a year and a half, Kashmir said. Our second round of pakoras had arrived, his story was moving on, and sex had to come into it. 'There was one place, a packing factory. There were girls there from many countries. I did it with one girl. She was a white girl but she could not speak English at all. We used to do it every day under the stairs in the factory. She did everything. In Punjab, girls never do everything. It was very good. My friends used to tease me. They also tried with others but they were not successful. One friend said to me, get me your girl. I said, up to you. He was not successful. But afterwards he was successful with another girl.'

All the while, Kashmir never stopped thinking of England. That's where he really wanted to get to. England had both money and Punjabis, and he could speak a little English too. He paid

€2500 to an agent to take him to Britain, but the agent took the money and disappeared. Then the man who had arranged their stay in Milan offered to send them to Britain. 'We gave him the money, cash in hand. He told us one day, early in the morning, to get up and be ready and a man will come to take us.'

'So that is how you reached here.'

'No, no.' It was never going to be that easy.

The man took them to Paris where they stayed at a gurdwara. 'They looked after us very nicely. We also did seva there. We did not have to do anything. Agents came to the gurdwara, they said they will take us to England.' They were taken to the port and packed into trolleys but then offloaded because someone tipped them off that trolleys were being checked. They waited for another day, another trolley.

'Next chance came after one week. Again we went in a bus and got into the line for the ferry. Then the agent said it is all right this time, you can go. Then we went into a different trolley inside a lorry. There were two others in the trolley with me. We made a little place inside the crates, and we lay down. Then I said it is now up to god. I started to say prayers.

'After a long time somebody opened the lorry door. We came out. The lorry was inside a godown. We were in England. We took a train to London. There we took another train to Charing Cross. Over there our people came to meet us. From there we went to Paddington, and from there we came to Southall.'

Southall was new home, and it brought new hope. Platefuls of pakoras later, we were walking down Broadway towards the Southall railway station. Kashmir was taking the train to visit friends in Gravesend. It was a Saturday, and there was no work for him. Until he could find busier employers, he had no choice but to rest.

I don't know a more heartening street than Broadway for a strolling Punjabi in England. To a Kensington Indian this is downtown Indian ghetto, and maybe some ethnic indulgence on a rare Saturday. To Kashmir and me this was natural habitat. Ghettos are reassuring places; they are your world that migrated, which makes them a comfortable place to occupy. I was pleased that

Indians had done to the place the English pronounced as 'sathal' (with the 'th' as in 'the') what the British had done by way of 'Cawnpore'. Punjabis now say it like 'south' plus 'hall' sequentially, and logically, and the white Brits have followed suit. Indians are American about these things, and they as good as renamed Southall, keeping just the English spelling.

Broadway consequently is more bazaar than street. A jalebi stall on the pavement, vegetable shops where vegetables do smell like themselves, a watch stall where a toy Daler Mehndi can be wound up to sing *Sadde naal rahoge te aish karoge*, jewellers, chaat shops, music shops competing in range, prices and decibels, and suitcases guaranteed for ten years that would last no more than two, edging away pedestrians on their land. Occasionally the bazaar attracts the always welcome white amid the bustling Indians. The life of a bazaar is so much more the people it gathers than the goods it's set up to move. Broadway is a 'mall road', and everyone knows that mall roads are meant for people to parade themselves before potentially noticing others. A bazaar is a place for familiar strangers; in Southall it's the place to feel at home with people you don't really know but who're off the same boat. It's a reassuring multiplication of the likes of yourself.

It's the place to be seen, to stare and be stared at. Indians love to look at Indians, to size them up, to slot them, to find in them material for opinion-making. Just to be aware of others and to think they might be aware of you can be treat enough. Nothing hurts more than a denial of existence in the eyes of some other; there can be too much of that in the mainstream. Southall is the place to forget you were once displaced.

Kashmir and I had turned right from Broadway on to South Street towards the railway station. Not a street that's as much of a mall road as Broadway, but with life enough by way of travel agents, restaurants, a desi supermarket and the new Himalaya cinema. And it has Suman Marriage Bureau, that oldest hope of turning stranger into spouse.

'Ever thought of marriage?' I asked Kashmir as we walked past.

'Yes, I have someone in Patiala. I plan to call her here.'

'And if you can't?'

'Then I will go back. But I will not leave her.' Kashmir did not connect his love for the Patiala woman with matters under a staircase in what he had called 'Milan area'. He was talking man's love here; those Milan matters were just a natural outpouring of Punjabi hormones.

'But some people marry here just to get legal.'

'I don't want to marry here.'

'You want to marry her.'

'Yes, and you know there are also big problems here. The girls over here, their style is much higher than ours. They think they are much above us. They don't like us. They call us "freshy".'

'But there are girls who will marry if you pay them.'

'Yes, agents told us. The girls want 10,000 pounds. Where to get the money? And it is big risk.'

'What's the risk?'

'There are two boys from Barking. Came here like us. Both of them agreed through agent. They said they will pay half now and half after marriage. Each fellow paid 5000 pounds to the girl. The girls said you go back, we will come and marry you and then we will come back. But the girls never went to Punjab. And they never called the two boys here. They never sent any papers. They lost 5000 pounds. And they lost England also. And after so much difficulty they had come.'

'Were they Indian girls?'

'No, white girls they had met. But Indian girls also do this. They take money, then they don't marry. So now we also don't marry. These girls, they do this just like doing a job. There are so many cases. Now we have become very careful.'

'What about meeting girls. Do you go and have a good time? You know, like in Milan.'

'You know our girls here, they want sixty pounds every time. On Peter Street. Then we are scared of infection also. But still our boys go. But they like more to go to white girls.'

'On Peter Street?'

'Yes, but they come to house also. That way it is good for everyone and cheaper also. In Gravesend also they come to houses. Ninety per cent of our boys like it.'

'But what about just meeting girls?'

'I go into town with my friends in Gravesend. We go to pubs, you know they have mixed pubs here. Our girls also come there. They just call us bastard and freshy. So we say bitch. And all the time there is too much fear of the immigration people.'

'You mean they might send girls to catch you.'

'Yes. Sometimes there are fights. Then you get exposed. Police comes, you get exposed to immigration. Then you also have to spend so much money on these girls. Then also nothing happens.'

'Do people feel really scared of immigration?'

'Yes, it is very dangerous for us. Every time you hear of raids. That means sometimes we cannot find work. And there is so much work out there, and we cannot do it.'

'But how do you find work?'

'There are people who take us. They say to us go here and don't go there.'

'How much money do you make?'

'In construction it is good. The company pays eighty pounds a day. But we get in hand only forty. Agents and company managers take the rest.'

'Did you get some good construction jobs?'

'Yes, in Wembley Stadium. For two months. Then regular fellows came back and I had to go. But still many people have work there. Sad thing is sometimes you do not do any work in the day. And weekend is difficult time, no work. We make about 200 pounds in a week.'

'Doing what?'

'Anything. I work in packaging all the time.'

'What are your expenses?'

'Rent we pay 125 pounds a week. Four of us share the rent. Then there is food and whisky. Then there is train tickets. Then we have to phone to Punjab also.'

'So what do you save?'

'We save about 150 a week.'

'Do you send money home?'

'Yes, to family, they had to pay back loan to agent who I paid in Patiala. I have paid the agent. I have helped family also.'

'Where do you keep the money?'

'Big problem. We have to keep in cash. We are always scared

of thief. So we take turns to be in the house, and nobody looks at other fellow's money. There is always good adjustment between all of us.'

'Do other Indians here help you?'

'These pukkas hate us. They tell us you have come and spoilt our work, we have spoilt the market. They just don't want to know us. White people are good to us, our Indians are more against us. But some are good also.'

'You got help from the gurdwara in Paris. Do you get help from the gurdwara here?'

'No no, they threaten us. They say if you come to us, we will report you to immigration.'

We had walked up the flyover and stepped into Southall station past the welcome sign in Punjabi 'Jee aayaan nu', put up there by a Sikh manager. I asked Kashmir as we sat down on a platform bench if he had a passport. Like I was some immigration officer.

'I have no passport since I gave it to agent in Moscow. Agents in Italy got me a passport there. But it was a risk. I came to England in trolley. Never used the passport I got in Italy. So no identity. Other boys also do not have.'

'Did you think of asking for political asylum?'

'No, they reject. They send us back. After spending so much money no one wants to go back.'

'How many are here in Southall like you?'

'Oh, thousands, there are thousands.'

'And women also?'

'Yes there are Punjabi women, three work with us. But they did not come like us.'

'How did they come?'

'They married pukka fellows here, then those fellows left the girls. They always do that. So girls are just living here and working in the factories. These fellows, they marry girls from Punjab, then they just leave them. Then they cannot get stamp.'

'And the people with you, some have been here a long time?'

'Some are here for eight, nine, ten, twelve years. Now they have become too old to marry anybody, and they are too old to go back. They send money, and they don't even know where it is going.'

'So it is work, work, work.'

'Work and whisky. We really love to drink. Who is there to say anything?'

*

The smell of alcohol and staled curries had by now wandered into the country meadow the wallpaper had tried to bring into this Southall sitting room. That aroma, garnished by presumable breaking of wind and perhaps multiplied sex, can be quite a force, particularly when closed windows feed it back on itself. I was reeling under its power as I waited for my Punjabi brothers from the next room, who like Kashmir had taken the trolley rather than a flight to Britain.

Stains of all kinds had added themselves to the heavy black and brown print of the carpet. The carpet too was of a colour that readily invited stains and suggested long periods of occupation of a place that would never be home. An empty bottle of whisky on the floor was the only thing in the room that looked new; there was probably something new in this respect every day.

An open window could have done something to clear the room's recent history. The air outside had been cold but invigorating; not even Southall streets could keep English air out. But maybe cold, fresh air came at a price; it would bring with it a bill for heating the room again. Or, this may not have been a calculated decision at all; home environment must be about the last thing on the minds of Jas and at least six others he was sharing the house with.

I was waiting for Jas on a sofa made of something synthetic; it was the only movable object in that room other than the bottle. Jas had asked me over, and we were going to talk about illegal immigrants and how they could be made legal. At the moment he was talking to some others in the room at the back.

After some waiting I wandered into the back room; among Punjabi males, no niceties stand in the way of doing some such thing. It was the bedroom in the sense that the room was a bed. The floor was covered by wall-to-wall bedding for seven or eight sleeping males. I asked for tea and we decided to have it right there. Jas was talking to two of his mates; the rest must have found weekend work or wandered out. I asked for tea and suggested we have it right there The two did not look that pleased to see me, and I returned to the room with the bottle.

Jas brought some tea in a bit. Like the Chandni Chowk tea, it was heavy on milk, long on boiling. The tea was a bond, so obviously was our language. But we were uncomfortably aware of the great divide between us. They were illegal, I was pukka. I felt almost guilty that I was legitimately in England. It meant I was occupying a dream they'd risked their lives for. I felt like a passenger in an air-conditioned railway coach looking at someone hanging on outside the locked door.

I'd met Jas through a family I've known for years in Southall. As with Kashmir, I needed a strong introduction to open illegal doors. So, to him too I wasn't some immigration officer in disguise. But Jas had not just been willing to meet me, he sounded keen. He said he wanted me to take a message to the outside world. Jas had told me on the phone in a nutshell what it was: they had so much money to give to the British government, if only it would please accept it.

Jas did almost all the talking. He said he was a computer engineer, and looked it in his wise-looking glasses over a square and sober face. He, even less than Kashmir, had been my idea of an illegal immigrant who sailed through Dover in an unobserved trolley.

'Main thing here is work permit,' Jas said. His life would turn one way or another on those two words. 'Just think what it would mean. You see how much tax the government would get through us. And with that, cheap labour. And whoever is here, even if he came illegally, he would have a status, he would have papers, he can apply for good jobs.'

'And what job would you do?'

'In computers.'

'But are you doing any computer work now?'

'Only a little. Basically, I go where they take me. Mostly farms and factories.'

'Who is "they"?'

'The agents.'

'Are they Indian?'

'Sometimes. But mostly they are white British people.'

'And there are enough people who will give you work?'

'It is human nature. If a company gets cheap labour, then it is human nature they will go for cheap work and save money and make more profit.'

'And you think the government will benefit more than you if you get work permits?'

'Of course. We have benefit here anyway. There is so much freedom. You can eat, drink, do what you like. Nobody asks you, nobody says what you are doing. And this place is much more safe than Punjab. You have full rights, you have full human rights. No problem with police, no racism, people are very kind, people are very fair.'

'But you are illegal, you have no rights here.'

'Even then, there are rights. But, of course, we are illegal, so there are big problems also.'

'Like what?'

'Like, you know, we do not get proper pay. We can work for ten hours and get only thirty pounds. And the agents, they take 50 per cent. Sometimes when it is very hard work they take more than 50 per cent. And this money, all is in black. The government getting nothing. If we have papers, government will know what is going on, they will have benefit of proper economy.'

'But the pukkas will say you are taking away other people's jobs for less money, you are ruining the market.'

'You think anybody will do the jobs we do? Show me one pukka who will do the job I do. Work so hard, never complain. We cannot say anything because we will get exposed. We just want to cooperate with government. Just give us work permits, then we will take care of everything.'

'Forget the government here, work permits will be good for you.'

'Of course, of course. So many of us people who come here are educated. But they are not getting proper work. One man is an electrical engineer. He cannot find work as electrician also. He works on field with me. And look at the others. They should at least allow us to get education. But everybody is afraid they will be exposed, means they cannot go and learn anything. We have technical graduates here, professionals, computer programmers. But they are working in packing, working in building. This kind of exploitation we face. Main thing is work permit. Otherwise you come here like number two, you live here like number two.'

'And where do you work?' I asked one of the other chaps I'd seen in the back room, they had both walked in to join us. He had the proverbial good looks of the truck driver on G.T. Road, a treat for a woman provided he was straight.

'Same thing, everyone works same thing. We go where agents send us. Mostly building.'

'What kind of buildings?'

'New buildings also, repairs of houses also. There are so many contractors.'

'You know anyone here?'

'I have some relatives.'

'In Southall?'

'Basically it is all of us. We have suffered coming here, only we know how we have suffered coming here. Pukkas don't care about us. So we look after one another.'

'And white people?'

'They are very good to us. Only white people are good to us.'

'Are there many Indians here?'

'Oh yes, so many, from India, from Pakistan. But we are not so many also. Most people are white, they come from Albania. We are nothing before them. You should see them. They do what they like. They get more money also.'

'So it's you and Albanians.'

'No, Chinese. There are too many Chinese.'

'Do you compete for jobs?'

'Yes but many pukka Chinese to help them. They get many jobs. You have Thai girls also, they do those jobs, you know.' He smiled the smile of one who knows. 'You have girls from Albania also. The girls do light work, they work in restaurants, they work in kitchens. Only Indian girls, Pakistani girls don't work like us.'

'Do you get along with the Chinese and Albanians?'

'We say hello at work. Then everybody goes back with their own group, we don't know where they go. But there is competition. But less competition in the summer. Then there is so much work.'

'How long have you been here?'

'Three years.'

'How long do you plan to stay?'

He looked surprised, like going back was not an option.

'Now I am here, I will stay. It is not easy to go back.'

'Why not?'

'What work I will do if I go back? And what people will say? They make so much fun of people who fail here, people who go back. Then you can never go out again. No chance after that. You should see those people. They can never do anything. And if you go back quickly, no money to pay agent also. My brother tried three times. Never succeeded, and family has paid so much.'

'But is it worth it here?'

'We are happy also. We only know about today. We don't know about tomorrow.'

'Do you know anyone who has gone back?'

'Yes, some fellows. They have been here for five years, six years, they have family in Punjab, they have gone back. They could not become pukka. So they went back.'

'So it is only single chaps who come here.'

'No, now the older men also come. Because it is easy for them. They get visitor visas. We can never get visitor visas. They come here, they work for two, three, four years, then they make some money and go back.'

'No one has asked you in three years who you are and what you are doing here?'

'No. People are very nice. And our people also, they don't tell.'

'And do you feel settled?'

'You can never have family life here. Agents, they give very false picture. They say good money, good houses, you will find many girls, you will marry, you will stay. But it is not like that. You go to girl here. What can you say to her? She will not look at you.'

Our gup-shup went on for some time till we decided to take it up another day. I hadn't asked the G.T. man his name, even if what he told me would now be his name. He came to see me to the door, and saw I had a car to get into. 'I want to drive a car here,' he said. 'Let us see, one day ...' He was unhappy, and I uncomfortable. Now he would see me drive off in his dream.

To a Degree

So it was time to go back, I said to Ujjwal, now that his degree was nearly done. It was the mean sort of thing an immigration officer might say. It didn't upset him; he was too cool to be upset by anything. 'We need permission to come here, not to go back,' he replied.

It wasn't something he had just thought up; he said it like he must have known well before he came to Britain that he'd never want to go back after it had offered him what it could by way of education. He wasn't here just to return to Gujarat with a British degree of sorts. An MSc in software engineering from the London Metropolitan University couldn't count for much in India, and he had no intention of testing its worth back home.

We were at the Sakoni restaurant on Ealing Road. Ujjwal was quite at home. He ordered his masala chai like he'd been promoting it proudly to others for years. His slight Gujarati build made him a Wembley natural. I looked behind his glasses and saw a winner's resolve in his eyes. He was determined to take from England more than he would give it. So far it was all give, and this bothered him.

'You see the fees we pay, the students from here pay so much less. So we are paying the universities. It is an income to government also. The governments must be paying universities, and because of us they will ask for less from government.'

'But the government allows you to work and earn money while you study. Twenty hours a week, isn't it?'

'Yes, officially twenty hours, but people work more for cash in hand.'

'How much do you earn?'

'The minimum wage is 4.50 pounds an hour, but most people pay less. You see everyone is getting a lot of workers now, students, illegal people. So many people are ready to work for less, for cash-in-hand. There is lot of competition, work is not easy.'

'How do you look for work?'

'I have been going to different areas. First to Wembley, then others. I give my CV, then I call them. I gave twenty CVs, then I got a call from a restaurant. So I work there as waiter on weekends when they need more people.'

'Is that okay money?'

'I get sixty pounds a week. That pays for my living charges here. But I am looking for work in city. I have been there and given my CV to many people. I told them I am ready to work cash-in-hand for less than 4.50 pounds, I can work at night also. I have not got a job in city, but I will get. The British people talk to you very nicely.'

'Any chance you will get work in software? That's your area, isn't it?'

'UK has no market in software. Here there is no development happening. No new companies, no new work. Not like India. Here, now, I can get labour work in offices and places like that. Because native British people, they don't like to do basic labour jobs.'

'So for work you will do just anything.'

'Anything. Tomorrow I am going to Heathrow. Going to hotels. I will ask there. At least someone can give me a rejection letter in writing.'

'Why do you want that?'

'Because with that letter I can get a national insurance number. I can show it to other places. It makes me proper you know, legal to ask for work. It can also help me open a bank account.'

'How will it help you open a bank account?'

'Because it is at least something. The banks here, they all want proof of residence before they open account. But we have no gas bills in our name. If there are twelve of us in this house, how can there be a bill in anybody's name? And banks want two utility bills in your name.'

'So what do you do?'

'We cannot just keep money inside pillows all the time. So we take rejection slips, because the letter comes to our address. That is what some people have done.'

'Did it work for you?'

'No, I haven't got a rejection letter in the post yet.' This was the first time I'd seen anyone look sorry over not getting one. But he had managed a bank account, he said.

'How did you manage that?'

'I got a provisional driving licence.'

'And that became proof of residence?'

'Yes. Because you know I don't have a car. Students don't get cars. And look at how I got it. Had to surrender my passport for one week. Then they give provisional licence and charge thirty pounds for it. It is one type of income for government here. Otherwise I have international driving licence even if I don't have a car. So I don't need provisional driving licence.'

'What were you doing before you got it?'

'Twice I had to go to broker to cash cheques. And I had to pay him commission.'

'It all sounds very difficult here.'

'But I will stay here. Everyone here I tell you, we have come to stay. Level of studies in India, too much. And money is not good in India.'

'But you are on a student visa.'

'Student visa? You know, I went to ask for delivery job in Pizza Hut. And the manager, he came on a student visa fifteen years ago. He is still on a student visa. You know how much money he is making? Because when you selling there, accounts are something else.'

'But don't you want a career in software?'

'Yes, if there is good money in it, why not? I could get a job, then get work permit. If I can get work permit for four years, that's all I want. Then I am here. Pukka.'

'You think you will get work and your work permit one day?'

'Yes, there are agents for that also. They get you work permit even if they don't get you work.'

'What do they charge?'

'Hundred, two hundred a month.'

'But whatever you do, you want to stay here.'

'Yes.'

He looked like he meant it. He had developed a certain ease with things British, and how to work them, and around them, that should have been deeply worrying to an immigration officer if only he could see now just who he had let past his little desk at Heathrow's Terminal 3.

The immigration officer had not counted on the determination that had brought Ujjwal to Britain. Ujjwal said he discovered the London Metropolitan University—one of those polytechnics now renamed universities—through a universities mela the British Council held in Ahmedabad. Ujjwal, who had a BE in computer engineering from Baroda, went to Ahmedabad for the mela because his father, a distributor with an electrical goods agency, had the money and because 'at the end of the day, pound is pound and rupee is rupee'. 'At the end of the day'—Ujjwal would be using London's language currency. Good British Gujaratis say that about three times a day to announce their comfort with cool English.

Ujjwal discovered in Ahmedabad that London Metropolitan University already had an agent in Baroda. There on, it all worked out smoothly; the admission to the MSc course, the visa. His father paid up £2400 as a third of the annual fee upfront, and arranged draft payments for the rest of the year. Foreign exchange was no problem, since India has those fabulous billions of it. Through the thriving agent network, Ujjwal found also an address for Nilesh who was running those thriving home–hostels for Gujarati students arriving in Wembley. And who could improve on £250 a month for a place to stay, with breakfast and dinner and friends from Gujarat thrown in, even if everyone slept a little closer to one another than they might have preferred?

Ujjwal was at home, and already earning enough to pay for himself. So was just about every other Gujarati student I met in Wembley. Whether they would stay on was going to be the great game played out between them and the immigration department.

Nilesh sub-let rooms in the ten or twelve houses he had rented to students from Gujarat. This was their home away from home. To Nilesh, their dreams had brought business; in their future lay his.

I never did find out whether he was Nilesh, Navin or Naved. When I met him he was Nilesh, but others spoke of Navin and

Naved, talking of the same chap. And there was more. 'Actually, he has got another name, Federico Fernando,' said my friend Vineeta who introduced me to him. 'He has that name on a Portuguese passport he got from an agent. Portuguese is EU, you know.' So is London, Wembley too.

Vineeta said she knew because she had seen the passport, and that was because she had rented some of her property to him in which he housed Indian students. She didn't know how Nilesh came to have that passport, she knew only that he arrived somehow, and somehow overstayed. Now that he was here, he'd found better names than Federico bhai.

I met Nilesh briefly a few times, and always only briefly. On a couple of occasions I met him with the woman who said she was his wife, though that was not something he ever said. She told me her name was Chanda, but she was probably Chanda only in the way that Nilesh was Nilesh, because another friend called her Chitra. With the arrivals from India these days, you never know who is who.

Vineeta had been telling me about Nilesh and Chanda as we walked down Ealing Road in Wembley to see them. Vineeta was only one of his landladies, and Nilesh just one of her tenants, because she too owned plenty of property around that area. But Nilesh was her tenant—and wasn't. 'Because he never takes the tenancy in his name,' she said. 'It is always in the name of one of his students. That way he does not have to pay council tax. And if there is a problem with the landlord, he can run away.' Vineeta had been thinking about his business because he was behind on rent. If he were to disappear, she might not even be able to name the man who owed her the money.

'He has 160, 170 students, you know,' she said. 'Can you imagine?' I understood that to mean, did I know how much money he was making? I did not have to wait long. 'You know how much money he is making?' Vineeta asked. She counted swiftly for me; £60 a week per student in some of the houses, £55 in others. In the house we were heading to, he had thirteen students, maybe fifteen, three to a small, very small bedroom. So £800 a week income, about £3500 a month and, of course, no receipts, which meant no taxes. He paid £900 a month rent and the usual bills for heating and electricity. He also spent on loaves of bread and milk for breakfast, and a Gujarati dinner of rice, dal, roti and shaak. But the net added up nicely, and this was just this one house.

'You should see him shop,' Vineeta said. 'He buys damaged oil tins that no one else will buy, he buys the bread from Kwik Save at just fifteen pence for a loaf. And he gets Chanda to cook.' Vineeta figured he makes £2000 a month from this one house. With many more properties with many more students around, Nilesh was in money. The business had to succeed. Where in London could a student find a deal this good? Everything but travel for £250 a month, or 200 for the student who let Nilesh use his name for the renting, and also play 'manager' of the house. His home hostel business was flourishing in Wembley.

We'd turned down Clayton Avenue and were there at last. Chanda, plump and unhappy, welcomed us at the door, and to leftovers from dinner for the students. 'We cook for fifteen people every day,' she said. 'There is always enough for one or two more.' We walked through a dark little corridor to the table by the side of the kitchen. Three students—two chaps and a girl—were talking at the table before our arrival bust up their meeting. The leftover dal and potato shaak waited for us in large pans. There was loads of rice on a kitchen plate.

Chanda heated the food and served generously, and I felt very much at home. I'd had my appetizer already on that walk round the corner from the VB Indian Foods Store. If you live in Wembley, VB is the tricolour of the tummy, though the dals and masalas at the new Fudco store have their loyalists. A cooked version of fragrances from VB was all I now needed.

I'd asked Vineeta just short of the door why she wasn't in this business herself. She didn't have time to answer then, but she couldn't wait to say why. She whispered to me a lot louder than she knew as we sat down at the table, 'He has the contacts in Gujarat. He has the agents, he is also an agent. The students come straight to him. They have his house number and telephone number. From the airport they come straight. It is good for students, cheap. And they have so many friends from first day they come here.'

Nilesh appeared briefly. He was slim, not very tall, and of

course he had a moustache, the subcontinental guide to the serious male. He had an abrupt way of talking and moving; at least he was always abrupt when I met him, and this time was no different. He quickly fished out his mobile phone, and with him you knew it would be one of the latest, with features that would have amazed me had he cared to show them. Someone wanted him on the phone, he said, and he was gone.

Chanda was not sorry to see him go. She'd done all the cooking and looked tired and hard done by. This was no way to spend evening after evening.

He was hardly gone before she began to complain. Not about work; it was Nilesh. She was convinced he was having an affair with a girl student in one of the other houses. 'Actually he is having an affair with two girls,' she said. 'But I'm not sure. One, I know, 100 per cent. Other one, I am 99 per cent sure.' So it is with suspicion in such matters; it parks very close to that figure, 99. The number gives it body, and the one per cent covers theoretical duty to think otherwise, and maybe, hope.

'I am going to leave him,' she said. 'He cannot do anything to me. Because he knows I can fix him.' There had been a quarrel over some money transfers, and there were things Chanda said she knew. The quarrels had led someone to invite Nilesh to the car park at the Sainsbury's store in Wembley and assault him. Nilesh had been left heavily, and very visibly, bruised.

Chanda was in the confessional mode appropriate for friends on a late evening after rice and dal. She could fix him because she was on pukka ground, she said. 'I have full rights to stay here now. I have got political asylum.' That clearly was not true, because I had gathered from Home Office figures that no one from India was getting political asylum. Who knows whether she could fix Nilesh, because perhaps he knew a thing or two about her as well.

Chanda said she had arrived from India at the time of those attacks on Christians in Gujarat. Her story was that she had declared at Heathrow that she was a Christian facing political persecution, and had asked for political asylum. I never heard her say a word about what persecution she had faced in Gujarat. If she did apply for asylum, then presumably her application went into processing stage. Whether her application had been turned down, or whether she did not apply at all, here she was, long past a visitor's stay. It's called disappearing into the system, or out of it.

But disappeared migrants do appear somewhere, and no Gujarati who disappears from the immigration system can disappear from Wembley for long. I had no idea how Nilesh and Chanda turned up in Wembley, only that they were now here. Together, or in such togetherness as they had found suitable, they were running the business of importing students and of maintaining imported students.

I couldn't begin to guess how many of the students appearing at their doors would later disappear. In Wembley, disappearing is good business.

~

KATHERINE AND CAB

Across from the bus garage on Ealing Road in Wembley, Katherine and King's College of London stood to make dreams of England come true. And for the chap I was talking to by the reception, who told me his name was Inder, it would make true his dream of driving a taxi in London.

Inder from Ludhiana could of course as easily have been Sarabjit from Jalandhar. Whoever he was, he was a student now with an advantage. He had come to Britain to the Thames Valley University for a £6800 course. Since he moved to Katherine and King's, he was paying only a little over £1000. With that difference he was 'getting a car to start a mini-cab', he was saying. Driving around London, even if that meant driving someone around London for money, sounded a lot better than sitting in a classroom here and then returning to Ludhiana.

In the hearing of the white lady at the reception, Inder gave me a lesson on his roundabout route to acquiring the taxi. 'You have to join a reputed university first for visa. You have to be there six months, because you have to pay half the fees first. Then you can go to a cheaper course.' That second move reduced costs, provided capital and gave him time through the day to start making money. 'But I do studies also,' he said, after a quick look at the young white receptionist. She was listening with open attention, and she represented establishment. It was fine for Inder to think and do, but not to talk. We talked a little further in Punjabi, and he was quickly gone.

That left me with the receptionist just within the shop-like shutters of the college. The place was making such an effort to look academic, white facade inwards. Just above the entrance by the side of the name 'Katherine and King's' sat a coat of arms in the shape of a shield, in the style of English knights advertising their lineage while protecting themselves from an unfriendly knight coming the wrong way. This was a coat of arms for academic knights. The upper half was divided in two sections, with three keys painted in the right half and three flower-like motifs in the left. The middle section tapering below featured a flat black graduation hat, a blank open book, and 'K&K' imprinted in knight font. On a Gujarati street across a bus garage, with a computer repair shop on one side and a fried-chicken outlet on the other, here was Britain being presented at its Englandest.

'Who owns the college?' I asked the receptionist.

'A Chinese lady,' she said. Predictably, the receptionist was East European.

'Is she Katherine?'

'Yes.'

'And King's?'

'It is Katherine King.'

I picked up a copy of the brochure from the reception desk. 'It's very simple,' she said in her East European English, before I had a chance to look at it. 'You get the application form on our website, and you fax it to us and send a payment of 150 pounds. We will send you a letter of acceptance on that basis. You take that to the British embassy in your country and you get the visa.'

'And if you don't?'

'We will return 50 pounds to you.' Not bad income at 100-a-head if enough people do no more than try.

I sat down to study the brochure. The first page asked the

question: 'Why to choose Katherine and King's College of London?'
Answer: 'An edge is given to you at Katherine and King's College
of London, which makes you stand out among the crowd.'

Admission itself would be no struggle. 'An acceptance letter
will be issued upon receipt of the application package,' the brochure
said. Some minimal education would be required, and this would
be checked on arrival.

The brochure promised free collection from the airport to the
college, or to student accommodation. And help with
accommodation. Cards on an accommodation board in the reception
area offered a choice of places at the usual £50–60 a week. And
once it has all proved suitably tempting: 'It is your wise choice to
choose Katherine and King's College of London as a significant
stop in your life journey. Wish you enjoy your stay here at
Katherine and King's College of London!'

The website had more. Students can work twenty hours a week,
and forty hours during holidays, it announced. 'In line with the
government initiatives to make studying in the UK more attractive,
there is a new policy on working visas after the completion of the
student's study. All students will be eligible to gain a further
twelve months working visa based on the employment being in
some way related to the preceding area of study. For further
information, please contact student service advisor.' Some courses
were as cheap as £1400 a year, which would in a way make the
fee for staying in Britain only a little more than 100 a month.
Once there, you could earn as you wanted. Who would clock
Inder's hours in his cab at twenty a week and forty during holidays?

If still in doubt, listen to Katherine King herself, principal, with
the qualification 'ACIS'. The college website quotes her as saying:
'Where there is a will there is a way.' Others, presumably college
academics of a sort, also speak up. Julie Samwise says: 'I ask
God, "How much time do I have left?" and God replies, "Enough
to make a difference".' Harry Lee says, 'The only real failure in
life is to stop trying.'

*

Course-hopping had given Ushani two years in London by now,

and still she had no husband. She looked betrayed by the absence of a suitable man. 'Why don't you suggest somebody, yaar?' she said to me as we sat down to lunch at Jashan, a restaurant on Ealing Road, together with our Gujarati friend Chanda.

Ushani had given herself time through steadily lowering costs. She got herself a transfer from the £7000 a year South Bank College to an £800 a year place in Ilford outside east London, with visa. 'And you know what? I never even have to go there.'

It surprised me that Ushani had not received a productive proposal for all of her two years here. She looked nice in a holdable sort of way, and she had the tough elegance of a Delhi girl—what more should a man want? Two blank years had not diminished her determination. Impatience rode piggyback on that determination, she wanted the stamp of permanence on her passport, or 'indefinite leave', as the Home Office so fuzzily calls its equivalent of the American green card. If she'd come here to stay and not study, then stay she would and study she would not. If she needed more time in Britain, she'd find it, and invite opportunity to do the rest. Living in Britain at present seemed only a state of non-return, but that was better than returning on a one-way ticket.

A Pakistani chap who was in the business of importing students and turning them into settlers had explained the game simply. Come as a student and take course after course. And after the courses, what? 'You think my students are such fools that in four years, five years, no one will like them?'

I caught Ushani staring at a couple of females who had taken the next table. They were obviously 'from here'; their made-in-young-Britain accents were unmistakable. So too was the look of envy in Ushani's eyes. They betrayed a dream that she would one day be pukka like them, that her charm would not be let down for ever by an improper visa. They in turn would have placed Ushani as an off-the-boat Indian. Not through her long brown slit skirt, almost a split skirt going by the daring of it, nor her beige sleeveless shirt, not her lovely oval face, it was her Delhi English that would bring the boat to mind. Delhi spoke in her voice. It's much easier to leave Delhi than have Delhi leave you, and not just by way of accent.

Our Guju-veggie lunch later, Ushani and Chanda took the bus

to a home for the elderly where some more caring at £6.90 an hour would buy more time. I walked the other way towards the London College of Business and Accountancy that Ushani had said she was considering for the next year if she still hadn't found anyone by then. She was praying she wouldn't have to spend another year substituting college admissions for a husband.

I took a short cut through the parking lot behind the Wembley High Road and then the stairs up to the road, and regretted it, as I always do. The stairs were lined with paan stains, not a pretty sight either here or at those right angles on stairs in a Delhi government building. And as usual there was fresh evidence on the sides of the stairs of kidney-processed beer from the previous evening. I tried to make the stairs in one breath, and failed again.

I found the college Ushani had spoken of just by Wembley Central Station, round the corner from Somali-owned internet cafes, next to a vegetable shop. Up two flights of stairs, a door in the corridor was marked LCBA, the London College of Business and Accountancy. The corridor was packed with Somalis visiting a centre there. This was more Mogadishu than London. I couldn't see Ushani ever attending college here, but then she only went to colleges she didn't have to go to.

I stepped in. A large man with a substantial beard rose from the computer and bore down on me at the reception. 'I'm Mohammed,' he said. I said I'd come to ask about admission. He gave me a brochure and pointed to a chair. Like the Katherine and King's brochure, this one was for the dream of some distant student, and wasted on me because I'd already seen the college. The college was one thing, its brochure another.

The cover showed a happy white boy carrying a happy white girl on his back. The Tower Bridge behind stood witness to where they are. Like K&K, this too had a coat of arms printed on the brochure, split into three sections. This one featured a graduation hat, a blank book with feather and ink pot, and what looked like a folder with the profile of a man and woman on it. Below these ran a wavy ribbon, the sort that things in Latin get written on. The words in English seemed a let down for the location: 'Excels in Education and Training'.

The cheapest course on an accompanying 'price list' was a

year's diploma in business administration at £2000. 'Is that negotiable?' I asked Mohammed before leaving. He had returned to his desk after handing me the brochure. 'The fee is not negotiable,' Mohammed replied, looking up. 'But it can be negotiated.' That offer stayed with me long after I left.

Several weeks later I mentioned to Ushani that I'd visited her dream college. I mentioned the fee. 'You never go by their price list,' she said. 'If I had to go there, I'd bring it down.' But she would not need to go to this college, she said. Or to any college. 'I'm getting married. I've met this really, really nice guy, yaar.'

Chanda later took some of the romance out of it. 'You know he is BSc honours in information technology. Born and brought up here. Parents are from Delhi but they came here forty years back. Whole family is pukka here.' Wouldn't Ushani like to go back to Jashan and have the same two girls at the next table again? Now she would have a passport like theirs. And unlike them, perhaps, a husband as well.

*

Britain used to have its universities, and separately it had its polytechnics until one day Margaret Thatcher decided to rename the polytechnics as universities. They came to be called the 'new universities'. So you have now the Thames Valley University, and the Hertfordshire University just north of London that I'd driven up to. A very university-like former polytechnic, and after Katherine and King's and LCBA, it looked like a proper place for study.

A lady at the reception in the students' office in the Mercer building asked me to wait for 'a lady in glasses with quite curly hair, if you see what I mean'. I saw what she meant when Alison Proctor finally turned up, but that was after a long wait. I'd asked at the reception to speak to someone about students from India and what they were paying to study here. It was a touchy subject, millions of pounds in income for the university depended on it. Some discussions had clearly taken place within on what to say to me, and mostly, I thought, what not to say.

I saw new money all around me as I waited in the Mercer building, one of three glassy new structures that had come up by the side of the old one. A tinted glass facade was held up by bright yellow frames, very new Britain. And this wasn't most of the new. The de Havilland centre, proclaimed proudly as a state-of-the-art learning centre, had just been built at a cost of £120 million.

Our meeting turned out to be a controlled quarrel. The British are particularly good at dressing quarrels politely. In time you learn to translate the verbal into the actual.

Alison had come accompanied by a young suited chap, a Mr Fletcher. They walked in like they were ready to leave. They looked more and more ready to go as they asked me what I wanted to ask. I raised a few simple questions. How many students did the university have? And how many foreigners? And what fees did the local British students pay, and what did foreigners pay? My questions, Proctor said, would be answered by the marketing manager, a Mr Donald McCloud, and he was not around that day. But they would get back to me.

Did I need a marketing manager to tell me how many students there are at the university, I asked.

'We have 22,500 students,' Proctor said, allowing the minimal to pass through. 'Of that about 3000 are international students. They come from eighty countries, but the number of students from China and India is significant. But we also have a lot of students from Pakistan, Sri Lanka and Bangladesh. And many British Asian students. We are very proud of our diversity.'

And the fee for overseas students? 'About 7900 pounds for a standard undergraduate international student.'

'What about a British student?'

'You say you have been a student here,' Proctor said, sharply. 'You should know.' She looked more than a little accusing, and looked more and more like she couldn't wait to see me leave. I replied that fees vary, and it was a while since I was a student in Britain.

'It's about 1100 pounds a year,' she said. 'But, don't forget, parents here also pay a lot of taxes.'

In the same classroom, a British student would be paying £1100 and an Indian student £7900. That was the simple explanation why the British had suddenly started to issue so many student visas. It was the reason Ujjwal was here, and why 'Nilesh' was in business. International students were being called in to pay to educate the British, and they were paying to build up the new universities. They had made more universities possible, they were giving the new universities a new look because they were paying for buildings and facilities that would remain in Britain long after they supposedly left. With so much foreign money, Brit students could be tempted to universities paying minimal fees. Useful, when not enough Brits want to go to university.

Taking the difference in fee at face value, Ujjwal's parents were paying also for the education of six British students they had never met and never would. On a rough calculation, the 3000 international students were bringing in 23 million pounds a year, about as much as the remaining 19,500 British students. Besides, the university was getting grants from the government, the taxpayer eventually. As Proctor put it, Brits were paying their fees that way too, and so their fee was not as low as it looked.

It was hardly surprising that Proctor and Fletcher did not want me airing these matters in India. If even a few potentially arriving Indians were to think they were being suckered, and choose some other place, those absences could add to significant losses.

'Do students find work here?' I asked. To my surprise, Ms Proctor began to offer a little more information.

'There is enough work in the area. But it is at the lower end, labour work in shops and warehouses and industrial areas. There is a lot of disappointment among students, because they come from well-respected families there, and they expect to pick up similar levels of jobs here. But we don't encourage students to come with that in mind, we want them to have their finances sorted out before they come. There are enough unscrupulous agents out there who say, don't worry, you will get a job there. But the cost of living here is very high, and working here can only give you those extras.'

Proctor was delivering a warning through me. 'It is very important that people who come this distance know what to expect. They should not come with inflated expectations, and we are very concerned that they come for the right reasons.'

Fletcher must have feared this would develop into a proper conversation. 'Thank you,' he said, and got up. There our meeting ended.

Hertfordshire University, I saw later, had appointed four agents, in Amritsar, Ahmedabad, Bangalore and Chennai. But this was not the only new university out to pull Indian pounds to Britain.

Middlesex University had set up a South Asia regional office in Safdarjang Enclave in Delhi that offered admission and accommodation. London Metropolitan University boasted 4000 international students, a great many of them from India. This university too was now suddenly a richer place. It had set up overseas offices in Beijing, Shenzhen, Delhi, Chennai, Dhaka and Lahore. And its old unlovely blocks had been given a dramatic new look by way of a centre designed by the famous architect Daniel Libeskind, the one who designed the memorial to the World Trade Center in New York, the Jewish Museum in Berlin and the Imperial War Museum in Manchester.

The coloured stainless steel panels that present a shining and ever-changing surface made this 'little jewel', as Libeskind called it, quite a landmark in a drab part of London. At the least they could have put up a plaque to thank Indian and Chinese students who paid so dearly to change the face of this university, as of so many others.

If, after all this, the British still cannot get themselves a decent education, no one can say many thousands of Indian parents did not do their bit to help.

LEGALLY MARRIED

When Manjula said she had found true love at last, no one took any notice; she found true love about three times a week. 'His name is Shakti,' she said. 'You must meet him, my other friends have all met him.' I said sure I would, as I had to the many other true loves of her life I never got to meet.

But it would be rude to appear to take her lightly. She didn't exactly make male heads turn, and she'd never had a boyfriend when some of her friends had got so far as to talk of ex-boyfriends. We would indulge the new loves of her life a little patronizingly. Now Shakti had come along.

But Shakti was for real. She met him at the Hare Krishna Mandir in Leicester, and everyone saw that they met again and again. In time she came to worship Shakti more than Krishna. She knew he was an illegal immigrant, but love can blossom independent of landing papers, or the lack of them.

Manjula's mum Preeti was getting more worried by the day over this true love at last. She asked me home in Leicester one evening to talk to Manjula and to Shakti. They turned up eventually. Shakti was a big and shifty guy with very short hair, and if he too had found true love, it didn't show. He did not look pleased with the summons. He was there because avoidance was not an option.

'How did you come to UK?' I asked.

'I came on a fake passport. I threw it away after I came here.' He obviously hated having to talk of the illegality of his arrival.

'Who gave you the fake passport?'

'There was an agent in Jaipur. I paid him eight lakh rupees. Plus the air fare.'

'You from Rajasthan?'

'Yes.' That much at least seemed true, because he spoke that kind of Hindi. He did not speak English at all.

'The passport must have been a good fake. Why not just use it, why did you throw it?'

'No, it is too risky. And anyway its date was running out.'

'So how do you plan to stay here now?'

'I will just stay. Maybe if I marry Manjula then I can stay.'

'You want to marry Manjula just to stay here?'

'No, but that way I can stay.'

Manjula heard, of course, but didn't look like she minded at all. After what I heard, I too wanted that meeting to end fast. I couldn't wait for him to leave before turning to Manjula. He had said what we'd been saying to her again and again, that he wanted to marry her just to settle here.

'I don't care,' she replied. 'I love him, and I'm going to marry him.' There is never anything left to say after a 'but I love . . .'

Shakti must have been very sure of that to have said what he did, the way he did.

Preeti's friend Raksha dropped in later that day; around Belgrave Road people always drop in without calling. Phoning first is too English.

Raksha was determined to save Manjula from herself. We all were, but there was nothing we could do. The only way to stop the marriage was to have him deported. She had called Crimestoppers, a substitute for calling the police in non-urgent matters. She gave them Shakti's name, his address, and told them he was an illegal immigrant, that he had arrived on a fake passport, and had said he did. The man on the phone took the information, thanked Raksha, and that was it. She thought he hadn't sounded interested. She was right. Weeks, and then months, passed by. Shakti lived freely in Leicester, and continued to work in a woollens factory along with many other illegal arrivals like him, and continued to see Manjula.

Manjula was now in a hurry to marry Shakti, and he was in a hurry to find, meet and marry. She told us he had asked her to introduce him to her friends. She did, and said he proposed to two of them. Then, he proposed to her younger sister. None of the others wanted to know him. But after all this, Manjula said she loved him regardless. She spoke of him in delirious excitement that must have felt like love but sounded all wrong.

Finally Preeti gave in, Raksha gave up, and before I knew it I was shopping for an engagement gift for the couple. I picked up some vouchers from Marks & Spencer, as dull and functional as a gift can get. I chose a card that said 'Tying the Knot' but I stopped even as I started to write something in the card. Dear Manjula and ... who? He had said his name was Shakti. But none of us knew his real name, unless he had used his real name on a false passport. Maybe he was Shakti, and had used another name for the passport. But Shakti is all I knew, and that's what I wrote.

I was back in Leicester the day of the engagement. Manjula glowed in the red sari she had managed to wrap around herself, a mother's caring quite obviously missing from the wearing of it. 'This is the happiest day of my life,' she said as I sat down on a floor cushion in the sitting room. Nobody else in the room said anything. There were just about a dozen of us. I looked around and thought of everyone not there; most of the close family and friends weren't. Preeti had not thought it the sort of engagement you make much of.

Preeti's boyfriend, very much a white Midlander, sat next to me, very all-seeing but saying nothing. I nodded to Raksha, who had tried so determinedly to stop the marriage. The next-door lady sat next to her on the sofa. A few others I didn't know had dropped in. Raksha's husband, a white Hare Krishna devotee, came a little later in his usual white dhoti and kurta. 'Hari bol,' he said. 'Hari bols' floated back to him.

Shakti walked in alone, camera in hand. He wore dark trousers and a light grey cotton jacket that sat so badly on him it was hard to believe it was his own. Getting into that jacket seemed the only special effort he made that day. He sat down on the sofa in a corner by the little bay window. He was with us and he wasn't. We all looked at him, he looked at no one.

It was about twenty minutes past the auspicious 3 p.m. that Manjula had found for this first formal connection to Shakti. She came down the stairs, holding two tiny red boxes in her hand—the engagement rings. She called Shakti up to her by the door and handed him one of the boxes. He took out the ring meant for her, and for the first time looked around. Manjula was waiting for him to put it on her finger, but he didn't know which finger it should go on.

Preeti stood up from the floor, held up her daughter's hand and presented the ring finger. He slid the ring on to her finger like he was placing it on some little stand so it doesn't fall off. Then it was Manjula's turn. He held out the forefinger of his right hand. Manjula struggled, but the ring did not get far. Preeti corrected the finger, but the ring wouldn't get on to his ring finger either, it was way too small.

'Didn't you check before buying your ring?' The question from the lady who had dropped in from next door seemed to burst the bubble of strained silence over what we were seeing. 'Take it back to them, they will enlarge it for you.'

Manjula didn't care about the misfit ring—she was a heap of ecstatic giggles. She reached out and gave Shakti a hug. She could have been hugging a tree for all the response she got. His turn now, the neighbour called out. Shakti made a move like he wanted to hug without touching, and since that was not possible he did something approaching a hug, and rapidly recoiled into his space. All of us came up to give each of the pair some gajar ka halwa. We took turns to take photographs for Shakti with his camera. The photography was the only thing he was taking seriously.

Lunch followed in the back room. Vegetarian, without onion and garlic, in the proper Hare Krishna way. Shakti sat by himself on a chair nearest the door. He finished fast and left first. Raksha had some quiet words to say later: 'Best wishes for indefinite leave to remain.' It was Shakti's big day: he had just got engaged to a British passport.

The engagement lasted. Manjula had time to 'see through' Shakti as everyone wanted her to. But she looked supremely happy. Shakti was not seen much, and it was Manjula who was now making arrangements for marriage. It was agreed that they should marry in Rajasthan. Months later, they did.

Manjula returned a bride, and Shakti returned later, this time on his own passport, to live in Britain legally. They would have to stay married at least a year for Shakti to stay on even if they divorced after that. How long they would remain married no one could say, but that you cannot even for love that blossoms legally.

*

Dinesh was going to 'expose' Shah Rukh Khan. Not only was he much better-looking than the Bollywood superstar, but once his new film was released the world would also see how much better an actor he was.

He looked film-set ready in the kitchen of my friend Sharda, whose daughter Anita he had proposed to. He was in an off-white silk kurta-pyjama, with a blue bandhni dupatta around his waist. It was more the dress for a village dance at a Bollywood studio than for a London kitchen. Dinesh did not think himself good-looking without reason. He was short, had clean, boyish looks that never fail to charm, and a winning sort of smile when he looked at mother and daughter. He did not smile at me, or even look at me.

I'd asked him what he did for a living soon after joining them at the table. That's when he said, looking pointedly at mother and daughter, that he would expose Shah Rukh Khan. He was the 'counter-hero' of a film being produced in London, he said. It would be released soon, and this film would show up Shah Rukh Khan for what he is not.

'I am going to create a new concept in Hindi cinema,' he said. 'You wait and see.' He would not only act, he would produce films and he would write the script, because the script in Bollywood cinema is rubbish.

'You mean you'll be hero, producer and scriptwriter?' I asked.

'Oh yes, why not.'

'But are you planning to do this in Bombay or here?'

'No, I plan to make the films here.'

'In Hindi?'

'Yes, in Hindi.'

'But won't that be expensive? I mean, it would take a million pounds, or maybe some big fraction of it.'

'That is not a problem, there are people here ready to finance my films.'

'Like who, Indian businessmen here?'

'Yes.'

'You know, I know most of them but I don't see any of them putting a few hundred thousand pounds into a film here.'

'That's because they haven't seen my ideas yet.'

It was beginning to seem like an act, and not a very good one. The mother had begun to find his outpourings of optimism worrying for some time now and she'd developed strong misgivings about the marriage to be.

Dinesh and Anita had met at the temple on Lady Margaret Road in Southall. Anita had called to tell me about this meeting with the man of her dreams. She had a role in the Krishna Leela at the mandir, and she ran into Dinesh just as she was heading for the changing room after the show. He told her he loved her role, they exchanged numbers, and it was not many days later that he told her he loved her. And she loved him, and didn't they look good together.

Within a month of meeting at the temple, they were talking

marriage dates, and Sharda had invited me to talk wedding matters through with them. Really, to check him out. Something told her, as it told me quickly, that this chap in the kitchen was not the hero Shah Rukh Khan was waiting to concede stardom to. Only Anita looked pleased. She was in love, and to her Dinesh was hero already. Marriage was due in a couple of months.

Dinesh was already very much at home. It was that sort of home too; Sharda was strong on entertaining, and her intimately lit lounge was designed for dissolving distances among people. The kitchen offered guests a parade of mostly successful experiments. All was as should be in this happy home except that the lovely Anita was pushing thirty and had not found anyone. Now that too seemed sorted, except that she had found a dubious hero.

'You see, he has no family here, we do not know where he is from, we do not know anything about him,' Sharda told me after the lovers left for an evening out in Anita's black convertible VW Golf. She had been asking Dinesh about himself, and what she heard made her uneasy. His story was that he was from Nepal, but had lived in India because his father was an officer with the Gurkha Rifles. They had been posted in Dehra Dun, where Gurkha Rifles is headquartered. He had tried to study in India, but family responsibilities came in the way just as he was about to complete his studies. He then went to Singapore, studied hotel management but stopped just short of completing his degree. He had now come to Britain to study. Where or what, he would not say. Sharda was becoming uneasy every time he took her daughter out, which meant really that she took him out, almost every day.

'Three weeks back I asked him to show me his passport,' Sharda said. 'He said, no problem, he will bring it the next day. He said the university has kept his passport. I asked him which university, he did not say anything to me. Then I asked, can I talk to your family in Nepal? I said, we cannot think of marrying unless we have met your family. He gave me the number. I called and I spoke to his mother. I told them that we are thinking of, you know, that he and Anita could get married. And you know what she said? She said, don't believe anything he says. And you won't believe, she said she will feel sorry for any girl who marries her son. This is his own mother who said this.'

'Did you tell him what she said to you?'

'Yes, I told him. He said, don't worry, aunty, my family is like that, they have always gone against me, they have gone against my studies, they want to go against my marriage.'

'And what does Anita say?'

'She is crazy about him, she believes everything he says.'

'What does he do here?'

'He works as a waiter. He says he is earning some money until his film comes out. After that I will be big. But it is not easy to become Shah Rukh Khan. Main thing is he has no job or qualification.'

'And Anita doesn't mind that?'

'No, she says she can work extra to earn for both, she says she will earn money to educate him if he does not make it in films, she says we can use our savings to put him in business. He says so many nice things to her, and she has gone crazy about him.'

'Does she believe everything he says?'

'No, she cannot. Because about his degree he was saying one thing, then he was saying something else. In front of her. I told him. And he said, sorry, he was telling lie about it. I asked him why did he tell lie? He said he was sorry about it.'

Sharda was determined to cure her daughter of this craze. They had a deal. He had lied about his university degree, and they would let that pass. But if he lied also about his passport, that would make him a pukka liar, and an illegal immigrant. It would mean he wanted to marry Anita because he wanted to settle in Britain. Maybe he really liked Anita too, it was hard not to, but it would mean he had a migration motive. So if he could produce the passport, the marriage was on, otherwise not.

He never did produce a passport. He would call Anita, he would text his love. But there was no university, no job, no passport, no qualifications, no money. And no sign of the film. Mother and daughter were devastated in their own ways. They left for Bombay on a six-week holiday, Sharda wanted to get the daughter's mind off her hero. The time away worked. They returned, Anita changed her mobile number, and there that non-story ended.

The search for someone eligible, and legal, for Anita began again, but this time it was not at the mandir.

Bollywood

NEHRU'S FOOTSTEPS

'Go beta, don't be nervous,' mum said, giving her seven-year-old a close hug. The little one looked unhappily at the dance floor as mum's hug wished away the nerves. Bollywood dancing was fine, but this was a Bollywood dancing exam.

It was being conducted on the floor of the Methodist Church hall in Finchley in north London. Diva Entertainments, run by Honey Kalaria, hired the hall once a week for Bollywood dance classes and the hall saw more people that one day than any other. If the priest at the church could ever have drawn as many youngsters as Honey, Britain would be a different country.

A teacher, very un-teacher like in her jeans and silver things hanging all over her, was lining up the kids in two rows of about seven or eight each. Two other teachers sat facing the rows at desks with open registers to write the marks, this was a real exam. I admired the kids braving it out there, and felt for the one who couldn't get herself to.

The teachers looked up, the kids looked around, and a slightly overpainted woman in jeans and bright orange T-shirt came bouncing into the room with a strongly stated announcement of youthful energy. This had to be Honey Kalaria. She was on the floor in no time. 'Okay,' she said, with a sharp clap, and all attention was instantly on her. She let forth a string of cheery nothings. The kids eased up, and the nervous one found the strength to abandon mum and return to the floor. 'What are those sparkling things up in the sky?' Honey asked brightly. They answered together. See, that's what they would get in class, she said, stars, not marks.

She was going to prepare them for the exam. A nod to a teacher, and the music began, 'Bole churiyaan, bole kangana ...' The five-to-seven-year-olds knew just what to do. They rose in a show of tip-toed nakhra, and offered teachers the come-on looks they'd been taught all term. This was a final refresher from Honey. 'From the neck, from the head, one-two-three, round and round, very-very good, one-two-three ...' The children began to gyrate hips that weren't there in the direction of a lover who wasn't.

Honey stopped the music to ask them to repeat what they would get stars for. They knew. The answer came in a chorus with every finger of Honey's hand that went up: Smiles; Energy; Sharp Moves; Timing; Classical Hands. The five things she taught them that add up to Bollywood dancing.

Now the exam began, and the kids had another go at putting them all together on their own. But not everyone was managing, and particularly not the seven-year-old last in. I saw a sinking look appear on her mum's face, though she had put on an encouraging smile, like she was drawing on her inner resources to find fortitude in adversity. Mum and daughter both looked relieved when it ended. The kids made their way back to the gallery where I sat with a lone dad and several mums.

The mums now took over. 'My girl, you know,' said one, 'she is so good, I tell you, she watches films all the time. Every new film she has to watch. She is six but she can teach me.' 'She used to be a classical Kathak dancer,' another mum was saying about hers. 'But she didn't like it. You know all that instrumental and classical, so boring. So she moved to this. Bit more interesting, no?'

Mums sound so much the same. 'This one gets nervous in a crowd. But at home, I tell you, she's so good.' 'My one is so fond of Bollywood dances and I am so fond of her. She is just dancing in front of TV every day. She watches every film.' In mums' gallery every kid was out-achieving every other.

The mum nearest to me was quiet, a bit stuck with lone dad and me. I asked her what had brought her and her daughter to Honey. 'I just love films, you know. She also. You know, we enjoy the music. And it helps to practise language also. And in this country it is a form of socializing. We go out as family to other families, then kids have something to do. Otherwise, you know, in this country for girls there are too many distractions when they grow up. We don't like that. This way, they get together in a cultural sense, you know, and have fun.' She seemed convinced her daughter would dance her way to goodness.

'It's nice to go to the films and learn this dancing,' said an unseen mum behind us who joined in, as mums do. 'When we came here, there was not that much of our culture. These days we feel so confident to talk about it.'

'Okay.' The command from the silvered teacher rose sharp above the talk. She was getting the next class into place for the bigger exam. The teenagers and twenty-somethings, who had rapidly filled up the gallery in the meantime, began to take position on the dance floor. The floor had filled up quickly and so had our gallery. If this was a bus, someone would have been asked to get off.

Honey took over from the teacher for this final rehearsal too. 'Come on, let's have a U with the bottom, nice and neat U.' The thirty-five or forty girls, and two or three boys in the class, followed Honey's U-turns to *Keh do na, keh do na, you are my Sonia*, the syllabus for this class. Honey led them through the song step by step, lachak by lachak. She showed them what to do, and she showed us in the gallery why she is such a popular teacher. 'To-the-left and to-the-right and nice-and-neat and punch-punch-punch and *keh do na, keh do na* ... Come on, you want the eyes on you at the next party, don't you?' After a pause, she asked, 'And who wants to be in Bollywood films?' I couldn't spot a hand that wasn't up. These must be among the world's most eager extras.

It was now between teenage hips and the two teachers at the desk, and Honey and I had time for a chat. We strolled over to the room behind the church hall, past a separate class for bhangra. 'That's mostly for older people because it's slow,' she said. 'Bollywood dancing, that's really fast.'

Honey looked very camera-ready as we sat down, and I felt I let her down because I didn't have one. But looking camera-ready must be standard appearance for her: she had the kind of good looks that get picked up more by cameras than people.

'I have offers already from the US to start dance academies

there.' She knew what she wanted to deliver, and she wasn't wasting time. 'Five years from now, I will have franchises worldwide. There will be 200 branches the world over.' In London she had only a dozen or so, and only something more than a thousand students. Her success in London looked humble before her ambitions. In true Bollywood style, she wouldn't take all the credit. 'I'm grateful to god,' she said, with a quick glance at the ceiling.

'Why has this whole Bollywood thing picked up so much now?'

'Some years back, parents were not very encouraging. Nowadays a lot of parents want their children involved. It's now accepted for kids to take part in Bollywood shows.'

'Why is that?'

'It's good for health, fitness, you make new friends, you gain more confidence. It's a good, enjoyable hobby. It gets them off the streets, so much better than going to a club.'

'Do Indian kids particularly gain confidence from this?'

'Dance is very psychological, a lot of it is in the mind. When you learn to let go in your mind, the body follows. Here children build dancing skills, choreography skills, then parents come to see. Some kids are not very confident, they don't open up. We encourage them, and they begin to open up, they begin to feel good. I can make anyone dance who says they can't, I guarantee that.'

'And how many kids get taken into Bollywood films?'

'I was privileged to give my students a chance to work in *Kabhi Khushi Kabhi Gham*. I had 900 artists who took part in *K3G*. Dancers, other roles. For *Mohabbatein* we provided 300 artists including twenty, thirty dancers. One little boy was first offered a role in *K3G*. But then they took the other one.'

'So you're sort of Britain's Bollywood studio?'

'If you come from India, you don't have to bring all these people. It cuts costs, works both ways. And people here have an opportunity to use their skills for Bollywood films, stage shows.'

'How do you teach so many?'

'I train teachers. Once they are up to a level, I let my assistants take over. I go to a class once every two, three weeks.'

'When did you begin yourself?'

'I came here from Malawi in the eighties. I was dancing to Bollywood songs when I was thirteen, when nobody was doing it. But even then I was quite a lot in demand. They call me Bollywood's ambassador to Britain.'

'Never thought of moving to Bollywood yourself?'

'Now that I have set up the academy, I can't leave it and go, or they won't trust you afterwards. I want people to know that we're here to stay.'

'And the kids here, you see them going more and more the Bollywood way?'

'Oh yes, yes. You wait, you haven't seen anything yet.'

We chatted on a bit. But the one thing that stuck in my mind was that she could make anyone dance. That included me. What if she taught me to dance like a dream and I became so good that I could partner her at a party? These were just the fantasies she had turned into business. Honey could make you shine, star-like, at parties, and then, who knows, even in Bollywood. She would get you noticed, at parties, on stage, on-screen, somewhere. Bollywood offered the dreams, Honey the technique to make them come true, at least as party dancer if not as Bollywood star. She would teach you to shine safely among your own. She had brought parents and kids to the same side.

The mums are counting their blessings, and Honey her success. A few years back, she began teaching just twenty-two students. Now, she has well over a thousand at something like £75 a term, three terms in a year. And that's not counting the money from her shows and from the extras offered whenever Bollywood came visiting and in need. Not good money if you're not the one making it.

It was the big evening when all that education would go public, in the five Honey commandments, in hip movement, in making eyes at that notional someone, in teasing meaning out of timing. Honey's students from her 'academies' in Finchley, Harrow and Ilford who'd been training for a year or more would compete at the big show at Acton town hall. It was time to show off.

As an Indian I knew my way to the hall, it's now an adda for events Indian. The hall had quite visibly been smart once. It was built when Britain still looked back to a sense of the grand, expressed usually as rounded lines with ornate interruptions here and there. But its doors open now to people quite different from those it was intended for. The days never come when you might see a few hundred white British mums head out, cameras in hand, to watch their kids do a Michael Jackson, but when little Nitesh is doing a Hrithik Roshan, you can count on mum with possibly two aunts and some cousins thrown in, for every Nitesh.

Diva Entertainments had prepared a poster exhibition in the foyer upstairs. A poster presenting an impish and animated Honey standing with a bunch of teenagers welcomed visitors. 'Fans drawn like bees to see dancing queen,' proclaimed the bold lettering across it. Another picture of Honey with her young dancers was pasted on another poster with the caption, 'Honey with her lucky, lucky sprogs.' 'Opportunity to be a star' said one, and another listed just what Honey could do to make that happen: 'Dialogue Delivery, Emotion, Voice Projection, Observational Skills, Mime, Impersonation, Diction, Hindi Language, Body Language and much, much more ...' Like, for example, 'Dance, Bhangra, Catwalk Modelling, Singing and Keep Fit.'

Honey's students 'have already had opportunities to work in Bollywood films, TV productions, stage shows, pop videos and next to superstars', a board by the collage of posters said. Amitabh Bachchan and Govinda appeared standing with Honey in a photograph, all Bollywood buddies. Another notice on the board said her shows were offered for 'Festivals, Melas and Corporate Events'. There was even a money-back guarantee from Diva Entertainments for making a Bollywood dancer of you; the bit that might have been of interest to me had I joined.

I moved on into the packed hall. Only a few seats at the back were vacant. Mums were lining the hall in scores all the way along both sides, little digi-cams in hand. Guest after guest at home would be shown the impressive steps their young are taking, and some day they could look back on their own early steps.

The show began. Lights. Mums' cameras. Action. Two large Indian flags danced on to the stage to a disco kind of *Vande Mataram*. Bollywood is India, and Honey was saying it loud; the first dancer of the evening was the Indian flag. She was doing more to connect youth here to India than those hundreds of sedative speeches by high commissioners that come, blabber and go.

In time, some young girls in lehenga-choli appeared from behind this nationalistic purdah to Bharatnatyamish movements, with more space between lehenga and choli than the Vishwa Hindu Parishad would have liked. The VHP would have to decide also whether to like the *Vande Mataram* part of the dance or dislike the dance part of it. The dancers were joined by some girls who had bared their navels between jeans and shirts instead of lehenga and choli— together they added up to another of those fusion things. The dance ended with one flag held the wrong way up. But these girls are British too, and we all knew they meant well.

The toddlers followed. The first team of four-to-seven-year-olds, who had only recently learnt to walk, gave us their post-feeding-bottle interpretation of 'Dil ye baichain ve ... aa ja saanvariya, aa, aa, aa ... tal se taal mila ...' Next came the eight-to-twelve-year-olds with their little feet pattering busily under looks of aching romance. Suddenly, a roar of applause broke out. The lehenga of one of the little girls had slipped, and she had caught it just in time, and in perfect time within her dance move without missing a beat. The little one had been practising enough to cover mum's failing with her narha.

We were moving up the years to more serious dancers. Someone was announced in as 'Hrithik Roshan in the making'. The spotlight picked up a plump little fellow, twelve or thirteen, strolling very slowly on to the stage, in crimson trousers and a silver-coloured shirt, black glasses, black gloves and a baseball cap reversed into cool black American. He walked silently to centre stage and stood still. So casual, see? Suspense. Then, with all the flourish he could unleash, he flung the cap dramatically downstage and began his dance. He lived up to the announcement and was unexpectedly quick for someone so obviously overfed. Another kid about the same age came next, announced as another Hrithik Roshan on his way; he was no slower, and you didn't want their mums fighting.

A bunch of girls who had set up their own Bollywood group 'Envy' was announced in. They were followed by many more groups. King's Crew—a bunch of Indian students from King's

College—Masti, Sahelis, Sens-Asians, Tempt-Asians. Bollywood must run a fair bit of their lives. The dancers from Ilford announced themselves: 'Let the battle begin ...' This was Honey's home ground, and they had a thing to prove. In ones and twos and more, they danced to the likes of *I am a disco dancer, Keh do na, keh do na, you are my Sonia, Choli ke peechay* ... One after another, Bollywood was taking them from Britain or reclaiming them as Indian, depending on how you looked at it.

In the end there were prizes for almost everyone. A great many went to Harrow, where Jawaharlal Nehru had come once for another kind of education. For Honey's dancers this was the discovery of another India.

*

Up in that studio at Honey's dance academy with a mirror for a wall at the far end, these were not just Bollywood dancers. They'd come to learn Bollywood acting, they could be stars one day. 'Remember what Honey told you about Tom Hanks?' the teacher was telling the class of about twenty, sitting on chairs along the walls, with the space in the middle meaningfully vacant. 'He spent a year meeting AIDS patients before shooting for *Philadelphia*. You see, that is acting. It's not something you just go and do out there just like that.'

A chap in the class who'd made it as an extra in a Bollywood film through Honey had known otherwise. 'We were only told five minutes before what to do,' he said. 'That was last year,' the teacher replied. 'Things will be different now.' It wasn't the best answer, but it was all she could think up.

The class was waiting for Honey at her flagship centre in Seven Kings in Ilford. For the glamour it was out to generate, the centre on Farnham Road at the end of a row of houses was unexpectedly unpretentious. Some East London neighbourhoods have the feeling of barracks about them, and Seven Kings is particularly barrack-like. It must be the smallness of the houses along wide roads, and the near absence of anything green. A board outside only called the place the Supplementary Education Centre. That was the boring adult education stuff. Honey Kalaria had taken a couple of rooms there for her office and dance lessons. Whatever went on here, it wouldn't be boring. The room with the mirror must be the only spot of colour for miles here, east of east London.

Honey walked in, as usual faster than necessary and after some rapid hellos, turned to the class, and to Hanks.

'When he was asked to do that role he spent a year going to all the hospitals that had AIDS victims. He saw their problems, their challenges, he saw how they behaved, how frail they were. He is such a great actor, and still he had to do all this. And which was the film with Brad Pitt? Yes, *Troy*. You think he went in and said I'm an actor, what do you want me to do?'

She waited for a reply. A white student in the class replied, 'No, he became more muscular to play the part.'

'Yes. He didn't just go and start doing something because oh, I'm so good.' And then she made her point. They must not leave at the end of a three-month term, they must stay the full three-year acting course. In that lay their hope, and her fee. Message given, Honey made her way out, just as fast as she'd come.

But Honey left some fresh ideas for learning to act. The teacher, very becoming in her blue denims and black shirt, set the class on the acting course. She was the picture of confidence, the sound of eloquence, she had to be. She was fair, almost white, between dark hair permed into too many curls.

She divided the class into groups. One group of two chaps and three girls went first, they were going to act out Honey's idea.

'What was the idea Honey gave you?' the teacher asked.

'It was like all her other ideas,' one of the chaps said. 'Pretend we've seen a UFO.' So they stared at a blank wall, swayed about in horror, and fell on the floor one by one according to who got overawed when by that sight.

Class over, some of us sat talking. The very Sikh-looking girl in the class saved me asking her that rude question, just what kind of actress she hoped to become. 'I qualified as a pharmacist, I work near Tower Bridge, and I'm bored out of my brains,' she said before I could say much. She didn't want to give her name, but since she was Sikh, it was a likely toss-up between Dolly and Pinky. She had bright eyes, and they were in search of something more than pharmacy could offer. She would be more than good enough to handle pharmacy, but pharmacy would never be good enough for her. She just wasn't made for too much of sameness.

'Why isn't pharmacy good enough?' I asked.

'It's good, but it's not creative.'

'Have you worked at more creative things before?'

'I did music when I was younger. My dad's very creative, he's a musician, and I used to sing shabads, sing in gurdwaras.'

'Now Bollywood's more interesting?'

'Oh yeah, I see all the films, stay up to date. I had an Indian channel, now I go to Upton Park to get my DVDs.'

'What do you like about Bollywood?'

'What I really like, whatever anyone says about Bollywood, is a degree of comfort in these films. They're melodic, they're colourful, they're about some ideal. You can't translate that into everyday life. But you do get transported into a different world. Films can be realistic and social and all that but there is a sector of arts that caters to all that.'

'What do you like best in this non-realistic sort of otherness?'

'The dancing, the choreography, the superb, superb dancing.'

'And what do you want to do with yourself in Bollywood?'

'Tell you the truth, I'm not looking for fame and fortune, but I'm so bored with pharmacy, I just want to build my confidence, learn to perform to a level.'

Others from the class were hanging around. I tried to guess which faces I might see on film posters that come up so quickly one above the other on every spare wall in Wembley and Southall. Maybe that girl in black, probably older than the rest, very actress-like in that curving style so outdated now but waiting to make a comeback, who knows. She was Pakistani, as I had guessed.

'I'm studying biomedical science, I'm taking a year off studies,' she said. Biomedical science sounded like it was to her what pharmacy was to the other.

'Is this your first go at acting?'

'No, I've always been into the performing arts. I've done stage plays, school plays, fashion shows.'

'Others in your family into the performing arts?'

'No, my dad's a teacher. He's from Pakistan.'

'So what language do you speak at home?'

'Punjabi, Urdu.'

'It's fine with your parents for you to learn Bollywood acting?'

'Oh yes.'

'Where do you want to take this?'

'I'd like a career in acting. I've done Bollywood dancing in the past.'

'You want to act in Bollywood films?'

'Yes, and also Pakistani TV plays. My uncle's in Pakistani TV plays.'

The white guy was of course the least expected figure in that room. 'Maybe not today, maybe not tomorrow, but I'll be one of the first guys here to break into Bollywood,' Wayne, as he was introduced, had announced earlier.

'What do you do otherwise?' I asked him now.

'I work in a factory in Walthamstow making installation tubes.'

'So how did Bollywood come into it?'

'This chap at work said to me, you should go to Bollywood.'

'Indian guy?'

'Muslim, to be honest.'

'You're keen on this sort of thing?'

'I've been acting since the age of ten. And I said to myself, I like Bollywood, I'd like to learn Asian culture.'

'What actually brought you to this?'

'There was the sixtieth birthday of this Trinidadian Indian, and they were dancing. I copied them. And they said, where did you learn to dance like that? I said, I just copied you.'

'So that was the inspiration.'

'Yes, then I just entered Bollywood dance in a search, and the first thing that came up was Honey. It was almost as if I was being led into something. And I said, why not Bollywood. Why not be the white man that breaks through into Bollywood?'

'Do you see a lot of the films?'

'I don't know that many Bollywood films, I don't know Hindi, but I can mime to songs.'

'You seem to enjoy this.'

'It's the biggest stress relief for me. I just have to do Bollywood dancing on Friday, Saturday and Bollywood acting Sunday.'

'But it's more than stress relief, isn't it?'

'It's very important to me. This is my last chance. Because I don't think I'll make it in the Western thing. But Bollywood, I feel it will come.' I couldn't share his confidence, but still, it was not as moony a bunch as I'd expected.

Shaban had more than an exaggerated swagger for age fifteen, for any age really.

'I've been doing Bollywood acting for a year,' he said. 'I've acted in a Bollywood show in Newcastle for a week.'

'Doing what?'

'I was a bus driver. A Jamaican bus driver. I had to speak in that accent.'

Shaban was a bit portly for fifteen, but he didn't think that would come between him and Bollywood heroism. He was cool, and that would make up.

'You speak Indian languages?'

'Yeah, I can speak Urdu and Gujarati. My dad's from Turkey, mum's from Gujarat. And I've picked up Hindi.'

'Through the films?'

'Been seeing films since I was five, six. Picked up the language there.'

'Who's your favourite?'

'Salman Khan. I see all his films. I like his style and his acting.'

'What's it been like, a year of Bollywood acting?'

'It's boosted my confidence. Earlier I was shy, not outgoing.'

'What brought you here to learn acting?'

'Earlier I was only doing Bollywood dancing, I used to be like every other guy, just copying what I saw on TV. Then I said to my mum I got this feeling that I want to be in Bollywood. So she found me these classes.'

'What now?'

'I'll be doing my acting and dancing classes for three years.'

'And then?'

'Hopefully I'll get into a Bollywood film. My two brothers, they also watch Bollywood films. But I'm much more into it. My brother also wants to join, but he's doing engineering. If I move into Bollywood, I'll just pull him into one of my films.'

Sheetal was waiting to talk to me, a little restlessly. She couldn't seem to stand still from the moment she'd walked in. And she didn't walk a regular walk either. Every step seemed a dancing step. Maybe it was those precarious heels; she had to move quickly from one to the other all the time to avoid falling. She was a party girl, every minute she wasn't at a party was that much life unlived.

'I just finished a job in a bank,' she said. 'Royal Bank of Scotland.'

'So, to dance, then?'

'No, I'm also studying accounts and financing for my banking skills. I'm also doing the beauty business, I do henna, you know, mehndi, aromatherapy, massage. Beauty is my side business, something to fall back on.'

'Going well?'

'Yes, that's going well.'

'Your first time, acting?'

'Yes, been doing Bollywood dancing. But had to stop because I have to go to aromatherapy classes. I'm also doing reflexology.'

'Always been interested in Bollywood?'

'I started singing since I was thirteen. Didn't keep it up, don't have the time.'

'What brought you to acting?'

'You see, I was this extra in a film *I: Proud to be an Indian*. And, you know Sohail Khan, he was running for the love of his life. And we were all running behind him.'

'Why?'

'We were cheering him on. Because he was so happy.'

'You liked that?'

'Loved it. We were there nine hours, we had to do it again and again. And I knew that this Bollywood is the only thing I really wanted to do.'

'That brought you to Honey ...'

'Yes, but I have these other things.'

'Think you'll stay the three-year acting course?'

'Of course.'

No, this wasn't a bunch that didn't know what they were up to. Maybe just the idea of what Bollywood was had succeeded in doing what the real Bollywood never would for them.

∼

Yash Blush

The little play the two girls had put up for Yash Chopra was almost done before he realized they were playing lesbians. In fact, I told him.

I hadn't managed to translate every word of their East Midlands Leicester English into mine, and I was in natural sympathy with Yashji's fellow Punjabi accent and lack of tuning to Indian teenager sounds in Leicester. He'd been watching the skit expressionless and, I thought, a bit bored.

'They're lesbians, you know, and one is getting jealous because she thinks the other girl is seeing a guy,' I whispered to him. It felt like ear-filling, snitching to teacher about class-fellow mischief. Yashji's face continued its woodenness, unless of course he was meaningfully impassive; with these film chaps you never know.

Yashji was chief audience among about thirty of us in a large upstairs room the local council had taken in the city centre for this meeting. A fairly good turnout by Leicester council standards. The council had invited singers, dancers and actors to show Yashji local talent and what Bollywood meant to British Asians. And who knows who Yashji might spot as just the one for his next film. One flick of his heavily ringed finger could mean a one-way ticket from a Leicester suburb to Bollywood fame.

The city council was hosting Yashji under a British Film Council tour of a picture-postcard selection of England and Scotland, and Leicester was the Indian flavour along the way. Yashji's *Dilwale Dulhaniya Le Jayenge*, *DDLJ* as rapid legend had made it, had showed Britain off to millions at no cost, and wouldn't it be nice if he came back with cameras for more? They weren't to know that he would one day bid salaam and namaste to England and head for Australia.

I'd come to the Yashji meeting with a friend and her two teenaged daughters, and their friend, a neighbour's daughter. This one was being sent out under watch because her mother had found out she was seeing a taxi driver. 'Her mum thinks it will take her mind off that guy,' my friend said. 'Stupid.' But if Yashji were to spot her, it would solve a lot of problems. Mum would pack the girl's bags happily for that Bombay flight. You never knew with

Bollywood, but at least she'd stop seeing the taxi driver. Serve him right if he got to see her one day only in a film at the end of fourteen trips from the bus terminal.

The lesbian skit was nearing its end. The girl in orange was the jealous one. She just knew that the other girl in the black shirt was seeing someone else, and a guy at that. No, said black shirt, they were just friends. No, no, orange knew better. And so it went on until confession. Not a performance that would lead either girl to speak of this hall in an interview one day as the place where Yash Chopra spotted her. The girls vacated the middle of the room for the next spot-me. Yashji did not join in the polite clapping. It was my fault.

A lightly built girl, too light for Bollywood, walked up to do a dance. Her blue sari would never fool Yashji's eyes, but then she'd never been taught that when you wear a sari you don't walk like you're wearing jeans. A friend switched on a tape for her. She swayed into some moony movements, then faded from the floor to join that vast population that once tried Bollywood. Another girl stepped up to deliver a dialogue in intended Hindi, and Yashji heard her out, more kind than interested.

Not everyone had to perform; you could sit there and hope to get seen as the face of the next film. A chap next to me was shifting about every now and then to catch Yashji's make-or-break eye. He was the lad of the times to detail—single earring, wet-look hair and baggy jeans with pockets by the knees that are always empty and still manage to bulge. 'Going to do something?' I asked. 'No, I'm here just, ya know, just ...' Just to be seen.

Finally it was time for Yashji to say something, and he had something to say.

'We believe in family,' he said. 'For us family is very important. We do not believe in showing sick emotions.' He did not look at either orange or black, but looked like he was looking away particularly from them. Then he turned to the moony dancer who'd disguised her jeans as a sari. 'You know, for dance, you need more light. Lot of lights.' His sets were coming back to his mind. 'For my dance I can have hundred lights, more than hundred.' He glanced up at the one or two lights on the ceiling and turned his eyes away. It was their most lowly moment since someone put them up there. But he wasn't going to leave without encouraging words. 'Very good, very good,' he said into the air generally as he got up to leave.

Good thing they couldn't hear what Yashji said to me as he left. 'These people, you know, very important. Look at the difference in price. Here one cinema ticket easy 500 rupees. This market has become whole territory. Like Delhi–UP this NRI market has become whole territory.' Yashji wasn't here talent spotting, or even location hunting. He was looking at the world where that easy Rs 500 a ticket comes from, and in hard currency. He was here to make his calculations.

The unspotted had begun to move towards the door, it was time to say goodbye to Bollywood. But wait, Yashji had something hot from Bollywood for them, a proper Bollywood script to work their acting skills on. 'It has English translation,' he said near the door, and handed out some copies. See what that meant? Young actors could take that script and act out a whole Bollywood film. A Bollywood script given to them personally by Yash Chopra, you know, the guy who made *DDLJ*.

I picked up a copy of the thick script, like an A4-sized book. The copies on offer were quickly grabbed away. But still, it was a script, not a contract. You spend years dreaming, hours grooming, then you're before that someone who could make those dreams come true. Then he's off, and it's all gone. Not the kind of sad ending Yashji would ever have liked himself.

I had left the room something of a hero for our three teenagers. They'd seen me talking to Yash Chopra himself, what's more, they'd seen him talk to me, and they saw as we got into the car that I had a script in my hands that had come straight from Yash Chopra.

'Can I see the script?' the youngest said.

'Let's wait till we get home,' I said. 'Then let's act it out.' Their squeals—of the brand that only girls aged fourteen to seventeen can produce—told me they could hardly believe this. We were going to do a Yash Chopra film of our own. In their squeals I heard also some surprise that I was not entirely boring after all. I felt myself rise in their esteem by the minute on our drive home.

We were home soon enough. My friend disappeared predictably

into the kitchen, which left us a cast of three girls and myself as hero in the sitting room. I placed Yashji's gift on the sofa where everyone could see it. The girls crowded around the script reverentially, like it was scripture.

'Yash Raj Films', it said on top. Then, *Darr*. That was our film. Produced and directed: Yash Chopra. Music: Shiv Hari. Below were the contents—written as reel number and footage, nothing as dull as chapter and page.

I leafed through some pages. The Hindi script was on the left column on every page, its English translation on the right. Whether Yashji had the translation done for the visit to London or whether this is standard Bollywood practice for a script, I do not know. Maybe the lines in English were intended to double as subtitles. The lines in Hindi were prefixed with letters like C.S. and L.S., which must have meant close shot and long shot. To us they meant simply the authentic touch.

'Why don't you read it loud?' I said to Bijal, the younger one. Like all fifteen-year-olds these days, she talked like she was twenty-five.

'Okay, here goes,' she said, and began reading.

'Kiran is lying and reading the letter.' She paused.

'Silly, read the thing on the right,' said sister Rupa.

Bijal read the opening lines of the script, the lines that Kiran was reading from the letter: '"My heart, I am far away from you but you are still in front of me. I feel as if I am looking at you."'

'Boyfriend's letter, wow,' said Rupa. She was always one to get straightaway into the sentiment of anything.

'Guys are never like that,' said the third one, the teenage neighbour in the wrong kind of love. 'Bet no one writes letters like that.'

'What's he say?' said Rupa.

Bijal read further. '"You are reading this letter sitting on a stone and all the things around you are coloured by your colour."'

Again she stopped. 'That's weird, what's he mean "coloured by your colour"?'

'It's because he's in love,' Rupa said matter-of-factly. She knew these things, and she had seen enough Bollywood films by now.

'Wait,' I said. 'Let's see what he says in Hindi.' I read a bit out.

'"Tum tanhayi mei ek pathar par bethi ye khat padh rahi hogi. Aur tumhare pass ki har cheez tumhare rang mei rang chuki hogi".' I repeated the line in my idea of how a Bollywood love line would get spoken. It went down well. It didn't matter that the girls didn't know Hindi, they knew enough Bollywood to know this was the real thing, a lot better than 'coloured by your colour'.

Bijal resumed with the letter Kiran was reading in the script, in English. '"The clouds must have spread like the kajal of your eyes."' Bijal wasn't impressed. 'Oh yeah? She must have put it on and washed her face.'

Bijal wasn't getting into the romance of it, and she was spoiling it for Rupa.

'Shut up Bijal, just read.'

'"You must be looking around and the entire earth is looking at your face. And I have become the sun and am kissing you."'

Now Bijal had to stop. 'So he's the sun, right? And so he's snogging her, right?'

'Come on, it's only a love letter,' said Rupa.

Bijal read on. The right column had gone blank but there was English on the left.

'"Kiran looks up. Kiran gets up. Kiran comes. Kiran comes. Kiran standing. Opens her buttons. Kiran opens the buttons. Kiran opens her dress. Kiran turns while removing her clothes."' Bijal finished reading it, her voice rising with Kiran's every action. The room was filled with the kind of high-pitched giggles teenaged girls produce from nowhere for moments like this.

'What's that?' mum's voice demanded from the kitchen.

'It's okay, mum,' Bijal shouted back.

Bollywood was supposed to be safe, family entertainment, and here we'd run into steam on page one.

'Let's skip this,' I said, back to boring ways. But the script had steered to safety anyway. Kiran was interrupted before she could remove any more clothes. She appeared now with female friends.

'Wait, there's a song,' I said. '*Jadu teri nazar.*'

'I know that one,' neighbour girl said, and began to sing it, really badly. Bijal stopped her with a 'shut up', exactly what I'd been relying on her to do. She read on but she'd begun to lose her way in the English of the script. This wasn't English as she knew it. She read the next lines from Kiran.

'I know, Sunil he here somewhere. But he is not coming in front of me.

'Second girl: "What is the reason for him to hide?"

'Kiran: "He gets enjoyment in worrying me."

'Third girl: "I know where Sunil is."

'Kiran: "If you know, why don't you tell me? Tell me where he is."

'Girl: "Here in the mirror of heart is his photograph."

'Kiran: "Oh, oh."'

Bijal figured I'd be more literate in this English, and gave me the next bit to read, marked "O.S." It stated the crux of the film. '"When love crosses the limit then it becomes a devotion and then when devotion is hurt then it becomes a madness. This is the story of such a madness which has the truthness of Laila Majnu's love and the pain of Romeo Juliet's love. It also has the suffering of Heer Ranjha's songs. It has something else also, which is not seen in today's love stories ... Fright ..."'

'That's why this film is called *Darr*,' I explained. 'See, *Darr* means fear.'

We were almost at the end of Reel 1, and Sunil had come into the story. I read on.

Sunil: 'May I come in, sir?'

O.S.: 'Come in.'

Officer: 'Sunil, the terrorist have kidnapped my niece's daughter. They have kept a clause that they will leave the child only if we release their leader or they will shoot the child. We must save the child and only you can do this work.'

Sunil: 'Where is the child?'

Officer: 'In the middle of the sea, in their boat. All the best ... all the best'.

End of Reel no. 1 at 738.10 feet. End also of our Bollywood adventure.

The girls vanished upstairs pretty soon for something or other but really to talk about the this-and-that of the day. The Yash spell hadn't lasted long. I realized right then that I'd never heard the girls discuss a Bollywood story; it was always only the dances or the clothes.

Between the usual household interruptions, I glanced at the script and read in it mostly its foreignness to the girls.

Getting the film into the fear mood, Sunil decides to give his fiancé Kiran a scare by stepping out of a cupboard.

Kiran: 'Sunil, idiot, shameless, always frightening me. I thought a dead body fell from the cupboard.'

Sunil: 'Are you a fool, you don't know this much, that from girls cupboards only old letters, old lovers and new sarees are found?'

Kiran: 'You old lover ... what if my heart had to fail.'

Sunil: 'How is that possible, your heart is with me?'

Kiran: 'Get lost! I am not talking to you. You are very bad. See how my heart is beating hard.'

Sunil: 'It is beating hard. Yes, yes.'

Love proceeds but never far from the stalking Rahul who's obsessed with Kiran. Sunil manages to get Kiran to a quiet house, she knows why.

Kiran: 'Mr Sunil Malhotra, the shine in your eyes and the smile on your lips state that your intentions are not noble.'

Sunil: 'Intentions are good but morals have changed.'

But Rahul calls just then to stalk her on the phone. 'Don't cut the line. I have to tell you a important thing. This Sunil is not capable for you.' He threatens to turn up on Holi, but when the day comes and he doesn't for some time, Sunil is free to flirt.

Kiran: 'From where are you coming behind me?'

Sunil: 'To take bath.'

Kiran: 'Have you gone mad?'

Sunil: 'It is great fun to take bath together after playing Holi.'

Kiran: 'You shameless creature.'

But Rahul appears in disguise and makes a pass at her. Then he calls again. Or has Kiran begun to imagine all this?

Sunil: 'What happen Kiran?'

Kiran: 'See, he is again doing phone to me.'

Sunil: 'Nobody is doing phone to you. Now you come.'

Kiran: 'You have not listen any bell.'

Sunil: 'No, I did not heard anything.'

Kiran: 'See, again the phone is ringing. Now have you listen anything? You don't get up. I know whose phone it is ...'

Sunil: 'I have disconnected the line. I never wanted that someone disturb you. I am not boaring you.'

Kiran: 'Sunil you save me. I don't want to be mad.'

Sunil thinks he and Kiran need to go away somewhere. But her sister-in-law Punam warns her of the pitfalls she may encounter. 'Kiran, you remember one thing. Until the fruit is on the tree it looks nice but when it came in hand then it is in mouth. The lovers also become like this after marriage.'

But go away they must. Clever Sunil lets out they are going to Goa, but he has a plan, as Kiran discovers at the airport.

Kiran: 'Well you tell me ...'

Sunil: 'Yes ...'

Kiran: 'That we came here but could not go to Goa. Why?'

Sunil: 'We are going to Switzerland and not to Goa.'

Kiran: 'Switzerland ... really. Then why you have taken the ticket of the Goa?'

Sunil: 'Because of that bastard we have to do like this. Till now he will come to know that we are going to Goa. He will be preparing for Goa and we will go to Switzerland.'

Kiran: 'You are wise.'

Stalking Rahul takes the wrong flight to Goa. The woman at the hotel reception tells him they aren't there: 'Here no Malhotra is staying. From where such people are coming?'

Rahul runs into an old and by now alcoholic friend Vicky being warned by a waiter that he is about to spill his drink. Vicky says 'If it is falling then let it fall down. This is my wine. What you have to do?' Vicky is dying: 'It is difficult,' he tells Rahul. 'My lever has totally gone. The condition of the heart is also like this. The battle of the rat and cat is started in my life. When the cat will eat the rat that God only knows.'

Vicky dies and Rahul gets word out that he died instead. Kiran's family call her on their honeymoon in Switzerland to give her the good news. And she tells Sunil.

Kiran: 'Sunil he has died.'

Sunil: 'Who?'

Kiran: 'That man who was phoning me. Just now brother has informed me by phone.'

Sunil: 'But I am having doubt.'

Kiran: 'Doubt for what?'

Sunil: 'Such a wicked man has died so easily.'

Sunil is right. The death was a trick to discover from her brother, whom Rahul knows, where Kiran is. Rahul heads for Switzerland and runs into Sunil, who does not know Rahul is the stalker.

Sunil: 'Friend, I am feeling very nice to meet you. If anyone met abroad then it looks very nice.'

Rahul: 'If our own are with us then the foreign is also looks like our own country.'

But in the end Rahul too dies, even though he had promised his long dead mother that he will marry Kiran.

Rahul speaks his last: 'Kiran, what reply I will give to the mummy? My life was started with your love and finished in your love only. I know that I am guilty ... but you don't hate to me. I love you Kiran ...'

The last of the script reads: 733.11 to 808.11. Different silent shots of the Rahul lying. Kiran is weeping including Sunil. Rolling titles starts. 'The End'. Reel no: 19 ends at 816.00 feet.

Our hopes that Yashji's script would inspire us had ended a little earlier.

PEE PRICE

The four chaps who stepped out of their vans one by one to pee by the side of the road to Nottingham were opening up a matter far beyond them and their bladders, or even between a man's needs on the one hand and countryside niceties on the other. They were raising an economic matter between India and Britain.

The men had stepped out of a white van, one of four parked on a lay-by on the road from Leicester to Nottingham. I had driven up and parked behind them a while back, but it was only when they opened their flies that the penny dropped on the economic meaning of this expression of their need.

Locating the vans had been a small triumph after I set out in search of them from Leicester. Dipesh was not sure I'd find them when I called him on his mobile. 'Basically we are filming all around Leicester, you won't be able to find us,' he said. Like all good Gujaratis in Britain, Dipesh did things either basically or literally. He sounded like he had very little time to talk, and hung up breathlessly.

I was looking for Dipesh because Ather Mirza at the University of Leicester had told me that Dipesh was de facto location producer for a new Bollywood film being shot in Leicester. Mirza had persuaded Dipesh to do some filming on campus so that Leicester University would be in a Bollywood film. This mattered enough to the university for Her Majesty's government to circulate a press release to mark the success.

'A new Bollywood blockbuster is being shot at the University of Leicester and in the city and county. *Raakh* which means Ashes, is being described as a "sophisticated gangster movie" and stars Sohail Khan, the brother of Bollywood megastar Salman Khan.' Mirza added his views in the press note. 'The University of Leicester is pleased to be playing host again to a Bollywood movie. India is the biggest film producer in the world—the potential to reach out to a global audience and showcase the university is huge.'

So that was why the university was such an eager extra. Leicester University, the one where DNA was discovered, needs students from India for it to keep going and growing. Every Indian student who watched *Raakh*, liked the look of its campus and came to join the university would bring a useful £8000 or so a year in fees, besides feeding the local economy for living expenses. The university was actively soliciting foreign students' fees, even if the students came with it. Who knows what undiscovered DNAs wait out there that Indian fees could pay to research. What better advertising at no cost than to get seen in a Bollywood film?

Dipesh and the film crew had done with the university campus and moved on. 'We are on Melton Road now, we are heading out on the road to Nottingham,' Dipesh had told me on the mobile. 'Basically we are in four white vans.' That had set me off on the van chase.

I had followed the signs to Nottingham, through the very Indian Melton Road into the countryside where England had begun to

reclaim itself. A ten-minute drive, and I spotted the white vans—
the film crew of *Raakh*. I parked behind the last of the vans.

Its rear doors were held wide open. A camera faced out, set to
shoot someone following the van. Half a dozen very Bombay
chaps sat around the camera, silently looking out. I was a little
taken aback by their motionlessness. They looked straight past
me. Like that camera, they looked programmed to focus on
something else. I came out of the car and walked on past them
towards the three vans in front. They did not look like just parked
vans, they seemed still in an odd sort of way, like everything
within was not as still as it seemed. Maybe the gangster movie
mood was getting to me.

I saw some chaps sitting in the next van looking blankly into
the countryside past me. Again, none of that Indian-I-presume I'd
have thought mandatory on a lay-by on the road to Nottingham.
I guessed they'd been warned about a pursuing journalist and told
they must give nothing away about the film. This was a gangster
movie and you didn't want the producer whining over whisky two
years later that no one would have guessed the end if it wasn't for
some journalist chap near Leicester. Or that the other film that
had stolen their story had come out first. Who knows who'd steal
what I might reveal?

I moved on to the front two vans like some peeping prowler.
I couldn't have looked inside them if I'd tried. Shirts, jackets, saris
on hangers had made purdahs of windows. But I sensed there was
someone inside and that they had seen me. This was becoming
like I-Spy, or Ice-Pice as we all renamed it.

I waited, and they waited. Then a youngish fellow stepped out
of the camera van. He had shoulder-length hair and trousers that
looked like pyjamas, more or less the uniform of the creative in
the cinema business. He walked up to me, and waited to be
spoken to. In my now suspicious mode, I thought a mobile or two
had got busy, and he had been sent out as official spokesman.

'So what's this film about?' I asked.

'It's underworld and love story mixed.' I must have nodded in
a so-what's-new way, because he added, 'But it's not the usual mix.'

'So what is it?'

'You know, a different kind of gangster movie.' In short, ask no
more. He was doing his PR job well.

'And what are you shooting here?'

'The don, you see he is from Leicester.'

'And will the film say he is in Leicester?'

'Yes, the story will show he is from Leicester.'

I asked because *Hum Dil De Chuke Sanam* had been filmed in Hungary and the story pretended it was Italy. I had attended a screening of the film in Budapest to which the Hungarian President was invited. He obviously had no idea that the film would show the wonders of his country pretending they belonged to Italy. Hungary offered the Europe look cheaper, and Italy was a better name. From the look of the President after the screening, I gathered he was not amused.

'And what are you shooting on this road?'

'This girl, you see, is getting to know this chap, so they are out on a drive.'

'The girl is going out with the don?'

'No, with this other chap.'

'Villain or hero?'

'No, not like that.'

I was asking the usual simplistic questions of a complex film. The shareef of Nottingham, or the badmash of Leicester ... wait and see. The hero might prove villainous, or the villain could emerge as hero. Bollywood separates them nicely, but this film was getting it all mixed up.

The spokesman was not keen to speak any further. Couldn't blame him. You don't wander on to the sets of a whodunit in curiosity mode and expect answers. He asked me to wait for Dipesh and the director, they had gone for a recce of the Nottingham road for some driving shots and to set the scene for some roadside action.

They drove up shortly in a silver-coloured Mercedes, old enough by now to have become one of the poor non-gleaming cousins from that family. Dipesh was every bit what I thought he would be: young, just short of bulky, smart leather jacket, smart accent, the man who knows how to play the role of the man in charge. He introduced me to director Hansal Mehta, a wide and amiable chap, and perhaps pushy in a more laid-back style. There was barely time for a hello, they had things to do.

Their arrival brought the still white vans to life. The two in front opened up like that horse the Trojans had discovered too late. The first yielded the heroine, in a lemon-yellow sari and all the facial paint mandatory for a star. A woman dresser carrying a little mirror followed her around. Perfecting is always a process; besides, new light and the outside air must call for new measures. Breeze is known to be disrespectful of hairstyles, and on a set there's always room for more paint.

'The heroine?' I asked one of the crew who had found a surprisingly idle moment by my side.

'Yes, yes. Isha Koppikar.'

'Is she famous?' I asked, suspecting it could be a rude question.

'Yes, very famous. She has done items.' Which meant something quick and spectacular, like something that the rest of the film was only an excuse to present.

The hero-like chap, or part-villain because this film was different, stepped out of Van Two, shadowed by a mirror in his dresser's hands. Hero and heroine stood on the roadside, each accepting final touches from the dresser. The hero was not satisfied with his hair, he never would be. He tossed his hair around, the dresser brushed them, then he tossed them some more. This went on for some time, well past the point when it seemed nothing more could be done or undone to it. Facial paint at least sticks, but that could hardly be a solution for a hero's hair.

Dipesh and Hansal squeezed into the camera van. It eased slowly out from the lay-by on to the two-lane highway. Girl and boy followed in Mercedes, boy driving naturally, under the gaze of the camera looking back at them. Girl liked boy but I gathered she wasn't so sure. I saw it as a film with a good deal of what is and also isn't. Gangster with a heart fights hero with a dark side over a woman who loves one but not entirely, cares for another but not that much, and in the end nothing is concluded. The off-beat genre, unless it was off the off-beat.

Their departure left me with three white vans for company. And a very relieved and, as it turned out, relieving crew. This is when the four men emerged from the vans to pee by the roadside and raise those crucial matters between India and Britain. There was an obvious matter of law here; a pissing extra would be of more than passing interest to a policeman, but the question here was more financial than it was legal or environmental.

Britain was not promoting itself as a location for filming for nothing. Filming here meant free advertising to seduce visitors and tourists. Efforts like inviting Yash Chopra to Britain and getting a British minister to attend promotional events at Bollywood were meant to bring new money into an industry badly in need of it. It should have meant hiring a film crew here, not flying everyone in, hiring equipment from production companies in Britain, not making cargo of it in Bombay.

By UK Film Council standards, a respectable production unit convoy should include mobile make-up studios, generators, cars for the stars, catering vans, lights, the works, and yes, mobile toilets. But the crew had brought just about everything with them, and the countryside was providing what they hadn't. Indian heroines can look better from inside a make-up van made from saris and coats on the windows than from mobile studios custom-designed to polish faces to cinematic looks. Finally, it wouldn't matter what kind of van or truck the paint was applied in before the camera was switched on.

Filming here should also have meant hotels for the crew so that some money was spent on local economy. The stars here had hotel rooms, the rest clearly hadn't woken up in a hotel room that morning. If nothing, the crew could have eaten out at local places to feed that business a bit, but I gathered through some chatting among the film crew that the *Raakh* unit had brought its own cook, so they were saving on that too. And it seemed a safe guess that the crew were not on a per diem they would go shopping-crazy on.

The Indian stars had been dressed on the roadside, and now its crew was peeing by it. The van the men had stepped out of announced it was from Rolfe St Garage in Birmingham. So some vans dealers had found customers for a couple of weeks. A couple of drivers too had found work. It meant that much more support for local business than it would otherwise have. But it could hardly be what the UK Film Council had in mind when it chose to promote Britain as a destination for Bollywood filming. UK Plc was not doing remotely near the business it might have expected. That roadside pee was far more meaningful for the country getting pissed upon than those doing the peeing would ever recognize. It meant something was working for their India but not for Britain.

*

He'd earlier wanted to film *Raakh* in Prague, director Hansal told me. 'It's a gangster film, you know. It has a very desolate, gloomy atmosphere.' I thought I saw the gloom in his mind's eye. The pleasant-looking clock tower in the Leicester city centre by the pavement where we stood talking was gone for the moment from his mind's scene. He looked like he was being tempted by dreams of far less cheerful sights. He was measuring British gloom against that offered by the Czech Republic.

Prague gloom was more promising, but at a price. 'And there were so many logistical problems in Prague. Language barrier, big thing there. And you know they have no experience in dealing with Bollywood kind of shooting, the kind of budgets we work on. The cost for shooting in Prague was working out to four to five crore rupees. They are used to Hollywood films, like Bond and all that. They talk in those terms.' The cheerful bit about the Leicester gloom was the lower costs compared to Prague. 'Here our total cost for three weeks of production will be under a crore, which is reasonable.'

Happily, Hansalbhai found Leicester at least partly as grim as Prague had promised to be. He offered a director's analysis of Leicester: 'The outskirts of Leicester are quite charming, they have this desolate, gloomy feel, it is overcast all the time, grey skies, but also there is good landscape, and a certain kind of isolated urbanization. Feels right for a film like this, a gangster film with a focus on relationships. A very complex matrix of relationships.'

The UK Film Council would hardly be pleased that someone thought Britain just the place for gloomy gangsters. It was not looking for Bollywood producers who would be drawn to Britain by promise of gloom, and then spend no money on it.

But a crore of rupees still seemed like a lot to middle-class me. Hansalbhai offered more director's philosophy. 'No, I do not make expensive films, only expensive-looking films. I do not cut corners, I cut costs. Money should be spent in front of the camera, not behind. Behind, we will have comfort, not luxury.' He sounded just the man for villainous heroes and heroic villains.

Maybe a crore wasn't bad for all of half of a feature film. Because Don would come here only after he found himself in danger in India. And Leicester brought other advantages. 'I have the stars captive here, they only go back to a hotel, not home.' Most of the remaining crew wouldn't go back to a hotel, but to a couple of houses rented for the shoot. Cheaper captives. 'The unit is not rushed, and it functions more efficiently this way.'

Hansal told me he had directed *Dil Pe Mat Le Yaar*, *Ye Kya Ho Raha Hai* and *Humraahi*. He had filmed a good deal of the first two in Mauritius, and *Humraahi* was shot in Rajasthan. When he talked like a man who knew how to get his money's worth, I believed him.

From where we stood, Hansal had his production boys in sight around the clock tower, there was going to be a scene of sorts around it. He wasn't particularly looking at them but he knew that they knew he could be, and that was good enough to encourage efficiency. He now wandered off to one of those what-next meetings with the crew, and I searched again for an opportunity to talk to Dipesh.

Everyone was hanging around the clock tower except the stars who could never be so commonly seen. A white chap who too obviously hadn't showered for weeks rode up on a bicycle unwashed in years. 'Spare some pennies,' he said, circling the crew, who must have appeared to him like tourists just off the bus. He had no idea of the kind of budget his potential donors were on. The bicycle man was finally cornered into a conversation by a policeman, and the crew was spared any more of their tiny contributions to the British economy.

Dipesh was near the clock tower, busy on the mobile. He signalled that he was on his way to the bench I'd found nearby. On the way to me he spoke to chaps from the crew, to the director, to the driver, but finally he was there.

'Busy?' I said.

'Oh, really busy. I'm the line producer.'

'Line? How line?'

'I do locations, management. I'm the producer of this film outside India.'

'So that's a line producer.'

'Yes.' He'd begun to look away from me already. He really didn't have time to educate me about these things.

'You a Leicesterwallah?'

'Yes I'm based here. Promoting East Midlands. I have an independent company, Siddhi Entertainments and Productions UK. I've got a lot of Bollywood films to the UK for filming. Four to Leicester in the last three years. *Is Pyaar Ko Kya Naam Doon*, *Aa Ja Re*, *Kyon Ho Gaya Na*. Now *Raakh*. I also do a lot of Bollywood shows here. I brought Hrithik Roshan and Aishwarya Rai here, to East Midlands.' It sounded like he'd said all he had to, to stop me wasting his time.

'Do the East Midlands authorities pay you for this?'

'No, but they should. Those people, they do nothing. They just talk. But they should pay me. Just kidding. But I do it because I live here. The producers pay me.'

'So you offered the location here to the *Raakh* people.'

'Oh no, they approached me.'

'What is it you offer?'

'It is a very good deal that we offer. Main thing is getting here. Once they are here we can arrange basic needs easy, and get public locations free of cost. They spend a little bit on staying and eating but it's not much because you get everything here and they get the cook from India. You can have full crew at very little cost.'

'Is that a lot of crew?'

'Yes, cameraman, his assistants, assistant directors, art directors, make-up people, dance people, production controllers, spot boys, everybody. You've had about forty-five people or so come in for this film from Bombay.'

'And what's in it for Leicester?'

'It comes on the world map. People come to know where Leicester is. People abroad say this film was shot in Leicester, tourist interest increases. I'm getting three more films in the next three months. Hotels here get business. It's good.'

Dipesh had been looking away firmly now, and he had to go. It was action time and he was done with his giving me something. He headed off to one of the four white vans I'd encountered on the road to Nottingham. The ones that *Raakh* did spend some money on.

Brideless

NEAR MRS

I can't remember another evening when I was turned down by so many hundreds of women.

The two marriage melas, or saathi sammelans I went to were crowded in just the right way. Hundreds of Indian women had turned up in search of husbands, many more than men in search of a wife. There'd never be a better chance to end my ongoing search for someone somewhere. For too long now I'd been to weddings as a guest. I was waiting for the day I could turn up for my own.

The two saathi sammelans were being held in Wembley. White Brits know of Wembley for all the wrong reasons. They visit the stadium, now very big and smart, to empty out their lungs over beefy chaps kicking a ball around to make their millions. They know almost nothing of the real Wembley, the land of dandia and garba, of chevdo and gaathia. To a football fan at his politest—if there is such a thing—our Wembley is just something ethnic on way to the stadium. To the Gujarati Londoner, this is Gujarat that somehow moved to within half an hour's drive from London from the usual eight-hour flight.

There would be some non-Gujaratis too, I'd been told, at these two conjugal bazaars, coming from London and outside. I picked my smartest shirt and jeans for my date with multitudes of single women.

It wasn't easy to find parking space for my ancient banger amid those Mercedes Benzes and BMWs at the school by the Alperton tube station that had been hired for the first sammelan. The schoolchildren had long gone home, to make way for a different species of girls and boys. A kindness of Indian tradition, that: as long as you're trying to be husband, you're a 'boy'.

'You candidate?' a Gujarati chap at the door asked from a crowded desk just outside the hall. I found the courage to say yes, and he let me in on a £5 ticket. I walked into the school hall, with no way to go but forward. Sitting in rows of chairs along each wall, watching everyone come in, were the girls, the boys, the parents—hundreds I saw at a glance. By the time I saw what I'd walked into, it was too late to turn back and run, so I just carried on forward through the inspecting rows on both sides. A catwalk almost, if one could walk like that. I saw unexcited looks all around the room; I had never been sized up and written off by so many so soon.

'You from Southall?' a woman behind the desk at the far end asked. My straight trajectory had brought me right before her. It was not a polite question. From Southall they come Punjabi, big and loud. Wembley is for Gujaratis, gentle and traditional. There must have been something Jalandhar-born about the way I walked.

'What your specifications?' the woman asked. She was matter-of-fact, like a woman behind a railway counter asking where I want a ticket for. 'What year you want?' I didn't know immediately what she was saying, so I just stood there. She had all sorts of lists and forms spread out before her. I looked at them, a little intimidated. But I didn't have to be sure of anything, and I didn't have to answer. She'd figured me out. She pointed me to the next desk with a little board marked '50 to 59'—for people born between 1950 and 1959, that is.

I had to walk a few steps again, this time to the lady behind the second desk. She wasn't wasting time either. 'What is your caste?' 'I don't know,' I replied. My £5 ticket said this was a social gathering 'for all single Asians to meet prospective partners'. 'Asian', as usual, meant nothing. Not Indian, not even Gujarati. I now understood the little caution a friend had sounded. This was a saathi sammelan for Gujarati lohannas. I'd decided to go anyway because I was Indian, and in need, and because the standard wisdom in advance of such meetings is that you never know.

But now I felt an outsider. 'You are Hindu Punjabi?' the lady asked. Nobody had ever called me that in India. Among Indians in Britain you get used to sub-Indian flags, and this was mine. HPs, we're sometimes called in Wembley; fellow Hindu foreigners. The lady was looking through her lists. 'We have one Hindu Punjabi girl here, but she's too young for you.'

'I was thinking of the Gujaratis,' I said.

'It is very difficult but I will try,' said the plain-speaking lady. I had made it through the gate, but I wasn't getting past the reception. I could of course go and sit and watch others walk in.

I did, next to a very expectant-looking family. 'Smile, for god's sake, smile,' the mother was telling her near-bridally dressed daughter in the front row. We sat there pretending we were not under watch, and trying not to be seen looking.

A volunteer who had been busy for a bit with a ghetto blaster on stage decided to get us all into the mood with some music for the occasion. '*Aaj main upar, aasmaan neeche* ...' She must have figured we needed some optimism.

Another young lady volunteer, very pert and pink, took the mike when the song got over. 'All you boys and girls please come up to the desk and register. Please stand up and mingle. Don't just sit there. Make the most of your time here. Parents, will you please sit down, encourage your children!'

My neighbour, the mother, again leaned towards the semi-bride. She nudged again but the girl wouldn't budge. A few other prodding mothers had been more successful. And so, a little more than before, the eligible abandoned the sides to brave the catwalk ground in the middle. It seemed to take the courage of a gladiator. A little more than before, boy began to meet girl. Some had even begun to talk.

Finally the mother had persuaded her daughter to leave her seat. Inspired, I too entered the maidan. I strolled up to pink-and-pert lady. 'Can you help me find a wife here?' I asked. 'I am Punjabi,' I added apologetically.

'Doesn't matter,' she said. 'Some girls won't mind, tell me who you like and I'll introduce you.' As every Indian male knows, this is the moment of cowardice. I was going to be brave.

'You see that lady in the black sari, I think she's wearing it really well.'

'Oh, she has three little children, she's just helping. She's ever-so-nice, you know. Anyone else?'

A lady in a darker shade of pink than hers passed by. 'She's graceful,' I said.

'Oh don't be silly, she's my masi.' This was going to be my evening of near Mrs.

'But it's good that you're asking,' she said. 'Now you're getting into the spirit of it. But what is your caste?'

I was lost for an answer, and she quickly lost interest.

I wasn't the only one getting nowhere. I ran into a Tamilian friend who runs a shakha of the Hindu Swayamsevak Sangh, the British wing of the RSS. 'I am looking, for my son,' he said. He too wasn't going to find a Gujarati daughter-in-law easily. Another looking-man joined our corner. 'All this is just moneymaking,' he said. 'Five pound per head makes it 1500 pounds here, take away a bit for hiring the hall and for snacks and they make a packet. I am going to the other sammelan.'

So were most others after some time. We were running out of time and faces here. A reverse flow began along the catwalk. Outside we were now a colourful procession along Ealing Road, and then right down Stanley Avenue to the other school hall, to see and be seen, in search of that that someone who would change our lives for ever. And the traffic thought we were just pedestrians.

This second gathering was announced in a leaflet I picked up at the gate of this school now as the 'Lohanna and All Hindu Gujarati Youth Sammelan, An Event Of Get-Together & Introduction Programme'. It was organized, the gossip on way from one school to the other had told me, by Jethalal Hindocha, a lohanna matchmaking rival to Madhuben Rabheru who had organized the first marriage mela.

A woman at a desk outside the hall was collecting £7 from every candidate (I'd become used to thinking myself a candidate) and handing out badges—a bright orange badge for age twenty to twenty-four, green for twenty-five to twenty-nine, blue for thirty to thirty-four, white for thirty-five to thirty-nine, and a very red for forty plus. On the badge we wrote our name, educational qualification and ticked either of two boxes 'Single' or 'Divorced'. 'Match Your Heart' a placard on the desk by the badges read. Within your colour range, of course.

She handed me a list of 'Girls 30–34'. I read some entries: '9/11/62 GMD 034 4.9 Chunilal Acc assistant OA level Middx'; and '5/16/62 GLF 449 5.0 Raja Office Secretary course Middx.'

The legend below explained some of the abbreviations.

GLD=Girls Lohanna Divorced

GLE=Girls Lohanna Engagement Broken

GLF=Girls Lohanna First Time

GMD=Girls Mixed Divorced

GME=Girls Mixed Engagement Broken

GMF=Girls Mixed First Time

'Mixed' meant anyone not lohanna. The GLF and whatnot was followed by identity number, height, surname, job, education and location. Someone was an accounts assistant, someone an office secretary, someone had done O Level at school and then A Level. Middx was Middlesex, the county that Wembley falls into, because, as the postman sees it, Wembley is not London.

I bought a list with about 250 entries. 'Refunds are not available for lists purchased,' the first page said on top. The list offered 250 potential wives for £2; I couldn't possibly haggle over that.

The girl put me down on another list, the one the girls would pay their £2 for. 'You are a BMD,' she told me. It sounded just a little better than that other three-letter abbreviation. 'You go look inside, and if you don't find anyone I'll introduce you to someone. But she's like this,' she said, and stuck her elbows outwards.

This sammelan, I heard someone outside say, was more organized. I saw as I stepped into the hall that the organizational skill lay in one simple act. A rope had been stretched halfway across the hall in order to separate parents from the boys and girls. The cordoned-off parents sat on chairs looking into the eligible half of the hall. As one of the boys, I walked past the parents, crossed the rope, smartly I thought, just as I caught that dreadful word on the mike here too—someone was asking us to go 'mingle'.

For once someone approached me—a man. 'I'm looking,' he said, 'for my sister. She's over there.' He pointed to her. His sister looked dark and bright and very attractive in her sea-green salwar kameez, or Punjabi suit as Gujarati women call it. 'O yes, I'd love to meet her,' I said. 'Tell me about yourself,' the businesslike brother said. 'Are you Hindu Punjabi?' 'Yes.' 'Actually my sister wants to marry a lohanna.' I felt quite let down by this Punjabi inclination to look Punjabi. He must have seen disappointment on my face. 'I don't mind as long as you're Hindu, you know. But it's her choice.' He walked back to her. Another potential wife lost.

A woman walked up, looking interested. She was more radiant than lovely, and had all the confidence I lacked. She was coming up to talk to me, and I felt a distinct rising of hope, I was getting mingled more with than I was mingling. After a rapid hello, she started to tell me about the next saathi sammelan she was organizing. She'd walked up to me to advertise her own sammelan, obviously confident that I'd leave this hall still single.

'I have a boyfriend and I told him I'm coming here just to advertise,' she said. 'But I'm also looking.' So she could replace her boyfriend, but the new one would have to be good, really good. We chatted a bit, then she left, saying 'I'll go chat up someone else now.' Two steps on, she looked back. 'I'm honest, you see.'

She left me floored, and I stood quite a while doing nothing. A suited lohanna took the mike on stage. 'Hey guys and girls! It's stupendous to see you mingling out there! Great, great! Just carry on!' Why couldn't I be like those guys who take the stage, take the mike, who have what it takes?

An announcement followed for someone who had been sought. 'Yogesh, will you please come to the stage. A really lovely girl wants to meet you.' Good for you, Yogesh, and damn you. I thought I saw many expressions around me saying just that. There must have been plenty of disappointed lohannas around me as well. Being a lohanna is a help, but not a guarantee. After the Yogesh announcement, came the song again, '*Aaj main oopar ...*' You had to be Yogesh this evening to enjoy it.

A queue was gradually forming to a side for the snacks and I headed straight towards it. It promised samosas and escape, and I wanted both. Someone father-like behind me was offering his views on the evening to his companion. 'UP ka avay chhe, Punjabi avay chhe, doctor avay chhe, dentist avay chhe. Moto problem chhe.' So, finding someone is a problem for everyone. But there was an edge to his observation. So many others have come here in search of single lohannas, when lohannas could not find enough of their own.

Picking up a white plastic plate with cold dhokla on it—I found no samosas at the table—I walked towards the very elderly and very wise-looking Hindocha who had organized this sammelan, and who seemed at last to be enjoying a free moment. 'It took me four years to find a match for my daughter,' he said. He knew just what to say to sad faces. It can take many sammelans for one saathi. 'What to do, there are no opportunities to meet others who are like you. Results usually take two to three months after a sammelan. But every week I get one or two calls from people marrying who met through my gatherings.' Good things always happen to others, don't they?

'Don't worry, we have your name,' Hindocha said. 'You will hear from someone.' I never did.

*

Right after he'd finished singing *Pukarta chala hoon main* very badly, the chap in the black shirt at least half covered in pink print asked our table at the mochi bar in Leicester if anyone was going to their marriage mela in Birmingham. Only I was interested, and this brought some beer-fuelled digs that I'd walk away with a mochi girl. That girl, like this bar, was really meant for a Gujarati male of shoemaker ancestry.

I must have been the only one thinking 'shoemaker' in the bar even though this was the mochi bar. It was run by an association of Gujarati Aryas, originally of the shoemaker caste. I used to be careful once to speak of this as the Arya bar because I didn't want to sound disrespectful. But very soon I was calling it the mochi bar like everyone else around Belgrave Road in Leicester, I didn't have to cover facts with a correctness they thought unnecessary. Naturally, someone at this bar knew about that coming together of Gujarati mochi singles in Birmingham. The singer gave me a number to call, and I was invited to attend after polite agreement that it would not be as a prospective groom.

A late start from London made me among the last arrivals at the smart new Shree Krishna Mandir on Henley Street in Birmingham. A young fellow was also walking towards the mandir hall through a crowded corridor as I headed in. I asked him if he was a mochi.

'We are all mochis, you know, shoemakers,' he said.

'And what do you do?'

'I'm a computer systems analyst up in Manchester.' He stopped to talk to someone, and I pushed through towards the hall.

It was a bright morning, made brighter by the weekend buzz around the temple. The weekend is when the business of life gets done. It's when the English rest or shop, go fishing or repaint the fence, do up an attic, do a roast, the rare one even goes to church. For an Indian, the weekend is the time to move from England to India. To the halls where everyone meets, to one another's houses, to Indian shopping for chat and chaat. It's the time to be with your own, or to look amongst your own.

A few hundred eligible mochis, expensively dressed, had crowded into the large hall under the white bud-like dome of the temple. The suits and silks in the hall, the shining cars outside, were quite unlike the picture of the mochi in India as I knew him to be—a man who often carried his workshop on his shoulder and who miraculously never seemed to notice the heat. These were well-heeled mochis.

By a side was the shrine, and some people had taken their shoes off for darshan. Shoes had brought everyone to this temple, not the shoes they arrived in, but the shoes their forefathers made, and even the shoes they did not—because whether they really made the shoes or not, they were the shoemaker caste.

Past the shrine, the eligible mochis had the hall to themselves; parents had been kept back in the corridor. That naturally didn't stop those closest to the door from happening to see what was going on within. The others just hadn't made the lucky front spot for the ringside peep.

There were 262 single mochis already in the hall, a male volunteer at the door told me as I was stepping in. Someone was keeping a watchful count. For a silly moment I was pleased at the even number, like there were just as many males and females, and everyone would necessarily leave the hall half of a pair. But it did appear a gender-balanced gathering. Through all the colours the one constant was the off-white badges everyone wore, each with a number that would lead back to the kind of CV that needs to be presented for marriage.

I heard numbers before I read them on the badges. 'One hundred and forty-nine,' a man on the stage called out. 'Eighty-eight,' he announced next. Everyone was a number, and he was calling out numbers that fronted singles who'd appeared interesting to someone. 'Nobody give your phone numbers, please.' This matchmaking must be done through official mochi numbers and processed through families, or it might be just another decadent party.

Had I been Eligible Mochi No. 263 this morning I'd have taken the number maybe of that woman taller than almost all the numbered men, made for a Punjabi. But height does not matter, and there were others. The more women I looked at in there, the more I wanted an off-white piece of paper with a number on it. But I'd been allowed in only as a witness to supervised flirtation. If my forefathers were shoemakers, I could have become a husband. But here I was badgeless, hopeless.

So I searched for a partner theoretically. Most of the girls were attractive, in the usual Gujarati way—pale, petite, permed. How about that light-eyed girl in the peach chania-choli with the large silver patches, or that bright-eyed woman in the yellow and red sari? As mochi, I'd have wandered past each one casually, made a note of the number when no one was looking, and gone straight to a volunteer. I'd have given my number, given hers. Her number would be called out and, who knows, they would call out mine, and we could live happily ever after.

I spotted the chap I'd met outside. Out of the corner of my eye, I thought I saw him looking around out of the corner of his. I had a better look at him now. He was slim, his jet black hair combed remorselessly back matching nicely with his moustache, the one thing so many Indian men have and the British don't. In his bright blue blazer and striped tie he was a picture of success. He looked a good catch for a sensible woman.

'What do you think of all this?' I asked.

'Mixed feelings, really.'

'How, mixed?'

'Well, it's a good idea if people can meet, nothing wrong with that.'

'But you're not very sure.'

'Well, yeah, it's this caste thing, you see. I mean by now we should be moving further and further away from it, right, but this kind of thing is only promoting that.'

'You said you're from the shoemaker caste.'

'Yes, shoemaker. Mochi.'

'But you're a computer analyst.'

'Yeah, but that's my work.'

'So in what sense do you think of yourself as a shoemaker?' I was squirming as I asked, but he seemed a lot more comfortable than I was.

'It's the parents. It's the whole community.'

'What does the community do?'

'Everything. We do our Navratri days together, we have our own temple where everyone keeps meeting. We keep meeting at weddings, when they happen within the community.'

'Do a lot of them happen within the community?'

'Well, most do, some don't. And there's always trouble with the parents when you marry outside the community.'

'You mean parents get upset if someone marries a Gujarati Hindu from another caste?'

'Oh yes, yes.'

'Are you here because you want to be here or because your parents want you here?'

'Well, it's for the parents, really. But there's no harm if you can meet somebody.'

'If you like a girl from another caste, would you marry her?'

'Well I don't know but if I marry within the community, right, my parents would be happy and I'd be happy.'

'Met anyone here?'

'Yes, I have, actually.' He led me with his eye to the girl facing us in the group to the left. The one in the peach and silver who I'd considered for myself only minutes back in my mochi dream world. 'She's just the kind of person I've been looking for.' There must be more who thought as he and I did. He couldn't hold back his smile when he spoke of her. And did I see a blush border the moustache, and a light in his eyes. 'I'll invite you to our wedding,' he said. He didn't have my address, and he didn't ask for it. He just wanted to share his joy with someone, and I happened to be around.

He'd given her number to his parents. They had spoken to her parents. Things had moved quickly and he looked impatient to announce the wedding. 'She's just finished college,' he said, looking again towards her, staring almost. An arranged marriage can sometimes be the same thing as love at first sight. But he was worried too, because he wasn't there yet. I had heard her number called out three or four times, and that may not have been all. He must have heard it far louder than I did. I left him hanging in that awful space between doubt and hope.

He was in love, but only because he was a mochi. Not that there was anything peculiarly mochi in his desire—shoes didn't come into that, the emotion wasn't informed by leather—but they couldn't have met without sharing family memories of shoemaker origins. For him, this was it, he'd found the woman of his dreams. After that, who thinks of the arranged time and place, or the given ancestry that made it possible?

For Dinesh Chauhan, who was managing the event and had invited me to it, theirs would be another happy story of shoemaker weds shoemaker, but he'd be just as happy if either was replaced by another mochi. Chauhan, young for a community leader and very proper in his grey suit, was off-stage now, and I sought him out in a corner past some girly groups and male conferences. In the given style of important people, he spoke to the point.

'We have a Mahasabha UK with nine constituent associations in Birmingham, London, Leicester, Bradford, Leeds, Preston, Wellingborough, Coventry, Greater Manchester. But our boys and girls in Birmingham will not know if someone from the community is available for marriage in London. Now introduction is available. So this is a sammelan for the candidates to come into contact.'

'Or they might never meet.'

'Yes, finding a suitable partner is a big problem because the people are scattered. In your area you may not meet person with right age and qualification.'

'You think this is a good way?'

'Oh yes, we cannot just have arranged marriages. Here they see each other first hand, they can talk and exchange views and hope to find a partner.' He surveyed the hall with much satisfaction. 'You see, they are mingling. Given the situation in this country this is a very viable way.'

'But is it necessary to call out someone's number on the mike?'

'Yes that is the way they have to contact a volunteer.'

'But then everybody knows that someone is interested in a particular person.'

'No, but we are not calling candidates on top of the stage. If somebody finds somebody likeable to talk to they have to go only to the volunteer. There are no obligations on anyone.' After a pause he said, 'You see the parents want to carry on the tradition. So we have this new mandir. The mandir is the central focal point for everybody to get together.'

'But what about other Gujaratis, other Hindus? Wouldn't they do?'

'We are doing this for the community but there are no restrictions with Gujaratis or Hindus.'

'But if you're doing this for the community, why not invite other Hindus?' I was making a daring suggestion—why not arrange for one Hindu to marry another Hindu?

'Hindus are most welcome. We can do that, but the Hindu community is so vast it is difficult to organize.' Chauhan had drawn the mochi circle, at least partly, he was suggesting, for logistical reasons. Only caste could give you manageable numbers to work with.

An elderly Gujarati in a suit (elderly Gujaratis have a way of getting even their suits to look Gujarati) walked up to call Chauhan away to attend to some matter that couldn't wait. Chauhan made his way to the stage and announced, 'You have been intermingling for two hours. Now the parents are coming in, as you can see. We will break for lunch now but after lunch you will get some further intermingling with each other.'

The parents were pouring into the hall fast, a 'what happened?' look on every face. The future of the family could depend on those last two hours. On numbers called and heard, or the numbers not

called. Some numbers I heard again and again, like the one that
had begun to sound peach, many I never did.

Some of the women in near bridal best were leaving the floor
like the bridegroom had failed to turn up. They'd stood two hours
waiting to be liked, minute after undesired minute, number after
another's number. All those days of preparing for this day—this
sari, no, that salwar kameez, those bangles, these earrings, the
nails just right, the hair ... no, that's never absolutely right but
still—and after all that, this silence.

Would this day ever end if your number didn't make it to the
mike? What an avalanche of undesire that would be to live with.
And other mochis would talk. You were there, and you're still
single? Want to think of marrying someone whom 150 men rejected
straightaway? Over lunch I began to not miss a number of my
own.

I decided to skip the post-lunch intermingling, but sought out
my near-bridegroom friend to say bye. He was heading out to the
parking lot, he wasn't staying for the post-lunch intermingling. He
looked defeated and rather white around his dark moustache.

'All well?' I asked.

'They said no. She said no.' He turned away and was gone.

Fast Work

'You will have three minutes each with twenty ladies,' Ann Little
told me when I called her. I don't know what she heard from my
silence over this, but she said, 'When you come to think of it,
three minutes is quite a long time in which to get to know someone.'
She was right, of course.

I had turned to the organization called A Little Creation. It was
a clever name, but one that must have been waiting to suggest
itself to someone by the name of Ann Little when she took to the
speed-dating business, unless Ann Little was her name for this
business.

I was running out of time and Indian women, and a friend persuaded me it was time to try my luck with English women. In any case, Indian women in England weren't Indian, really, they were first Gujarati or Sikh. And it wouldn't have been possible to be just Gujarati or Sikh. The Chha-gam Patels would not invite me for their matchmaking parties if I wasn't one of them, the Charotar Patels would leave me out of theirs. Jat Sikhs sought jat Sikhs, ramgarhia Sikhs looked for and found their own. As none of the above, I found no one among them. There's nothing quite like the desire to marry to teach an Indian how much a foreigner he can be to other Indians.

I had slipped into the lohanna bazaar twice, but where could I hide my un-lohannaness? Maybe it was me, not the Hindu Punjabi in me that turned all those faces away. But usually I never got that far, I just bumped into one closed door after another. It hurt that I was dismissed before I'd had a chance to prove myself unworthy.

It was time for A Little Creation. A friend showed me the way at the very suburban-yuppy David Lloyd's club in Harrow. We found the Ann Little posters pasted just above the Internet access points by the pool and bar. 'A Little Creation presents fun-dating', the poster read in many colours. The logo was the silhouette of a joyous couple, with a clock on the side to remind you that time was running out. The couple and the clock worked, I called Ann Little and before I knew exactly what I was letting myself into, I was speed-dating.

I went in my coolest blue shirt and casual–smart black trousers, two pleats to each side. You can't let the wrong clothes come in the way of twenty possibilities spread evenly across an hour. Twenty was a lot less than the hundreds at the Gujarati saathi sammelans, but here I would get to talk to every one of the twenty, which was about twenty more than at the Indian melas.

Ann Little was easy enough to find at a table by the Internet point. 'And you are ...?' she asked, with the distant ease of a receptionist. She peeled off a sticker with my name on it under the colourfully lettered 'Fun-Dating'. I stuck it on my shirt as instructed.

'Let me explain what happens,' she said briskly. 'You see these twenty tables, each has a number. The ladies will just sit at their table. We think it is more appropriate for the men to rotate. Every three minutes someone will blow a whistle, and you move to the lady at the next table. You start at table 7. Take this coupon. It will get you your first drink at the bar free. We find that people usually need it.'

Ann also handed me a little eight-page booklet, some blank post-it notes and a pencil. 'Those blank ones are in case you want to make some notes about a lady. On the form, you enter the name of every lady you meet. If you would like to see her later, tick the box to the side. The form will tell you more. And have a great evening.'

Ann was right about the drink. My beer at the bar went down at speed as I waited for the rotation to begin. I saw others with 'Fun-Dating' stickers at the bar making rapid progress with theirs. We all looked away from one another. The men were all alone, the women all in groups. The agony of waiting was relieved a little by the knowledge that I didn't have to approach the women at the bar, I'd be moved past every one of them like the needle of the clock that A Little Creation seemed so fond of. For the first time, I was at a crowded bar knowing I would talk to every woman there. Going up to Ann Little had taken courage; going up to the women would be pre-arranged routine. A Little Creation had institutionalized the pass and rotated it into spinning-wheel inevitability. I was urgently arguing its advantages to myself, to work myself into an upbeat state I didn't feel.

As the beer disappeared from the glass, I turned to a snapshot account of speed-dating in the booklet Ann Little had provided.

HELLO AND WELCOME TO FUN-DATING!

The aim of the evening is to ensure that we all have a great time. You will be meeting like-minded people in a relaxed atmosphere and the emphasis of tonight is to have fun.

Fun-dating at speed is a great way of meeting and chatting to people that you might never get the opportunity to talk to in normal circumstances. You would have three minutes to decide whether or not you would like to get to know a person better and then move on.

Fun-dating at speed also gives you a fairly quick escape route if you need it! I wonder how many of you have been on a blind date and within three minutes you have wanted to leave? Well at Fun-dating you can! You just move on to your next date.

Our function room tonight is exclusive to 'fun-daters' and there is a cash bar open throughout. Once the dating is over, there is the opportunity for everyone to stay and chat at the bar and to carry on talking to the new friends that you have met. It really is very informal and relaxed.

Thank you for coming along tonight and who knows it could be the first three minutes of the rest of your life!'

Too soon, a whistle started my first three-minute date. I walked up and sat down across a lady at table 7. She was sharp and elegant in that chiselled English way. I wish I could say she'd been waiting for me.

She spoke first, thankfully. 'Have you done this before?'

'No. And you?'

'A couple of times. It's not so bad. Okay, now let's see where we start.' She glanced at a printed green sheet placed on the table to guide women on what they could talk about over three minutes.

'You go to a gym?' she asked. She spoke like someone situated unerringly on a socially pleasant plateau.

'Sort of, sometimes.' I could see that she did.

'And what do you do?' she asked.

'I'm a journalist.'

'Who for?'

'Just write articles here and there, in India, in some other countries.' So I was not BBC or anything proper like that. I felt my score drop. The marginal man. I wasn't giving her anything that would make me respectably introduceable to her friends. Now I took some initiative, I wanted my ninety seconds.

'And you?'

'I'm a nurse. Up at Clementine Churchill.'

'Yes, that's just round the corner, isn't it?' I'd been given only a few seconds to be scintillating, and was failing badly.

'Yes, and there's lots of us from there around today. We're all friends, we all came here together.'

'Lots of nurses here, is it?' I had no idea why that should make me nervous, but it did.

'Oh yes, lots. But that's your whistle.' I thought she'd been a bit quick to point my attention to it. The man ahead of me had moved on already, and I replaced him across from the lady at table 8.

I was now opposite another nurse, the first 'Hi, I'm so-and-so' confirmed. Everyone had a name tag, but it was still polite to engage in unassisted introductions. I decided to be brave, and looked straight at her. She was pretty and bright in her turquoise blue dress. Streaks of grey in the sheer drop of her hair to the shoulders added anchor to her good looks. She was a woman fighting off experience with spirit.

I found myself carrying table 7 to table 8. Clementine Churchill.

'That hospital's more like a hotel,' I said.

'Oh ya, it is really very nice. But, you know, when you work somewhere, it's just work.'

'Of course,' I said, and went blank.

She didn't. 'Do you think there's something really very sad about all this, the way we are meeting. You know, meeting like this just because we couldn't find anyone otherwise?'

'Yes, it is sad. It means, I suppose, that the magic didn't work for us, chance didn't sort of deliver anything. So you play a numbers game, and hope something happens this way.'

'How long have you been on your own?' she asked.

'Oh, long.'

'Which means?'

'Years, many years. And you?'

'I broke up with my boyfriend last month.' She needed someone faster than I did, but she didn't need me, and it didn't take perception to tell.

This time I heard the whistle. The whistle-blower was walking right by our table, a twenty-something given charge of moving twenty men every three minutes.

I left table 8 with a feeling of some indignity. I was leaving tables, and would leave another eighteen because someone would blow a whistle in my ears. I wished Ann Little had found other ways to mark the passage of time. But at least my three minutes at table 8 had not come off the green sheet here.

I would never recall everything said at every one of those twenty tables. I never did make notes on those blank slips of paper—couldn't, in those three minutes of throwing up some talk, anything, and couldn't in-between. After the first couple of conversations, I really stopped listening. There was nothing to note, nothing to say. Okay, you have three minutes to be scintillating in, or ninety seconds, and your time begins NOW. Under such pressure, I developed even more cramps between my ears than usual.

But through those three-minute multiplications, what got said didn't really matter. It was the expressions I found myself reading, and figuring whether there would be anything to read there or not. Looks say so much, and every three minutes they were saying 'no'. Ann was right, three minutes really is quite a long time. The real choices had been made already in those quick glances at the bar. This business is so fast it's over before it begins.

So I knew the Cypriot girl was from Cyprus only because we had to say something for three minutes. But a shutter had dropped over her grey eyes before I could sit down. Before those eyes three minutes was a very long time. I had no idea what to say to her, and no particular desire to say anything. I found myself longing for the whistle, because this time the indignity would bring escape.

We found no room for those social rituals that hide the hard decisions, or for those playful nothings that really bring two people that one step closer. We were meeting with raw purpose, and when we saw we were getting nowhere, no one cared if it showed. I began to feel like a train passing through stations; I stopped at platforms to stare at faces, exchanged a word or two, then moved on to the guard's whistle. I went past the Greek lady who said she has a store selling designer stuff, past the schoolteacher from Ireland, the management consultant handling male resistance to her at an office in Newcastle, the Essex-like girl who so, so, loves to travel and has been almost everywhere and couldn't wait to go everywhere else.

One table I remember well; here I met a Gujarati girl. 'I'm a Prajapati, you know, from the north of Gujarat. Saurashtra. But that is my family. I'm from Kenya. But to tell you the truth, I do not want to meet a man from my community. I would like to go out with a white guy. But I did not really come for myself. My friend, he is just going through a divorce. So I brought him here to meet girls, then I said why not join myself also.'

I'd found no time to look at the men in the circle and had no idea who he was, or even what she was really saying. But about halfway through my table tour I figured who was behind me. He spoke to me after a quick whistle to draw my attention, in obviously Pakistani Punjabi. 'Tusi kidi laini ay?' ('So which one are you going to screw?') I must of course have been just as obviously Punjabi to him. I only had time to say that I thought neither of us would get anywhere with anyone this evening.

Towards the end of the circle, I began to notice also the guy in front of me. Everyone did. I'd seen him at the bar. He was the picture of the regular English football fan, sort of bulky but with a sporty manner, he probably had the cross of St George on his car outside. But as he progressed along the circle he had become more and more unsteady. He'd been speed-drinking longer and at greater speed than anyone else, and he was now getting slower and slower off each table. I was never more sympathetic towards someone who had had more than he could handle.

And never before did I think it would be such a relief to sit at a table only because it was called table 6. The round was done, and fast enough, perhaps, the evening was over. I was on my own at the end, as I was at the beginning. Only now I felt my ineligibility wasn't Indian any more, it had gone, as they say, mainstream.

*

The first woman I saw on my big evening out just happened to catch me admire my moustache in the ladies toilet. I apologized rapidly and walked out fast, lucky not to run into a second woman walking in. But the place was seriously dark, and she could have excused the intrusion.

Everything was dark about the Turnmills Club on Clerkenwell Street, across from Farringdon station on one side, and the offices of the *Guardian* on the other. The facade was painted black, the name of the club that spoke through little fluorescent tubes too also managed to look dull. It was right enough for a nightclub, though, which it would become again after our Asian speed-dating event got over.

I half-guessed my way towards the party hall downstairs in the basement. The light along the way was a shade between diffused and disappeared. But it was just right for the occasion. It would fade out our imperfections and create the 'atmosphere' the electricians must have been instructed to wattage for. The rewards were greater than the risk of walking into the wrong toilet. This had promised to be a particularly rewarding evening because Apna Speed-dating was going to put me on a circuit created especially for Hindu Punjabis. After the misadventures with Gujarati lohannas and white English nurses, this would be home turf.

The Apna website had announced the event would be for 'H/P & Separate Muslim'. Hindu Punjabi and a separate Muslim event, that is, at the same place, at the same time. Nothing gets the Hindu parent more worried than the fear of a daughter taking off with a Pakistani, since at an event like this Muslim would really mean Pakistani. And what if circuits got mixed up somehow? I reminded myself I was here as searching male, not as worrying parent.

I joined a queue headed downstairs to a desk where a chap and a girl were ticking arrivals against names. The bare shoulders and glance-stopping silhouettes descending before me looked good. The girl at the desk marked what she thought was my name on what I guessed was a register, and gave me a coupon for the first free drink at the cellar bar. Everyone knows the need for that one.

I said hello to the chap beside her, he was the one I'd spoken to on the phone earlier. Even in the darkness of the Turnmills basement, I could see he was Pakistani. What would parents of Hindu Punjabi girls have to say to their daughters descending into a dark basement for a group date being managed by a Pakistani, and with lots of Pakistani males around at a simultaneous event at the same place? I guess it wouldn't be 'have a great night out, darling'. I groped my way towards the bar, mainly to work myself out of a vicarious parental mode.

Beer in hand, I entered the dating room. Tables were set and numbered, with two chairs facing one another at each table. This is where Apna would play us in three-minute slots. The clock on the Apna website, quite the favoured emblem of speed-dating managers, had suggested alarmingly what these could be. 'It's time', the clock declared, with only 3, 2 and 1 etched on it in place of the usual twelve hours. Three, a couple appeared sitting across one another. Two, they got closer. One, they were holding hands. This wouldn't be everyone's story that evening, not even in those promised twenty-seven three-minute attempts. All of us knew we were always likely to fail that against the clock, but we were there for what could be.

Many more who had made it down into the darkness were now hanging around the paired chairs. That was the idea. 'It's the ice-breaking time,' a girl with papers and lists in her hand announced a few times through a quick tour of the room. The website had announced this as a new feature. 'New: Ice-breakers are being introduced at all our events from May onwards, these will help you get relaxed and put you in a positive frame of mind before the dating gets underway, please ensure you arrive at the specified time to take part in these activities.'

There was no separate breaking of ice for Muslims and for HPs. I ventured a hello and parked myself at the nearest table, and I saw eventually that I'd joined two chaps with Muslim names, Pakistanis clearly, breaking ice with two girls with Hindu names. The two Pakistanis looked everywhere but at me, they wanted me to be anywhere but there. We chatted for a while, and then I got up and strolled towards the lady with the lists.

'Are the Hindu and Muslim events separate?' I asked.

'Yes they are, but we are going to have some Muslim tables in the Hindu room. Excuse me.' She was off, this was not something she wanted to talk about. After breaking ice, some Pakistanis and Hindu Punjabis would again be speed-dating in the same room.

I looked around the room at the guys. An Indian can usually tell Pakistani from Indian about nine times out of ten; a good many chaps chatting around were obviously Pakistani. There were Hindus too, and a turbaned Sikh. I walked up to a chap with a Hindu name on his sticker. 'Where are you from?' I asked, which could mean something as usual as where in London, a fairly dull opener of a question. But he was only a male, so it was okay. He looked past me and walked towards the bar. I followed. 'What's your drink?' I asked. Now he walked away from the bar. He wouldn't say a word, not to me.

In the dark, I tried to read stickers on the women without appearing like I was staring at their breasts. Couldn't find a Muslim name immediately; maybe they were in some other room. A religious mix should be something to be pleased about, and maybe this one had the innocence of a cross-religious togetherness we could all smile upon. Togetherness in itself seems such an ideal, separation such a shame. But the method here seemed dubious, and at the least at variance with the announcement. The Hindu–Muslim divide in matters sexual is issue enough; between Indians and Pakistanis it can be the stuff of family destruction.

The dating began sharp an hour behind schedule. I began at table 1, and I was to move down to table 27 in three-minute rides. I had a scorecard in my hand from the front desk, so had all the girls. My curiosity had taken over my need for a woman in my life. I just wanted to see who these Indian girls were at this kind of event.

I began with a nursery schoolteacher, light and pretty, whose parents she said had come to Britain from Mauritius. She was renting a flat in smart Notting Hill with a friend. But Notting Hill was not a good place to meet others ethnically like her. 'It's always nice to meet Asians,' she said. 'There's just so much more you can share, it's not the same with the whites, is it?' Her parents weren't in London, so how would she ever meet anyone if not this way? She'd seen an ad for the event in *Metro*, the free morning newspaper distributed on the Underground.

'Well, you've been looking around for an hour,' I said. 'Seen anyone interesting?'

'No, not really, but let's see how it goes.'

The girl at table 2 had invested in a strikingly short dress. The shortness of her skirt would show particularly to the male across. This was the barest at a generally bare evening. The dress code that evening was minimal, I was seeing bare legs and shoulders all over the place. Only one girl wore Indian, a churidar-kurta.

Table 2 was a personal assistant to a manager at an IT firm, and she looked most relieved that she did not have to put up with my Indian accent for more than three minutes. 'Such a desi,' I could hear her saying later.

The next girl was Gujarati. And why was she here? 'I really like Hindu Punjabi boys,' she said. 'I think they're so sexy. But there seem to be hardly any around today.' The ice-breaking hour had dashed her hopes already. In the rush, I had no time to feel pained that she seemed to exclude me.

Table 4 was also Gujaratan, and a speed-dating veteran. 'Been to many of these, you know, speed-dater and some others.'

'Didn't find someone?'

'No, not really. It's not easy, you know. Guys, you know, they're so vague.' She held her scorecard with a practised hand. After I moved to table five she'd mark me in the 'No' box, if she cared to do even that. She must have crossed a hundred speed-dating NOs by now. At least she could never say she'd been short of choice.

I was not doing a very good job with my scorecard. I saw later what they meant by tip number four on the website: 'Try and keep notes of your dates, adding comments in the space provided on your scorecard for people that have impressed you. This will remind you later of who they were.'

Table 10 was unforgettable, though, and not because the bareness of her back went down that extra half-mile. I only had to say 'Hi' before she said, 'You're from India.'

'Yes. The accent, is it?'

'When did you arrive?'

'Been here ten–twelve years.'

'What? Ten years? And you talk like an Indian?'

'What else?'

'But ... ten years? You didn't change?'

I said this was one failing that didn't embarrass me.

'But you must be from India,' I said.

'Yes, I only came here three weeks back.' Already she sounded far less Indian than me.

'And how long are you here for?'

'Only another three weeks.' I did not ask the rude question:

what was she doing speed-dating here then?

She sounded Delhi to me, and I was right. 'Why don't you go back and start speed-dating in Delhi.'

'It would never work there.'

'Maybe not if people just pay over the phone and walk in like here, but if you pre-select a group and put them together, it might.'

But she was here thinking London, not Delhi.

'What brought you to London?'

'I'm a fashion designer, here for a course.' She looked like a woman with other designs. I moved on, and so did she, whether in Delhi or London I don't know.

The transfers came to an abrupt end at table 17. Someone suddenly announced an invitation to the Anexo bar next door, with offers of coupons for two drinks for the price of one. It was a relief, and I didn't mind missing women 18 to 27. This would be a free-for-all party, no one was even pretending any more that Hindus and Muslims would be separate there.

'Maybe they should have just parties instead,' the private secretary, table number whatever, said as I walked upstairs with her. Apna was a few steps ahead of her. Their next event was going to be a party, the website had said, with no separateness announced. 'Summer Bonanza All Asian Mixed Speed-Dating Event, Tickets on sale below ... Meet and Date up to 30 People, From Only £15 ...' The usual promise had been tagged on: 'Imagine a room full of between 15-25 eligible singles who want to meet someone like you ... No pressure, it's fast it's fun and you could meet the one!' Apna was also offering 'limited spectator/chill-out zone tickets (£15.00 each)' in case you wanted to observe the dating and not join in.

Almost none of the Hindu girls walked into the bar next door, all of them just seemed to be leaving. That should have reassured the VHP. Maybe they were waiting for the one-to-ones later from the scorecards we'd handed in before leaving. But my guess was there wouldn't be much of that.

That left four of us Indian males at Anexo to brood over the evening, and I exchanged names with them more happily than I had with the girls. About the quietest-looking was a chap to my side, Rakesh. He was twenty-four, he said, and he'd been pushed by friends to attend the event because he was still a virgin. 'I've always been shy of talking to girls.'

'So how did you get on this evening?'

'How can you talk to these girls? They all wear, like that.' He made a horizontal move of his hand at chest level in line with the low-cuts of the evening.

'That's good man, that's good.' This was Jaz, the Sikh. It's hard to find a young Sikh in London who's not called Jaz. Jasminder, Jaspal, Jasbir—they're all Jaz.

Jaz was taking Rakesh under his wing. 'You know I was shy like you once. And look at me now. It's a phase, man. It's just a phase.'

'I'll tell you what,' said the fourth, Mukul. 'You come with me to Sports Cafe at Piccadilly. Polish, Hungarian, Chinese girls. I'll make any one of them shag you.' We were all getting quite concerned about poor Rakesh's virginity. He listened quietly and looked like he just wanted to go home and wished he hadn't left it at all.

Mukul was resigned to a wasted evening. 'I won't get anyone tonight,' he said, in a loud funky-punky kind of accent that belonged nowhere. He'd come from Bangalore three years back.

'You just came from India,' he told me. 'I can tell.'

I delivered the shock to him now. 'You been here ten–twelve years? You still not managed to change? I can't believe it.' I believed that he couldn't, he looked very open-mouthed.

'Why do you think you won't get anyone?' I asked him.

'I can tell, I can tell,' he said.

'How many girls did you tick?'

'Just four, five. You have to be selective.'

'I ticked everyone,' said Jaz. 'If I give seventeen girls the chance to have me, I have a better chance. Mark just three, four, less chance. But you,' he said, turning to me. 'You should not look so Indian, man. I have a Pakistani friend, he couldn't get no girls. Then I told him to shave off his moustache and he got plenty girls. You should shave off your moosch.'

He didn't make the connection that his own moustache was probably bigger than mine. With a beard for company, a moustache is probably not a moustache. I hadn't expected the evening to begin and end with my moustache. But somewhere I knew through arguing hope to myself that if I did meet Hindu Punjabi girls this evening, we wouldn't emerge a Hindu Punjabi pair. It wasn't just the toilet that I got wrong.

~

LUCKY DUCKY

We'd meet, we Indians, some Pakistanis maybe, at a place as white English as it could possibly get. Ask a tourism consultant in London which part of England is most England-like if you had just a day to visit, and Henley is what you'll hear.

It's the kind of place nature custom-designs for tourism boards, a picture postcard waiting to be walked into. Wooded hillside descending into a meadow right down to the clear waters of the Thames, the rafters by the pretty white boats under the ancient stone bridge which you must cross to enter the village street for the tea houses with the hot scones, the ones right by the old clock tower in the square ... Maybe it wanted something they could have called cobbled, but even Henley can't have it all.

They must have added 'scenic drive from London'. I was there in less than an hour. I put aside the map that would tell me where to go from the parking lot, because a more interesting possibility arose by way of an Indian girl who emerged from a red Renault two cars away. She must be headed for the party—why else would an Indian be in Henley, and she wouldn't be in that high black skirt and little yellow number if she was a tourist. She'd come looking for a someone, as I had, though she didn't look half as tentative as I felt. In fact she looked assured in a defiant sort of way. She surveyed the surroundings and dared Henley to be good enough for her.

I was going to pay £35 to meet single women in Henley this afternoon, and I could get my money's worth starting now.

'Hi, do you know where we have to go?' I asked.

'No, I don't come here every day.'

I had to be clumsy, and she had to be clever. It's the way it is with women like her—you can tell. And it must be something about chaps like me too, and no doubt she could tell. I've often wished it was only my Indian accent that puts Indian girls off so quickly; that I can't help where I'm from is a little better than I can't help who I am.

By now the girl who'd been driving the Renault had stepped round. She held out her hand straight to me in a warm handshake. 'Hi, I'm Neera.' My spirits were restored a little. Perhaps she knew that any male her companion spoke to needed instant restoration. The power women can have, one way or another.

'Let me see the map,' she said. I stood so I could be seen to be looking at the map while I could also have a good look at her, the usual sly male thing to do. She was wearing a black blouse made from the kind of cloth a proper Indian tailor would use only for a dupatta. The blouse ended its descent some distance above a blue skirt streaked with yellow, which left room for plenty of midriff and more in-between. I thought it proper to move vision to her hair. They'd wound themselves into a bunch of rather complicated curls. They began black and turned blonde by the time the curl played itself out. It must have taken some doing. But I saw them only vaguely. I developed the kind of camera focus that would make everything a blur except her navel. Like all men in my position, I forgot that when you pick that way of looking, women always know.

'That way,' she said, and placed the map back in her bag. She pointed to a path along the river. I felt momentarily awkward that I hadn't looked at the map at all. The three of us walked on together, and I was much relieved by the comfort of what must at least appear a group.

Another picture postcard from the set at the tourism office presented itself. We passed toyland boats blown to life-size moorings on the riverside, with names like Sundown Lady and River Lark. A couple of them sailed by carrying men in hats. Two women went past on a polished wooden deck, inviting the afternoon sun to brown their legs just a little. Trees stood above tipsy reflections on the banks until a boat came along and bust it all. Ducks and swans rode the wake; they were the smaller bits that completed the picture. We were paying for the prettiness of the place. The Patel couple who had arranged the singles party presumably included a 20 per cent romantic-setting surcharge.

The map had drawn us to a point across from what was marked as a chalet on Rod Eye Islands where Mr Patel had told me on the phone the singles party was happening. He said chalet like he'd like me particularly to notice the 'ay', and that he was sophisticated enough not to pronounce the 't'. Five or six others were waiting for a boat to take us over to the shall-ay.

A slim Sikh in a light jacket and an elegant-almost-rakish turban had taken over this little pre-party.

'Why don't I grab a duck and ride over?' he said.

'They took one look at you and swam away,' a plump girl with her back to us replied.

'Let's all jump into the water,' he said.

'Yeah, like that would get rid of the ducks, right?'

I got the sick feeling that these and the like would be the clever lines of the day, and they would fail me all afternoon. This was going to be the slim Sikh's day, not mine. I settled into the sinking feeling that his £35 was going to work a lot better.

He was splashing out the GSOH I'd seen advertised in those Asian matrimonial and dating ads: Good Sense of Humour. White seekers in the *Guardian* and the *Sunday Times* struggled to write clever things about themselves. Indians simply wrote GSOH, and left it to you to discover in person how clever they really were.

The Sikh with dash introduced himself as Lucky. Lakhvinder, I presumed. This afternoon you had to strike the cool mode rapidly, and Lucky was on target before we'd even got to our dream island. He had put us all under pressure to produce GSOH, and pretty soon. I began to feel inadequate for not suggesting that we cross over on a duck's back.

The arrival of the boat to the chalet lifted the pressure. The white boatman led every girl into the boat by hand. 'C'mon, darling', 'Come, love', he went. The little boat rocked with every new passenger, and girls like protection at moments like this. He would have something to say about these Asian singles at his pub.

Our voyage lasted only a few yards. Over on the island a

woman, the female Patel host clearly, marked us off on a list and collected the money. She was a lovely girl with straight black hair, but I was looking at her because I couldn't bear to look in the direction of the seventy or eighty Indians, Asians, already out there on the lawn watching new boat people like us come in. They were sizing up everyone who came off the boat. We were mighty late, and the later you arrived, the more scrutinized you'd be as you got off that boat.

I crossed the lawn and walked into the chalet kitchen because it was too frightening to just walk into one of those groups on the lawn. A good decision, I concluded, because it was a friendly lot in there. Everyone introduced themselves cheerfully as some Patel or other. One was serving, someone was setting up the barbecue, one was in charge of the bar. The Patels had come together to take care of everything between them. Who better than Gujaratis as exterminators of overheads?

Some quick beers later I ventured into the lawn, like a batsman stepping out to face the test. About fifty women stood around to whom I could say hello to. So, who in the fifty, I thought—maybe even, who all? The thought made me just the kind of chap feminists are so right to despise. Funny how hormonal honesty keeps getting in the way of feeling the right thing.

I walked into the nearest group, and into instant hostility. I said hi to a chap in the group with crew-cut hair, in a long creased shirt drooping low over his trousers, very deliberately casual for a day like this. He did not reply. 'Go pick up someone somewhere else,' his body language said. There were girls in the group, and he had been talking happily to them.

'Ever been to the Regatta around here?' I said generally to everyone.

'Woz that?' said a less unfriendly chap in a sleeveless shirt.

'You get lots of boats and there are races and things,' said a round sort of girl. Lucky, if he'd been around, might have suggested a race on ducks' back. But he must have thought up new clever lines by now.

Our group broke up quickly. The rounded girl had no further interest in muscled chaps getting into boats to out-row one another. I moved over to the barbecue, as pleased to leave as long shirt must have been to see me go. The barbecue was by a highish wall, right below the gaze of two girls sitting on it, one of them Sikh—because I knew she couldn't be anything but. I thought I'd seen her before. She wore a skirt, and sat unfortunately at near eye level.

'I teach in some colleges,' she was telling her friend, and some of us who'd gathered round. 'Been doing some seminars with business people. Really planning to set up my own consultancy.'

'Do you find a lot of the usual, you know, all family businesses?' I asked. I was painfully aware how dull this was after Lucky.

'Oh yeah, but that's also the strength. Because you can have compact management, you can save costs, be more competitive.' Her toes were right there before me. The paint had begun to chip off the nails and I was surprised she had not provided necessary replenishment for a day like this, and then sat where she had. Maybe she didn't really care, maybe she really was mostly mind.

'But doesn't it mean that if you do things that way your business will stay small?' We were reproducing every bit of stock wisdom on Asian businesses.

'No ... well, yes. Corner shops and stuff but you have big ones also in family business. But they've got to get more professional. Can't go on and on like that.'

'But do they want to change?'

'That's the thing. There's always resistance to change. But when you tell them there are efficiency models, and that's gonna make you more productive and you're gonna get more profit, then they listen.'

'Sounds good for your consultancy.'

'Yeah, I'm getting like really good response.'

The others in the group had not joined the conversation in this split-level seminar. It was not the stuff dates are made of. Soon, this group too scattered.

'You picked your spot,' the chap in the long shirt said to me as I ran into him again around the barbecue. Now that no girls were around him, he was a lot friendlier. He lowered his voice. 'Look what I got.' He produced a piece of paper with six female names, with phone numbers. 'Guess I'm sorted for the next six months.' I was having a listless day.

I guessed that everyone thought everyone else was having a great time, but that no one really was. Even Lucky was now eating quietly. Over some of the afternoon we all joined some group or other. Everyone worked at generating something to say, but it didn't look like coolness and cleverness were flowing on that lawn. You clocked some reasonable minutes saying just anything, and asked for a number. Things—if anything—would happen only later depending on who you called, whether it was a real number, and what you heard back.

If that island had hosted some Asian chemistry, it had passed me by. And such as it was, it was over. The flirtation groups had almost all broken up. Over barbecued chicken, pulao rice and salad we were now divided into male groups separate from female groups. The chaps were drinking beer; the girls were engrossed in conversations, presumably about how vague the guys were.

It wasn't much later that the boat chap began to get the first Asian singles off the island. Everyone wanted to go; it would be nice to lose ourselves in London again.